William Wordsworth's *The Prelude*

A CASEBOOK

WEEK LOAN

WILLIAM WORDSWORTH'S

The Prelude

◆　◆　◆

A CASEBOOK

Edited by
Stephen Gill

OXFORD
UNIVERSITY PRESS

2006

OXFORD

UNIVERSITY PRESS

Oxford University Press, Inc., publishes works that further
Oxford University's objective of excellence
in research, scholarship, and education.

Oxford   New York
Auckland   Cape Town   Dar es Salaam   Hong Kong   Karachi
Kuala Lumpur   Madrid   Melbourne   Mexico City   Nairobi
New Delhi   Shanghai   Taipei   Toronto

With offices in
Argentina   Austria   Brazil   Chile   Czech Republic   France   Greece
Guatemala   Hungary   Italy   Japan   Poland   Portugal   Singapore
South Korea   Switzerland   Thailand   Turkey   Ukraine   Vietnam

Copyright © 2006 by Oxford University Press, Inc.

Published by Oxford University Press, Inc.
198 Madison Avenue, New York, New York 10016
www.oup.com

Oxford is a registered trademark of Oxford University Press

Library of Congress Cataloging-in-Publication Data
William Wordsworth's The prelude : a casebook / edited by Stephen Gill.
p. cm.—(Casebooks in criticism)
ISBN-13 978-0-19-518091-6; 978-0-19-518092-3 (pbk.)
ISBN 0-19-518091-7; 0-19-518092-5 (pbk.)
1. Wordsworth, William, 1770–1850. Prelude—Handbooks, manuals, etc.
I. Gill, Stephen Charles.   II. Series.
PR5864.W554 2006
821'.7—dc22   2005028827

1   3   5   7   9   8   6   4   2

Printed in the United States of America
on acid-free paper

Acknowledgments

The editor and publisher thank the following for permission to use copyright material.

M. H. Abrams, excerpt from *Natural Supernaturalism: Tradition and Revolution in Romantic Literature*. Copyright © 1971 by W.W. Norton & Company, Inc. By permission of W.W. Norton & Company, Inc.

Jonathan Bate, excerpt from *Romantic Ecology: Wordsworth and the Environmental Tradition*. New York: Routledge (1991). Copyright 1991 from *Romantic Ecology: Wordsworth and the Environmental Tradition* by Jonathan Bate. Reproduced by permission of Routledge/Taylor & Francis Group, LLC.

Howard Erskine-Hill, excerpt from *Poetry of Opposition and Revolution: Dryden to Wordsworth*. New York: Oxford University Press, 1996. By permission of Oxford University Press.

Richard Gravil, " 'Some Other Being': Wordsworth in *The Prelude*," *The Yearbook of English Studies* [The French Revolution in English Literature and Art, Special Number] 19 (1989). With permission of Richard Gravil.

Geoffrey H. Hartman, excerpt from *Wordsworth's Poetry, 1787–1814*. Cambridge, Mass.: Harvard University Press (1987, © 1971). By Permission of Geoffrey H. Hartman.

Mary Jacobus, excerpt from *Romanticism, Writing, and Sexual Difference: Essays on The Prelude*. New York: Oxford University Press (1989). By permission of Oxford University Press.

Alan Liu, excerpt from *Wordsworth: The Sense of History*. Stanford, Calif.: Stanford University Press (1989). By permission of the Board of Trustees of the Leland Stanford Junior University.

Anne K. Mellor, excerpt from *Romanticism and Gender*. New York: Routledge (1993). Copyright 1993 from *Romanticism and Gender* by Anne K. Mellor. Reproduced by permission of Routledge/Taylor & Francis Group, LLC.

Lucy Newlyn, excerpt from *Coleridge, Wordsworth, and the Language of Allusion*. New York: Oxford University Press (1986). By permission of Oxford University Press.

Christopher Ricks, excerpt from *The Force of Poetry*. New York: Oxford University Press (1987). By permission of Oxford University Press.

William A. Ulmer, excerpt from *The Christian Wordsworth 1798–1805*. Albany: State University of New York Press, 2001. By permission of the State University of New York. All rights reserved.

Susan Wolfson, excerpt from *Formal Charges: The Shaping of Poetry in British Romanticism*. Stanford, Calif.: Stanford University Press (1997). By permission of the Board of Trustees of the Leland Stanford Junior University.

Jonathan Wordsworth, excerpt from *William Wordsworth: The Borders of Vision*. Oxford: Clarendon Press (©1982 by Jonathan Wordsworth). By permission of Peters Fraser Dunlop on behalf of Jonathan Wordsworth.

Contents

William Wordsworth's *The Prelude*

A CASEBOOK

Wordsworth has transformed the inherited language of poetry into a medium adequate to express new ways of perceiving the world, new modes of experience, and new relations of the individual consciousness to itself, to its past, and to other men. More than a few English writers, Wordsworth has altered not only our poetry, but our sensibility and our culture.

M. H. Abrams

Introduction

STEPHEN GILL

◆   ◆   ◆

Prelude

THE TWO GREAT critics who defined the terms in which much of the debate about Wordsworth's achievement has been conducted were in agreement about his stature. "In imaginative power," Samuel Taylor Coleridge declared in *Biographia Literaria* (1817), "he stands nearest of all modern writers to Shakespeare and Milton." "I firmly believe that the poetical performance of Wordsworth is, after that of Shakespeare and Milton . . . undoubtedly the most considerable in our language from the Elizabethan age to the present time," Matthew Arnold echoed in 1879.[1] As to the merits of *The Prelude*, however, they disagreed completely. Coleridge was so inspired by a private recitation of the poem that he wrote his own verse tribute, "To William Wordsworth." In his judgment, Wordsworth's "prophetic Lay,"

> An Orphic Tale indeed,
> A Tale divine of high and passionate Thoughts
> To their own music chaunted!

enrolled him in the "Choir / Of ever-enduring Man," the "truly Great," who have "all in one Age and from one visible space / Shed influence."

To Arnold, on the contrary, it seemed rather that *The Prelude*, together with *The Excursion*, another of Wordsworth's "poems of greatest bulk," was likely to hinder recognition of its author as one of the truly great. These long poems were "by no means Wordsworth's best work," he pronounced. 'His best work is in his shorter pieces."[2] Over time it is Coleridge's rather than Arnold's assessment that has been confirmed. While few readers today (it is probably safe to venture) will find themselves "in Prayer" at the close of *The Prelude*, as Coleridge did, it has come to seem Wordsworth's richest, most rhetorically sophisticated achievement, of all his poems the one that offers the most varied poetic pleasure.

There has always been something odd, though, about *The Prelude*, and while the scholarly investigation that has accompanied the poem's rise in reputation has accounted for some aspects of the oddness, it has not smoothed it away entirely. The many-sided oddness of *The Prelude* still confronts all new readers who probe into the poem at all and remains even now part of its essential being. And the oddness is? At least the following facts about the identity of what is routinely—and rightly—referred to as one of the greatest of Romantic poems: (1) that there is not one *Prelude* but many; (2) that the poem known by this title evolved over many years during the poet's lifetime and has continued to evolve until practically the present day; and (3) that the poem that student readers are most likely to encounter, and that has given rise to the critical discourse exemplified in this collection of essays, was never authorized by the poet, exists in no incontrovertibly established text, and was not even known about until three-quarters of a century after the poet's death and the appearance of the poem he *did* authorize for publication.

The first part of this introduction is an attempt to put flesh on the bare bones of the three statements just made and in so doing to trace the coming into being of the poem on which all of the essays gathered in this volume focus and to which most scholars and readers still refer with unmisgiving certainty as *The Prelude*.

The First Appearance of the Poem

The oddness was there right at the beginning when the poem was first published in July 1850, three months after Wordsworth's death. The title page read *The Prelude, | or | Growth of a Poet's Mind; | An Autobiographical Poem; | by | William Wordsworth*. A posthumous poem that was a prelude? To what? The autobiographical poem's chronicle of events in the poet's life that have contributed most significantly to the formation of his creative powers ends with the excitement of the summer of 1798, when Wordsworth and Coleridge had been busy compiling the first *Lyrical Ballads* collection. Since every reader knew that Wordsworth's career really began with that volume, they might reasonably have assumed that the title of this new, posthumous poem, *The Prelude*, situated it as prelude to the whole of Wordsworth's increasingly illustrious career after the appearance of *Lyrical Ballads* in 1798. If so, was it not puzzling that Wordsworth should have held back from publication a work that both explained and, through the originality and quality of its verse, exemplified all that he had pronounced on over the years about the importance of the creative imagination? What followed the title page, however, appeared to clarify matters. Serious readers would have recalled that in the Preface to *The Excursion*, the long, quasi-dramatic philosophic poem he published in 1814, Wordsworth had revealed (1) that it, *The Excursion*, was only part of a planned three-part philosophic work to be called *The Recluse* and (2) that another poem anterior to the whole philosophic project had already been completed, a review of the growth of the poet's mind to the moment when he "retired to his native mountains, with the hope of being enabled to construct a literary Work that might live."[3] This was not, in fact, an accurate account of events. The evidence is overwhelming that *The Recluse* was not conceived of as a result of the poet conducting a review of his own powers in an autobiographical poem, but was already in existence as an ambition by the summer of 1798 and that the autobiographical poem originated, at least in part, in Wordsworth's sense of frustration that he was not making headway with the philosophic one. But if Wordsworth's 1814 explanation is not historically reliable, it has a persuasive narrative logic to it: poet retires to native mountains to consider his poetic future; a review of his powers gives confidence; a grand project is conceived; here, in 1814, is the first fruit of that moment of poetic dedication. So satisfying was this story that by way of introduction to the 1850 *Prelude* for younger or newer readers, the editors repeated the poet's 1814 revelation word for word, just adding by way of clarification that *The Excursion* was the only part of the great *Recluse* project ever completed.[4]

In answering one question, though, this apparent clarification raised another. The *Prelude* was preparatory to another, more important work. It had been written in a spirit of self-examination, to "examine how far Nature and Education had qualified him" to construct a work of enduring value. But Wordsworth had never completed the task he had set himself—to write *The Recluse*. The noble duty invoked at the close of *The*

Prelude had been at best only partially fulfilled, it seemed. Had he been mistaken, then, in concluding that Nature and Education *had* fitted him for his special task? Surely not. By the time of his death, the figure of Wordsworth (Victoria's poet laureate since 1843) had assumed an aura almost of sanctity, so often had it been repeated that his poetic endeavors had been devoted to the noblest goals.[5] Nonetheless, *The Recluse* had not been written. How strange that his executors should have authorized the publication now, when Wordsworth was barely in his grave, of a poem whose title could not but direct attention to what he had *not* achieved, to failure.

The title, in fact, was a problem, but this was not divulged in 1850. The prefatory words already mentioned that drew attention to the poem's place in Wordsworth's work overall did not reveal that the poem lacked an authorized title. Having recapitulated Wordsworth's own 1814 account of the relation of the autobiographical poem to *The Recluse*, the editors in 1850 added: "It will thence be seen, that the present Poem was intended to be introductory to the RECLUSE," a comment that so clearly indicated that the title, *The Prelude*, meshed with Wordsworth's thinking about the poem that there was no reason for it to enter any reader's mind in 1850 that it had not been settled on by the author half a century earlier.

A year later, however, in his biography of his uncle, Christopher Wordsworth revealed the truth. Having recounted the early history of the poem's composition and its relation to that of *The Excursion*, he continued:

> Its title, 'The Prelude,' had not been fixed on by the author himself: the Poem remained anonymous till his death. The present title has been prefixed to it at the suggestion of the beloved partner of his life, and the best interpreter of his thoughts, from considerations of its tentative and preliminary character. Obviously it would have been desirable to mark its relation to 'The Recluse' by some analogous appellation; but this could not easily be done, at the same time that its other essential characteristics were indicated. Besides, the appearance of this poem, *after* the author's death, might tend to lead some readers into an opinion that it was his *final* production, instead of being, as it really is, one of his *earlier* works. They were to be guarded against this supposition. Hence a name has been adopted, which may serve to keep the true nature and position of the poem constantly before the eye of the reader; and 'THE PRELUDE' will now be perused and estimated with the feelings properly due to its preparatory character, and to the period at which it was composed.[6]

Christopher Wordsworth's uneasiness is plain. There is something odd about this publication, and the reader needs to be alerted. Although the poem occupied Wordsworth for much of his life, it seems that it retained its "tentative and preliminary character." It never had a title. Although prepared for publication at the height of the poet's maturity and now published at his death, *The Prelude*, the reader is cautioned, is not a late production, but 'one of his *earlier* works.'

One of his earlier works it may be, but it is also a Victorian poem, and this dual identity is an aspect of its oddity that played a part in determining the evolution of the poem's reputation. When Jerome McGann omitted *The Prelude* from the *New Oxford Book of Romantic Period Verse* in 1993, he did so because his intention in compiling the anthology was to give a generous representation of what was actually being read in the period. *The Prelude* was not read in the period, and by adhering strictly to this criterion McGann drew attention to what was most striking about the poem's publication, namely, that at the moment when it entered cultural circulation it did so both as a document about history and as a historical document.[7] *The Prelude* told of the past sixty years and more earlier, of the French Revolution, of Robespierre and Napoleon, of Pitt and Burke, and it did so as a participant, so to speak, in the historical moment it documented. This was not an imaginative recreation of the past, but a voice from that past. *Barnaby Rudge* (1841) and *Vanity Fair* (1847–48) are set in the past (in the period of Wordsworth's youth and early manhood, as it happens), but everything about them speaks of their composition in the present. They are Victorian historical novels, to be read as documents not of eighteenth-century or Regency culture, but as voices of the 1840s.

How very different was the poem presented to the reading public in 1850. Addressed throughout to Coleridge, it concluded (XIV, 432–56) with a stirring rededication of the two friends to their task:

> Oh, yet a few short years of useful life,
> And all will be complete, thy race be run,
> Thy monument of glory will be raised;
> Then, though (too weak to tread the ways of truth)
> This age fall back to old idolatry,
> Though men return to servitude as fast
> As the tide ebbs, to ignominy and shame
> By nations sink together, we shall still
> Find solace—knowing what we have learnt to know,
> Rich in true happiness if allowed to be

Faithful alike in forwarding a day
Of firmer trust, joint labourers in the work
(Should Providence such grace to us vouchsafe)
Of their deliverance, surely yet to come.
Prophets of Nature, we to them will speak
A lasting inspiration . . .

Coleridge had listened to a version of this exhortation in 1807, but by the time anyone could read it he was long dead, as much a historical figure as Robespierre, and the aspiration the passage voiced was long in the past, too. Had *The Prelude* been published in 1807, these concluding lines would have spoken to the present about the future: in 1850 they spoke to an unimaginably different present only about the past. To do so was a proper poetic function, but not one that Wordsworth thought himself as undertaking when, having "retired to his native mountains," he began to "take a review of his own mind."

For Wordsworth's more devoted readers, the emergence of *The Prelude* would obviously have been welcome. The poem's existence had long been known about through published extracts and from mention in essays and memoirs by Coleridge, De Quincey, Hazlitt, and others of Wordsworth's acquaintance. Now here it was, at last. But it must also have been discomfiting in a way that hindered the growth of the poem's reputation.

Ever since his career had begun to establish itself, Wordsworth had sought to control how his work was to be perceived. In the preface to *The Excursion* in 1814, he declared that all of his poems had a relation one to another like the diverse architectural features that make up a gothic church, a relation that would become apparent to the "attentive reader" once the minor pieces "shall be properly arranged." A year later they were "properly arranged," in a two-volume collection organized on a classification principle of Wordsworth's own devising that was buttressed by a substantial critical-theoretical defense in prose of its rationale.[8] Though much strained, the system remained essentially intact until Wordsworth's death. The collective volumes expanded from four (1820) to five (1827) to six (1836) to seven (1846), and for each fresh edition new poems were incorporated into the existing classificatory order and the whole corpus was revised. The text of each new collective edition superseded that of the previous one. After 1836 the pretense that any more of *The Recluse* would appear was abandoned; in 1842, long-suppressed early works were admitted to the canon, accompanied by personal remarks in a tone that suggested a poet clearing his desk.[9] A fully revised edition in 1845 confirmed the architecture of Wordsworth's achievement, and in 1849–

50 a six-volume collective edition that embodied it was overseen by the poet for the last time.

This process of continually revising text and simultaneously adding titles to the canon conveyed the impression that Wordsworth's oeuvre was organically unfolding throughout his lifetime, but also that he was in charge. What he, the poet, authorized as the canon, was the canon. Now, in 1850, readers who had barely had time to examine the most recent collective edition were suddenly required to adjust very radically their sense of what the Wordsworth canon was by absorbing into it thousands of lines of verse that, it was revealed, had always existed alongside the authorized, admitted canon. T. S. Eliot's insight about a larger body of work is true about the smaller:

> What happens when a new work of art is created is something that happens simultaneously to all the works of art which preceded it. The existing monuments form an ideal order among themselves, which is modified by the introduction of the new (the really new) work of art among them. The existing order is complete before the new work arrives; for order to persist after the supervention of novelty, the *whole* existing order must be, if ever so slightly, altered.[10]

What had been thought of as Wordsworth's complete life's work had to be reconsidered after the publication of *The Prelude*, not least because its autobiographically revelatory character had implications for understanding the whole of Wordsworth's career. "Tintern Abbey," for example, in print since 1798, became the richer once *The Prelude*, and the first two books in particular, were available to contextualize where and how the poet became "a worshipper of Nature," but the poem *Guilt and Sorrow*, not published until 1842, also assumed a more powerful character once the poet's account of his radical years in books 9–12 of *The Prelude* could shed light on it. *The Prelude* wasn't just to be added to the canon as a late accretion. It was destined to alter that canon completely, both by taking up its place in its historical development and thus reshaping apprehension of what that had been, and by acting as a commentary upon it.

The Emergence of the Poem after 1850

The Prelude is a long and complex poem, and Wordsworth's oeuvre was already daunting in size, so it is perhaps not altogether surprising that it took time for the poem to win readers and to figure much in critical discourse. But there was another factor that hindered the growth of the *Prelude*'s reputation, one that it is easy to overlook in a brief reception history—the law of copyright. *The Prelude* remained under copyright protection until 1892, the property of the Wordsworth family and of the publisher Edward Moxon and his successors. What this meant in practice was that up to the turn of the century, the poem could not be included in any of the numerous editions competing for readers (or at least purchasers): handsome collected works; pretty gift-books; selections. There is nothing from *The Prelude* in Matthew Arnold's 1879 selection. As already indicated, Arnold explained the absence by a critical justification, and it is a plausible one, given the argument proposed by his prefatory essay, but what needs also to be recognized is that Arnold's selection, being issued by Macmillan, could not include anything from *The Prelude* that was not already in print and out of copyright. Whether Arnold's selection was quite as influential as is always maintained is perhaps a question, but what is not in doubt is that it was reprinted in huge quantities over many years. The house of Frederick Warne, another big player in the publishing market, had no choice but to admit that its "Albion Edition" was not actually complete, but it only did so with the barefaced assertion that what was omitted was of no account. The "Publisher's Preface" read:

> The present Edition of Wordsworth has been carefully revised, and numerous additions have been made to it. It now comprises all the Poet's best and finest poems (with his latest corrections), and is indeed complete, with the exception of "The Prelude," his last work, which was published after his death, and is not generally considered equal to his former poems.

Of course this was sour grapes—even if *The Prelude* had been hailed at once as Wordsworth's greatest work, the "Albion Edition" could not have included it—but, to put it no more strongly, it cannot have helped the poem's reputation to have this dismissive judgement broadcast until at least the 1920s.

Nonetheless, *The Prelude* did eventually feature with increasing visibility in the developing critical debate about what Wordsworth amounted to. For those prepared to disregard Arnold's warning that Wordsworth's philosophy was emphatically not the core of his achievement, the poem could be turned to as an ever-present help in times of confusion caused by the profundities of the poet's thought. Whereas the historian Thomas Babington Macaulay was disappointed at finding "the old raptures about mountains and cataracts; the old flimsy philosophy about the effect of scenery on the mind; the old crazy mystical metaphysics," one of Arnold's successors as professor of poetry at Oxford, John Campbell Shairp, welcomed *The Prelude* for revealing in full what the poet's disciples could previously only glimpse in part, the philosophical foundation to his utterances about the material world:

> when, after his death, 'The Prelude' was published, they were let into the secret, they saw the hidden foundations on which it rests, as they had never seen them before. The smaller poems were more beautiful, more delightful, but "The Prelude" revealed the secret of their beauty. It showed that all Wordsworth's impassioned feeling towards Nature was no mere fantastic dream, but based on sanity, on a most assured and reasonable philosophy. It was as though one, who had been long gazing on some building grand and fair, admiring the vast sweep of its walls and the strength of its battlements, without understanding their principle of coherence, were at length to be admitted inside by the master builder, and given a view of the whole plan from within, the principles of architecture, and the hidden substructures upon which it was built. This is what 'The Prelude' does for the rest of Wordsworth's poetry.[11]

Readers less inclined to venerate Wordsworth as a sage could study the poem for what its subtitle claimed to offer, an account of experiences the poet believed had shaped his creative being. At this distance in time, the following may seem a rather silly statement to make, but the fact is that the originality of the contribution of Emile Legouis's *La Jeunesse de William Wordsworth* (1896) to Wordsworthian scholarship lies in its determination to take the poem seriously as source and interpretative guide and that it stresses, as *The Prelude* does, that there can be no understanding of the work of Wordsworth's maturity in the "absence of any adequate endeavour to analyse the moral crisis of his early manhood."[12]

Toward the end of the nineteenth century, understanding of the composition and textual history of the whole of Wordsworth's oeuvre was enormously advanced by the pioneers of Wordsworthian scholarship, William Knight, Edward Dowden, and Thomas Hutchinson, and each made his own contribution to knowledge of *The Prelude*. Gradually it did displace *The Excursion* in critical discussion.[13] In none of the important contributions to the unfolding debate, which M. H. Abrams has felicitously called the "Two Roads to Wordsworth," however, is there any sense that the poem is being looked at from a new perspective.[14] Paradoxically it was not until the age of high modernism, when Romanticism was generally regarded as a spent force, that anything happened to redirect attention to *The Prelude* both as poetic text and as a document in the poet's history.

In 1926 Ernest de Selincourt, professor of English at Birmingham University, published an edition of *The Prelude* in which not one but two texts were presented, that of the first edition of 1850 and an editorially constructed text dated as 1805.[15] De Selincourt was a friend of the Wordsworth family and had been given access to all the *Prelude* manuscripts that survived in their possession. Listing and describing them, thirteen in all, De Selincourt was able to trace the evolution of the poem from fragments found in notebooks in use in 1798–99 to a whole in thirteen books in fair-copy manuscripts of 1805–6. Many previously unpublished passages were adduced that had a bearing on the poem's composition; photographs of specimen manuscript pages suggested how laborious the labour of textual analysis and reclamation must have been.

That Wordsworth had completed the poem long before it had been published and that he had revised it over the years was not news—it had been revealed in the preface to the first edition, mentioned in the official biography, and enlarged upon in the editorial work of the later nineteenth century.[16] Nor did De Selincourt feel the need by this date to argue for the poem's importance: "*The Prelude*," his introduction began, "is the essential living document for the interpretation of Wordsworth's life and poetry; any details, therefore, that can be gathered of the manner and circumstances of its composition must be of interest alike to biographer and critic. But of more vital importance than these is a knowledge of its original text." And what De Selincourt was able to reveal, with a spectacular display of scholarly fireworks, was that such knowledge was recoverable. At last readers had access to the poem on the growth of the poet's own mind written at the height of his powers.

This was a momentous event in *The Prelude*'s history. De Selincourt's edition put all later scholars and critics in his debt. But it had its down side, too. In his long and forcefully argued introduction, De Selincourt compared the 1805 and 1850 texts. Some revisions, he thought, unquestionably added "strength and vividness" to verse that by 1850 "had reached a high level of workmanship"; others were evidence of loss of imaginative vigor and confidence. In the end the scales tip decisively toward 1805. Though the section "Comparison of Texts" begins "No one would doubt that the 1850 version is a better composition than the A [1805] text," it concludes with an endorsement of what is termed "the original *Prelude*" as the "frankest and most direct confession" of the sources of Wordsworth's greatest poetry, that of the decade 1798–1807.

The comparison of the two texts was well done: what was not helpful about it was that it put blinkers on further approaches. It ought to be possible, the editor argued, to construct a single, ideal text of *The Prelude*, one that would accept revisions "Wordsworth might have made (and some he certainly would have made), had he prepared the poem for the press in his greatest period" while "most firmly reject[ing] all modifications of his original thought and attitude to his theme." But this ideal text was not what the augustly scholarly Oxford University Press edition offered with its two texts printed in parallel, nor did the confident assertions about Wordsworth's "greatest period" or his "original thought and attitude" do anything but bolster the impression that *The Prelude* existed in two versions, 1805 and 1850, between which a choice had to be made. In his magisterial study *The Mind of a Poet* (1941), Raymond Dexter Havens refused to be coerced by De Selincourt's favoring of 1805. "By '*The Prelude*' is generally understood *The Prelude* of 1850," he declared. "It has always been so; presumably it always will be so."[17] Twenty-two years later, in another book solely on *The Prelude*, Herbert Lindenberger sounded less confident: "Like *Hamlet*, *The Prelude* exists in two versions, neither of them altogether satisfactory," but as the title of his appendix, "1805 or 1850?" reveals, the terms in which the text of the poem is being discussed are still those laid down by De Selincourt in 1926.[18] And so it continued. "1805 or 1850" was still a choice eminent scholars were prepared to dispute over twenty years later, when they engaged in what the periodical *The Wordsworth Circle* reported as "The Great *Prelude* Debate."[19]

Ironically, it was the publication of a revised edition of De Selincourt's monumental work that loosened the hold of this 1805/1850 opposition. In 1959 Helen Darbishire issued a corrected and greatly augmented second edition of the parallel text *Prelude* in which she revealed the existence of still more early manuscripts. One in particular seemed of especial interest as "representing Wordsworth's first coherent attempt to embark upon the poem which afterwards became *The Prelude*," and it was transcribed in full as an appendix.[20] This and the mention of other fresh material from 1798–1800 indicated that, after all, the early history of the autobiographical poem was not, as yet, settled. By 1964 J. R. MacGillivray had concluded that two versions of *The Prelude* existed earlier than the 1805 text and that in one of them, what he called the two-book "proto-*Prelude* of 1798–1800," could be discerned "a much more unified theme and a much stronger sense of formal structure than in the poem completed first in 1805 and published in 1850."[21] Prompted by MacGillivray, scholars proceeded to recover what is now generally known as *The Two-Part Prelude*. In 1970 Jonathan Wordsworth argued that it offered "in a simpler and more concentrated form most of what one thinks of as best in the thirteen-Book poem."[22] It was given full-dress scholarly honors in the Cornell Wordsworth series in 1977 and disseminated more widely in 1979 in a Norton Critical Edition.[23]

Like *The Ruined Cottage*, another poem not published by the author or prepared for publication by him, this autobiographical poem in two parts has become an accepted title in the Wordsworth canon. Two other bodies of verse—both highlighted by MacGillivray—have not quite coalesced (or been coerced) into versions that can legitimately claim critical attention to the same degree, but they have attracted strong advocacy.

What Helen Darbishire had transcribed in the appendix to her edition was the earliest material that could be identified as unquestionably belonging to *The Prelude*, that is, tentative and incomplete passages about childhood experiences, beginning "Was it for this," that were later embedded in book 1. This body of verse had been looked at afresh and edited by later scholars, but always as if it were a stage on the way to the more developed material emerging from it. One of them, however, Jonathan Wordsworth, was to go a step further on renewed consideration of the significance of this manuscript. Accounting for his decision to include the "Was it for this" material as one of the four texts (1798, 1799, 1805, 1850) presented in his Penguin *Prelude* in 1995, Jonathan Wordsworth argued that "Short as it is, it takes for its theme 'The Growth of a Poet's Mind,' containing in embryo the discussion of education through nature central to all later versions," and so warrants presentation "as a separate annotated version of *The Prelude*."[24]

Equally boldly, Duncan Wu has presented another separate version of the poem. However one interprets the material, it is clear that Wordsworth's autobiographical poem did have its first textual (as opposed to merely conceptual) identity in the verses "Was it for this" entered into a notebook in late 1798. It is also clear that Wordsworth did round off the autobiographical poem in two parts in 1799 and had it copied out neatly. Scholars may debate how for how long Wordsworth considered this two-part work "finished," and there is nothing in his letters to settle the matter one way or another, but at least the poem itself exists, and it reads like a self-sufficient, artistically coherent whole. Very quickly after its completion, however, Wordsworth was back at work on his autobiography, and by early March 1804 he was declaring himself confident of finishing "in two or three days time" a poem in five books.[25] Within a very short time that notion, too, was superseded by a still grander scheme, and since no single manuscript authority exists for the putative five-book version, scholars have been content to accept that, although it could perhaps be notionally reconstructed, the version probably was best regarded as a slightly vexing episode in the poem's textual history. Duncan Wu, however, believing otherwise, has reconstructed the poem as it was before Wordsworth expanded it beyond a five-book structure and, presenting it in 1997 as an edition of *The Five-Book Prelude*, has declared it "the great work of Wordsworth's poetic maturity."[26]

So far I have discussed only the proliferation of versions that has come about because of renewed work on the manuscript evidence of the poem's development up to 1805, but the post-1805 materials have also yielded fresh information, which refines and to a degree complicates the history of how the autobiographical poem evolved after the moment at which Wordsworth first declared it finished. From detailed study of the revisions made to the two fair copies of the thirteen-book poem (manuscripts A and B) and their relation to a further fair copy of 1819 (manuscript C), Mark L. Reed has argued that the C-stage of the poem should be regarded as something more than a gathering of revisions that matter only as harbingers of the evolving text of 1850: "This record does not constitute an approved finished form of *The Prelude*. It does, however, represent a distinctive stage of the poem's development which deserves study in its own right, and neither its extent nor its individuality has been sufficiently recognized."[27] Reed's volume in the Cornell Wordsworth series accordingly offers a "reading text" of the 1819 *Prelude*.

Reed's meticulous analysis of the two earliest complete manuscripts of the thirteen-book poem has demonstrated that there is no single source for what is always called "the 1805 text." It is an editorial construct embodying countless decisions on verbal details and questions of punctuation. Reed's 1805 *Prelude* is not identical to De Selincourt's or to Darbishire's or to that of the Norton Critical Edition. The Cornell volume, though, is dealing with a version of the poem that never did achieve the fixity of print, so a degree of variation between edited texts might be expected. But surely the integrity of the 1850 first edition *Prelude* is unimpeachable. Didn't the poet himself prepare it for publication? Though final revision took place more than three decades after the poet first declared the poem complete, it was his revision, and the fact of posthumous publication cannot rob it of its status as an "authorized text."

The answer is, yes and no. De Selincourt had shown in 1926 that Wordsworth's final revision of *The Prelude* dated from 1839, but also that those who saw the poem through the press in 1850 (his relatives and executors) made numerous corrections and alterations. Even they were insufficient, and it was recognized at once that the 1850 text was defective—corrections were made for the second edition of 1851. What W. J. B. Owen was able to show, however, in his edition of the poem for the Cornell Wordsworth series, is that there is not even security in looking to the poet's manuscript of 1839 for a satisfactory final authorized text. This is an unreliable manuscript that has frequently to be corrected and supplemented by reference back to the previous full copy of 1832 and occasionally further back still. The result, as Owen explains, is that "the reading text of the 'final' version of *The Prelude* in this edition is an eclectic one," the construction of an editorial procedure designed "to provide such a text as Wordsworth would have approved for his final version of the poem."[28] In short: (1) The first edition *Prelude* of 1850 does not represent Wordsworth's final authorized version; (2) Wordsworth's final authorized version does not exist in any wholly reliable state, though later editorial intervention can bring us close to it; (3) what is generally being referred to as "the 1850 *Prelude*" is, in fact, a version of the poem that dates substantially from 1839.

A Resting Place

Bibliographical material in any quantity tends to be hard to digest, and so a review of the uncontested facts about *The Prelude* 1798–1850 might be helpful at this stage:

1. The autobiographical poem had its origin, in a not entirely clear way, in Wordsworth coming to believe in 1798 that he was called to the high task of writing *The Recluse.*
2. Recollections of childhood joys and fears were composed over the turn of 1798–99 in the 'Was it for this' manuscript.
3. By the end of 1799, a poem in two parts had been completed, beginning with 'Was it for this' and ending with an address to Coleridge. The poem exists in fair-copy manuscripts.
4. By March 1804, Wordsworth declared himself close to completing a poem in five books. This version can only have existed as a discrete version for a short time, and it does not exist in any one manuscript copy; but what the five-book poem would have consisted of had it been stabilized as a version in a fair-copy manuscript can be reconstructed with a high degree of certainty.

5. By the summer of 1805, Wordsworth had completed a poem in thirteen books. It exists in two fair-copy manuscripts. There is no single, unimpeachable text of this version, as Wordsworth subjected it to revision even as the manuscripts were being made. The poem was referred to as "The Poem to Coleridge" and/or variants on "Growth of the Poet's Mind."

6. In 1814, in the preface to *The Excursion*, Wordsworth revealed the existence of the as-yet-unpublished autobiographical poem and gave a not-wholly-reliable explanation of its relation to the philosophic project of which *The Excursion* was a part-offering.

7. Over the next twenty-five years, Wordsworth returned to the poem from time to time. Extensive revision made in 1819 can be identified from manuscript evidence, and it has been presented as a version of the poem worthy of independent recognition.

8. In 1839 Wordsworth completed a final revision of the poem, now divided into fourteen books, and it seems likely that he settled on publication only after his death (at sixty-nine he had already outlived most of his friends from the years chronicled in the autobiographical poem).

9. On his death in 1850, his widow and executors published a version of the poem in fourteen books and gave it a title whose significance was explained in an editorial preface.

This is only a summary, but it's a lot to take in. To some readers, however, bibliographical material of this kind may seem not just indigestible but entirely at odds with the kind of direct, readily accessible pleasure Wordsworth would have wanted them to take from his work. The one necessity of the poet's art, he declared, was that of "producing immediate pleasure," and it was not to be thought a degradation:

> It is far otherwise. It is an acknowledgment of the beauty of the universe, an acknowledgment the more sincere, because it is not formal, but indirect; it is a task light and easy to him who looks at the world in the spirit of love: further, it is a homage paid to the native and naked dignity of man, to the grand elementary principle of pleasure, by which he knows, and feels, and lives, and moves.[29]

Magnificent—but how does talk of versions and revisions and manuscripts square with it? Isn't textual scholarship poetic pleasure's death-watch beetle?

One way to respond to this anxiety would be to insist that bibliographical innocence is not an option. Facts about the poem's history were broadcast even before it was published; a recapitulation of them formed part of the first edition text; scholarly labors have uncovered many more; within the poem itself, reference is made to the history of its composition (see, for example, the opening of book 7). Once there was one version of *The Prelude*, now there are many, and there's no going back.

But this is not the response to make, or rather, not the tone in which to make it. The declaration that innocence is not an option carries more than a hint of wistfulness that it would be preferable if it were, but this notion is a siren call to be resisted. Bibliographical and compositional history of the kind being discussed here is not a limiter on aesthetic enjoyment but the generator of more. No matter where one begins with the poetry (provided one does begin with the poetry and not with writing about it), scholarly discoveries made since the *Prelude*'s first publication open up intriguing possibilities for exploration. What is the organizational principle of the two-part work of 1799, and if it's the case, as editors claim, that the poem can be regarded as an independent creation, what happens to it when it is subsumed into a larger whole? Which is . . . in five books? In thirteen? What was so important that, within the space of of a few weeks in 1804, Wordsworth went from thinking that five books would serve to realize his intentions to recognizing that his poem would need many more than five books, were it to do justice to themes that were emerging? Had he not known what he was aiming for when he returned to the poem after its 1799 moment of stasis and dismembered it? How did the differing functions of the poem over time affect the evolution of its formal properties? Clearly, what an autobiographical review of the growth of a poet's mind meant in 1799, when the poet in question was practically unknown, must have been very different from what it was in 1805, when he was on the way to becoming poetically notorious, and different again from what it was in 1839, when he was garlanded with honors. Throughout his writing lifetime, Wordsworth the poet had a public self, but also a private self inscribed in an autobiography he wouldn't publish and so could change. Did the poem age with its creator? What did the old poet do to his younger self's words? These are just examples of questions provoked by the existence of multiple texts of *The Prelude*. They are not at all at odds with the elementary pleasure to be gained from the poetry because pursuing them demands ever closer engagement with the poetic text in whatever version.

A reader, however, has to start by getting to know one version. In time, the idea that it is *the* one correct, or ideal, or authorized version will give way to a slightly unsettling but ultimately invigorating sense of the multiple invitations offered by Wordworth's autobiographical poem(s). But one has to begin somewhere, and for student readers this is most likely to be with the thirteen-book poem of 1805. Texts are widely available, with differing degrees of textual and explanatory annotation. On the shelves of research libraries will be found the two volumes edited by Mark L. Reed as part of the Cornell Wordsworth series. Most graduates, let alone undergraduates, will find them daunting, but what can be safely asserted is that they provide the textual evidence for every issue a student might want to follow up about the development of the poem to its thirteen-book form. In campus bookstores, scholarly editions of *The Prelude* that contain the complete 1805 text include the Norton Critical Edition, edited by Jonathan Wordsworth, M. H. Abrams, and Stephen Gill; the Penguin edition, edited by Jonathan Wordsworth; and my own, *Wordsworth: The Major Works*, a selection representing Wordsworth's variety, which is now a volume in the Oxford University Press World's Classics series.

There are, moreover, very good reasons why a version of *The Prelude* that was unknown before 1926 should have become the default version of *The Prelude* for academic courses and critical writing on the Romantic period. It was the first version of the poem Wordsworth declared "finished" (letter 3 June 1805) and there is little later variation from its structural template. It is formally much more ambitious than the versions in two or five books, but more important, it is successfully ambitious. It was, the poet declared, "a thing unprecedented in Literary history that a man should talk so much about himself," but this much-quoted remark is a great misleader.[30] *The Prelude* is not *talk*, but a highly wrought structure that is extremely conscious of itself as, on the one hand, poetically groundbreaking ("a thing unprecedented") and, on the other, as embedded in the epic genre excelled in by the only poet Wordsworth wanted to outperform—Milton. Apparently rambling—at one point Wordsworth likens its progress to the meanderings of a river—the thirteen books in fact have a very strong architecture, because however elusive the emergence of the theme (the growth of the poet's awareness of his creative power), signs of it are always looked for and tracked through actual circumstances. A poem that continually aspires to the affirmation of the transcendent ("Our destiny, our nature, and our home / Is with infinitude, and only there" [VI, 538–9]) is firmly grounded on real events, in the real world ("which is the world / Of all of us, the place on which in the end / We find our happiness, or not at all" [X, 725–7]). Childhood raptures and terrors among lakes and mountains; life as a Cambridge student; walking across France and the

Alps; the shows of London; war and its victims; hallucinations on Salisbury Plain; climbing Snowdon at night—*The Prelude* emphatically gives the lie to its creator's remark that his life had been "unusually barren of events."[31] Wordsworth is marvelously good at re-creating experience. "A meditation rose in me that night / Upon the lonely mountain when the scene / Had passed away," begins the passage after the description of the climbing of Snowdon that opens Book 13, but most readers, I suspect, would hardly take in a word of the meditation were it not for the vividness of the account of the experience on the mountain that has preceded it and to which it refers. As a poet, Wordsworth tended to cling to the palpable, Coleridge noted.[32] To which one can only add, thank goodness he did.

Finally, there is a strong case for saying that not the least of the attractions of the 1805 version of *The Prelude* is the way it registers politics. In his letter of 1 May 1805 (see n. 30), Wordsworth remarked to Sir George Beaumont that he had thought he might have success in an autobiographical venture, "as I had nothing to do but describe what I had felt and thought [and] therefore could not easily be bewildered." This is breathtakingly ingenuous. Wordsworth had been bewildered. Writing in 1804–5 about events of a decade earlier was the primary way in which Wordsworth was attempting to rescue himself from what bewilderment persisted, and no aspect of the task was easy. When living in France in the early years of the Revolution, the young radical had had no doubts about his allegiances—"my heart was all / Given to the People, and my love was theirs" (IX, 125–6). But as his country and France went to war, as radical politics was stifled, and as the degeneration of the French experiment cast a pall over hopes for human betterment, Wordsworth was in torment. The great poet who came into being with *Lyrical Ballads* was formed in the torment, and *The Prelude* is a meditation upon the process. But it is also, wonderfully, a record of the torment itself, as it was then, in the 1790s, and as it still lingers now, a decade later. *The Prelude* is a poem about the politics of the British response to the French Revolution and its aftermath, written by an eyewitness in France and London. But it is also a poem about the politics of the moment when Britain was facing its first serious invasion threat in nearly eight hundred years, in the face of which patriotism was not something of which to be ashamed. As an account of one man's bewilderment at a moment of national crisis, which matters because the profundity of the self-examination brings into focus the experience of a whole generation, there is nothing else like it in Romantic poetry.

The Essays

All the essays selected for this volume date from the later part of the last century and the beginning of this one, and the introduction so far has, I hope, indicated why this is so. It is not that there is no earlier writing about Wordsworth that can claim our attention today. Edward Dowden's *The French Revolution and English Literature*, for instance, dates from 1897, but it is very fine, a chastening reminder that the informed and nuanced reading of literary texts in or against or through history is not solely a late twentieth-century phenomenon. A. C. Bradley's "Wordsworth," published in his *Oxford Lectures on Poetry* in 1909, is profound without being heavy, another very important milestone in the development of Wordsworth's reputation. A few more books and essays could be mentioned. So a responsible collection of critical pieces about Wordsworth designed to be of use to today's students could properly reach back into the later nineteenth century at least and ought really to go further back still, to Coleridge. But this is not true of *The Prelude*. Writing that remains of value on the poem (rather than on Wordsworth's work as a whole) postdates Helen Darbishire's 1957 revision of De Selincourt's parallel text edition of *The Prelude*. It is not simple cause and effect, but it is clear that the mass of new material the 1957 edition presented, tantalizingly rich in prompts for still further investigation, intensified scholarly attention to *The Prelude* and hastened recognition of it as central to Wordsworth's achievement.

The essays chosen represent work of only a forty-year span, but the selection does not pretend to add up to a specimen account of the critical developments over the period, which are detailed in Keith Hanley's contribution to the *Cambridge Companion to Wordsworth* or in John Williams's excellent analytical survey in the Palgrave Critical Issues series.[33] What this volume aims to do, both in the selection and the grouping of the essays, is to offer those students who are new to *The Prelude*, or those who are familiar with it but daunted by its size and idiosyncrasy, ways into reading it with most enjoyment. My selection criteria have been quite simple. (1) The pieces included have to focus on *The Prelude* and must be self-contained—the result of this practical restraint is that many fine works on Romanticism or even on Wordsworth are not represented other than in footnote citations. (2) The essays must be lucid. (3) They must be of use. *The Prelude* is a complex poem, and it does not reveal intellectual weakness to confess that one is having difficulty making sense of the verse in much of book 8, for example, or that one is getting lost in the chronological confusions of book 10. All of the pieces included in this collection will, I hope, be found to offer help of different kinds for the fuller reading of the poem.

The Prelude is, first and foremost, a work of literary art. It deserves examination in a spirit of "tender vigilance" (to borrow a fine phrase of Richard Cronin's),[34] and so it is with deliberation that I have placed first five essays that focus in differing ways on poetic form and language. The next group of four essays is characterized by concern with the primary concepts that insistently emerge in all discussions of *The Prelude*—Nature, Imagination, God. Essays in the third and last cluster dwell on diverse issues, each one of which is important enough to deserve a casebook of its own—questions essentially of the politics of identity and nation, of history, and of ecology.

Group 1

"Poetry is precisely, and inescapably, defined by its formed language and its formal commitments," declares Susan Wolfson, and her statement of a fundamental truth is the starting place for this collection of essays.[35] *The Prelude* is a long, varied, complex autobiographical reflection, but that description would fit Coleridge's *Biographia Literaria*. What defines *The Prelude* as different, of course, is its medium. In every line the poet is struggling with the "formal commitments" of blank verse, which he described as "infinitely the most difficult metre to manage."[36] Assessing those formal commitments, which means becoming responsive to the demands of the blank verse itself, is the first challenge facing every reader of it.

Considered in its historical context, it becomes apparent that the choice of the verse form itself meant something—that is, Wordsworth didn't just move on to blank verse because he had mastered the Spenserian stanza in his *Salisbury Plain* poems of 1793–95. To Milton, blank verse represented "ancient liberty recovered to heroic poem from the troublesome and modern bondage of rhyming," and scholars have traced how in the century following *Paradise Lost* the verse form itself became associated with ideas of liberty and national identity.[37] But when the Whig politician Charles James Fox told Wordsworth in 1801 that he was "no great friend to blank verse for subjects which are to be treated of with simplicity," he revealed that those ideas tended also to identify blank verse solely with the elevated and heroic.[38] Milton wanted to pursue "Things unattempted yet in Prose or Rime."[39] So did Wordsworth, but in addition to pursuing what he considered "in truth heroic argument" (*Prelude*, III, 182), in verse that was to be elevated but not Miltonic pastiche, what he also wanted to write about included bird-nesting escapades, skating, and watching jugglers in London streets, things not at all heroic.

For readers today, however, what will most likely seem problematic is not the historical significance of the choice of the verse form (although this is a very intriguing topic to follow up), but the nature of the verse form itself and the overall poetic structure it serves. The opening essays have been chosen because, in differing ways, they all illuminate the formal properties of the poem. In two remarkable articles in 1971 Christopher Ricks took issue with Matthew Arnold's dictum that Wordsworth "has no style," and they remain the finest writing yet on central elements of Wordsworth's poetic manner.[40] Implicitly admonishing Arnold, Ricks declares: "So simply lucid is Wordsworth's speech that it can constitute a temptation: we may not pay sufficient attention to the very words," and the complementary essays are exemplary (in all senses of the word) as demonstrations of how we might rise to the challenge, which, as Ricks sums it up, "both meets and makes high demands").[41] The one included here, "William Wordsworth: 'A Pure Organic Pleasure from the Lines,'" is a subtle and far-reaching account of how Wordsworth manages the basic unit of the verse, the line. Its complement, "William Wordsworth: 'A Sinking into Ourselves from Thought to Thought,'" a revelation of what rests on Wordsworth's use of prepositions, can be read in Ricks's collection of essays, *The Force of Poetry* (1984).

In another comparable (and to my mind very much underrated) study of the intricacies of Wordsworth's verse, Robert Rehder has tried to demonstrate the ways in which certain of Wordsworth's characteristic rhetorical strategies, in particular his deployment of long sentences, arise from a "concern to mark nuances" in "his recognition of the ever-changing data of consciousness."[42] The formal challenges Wordsworth struggles with, Rehder argues, take the shape they do because what he is trying to embrace as subject matter is resistant and because the very attempt to embrace it is revolutionary: "Wordsworth is the first of many poets to attempt in his poetry to take full possession of his own life."

It was, Wordsworth confessed, as mentioned earlier, "a thing unprecedented in Literary history that a man should talk so much about himself,"[43] and Rehder is justified in placing the emphasis he does on the originality of Wordsworth's autobiographical project. But what needs constantly to be kept in mind also is that if the attempt to take possession of his life brought Wordsworth's autobiographical poem into being, it was not in a single act of comprehensive mastery, at the end of which the poet could declare the process of possessing complete. Taking possession involved continuous, life-long activity, the return to previous attempts at mastery. As Susan Wolfson has put it, very finely, "Manuscripts as well as memories constitute his past, and textual revision reduplicates, perpetuates, and enters into recollection."[44] Wolfson's essay, "Revision as Form: Wordsworth's Drowned Man," traces the evolution and shifting identity of a particularly fascinating passage of childhood memory and is included here for two reasons. First, because it demonstrates entirely persuasively the truth and importance of her declaration that "revision is not just compositional; it is the very trope of autobiography, a resistance, in events large and small, to arresting and fixing phantoms of conceit in a final frame of autobiographical argument." Second, because it is such a fine practical example of the rewards of intense scrutiny of the poetic text through its evolving manifestations as the poet repeatedly attempted to take a secure hold on his past.

Mary Jacobus's essay, " 'Dithyrambic Fervour': The Lyric Voice of *The Prelude*," directs us through minute and highly informed scrutiny to details of the text while developing ever more wide-ranging consideration of their meaning. Distinctions between the dithyrambic and the Orphic in classical poetry are likely to be lost on most modern readers, as is the significance of Wordsworth's allusion to Theocritus and the story of Comates in *Prelude*, book 10, and it is not the least of the virtues of Jacobus's piece that it so accessibly unfolds what otherwise tends to lie inert in footnotes. In the unfolding of the local, however, what Jacobus does is indicate the enormous importance of the range of rhetorical choices made, and strategies employed, in the poem overall. Unpacking in effect Matthew Arnold's comment, "It might seem that Nature not only gave him the matter for his poem, but wrote his poem for him," Jacobus suggests with great subtlety the kinds of anxiety at work in a poet powerfully aware "of the dread that poetic individuality might be lost" and what it might mean for understanding the actual practice—the formal characteristics of the verse—to suggest that "Drowned neither by the voice of the Sublime—Milton's voice—nor by the clamour of all the other voices by which the poet risks being possessed, the voice of nature permits a loss of individuality which is at once safe and unifying."[45]

At a crucial juncture in her argument, Jacobus declares, "The function of *The Prelude*'s apostrophes is to constitute the voice of the poet: the function of its addresses to Coleridge (and to some extent, Dorothy) is to save it by domesticating it." The next essay, by Lucy Newlyn, focuses on this vital element in the shaping of *The Prelude*, namely, that it was addressed to somebody; that for Wordsworth, taking possession of his own life involved explaining it to a beloved and ideal reader—Samuel Taylor Coleridge.

As the autobiographical poem began to materialize, Wordsworth's most ambitious work to date, Coleridge was literally a presence. The earliest childhood memories in book 1 were sent to him in a letter as early as December 1798. In January 1804, as Coleridge was preparing himself to leave home and family for the Mediterranean, he listened in the emotionally charged landscape setting of a high point above Grasmere to Wordsworth reading "the second part of his divine Self-biography."[46] A year and a half later, Wordsworth had finished the poem, now in thirteen books, but it could not be regarded as truly completed until Coleridge had received it. The ceremony of completion—for that is what it was—took place in January 1807, as Wordsworth recited the whole poem to his friend, now, it was hoped, "in renovated health." During 1797–98, Wordsworth and Coleridge came to conceive of their friendship as not just a personal boon but as a providential gift that pledged them to high endeavors. So, in the closing section of his poem, Wordsworth recalled the joyous summer when together they "wanton'd in wild Poesy" (XIII, 414), and dedicated them both anew as "joint-labourers in the work, (Should Providence such grace to us vouchsafe) / Of [Man's] redemption, surely yet to come" (XIII, 439–41).

If the flesh-and-blood Coleridge was a spectator at important moments in the history of the poem's reception, the idea of Coleridge was active throughout its evolution. What was known in the Wordsworth circle as "the poem to Coleridge" was "to" him in a double sense. The poem was a gift, it was Wordsworth's "offering of my love" (XIII, 427), but it was also "to" Coleridge in that it was addressed to him. The language of the poem, its rhetorical strategies, decisions at to what to include and what exclude, its whole shape and texture in fact, are determined by thoughts of the addressee, namely, in the words of the preface to *The Excursion* (1814), that "dear Friend, most distinguished for his knowledge and genius, and to whom the Author's Intellect is deeply indebted."

At the close of book 1 of *The Prelude*, Wordsworth signals that he recognizes that the task of trying "To understand myself" is inextricable from that of enabling Coleridge "to know / With better knowledge how the heart was fram'd / Of him thou lovest" (I, 656–8). What Newlyn's essay does is demonstrate just how complicated this apparently simple declaration of intent turned out to be. " 'A Strong Confusion': Coleridge's Presence in *The Prelude*" is a searching analysis of the needs that determined

Wordsworth's construction of Coleridge in the poem, a guide to an omnipresence felt from the first moment of address at line 55 of book 1, to the last, in the poem's closing lines.

Group 2

The most appropriate text with which to launch the introduction to the second group of essays comes from Thomas Carlyle's *Sartor Resartus* (1833–34), a philosophical-fictional extravaganza that makes a bridge between the Romantic and early Victorian periods. In the chapter headed "Natural Supernaturalism," Carlyle's mouthpiece, supposedly a German Professor of Things in General, delivers a great truth about the factors that limit Man's life on earth, those "two grand fundamental world-enveloping Appearances, SPACE and TIME":

> These, as spun and woven for us from before Birth itself, to clothe our celestial ME for dwelling here, and yet to blind it,—lie all-embracing, as the universal canvass, or warp and woof, whereby all minor Illusions, in this Phantasm Existence, weave and paint themselves. In vain, while here on Earth, shall you endeavour to strip them off; you can, at best, but rend them asunder for moments, and look through.[47]

Scooping together most of the key texts of Romanticism (Wordsworth's "Intimations of Immortality" most obviously among them), Carlyle voices many of their profoundest concerns. What is the very beauty of the material world but a prison house that closes about us? What can we ever know about the transcendent world beyond the veil? Close bound by space and time, by what power, if at all, can we "rend them asunder for moments, and look through"? And at the heart of it all, the question, on what can morality be grounded in "this Phantasm Existence"?

Each of the essays in this group considers Wordsworth in relation to these questions, and for each writer what is also in play is the struggle to define most exactly what kind of poetical phenomenon Wordsworth is. It is a question that has been exercising readers ever since Wordsworth prefaced the monumental *Excursion* in 1814 with revelations about poetic ambitions that made Milton's seem modest. What kind of poet-prophet was this who could, "unalarmed," "tread on shadowy ground . . . sink / Deep— and, aloft ascending, breathe in worlds / To which the heaven of heavens is but a veil"? It is, William Hazlitt declared in a review of the poem, "as if there were nothing but himself and the universe." Matthew Arnold in the next generation picked up on Hazlitt's comment, "His mind is, as it were, coeval with the primary forms of things, his imagination holds immediately from nature," when, struggling to characterize Wordsworth's power, he plumped for "Wordsworth's poetry, when he is at his best, is inevitable, as inevitable as Nature herself."[48] All the major Wordsworth critics in the later nineteenth and early twentieth centuries—Leslie Stephen, Walter Pater, A. C. Bradley—followed suit, as if impelled to try to refine a critical formulation that would be applicable to this or that poem and yet also adequate to represent what overall the phenomenon "Wordsworth" essentially is. When Geoffrey Hartman declares "it is certain that he is not a mystic or even a materialist," the same compulsion is at work. "If Wordsworth must be labeled," he continues, "it would be better to call him a radical Protestant whose mind is in love with works . . . yet cannot subdue or bind itself to natural objects."[49]

It is fitting that the second group of essays should open with an extract from Hartman's *Wordsworth's Poetry 1787–1814* (1964, 1971), because it has been unquestionably one of the most influential books in determining a whole movement of critical thought. Within Christian discourse, the progress of a soul has necessarily entailed releasing the self from the bonds of nature for enjoyment of the freedom of the greater not-nature, and a great many of Wordsworth's utterances could be marshalled to demonstrate his comfortable relation to this tradition of spiritual enlightenment. For example, this comment to fellow poet Walter Savage Landor, which Wordsworth made in the course of a letter (21 January 1824) about religious poetry:

> Even in poetry it is the imaginative only, viz., that which is conversant with, or turns upon infinity, that powerfully affects me,—perhaps I ought to explain: I mean to say that, unless in those passages where things are lost in each other, and limits vanish, and aspirations are raised, I read with something too much like indifference—but all great poets are in this view powerful Religionists.

What is so important about Hartman's work—what made it controversial in 1964 and what flags it still as a landmark study—is that it problematizes in every particular the primary coordinates of an utterance such as this—the Self, Imagination, the Infinite, and Poetry. While confirming the centrality of the "movement of transcendence" in Wordsworth, Hartman searchingly examines "the deeply paradoxical character of [his] dealings with nature." *Wordsworth's Poetry* ranges across the whole of Wordsworth's most creative years and makes its impact in part from the comprehensiveness and thoroughness of its exploratory procedures, but, as it happens, the extract—chosen for inclusion here because it centers on *The Prelude*—does exemplify the quality of the book as a whole. "The Via Naturaliter Negativa" has a proposition to pursue, namely, that "Wordsworth thought nature itself led him beyond nature," but it is pursued not with Procrustean determination, but rather a scrupulous attention to the workings of the poetry that illuminates specifics even as it constructs the overall argument.

Hartman's essay is followed by an excerpt from another landmark in Romantic scholarship, M. H. Abrams's *Natural Supernaturalism* (1971). Taking his title from the phrase of Carlyle's that most succinctly defines the "cardinal endeavor" of the great Romantics, which was "in diverse degrees and ways, to naturalize the supernatural and to humanize the divine," Abrams examines the reversion in much Romantic writing "to the stark drama and suprarational mysteries of the Christian story and doctrines and to the violent conflicts and abrupt reversals of the Christian inner life, turning on the extremes of destruction and creation, hell and heaven, exile and reunion, death and rebirth, dejection and joy, paradise lost and paradise regained." Since they lived inescapably after the Enlightenment, however, Romantic period writers, Abrams argues, had to revive "these ancient matters" with a difference. They "undertook to save the overview of human history and destiny, the experiential paradigms, and the cardinal values of their religious heritage, by reconstituting them in a way that would make them intellectually acceptable, as well as emotionally pertinent, for the time being."[50]

Whether or not its thesis is accepted in full, the lucidity with which *Natural Supernaturalism* deploys complex materials ensures that the book remains of enormous value to every student of European Romanticism, not least on account of the range and historical depth of the texts that are cited; the excerpt included here has had long-lasting influence on study of *The Prelude*. Arguing that "A supervising idea . . . controls Wordsworth's account [of his growth] and shapes it into a structure in which the protagonist is put forward as one who has been elected to play a special role in a providential plot," Abrams traces the "radically achronological" presentation of the poem's spiritual journey, which opens "not at the beginning but at the end," and argues that "the Wordsworthian theodicy of the private life . . . translates the painful process of Christian conversion and redemption into a painful process of self-formation, crisis, and self-recognition, which culminates in a stage of self-coherence, self-awareness, and assured power that is its own reward."

Both of the essays that follow are in dialogue with Hartman and Abrams and in differing ways complement them. Jonathan Wordsworth examines afresh and in detail a section of the poem that is very important to Abrams's argument; William Ulmer concentrates on examining the fit between Abrams's overarching formulations about Romantic theodicy and the specifics of Wordsworth's poetry.

There are two mountain-top scenes in *The Prelude:* the crossing of the Alps in book 6 and the climbing of Snowdon that opens book 13. In the writing of the crossing of the Alps—not at all the same experience as actually crossing them—Wordsworth is seized by such tumultuous feelings as he tries to interpret what he recollects that, in a mysterious fashion, he is both blocked and thwarted by Imagination while being granted by it a revelation of Man's true home, "with Infinitude" (VI, 539). The ascent of Snowdon is also, like the crossing of the Alps, an account of expectations disappointed and of abundant recompense granted in a moment of epiphanic revelation, but here the meditation on Imagination that follows is eloquently assured. Both of these episodes are keystones in the structure of *The Prelude,* but it is in the ascent of Snowdon that the poem's major concerns come together and are restated in such a way that its concluding lines, which reaffirm the poet's fitness for this vocation and the value of it, seem not magniloquent, but justified.

That, at least, is what Wordsworth would have his readers assent to, and it is what Abrams endorses in his sympathetic exposition of the poem's final book. Jonathan Wordsworth, however, shows some resistance to the argumentative drive of book 13, and it is one of the chief strengths of his essay that, while acknowledging its greatness, it probes the poetry so carefully. What the poet asserts about Imagination; how it is embodied in figurative language; what moral and/or social good is said to follow from the exercise of this power—all these are scrutinised in criticism that generates a continuous flow of insights from a rare combination of wide-ranging scholarly command and pertinacious attention to textual detail.

Hartman, Abrams, and Jonathan Wordsworth write about revelation, transcendence, infinitude, invoking the conceptual paradigms (Fall, Redemption) and the lexicon of the Christian tradition in which Wordsworth's poetry was situated historically. Wordsworth was not Shelley—even in his red-hot republican years it was not conceivable that he would write *The Necessity of Atheism*—and few if any would dissent from the claim that *The Prelude* belongs to the tradition of English Protestantism.[51] But equally, it is true to say that few would regard that claim as any great matter. The radical humanism of Wordsworth's work is what commends it to most modern readers, and for those who are troubled by the role of the Christian God in the poem, Abrams has provided so intellectualy persuasive and imaginatively satisfying a model for understanding it that it is as if questions about the religious dimension of *The Prelude* have been put aside as settled.

William Ulmer argues that this quiescence needs to be disturbed. His essay is tactful and diplomatic; this is not an assault on M. H. Abrams by a pretender to his intellectual throne. And it is circumspect in its aims; "Soul's Progress: The Faith of *The Prelude*" is neither a belatedly Victorian attempt to claim the poet for this or that denominational identity nor a twenty-first-century neo-Christian reading of the poetry as doctrinal succor in a godless age. What Ulmer's essay does do is reopen important questions. What part was played by the religious culture in which Wordsworth had been nurtured when he came to shape the autobiographical poem? Given that it is hard to disagree with Abrams's contention that God does "nothing of consequence" in *The Prelude*, can it be thought of as a Christian poem? Is there a fundamental incompatability between humanism, as Wordsworth would have conceived of it, and Christian revelation? As he explores how "the faith of *The Prelude* marries Wordsworth's assurance of spiritual purpose to his humanistic reverence for the 'mind of Man,' " Ulmer's essay brings these and other questions into focus, and it has been included both because it serves to underline their continuing importance and for the pragmatic reason that it may be of assistance to readers today who are less familiar than earlier generations with the language of the Bible and the Prayer Book in which the poem is steeped.[52]

In tracing Wordsworth's attempts to identify the preeminent formative moments in his life, those that have contributed most to the evolution of his creative being, Abrams and the other scholars discussed here follow Wordsworth's own choice of topics and language. Events through which Nature acts out on the child her ministry of love and fear; crossing the Alps and climbing Snowdon; loss of faith and restoration—these are the defining elements in the progress of the soul in *The Prelude,* and what they confirm is that it is possible to identify a "true self." A vital declaration in book 1 (356–62) images the "mind of man" as composed, like music, of discordant elements that are reconciled:

> Ah me! that all
> The terrors, all the early miseries,
> Regrets, vexations, lassitudes, that all
> The thoughts and feelings which have been infus'd

Into my mind should ever have made up
The calm existence that is mine when I
Am worthy of myself.

Anne K. Mellor's essay has been included to round off this group because it challenges so cogently such a passage as this one and the many
others like it that constitute the poet's own commentary on his providen-
tially ordered life story. The chapter in *Romanticism and Gender* from which
this extract is taken contrasts the ways of "constructing the self" taken by
William and Dorothy Wordsworth; it needs to be read in its entirety for
the persuasive force of Mellor's interrogation to be felt to most effect, but
the section on *The Prelude* can stand alone. It introduces ways of thinking
about the nature of the gendered self in accounts of the evolution of an
artist that have a bearing not only on *The Prelude* but also on such decidedly
masculine autobiographical fictions as *David Copperfield* and *A Portrait of the
Artist as a Young Man.*

It needs to be recognized, Mellor argues, that Wordsworth's conviction
of the "enduring coherence of his self," as linguistically constructed in *The
Prelude*, is "not the 'higher'—and potentially universal—self he dreamed
of, but rather a specifically *masculine* self." Keeping in view the loftiest conception of the self, by "deliberately denying his material physicality, even
his mortality, Wordsworth represents his poetic self as pure ego, as 'the
mind of man,' " but the cost is inscribed in the poem. Wordsworth's "sublime self-assurance is rendered possible . . . only by the arduous repression
of the Other in all its forms" and by a continual struggle to control female
Nature. Examining Wordsworth's gendering of Nature, Earth, Soul, Imagination, Self, Mellor concludes that "Wordsworth's attempt to represent an
autonomous self with clearly defined, firm ego boundaries, a self that
stands alone, 'unpropped' (III, 230), entirely self-sufficient and self-
generating, both unmothered and unfathered, is undercut by Wordsworth's
own slippery pronouns as a heuristic fiction, a 'story.' "

Group 3

John Williams has observed accurately that historical fluctuations in Wordsworth's reputation have "from the first been predicated on a controversy
over quality, and over where and how to locate the political and religious
themes that inform the work."[53] The essays in group 2 have been loosely

concerned with the latter; the three that open group 3 are directly concerned with the former.

Political history is inescapable in *The Prelude,* by which I mean quite simply that the poem is dense with reference to historical events. For the actuality of many of the most interesting things that Wordsworth tells us about his own life his words are the only evidence. Did he really steal a boat on Ullswater? Had he really never heard a woman swear before he went to London? Did he really have visions of Druids as he crossed Salisbury Plain? We cannot know for sure: there is no corroborative evidence. But there is no uncertainty about the fall of the Bastille in 1789, or the outbreak of war between Britain and France in 1793, or the death of Robespierre in 1794, or the coronation of Napoleon as emperor ten years later, and it is references such as these that are the matrix in which the autobiographical poem is set.

The Prelude; or Growth of a Poet's Mind is the wording on the 1850 title page, to which in any ideal edition of the poem an editor would be tempted to add: "In particular during the fifteen foundation years of modern European history." To which might further be added, in smaller print perhaps but large enough to signal its importance, "An eyewitness account from one who was there." Without question the French Revolution was, in Shelley's words, "the master theme of the epoch in which we live," and Wordsworth was there.[54] He alone of all the major poets of the period was actually in France, not at the center of things for long, but close enough to experience the jubilation of a people "when Europe was rejoiced, / France standing on the top of golden hours, / And human nature seeming born again" (VI, 352–4); close enough to feel at one with them and to be able to declare that their cause was his: "my heart was all / Given to the People, and my love was theirs" (IX, 125–6). When the Pitt government declared war on the fledgling republic in 1793, Wordsworth was back in England, but he still had the dust of France on his shoes and—painful to acknowledge though he later found it—as he joined the congregation in a village church, his prayers were for French victory and "the day of vengeance, yet to come" (see X, 245–74). How different was the situation ten years later, when the poet, together with the great majority of his able-bodied countrymen, enlisted in the militia and regularly turned out to drill in preparation to resist the threatened French invasion.[55]

Political and military history will have a bearing on almost any poem written between 1793 and 1815. With *The Prelude* they determine its subject matter and its structural evolution. The poem chronicles Wordsworth's life from birth in 1770 to the publication of *Lyrical Ballads* in 1798, and its account of the 1790s tells of youthfully idealistic commitment to the French Revolution being dashed, then revived, then dashed once more, and of the poet's intellectual and emotional impasse before a breakthrough into a new sense of how hopes for Mankind might be imagined and realized. But it also registers his developing conception over the six years of the poem's composition of what the politics of the revolutionary years from 1789 onward had really meant *then* and still meant *now.* Such complexity serves to make *The Prelude* one of the key documents of the entire Romantic period and an entirely original and enormously rewarding poem, but there is no doubt that it demands a great deal of its readers. It requires attention to three strands of historical material: (1) the chronology of historical events, for which all of us need help from footnotes to a greater or lesser degree; (2) Wordsworth's account of these events, which is anything but straightforward; (3) Wordsworth's meditations on their inherent significance at the time they were experienced, their signifcance at the present moment of composition of the poem, as it now seems to the eye of retrospection, and the relation between the two. The essays by Erskine-Hill, Gravil, and Liu have all been included for their practical value in helping readers meet these demands.

Howard Erskine-Hill's book *Poetry of Opposition and Revolution* rests on an assured grasp of the intricacies of British politics since the Glorious Revolution of 1688 and an acute sense of the political meanings of the linguistic choices open to a poet in the late 1790s, and both of its chapters on "The Politics of *The Prelude*" can be recommended. The excerpted section from 'Wordsworth and the Conception of *The Prelude*' is included here because it directs attention to the political contexts of the poem's first coming into being. Most accounts of the evolution of the poem understandably emphasize that the expansion of the structure to thirteen books was the moment when politics entered the poem, but, as Erskine-Hill points out, the poem had its genesis in the politics of a period characterized by Wordsworth as "these times of fear, / This melancholy waste of hopes o'erthrown" (II, 448–9). The poet's return to childhood is motivated by the desire to answer as fully as possible the question "Was it for this . . . ?" The opening books track back to infancy, but the driving force is not nostalgia but the need to make sense of now, that is, the situation in 1799, the year in which Napoleon subjugated the Swiss and which Wordsworth in later life always dated as the moment of his final disillusion with the French Revolution. The question that remained was, what, if anything, survived of the hopes the Revolution had once embodied?

That it is a struggle to meet the question candidly is apparent in books

9–11, not least from the manner in which the chronological narrative that is necessary if the growth of the poet's mind is to be charted as a progression from one state to another strains against memories and reflections that will not conform to the discipline of chronology. But evidence of the struggle does not indicate a failure of art—on the contrary, the struggle at the moment of writing needs to be recorded in the verse as well as the torments of a decade earlier, and it is the poet's determination to encompass as much as possible that makes "the Revolution books," as Alan Liu observes, "among the most difficult sections of the poem to grasp as a whole." But they can be grasped, once the "design" (Liu), the "architectonics" (Gravil), of the Revolution books is appreciated.

Gravil's analysis of "what is created in the rhetorical structure of books 9, 10, and 11" scrutinizes the language of Wordsworth's self-assessment in such detail that it will be difficult to follow without quite a good grasp of the shape and content of these books.[56] Once these have been registered, however, at least in outline, the rich seams of Gravil's essay can be mined. Recognizing that the Wordsworth of 1804–5 is trying "to tell the truth twice: the truth of enthusiasm and the truth of disenchantment," Gravil adroitly probes the poet's representation of his past and present selves. His method, moreover, is exemplary of the rewards possible from one kind of critical approach strenuously pursued, for his challenges not just to accepted readings of the self-representation, but also in a sense to Wordsworth's own readings of it, are grounded not on the deployment of historical or biographical information from outside the text, but on an openness of response to the possibilities of meaning presented by the poem's language itself.

Alan Liu is also eager to understand the imaginative processes at work in Wordsworth's historical retrospect; his *Wordsworth: The Sense of History* is the most ambitious book on the subject yet. Excerpting from it is very difficult because Liu's study is so densely woven—his persuasiveness in large part arising from a cumulative procedure of argument and illustration—but the extract on *The Prelude*'s Revolution books can stand independently.

Liu scrutinizes the same section of the poem as Gravil, with a comparable determination to resist reinscribing the contours of his past that the poet has already mapped out, but Liu's approach is quite different. Taking up Wordsworth's image of himself in France as being like someone who "had abruptly pass'd / Into a theatre, of which the stage / Was busy with an action far advanced" (IX, 93–5), Liu analyzes the genres through which the poet attempts to give shape to his experiences—the tour poem, romance, drama, epic, lyric: "Wordsworth engages the reader in his younger self's perpetual confusion about the kind of agon the Revolution is and the kind of narrative appropriate to tell it." Identifying what he terms the "contest of genres," those genres that "cannot comprehend the Revolution as historical phenomenon," Liu sees Wordsworth moving inexorably toward lyric, whose function "is to sound the death of history" in a vision of peace that reconciles and restores.

In all the essays in group 2 and those discussed so far in group 3 the word Nature appears. It is the most Protean of terms—Nature is a power whose tutelary presences are the "Souls of lonely places" (I, 493), but also a power contrasted to the civilized: "To Nature then / Power had reverted; habit, custom, law / Had left an interregnum's open space / For her to stir about in uncontroll'd" (X, 609–12). But Nature is also "The Earth," whose "common face" spake to the poet "rememberable things" (I, 614–16), through whose beauty he as a child "held unconscious intercourse / With the eternal Beauty" (I, 589–90), and it is on his sense of the word *Nature* that the last essay in this collection focuses.

In the closing lines of *The Prelude* Wordsworth refers to himself and Coleridge as "Prophets of Nature," and by this stage of the poet's unfolding of the design of his life the appellation seems entirely appropriate. The poet's childhood is said to have been blessed by Nature. Truths come in revelation among the Alps (book 6) or on Snowdon (book 13); he dates his vocation as a "dedicated spirit" from the moment of an epiphanic vision experienced on an early morning walk (IV, 330–45):

> The Sea was laughing at a distance; all
> The solid Mountains were as bright as clouds,
> Grain-tinctured, drench'd in empyrean light;
> And, in the meadows and the lower grounds,
> Was all the sweetness of a common dawn,
> Dews, vapours, and the melody of birds,
> And Labourers going forth into the fields.

Clearly it cannot be wrong to join Shelley terming Wordsworth a "Poet of Nature."[57]

If it were to be objected that, since *The Prelude* is where Wordsworth defined the terms in which his career and identity were to be discussed, of course all quotations from it will confirm the rightness of the "Prophet of Nature" formulation he arrives at, the 1798 *Lyrical Ballads* volume might be adduced to counter the objection. Here, on the one hand, are poems about rural people and lives hard struggled through in the eye of Nature, and on the other, lyrics celebrating rhapsodically the coming of Spring, when "every / Flower enjoys the air it breathes" ("Lines Written in Early Spring") and declaring that in "nature and the language of the sense" this poet, "so long / A worshipper of Nature," finds "The guide, the guardian of my heart, and soul / Of all my moral being" ("Tintern Abbey"). The claim to be Nature's priest could hardly be put more unequivocally.

Much of the rest of Wordsworth's oeuvre flows in one or other of the directions marked out by this unpretending but highly significant volume. One movement consists of poems and prose about rural figures in their world and/or about the natural world itself—"The Old Cumberland Beggar," "Michael," "The Brothers," "Ode: The Pass of Kirkstone," *The River Duddon* sonnet sequence, the *Guide to the Lakes,* and many more. The other consists of all those poems in which the poet speaks of his response to the natural world and why it matters—from "Tintern Abbey" through the "Ode: Intimations of Immortality," "Elegiac Stanzas . . . Peele Castle," the ode "Composed Upon an Evening of Extraordinary Splendor and Beauty," the poems about the River Yarrow, and, of course, *The Prelude* itself.

Further titles could be listed, and more evidence of different kinds could be marshalled. Among the latter would be Wordsworth's letter of 14 January 1801 to the statesman Charles James Fox about the significance for contemporary politics of his English pastoral "Michael," or the seventy-five-year-old poet's explanation of his resistance to classroom teaching—it came, he said, "from one who spent half his boyhood in running wild among the Mountains."[58] The sum total would confirm general assent to the proposition that Wordsworth was a Poet of Nature and that his treatment of rural life and landscape is enormously significant not just for the history of English poetry but for British culture more largely.

Questions begin to niggle, however, about every aspect of the proposition to which general assent could readily be given—and they have done so ever since Wordsworth felt compelled to write a second version of the Preface to *Lyrical Ballads* in 1802 to clarify, supposedly, problems about the first of 1800. Is what Wordsworth felt about Nature translatable to other human beings as a value for them, or is it the peculiar possession of a special sensibility only? How can "nature and the language of the sense" be a source of moral guardianship? Or even: can loving the beauties of nature really do you any good? Does a poet who is educated at St. John's College, Cambridge, have any standing when he declares it better for the Old Cumberland Beggar to "Struggle with frosty air and winter snows" than to enter the workhouse? What vision of rural life is being promulgated by this poet in 1798 who exactly twenty years later was electioneering on behalf of the Lowther family, the biggest landowners in the Lake District?

During his most creative years, all these questions were troublingly glimpsed and thereafter brought into sharper focus by Wordsworth himself. They figure in *Home at Grasmere* (1800), where for the first time they are posed as questions rather than being only possibilities latent in the verse, as they are, for example, in "Tintern Abbey." *Home at Grasmere* is a celebration in reverent wonderment of the providence that has brought the poet to this paradisal spot, but it is also an acknowledgement of the dangers of selfish withdrawal, bad faith of various sorts, illusion and denial. The questions were explored further throughout the evolving *Prelude*—in fact, the wrestle with these questions determined the expansion of the poem from two to five to thirteen books. And they have remained central to the debate about Wordsworth's overall achievement and historical stature that has continued to this day.[59]

The questions are big ones, and consequently the parts of *The Prelude* in which they are the central subject matter, rather than observations arising *en passant,* are difficult. Book 8 in particular—its 1850 subtitle is "Love of Nature Leading to Love of Man"—is a challenge. Jonathan Bate's essay has been included because it attempts to recover what is most valuable about Wordsworth's struggles with these issues in a sympathetic, recuperative reading of books 7 to 9. Locating Wordsworth's revisioned pastoralism in relation to both the history of classical pastoral, from which it is too often damagingly wrested, and to the environmental and ecological concerns of our own day, Bate suggests ways of recognizing what he calls the radical humanism of book 8 and what its place would be in a fresh conception of politics: "To go back to nature is not to retreat from politics but to take politics into a new domain." Wordsworth's poetry, he declares, offers a "vision of "fullness and completeness of life.' " The quoted words are William Morris's, and in recalling them Bate restores for a moment a late nineteenth-century sense of the possibility of the good life, but he does so deliberately to point to its appositeness for the twenty-first.

Notes

1. Samuel Taylor Coleridge, *Biographia Literaria,* ed. James Engell and Walter Jackson Bate, 2 vols. (Princeton, N.J.: Princeton University Press, 1983), 2:151. Matthew Arnold, ed., *Poems of Wordsworth* (London: Macmillan, 1879), x.

2. Samuel Taylor Coleridge, "To William Wordsworth, Composed on the Night after his Recitation of a Poem upon the Growth of an Individual Mind," in *Poetical Works*, ed. J. C. C. Mays, 3 vols. (Princeton, N.J.: Princeton University Press, 2001), vol. 1, pt. 2, 817. Arnold, *Poems of Wordsworth*, xi.

3. At the time of writing, *The Excursion* has not appeared in the Cornell Wordsworth series. Readers who want to find the Preface in its entirety will need to consult vol. 5 of Wordsworth's *Poetical Works*, ed. Ernest de Selincourt and Helen Darbishire, 5 vols. (Oxford: Clarendon Press, 1941–49).

4. The editors were effectively Wordsworth's nephew, Christopher, his son-in-law Edward Quillinan, John Carter, his long-time secretary, and Mary, his widow. In the preface to *The Prelude* they conscientiously point out that "The First Book of the First Part of RECLUSE still remains in manuscript." This manuscript poem escaped from family control and was published in 1891 by Macmillan under the title *The Recluse*, which makes things very confusing for students who read that Wordsworth never did write *The Recluse*. In manuscript the poem's subtitle is "Home at Grasmere," and it is under this title that the poem has entered the Wordsworth canon. For full details see the Cornell Wordsworth series volume *Home at Grasmere*, ed. Beth Darlington (Ithaca, N.Y.: Cornell University Press, 1977).

5. For a full account see Stephen Gill, *Wordsworth and the Victorians* (Oxford: Oxford University Press, 1998).

6. Christopher Wordsworth, *Memoirs of William Wordsworth*, 2 vols. (London: Edward Moxon, 1851), 1:313. Mary Jacobus discusses the passage and the act of naming the poem as "at once a legitimation, an act of propriety, and an appropriation" in *Romanticism, Writing, and Sexual Difference: Essays on "The Prelude"* (Oxford: Clarendon Press, 1989), 188–9.

7. Jerome J. McGann, ed., *The New Oxford Book of Romantic Period Verse* (Oxford: Oxford University Press, 1994).

8. *Poems*, 2 vols. (1815). For the new "Preface" and the "Essay Supplementary to the Preface" see *The Prose Works of William Wordsworth*, ed. W. J. B. Owen and Jane Worthington Smyser, 3 vols. (Oxford: Clarendon Press, 1974), 3:23–107.

9. In collective editions from 1820 on *The Excursion* was subtitled "A Portion of the Recluse," but with the 1836 edition the subtitle was excised. In 1842 Wordsworth gathered together *Poems, Chiefly of Early and Late Years*, in which he included a revised version of the Salisbury Plain poems written in the 1790s, now entitled *Guilt and Sorrow; or, Incidents upon Salisbury Plain*, and a revised version of his 1797 drama *The Borderers*.

10. T. S. Eliot, "Tradition and the Individual Talent," in *Selected Essays*, 3rd ed. (London: Faber and Faber, 1951), 15.

11. *Life and Letters of Lord Macaulay*, ed. George Otto Trevelyan, 2 vols. (London,

1876), 2:279. J[ohn] C[ampbell] Shairp, *On Poetic Interpretation of Nature* (Edinburgh: David Douglas, 1877), 265.

12. Emile Legouis, *La Jeunesse de William Wordsworth* (Paris, 1896); trans. J. W. Matthews as *The Early Life of William Wordsworth 1770–1798: A Study of "The Prelude"* (London, 1897); reissued with new introduction by Nicholas Roe (London: Libris, 1988), 12.

14. M. H. Abrams, "Introduction: Two Roads to Wordsworth," in *Wordsworth: A Collection of Critical Essays* (Englewood Cliffs, N.J.: Prentice-Hall, 1972), 1–11.

15. *The Prelude or Growth of a Poet's Mind,* ed. Ernest De Selincourt (Oxford: Clarendon Press, 1926).

16. For an account of the editions published by Knight, Dowden, and Hutchinson, and of the labors of other scholarly pioneers, see Gill, *Wordsworth and the Victorians.*

17. Raymond Dexter Havens, *The Mind of a Poet,* 2 vols. (Baltimore: Johns Hopkins University Press, 1941), xiii–iv.

18. Herbert Lindenberger, *On Wordsworth's Prelude* (Princeton, N.J.: Princeton University Press, 1963), 295–9.

19. *Wordsworth Circle* 17 (1986): 2–38. An important discussion of the issues involved is Zachary Leader, *Revision and Romantic Authorship* (Oxford: Clarendon Press, 1996), 19–77.

20. Ernest De Selincourt, ed., *The Prelude or Growth of a Poet's Mind,* 2nd. ed., rev. Helen Darbishire (Oxford: Clarendon Press, 1959), xxvi.

21. J. R. MacGillivray, "The Three Forms of *The Prelude,*" in *Essays in English Literature from the Renaissance to the Victorian Age, Presented to A.S.P. Woodhouse, 1964,* ed. Millar Maclure and F. W. Watt (Toronto: University of Toronto Press, 1964), 229–44.

22. Jonathan Wordsworth, "The Growth of a Poet's Mind," *Cornell Library Journal* 11 (1970): 8.

23. *The Prelude, 1798–1799,* ed. Stephen Parrish (Ithaca, N.Y.: Cornell University Press, 1977); *The Prelude 1799, 1805, 1850,* ed. Jonathan Wordsworth, M. H. Abrams, and Stephen Gill (New York: Norton, 1979).

24. Jonathan Wordsworth, ed., *The Prelude: The Four Texts (1798, 1799, 1805, 1850)* (London: Penguin Books, 1995), xxvi.

25. Wordsworth to S. T. Coleridge, 6 March 1804, in *The Letters of William and Dorothy Wordsworth: The Early Years 1787–1805,* ed. Chester L. Shaver (Oxford: Clarendon Press, 1967), 452. Future citation to *Letters.*

26. Duncan Wu, *The Five-Book Prelude* (Oxford: Blackwell, 1997). The groundbreaking article on the poem was Jonathan Wordsworth, "The Five-Book *Prelude* of Early Spring 1804," *Journal of English and Germanic Philology* 76 (1977): 1–25.

27. Mark L. Reed, *The Thirteen-Book Prelude,* 2 vols. (Ithaca: Cornell University Press, 1991), 1:82. All quotations from and reference to the thirteen-book poem

will be to this edition. As Reed's text differs slightly from others, readers may find that line numbers given in my introduction don't exactly match those in other generally available edition of *The Prelude,* but these differences are too slight for there to be any difficulty in locating a passage.

28. W. J. B. Owen, ed., *The Fourteen-Book Prelude* (Ithaca, N.Y.: Cornell University Press, 1985), 11.

29. From the Preface to *Lyrical Ballads* (1802 version). See *Prose Works,* 1:139–40.

30. Letter to Sir George Beaumont, 1 May 1805, in *Letters,* 1:586.

31. Letter to Anne Taylor, 9 April 1801, in *Letters,* 1:452.

32. In "My First Acquaintance With Poets" (1823), Hazlitt reported Coleridge as lamenting in Wordsworth "a something corporeal, a *matter-of-fact-ness,* a clinging to the palpable." *Complete Works of Williams Hazlitt,* ed. P. P. Howe, 21 vols. (London: Dent, 1930–34), 17:117.

33. Keith Hanley, "Textual Issues and a Guide to Further Reading," in *The Cambridge Companion to Wordsworth,* ed. Stephen Gill (Cambridge: Cambridge University Press, 2003), 246–64; John Williams, *William Wordsworth* (Basingstoke, England: Palgrave, 2002).

34. Cronin uses the phrase in the course of an eloquent call for a reinvigorated formalism in his *The Politics of Romantic Poetry: In Search of the Pure Commonwealth* (Houndmills, Basingstoke, England: Macmillan Press, 2000): "in the criticism of Vendler and O'Neill poems are examined with a tender vigilance that is both the index of the delight that they take in the poems, and the means by which they share it with their readers" (13).

35. Susan J. Wolfson, *Formal Charges: The Shaping of Poetry in British Romanticism* (Stanford: Stanford University Press, 1997), 3.

36. Wordsworth to Catherine Grace Godwin [spring 1829]. *The Letters of William and Dorothy Wordsworth: The Later Years, Part 2, 1829–1834,* ed. Alan G. Hill (Oxford: Clarendon Press, 1979), 58.

37. Milton defended the verse form in prefatory words to the second edition of *Paradise Lost* in 1674. *The Poems of John Milton,* ed. John Carey and Alastair Fowler (London: Longmans, Green, 1968), 457. For the debate about blank verse see David Fairer, *English Poetry of the Eighteenth Century 1700–1789* (London: Longman, 2003), esp. 148–50.

38. Charles James Fox to Wordsworth, 25 May [1801], quoted in Christopher Wordsworth, *Memoirs,* 1:171.

39. *Paradise Lost,* I, 16.

40. Matthew Arnold, ed., *Poems of Wordsworth* (London: Macmillan, 1879), xxi.

41. Christopher Ricks, *The Force of Poetry* (Oxford: Clarendon Press, 1984), 127.

42. Robert Rehder, *Wordsworth and the Beginnings of Modern Poetry* (London: Croom Helm, 1981), 84.

43. Wordsworth to Sir George Beaumont, 1 May 1805, in *Letters*, 1:586.

44. Wolfson, *Formal Charges*, 104.

45. The quotation from Matthew Arnold is found in Ricks, "William Wordsworth: 'A Sinking Inward into Ourselves from Thought to Thought,' " in *The Force of Poetry*, 117.

46. *The Notebooks of Samuel Taylor Coleridge*, ed. Kathleen Coburn (London: Routledge and Kegan Paul, 1957–), vol. 1, entry 1801.

47. Thomas Carlyle, *Sartor Resartus*, ed. Kerry McSweeney and Peter Sabor (Oxford: Oxford University Press, 1987), 197.

48. The essentials of Hazlitt's three-part review are found in Robert Woof, ed., *William Wordsworth: The Critical Heritage, Volume I: 1793–1820* (London: Routledge, 2002), 366–81; my quotations pp. 371 and 369. Matthew Arnold, ed., *Poems of Wordsworth* (London: Macmillan, 1879), xxii.

49. Geoffrey H. Hartman, *Wordsworth's Poetry 1787–1814* (New Haven, Conn.: Yale University Press, 1964; 2nd. ed. 1971), 350.

50. M. H. Abrams, *Natural Supernaturalism: Tradition and Revolution in Romantic Literature* (London: Oxford University Press, 1971), 68, 66.

51. Lucy Newlyn, " 'The Noble Living and the Noble Dead': Community in *The Prelude*," is a recent repositioning of the poem in the tradition of *Pilgrim's Progress*. See *The Cambridge Companion to Wordsworth*, ed. Stephen Gill (Cambridge: Cambridge University Press, 2003), 55–69.

52. Quotation is from William A. Ulmer, *The Christian Wordsworth, 1798–1805* (Albany: SUNY Press, 2001), 140.

53. Williams, *William Wordsworth*, 225.

54. Shelley to Lord Byron, 8 Sept. 1816, in *The Letters of Percy Bysshe Shelley*, ed. Frederick L. Jones, 2 vols. (Oxford: Clarendon Press, 1964), 1:504.

55. For a fascinating account of the very real invasion threat and British responses to it, see Alexandra Franklin and Mark Philp, *Napoleon and the Invasion of Britain* (Oxford: Bodleian Library, 2003).

56. Gravil uses primarily the 1850 text of *The Prelude*, but this will not present any difficulties in practice to a reader using it with only the 1805 text to hand. The important difference to have in mind, of course, is that for the fourteen-book poem of 1850, book 10 of the 1805 text was divided in two at line 567, so that line 568, "From that time forth . . ." becomes the first line of book 11 of the 1850 text.

57. The opening words of Shelley's sonnet "To William Wordsworth."

58. Letter to Hugh Seymour Tremenheere, 16 December 1845, in *The Letters of William and Dorothy Wordsworth: The Later Years, Part 4, 1840–1853*, ed. Alan G. Hill (Oxford: Clarendon Press, 1988), 733.

59. My *Wordsworth and the Victorians* (Oxford: Clarendon Press, 1998) traces the line of the debate during Wordsworth's later life and after his death.

William Wordsworth

"A Pure Organic Pleasure from the Lines"

CHRISTOPHER RICKS

❖ ❖ ❖

THERE IS REASON to think that Wordsworth was aware of a discussion about the difference between poetry and prose in Erasmus Darwin's *Loves of the Plants;* aware, too, 'almost certainly', of an article in *The Monthly Magazine* for July 1796 on 'Is Verse Essential to Poetry?'[1] Such arguments are ancient, and usually yield only to fatigue. Robert Lowell said, 'I no longer know the difference between prose and verse'.[2] T. S. Eliot towards the end of his life declared: 'the moment the intermediate term *verse* is suppressed, I do not believe that any distinction between prose and poetry is meaningful'.[3] That was in 1958; but thirty years earlier, when the usual arguments were being rehearsed in *The Times Literary Supplement,* Eliot had come up with a very suggestive formulation: 'Verse, whatever else it may or may not be, is itself a system of *punctuation;* the usual marks of punctuation themselves are differently employed' (27 September 1928).

The punctuation of which poetry or verse further avails itself is the white space. In prose, line-endings are ordinarily the work of the compositor and not of the artist; they are compositorial, not compositional. Without entering into some traditional problems of distinction, and without claiming here[4] that it is line-endings alone which importantly distinguish poetry (or at any rate such poetry as is not also verse) from prose, one may at least urge that the poet has at his command this further 'system of punctuation'. The white space at the end of a line of poetry constitutes some kind of pause; but there need not be any pause of formal punctuation, and so there may be only equivocally a pause at all. A non-temporal pause? Unless the rhythm or the sense or the formal punctuation insists upon it, the line-ending (which cannot help conveying some sense of an ending) may not be exactly an ending. The white space may constitute an invisible boundary; an absence or a space which yet has significance; what in another context might be called a pregnant silence.

Just how much a line-ending may effect has been finely shown in two classic passages of literary criticism. Dr. F. R. Leavis commented on two lines from Keats's 'To Autumn':

> And sometimes like a gleaner thou dost keep
>   Steady thy laden head across a brook;

'As we pass across the line-division from "keep" to "steady" we are made to enact, analogically, the upright steadying carriage of the gleaner as she steps from one stone to the next.'[5] The perfect steadiness of rhythm matches the simply steady movement of the syntax; the sense that such steadiness has to be achieved, that it is laden and not just casual, is enforced by the line-ending, across which—it stands for the unseen brook which we are *not* looking down at—the steady movement must be made.

Such a line-ending creates its effect mimetically and without recourse to any type of ambiguity. But a line-ending—and here the classic piece of criticism is by Donald Davie—may create its significance by a momentary ambiguity:

> Then feed on thoughts, that voluntarie move
> Harmonious numbers; as the wakeful Bird
> Sings darkling, and in shadiest Covert hid
> Tunes her nocturnal Note.
>   (*Paradise Lost,* III, 37–40)

The language is deployed, just as the episodes are in a story, so as always to provoke the question 'And then?'—to provoke this question and to answer it in unexpected ways. If any arrangement of language is a sequence of verbal events, here syntax is employed so as to make the most of each word's eventfulness, so as to make each key-word, like each new episode in a well-told story, at once surprising and just. The eventfulness of language comes out for instance in 'Then feed on thoughts, that voluntarie move', where at the line-ending 'move' seems intransitive, and as such wholly satisfying; until the swing on to the next line, 'Harmonious numbers', reveals it (a little surprise, but a wholly fair one) as transitive. This flicker of hesitation about whether the thoughts move only themselves, or something else, makes us see that the numbers aren't really 'something else' but are the very thoughts themselves, seen under a new aspect; the placing of 'move', which produces the momentary uncertainty about its grammar, ties together 'thoughts' and 'numbers' in a relation far closer than cause and effect.[6]

Before now pointing to the kinds of effect, subtle and various, which Wordsworth achieved with line-endings, I need to suggest some of the ramifications. For the use of line-endings can be a type or symbol or emblem of what the poet values, as well as the instrument by which his values are expressed.

First there is Wordsworth's commitment to those ample relationships which yet do not swamp or warp the multiplicities which they accommodate.[7] No fragmentation into separateness; but also no dissolution within a greedily engrossing unity. Such a commitment asks an analogous literary feat: that the relationship between the line of verse and the passage of verse be just such a relationship. The poetic achievement is itself to embody the values to which the poet has allegiance. The separate line of verse must not be too simply separate, and yet it must have its individuality respected. Nothing must be viewed 'In disconnection dead and spiritless' (*The Excursion*, IV, 962). Everything must be free, 'Itself a living part of a live whole' (*The Prelude*, III, 625). The might of poetry is, like that of mind and world, a 'blended might',[8] something which overrides 'our puny boundaries' (*The Prelude*, II, 223).

'Beyond, though not away from': Geoffrey Hartman's shrewd paradox is therefore as right for the verse as for the vision. Beyond, though not away from: such, after all, is the relation of tenor to vehicle within a metaphor, and such is the relation of verse-paragraph to verse-line, or of poem to verse-paragraph. Wordsworth said:

The Imagination also shapes and *creates;* and how? By innumerable processes; and in none does it more delight than in that of consolidating numbers into unity, and dissolving and separating unity into number. (*Preface to Poems*, 1815)

'Consolidating numbers': the words cannot but bring to mind the other sense of *numbers*, 'harmonious numbers', that poetic imagination which consolidates numbers into unity by creating poetic numbers within poetic unity.

So it is not surprising that a characteristic Wordsworthian effect should be that in which line gives way to line with the utmost intangibility of division. James Smith has written exquisitely of 'Michael':

> The verse of the poem is a delicate thing. It has almost ceased to beat, and seems maintained only by the flutter of tenuous hopes and sickening fears.
>
> >   the unlooked-for claim
> >   At the first hearing for a moment took
> >   More hope out of his life than he supposed
> >   That any old man ever could have lost.
>
> Wordsworth, who was so often an imitator, here speaks with his own voice; and the verse is the contribution he makes to prosody.[9]

Yet Wordsworth made more than one contribution to prosody (even though we might agree that this was his greatest); and similar considerations bear upon verse of a quite different tone and tempo.

>   and oftentimes
>   When we had given our bodies to the wind,
>   And all the shadowy banks, on either side,
>   Came sweeping through the darkness, spinning still
>   The rapid line of motion; then at once
>   Have I, reclining back upon my heels,
>   Stopp'd short, yet still the solitary Cliffs
>   Wheel'd by me, even as if the earth had roll'd
>   With visible motion her diurnal round;
>   Behind me did they stretch in solemn train
>   Feebler and feebler, and I stood and watch'd
>   Till all was tranquil as a dreamless sleep.
>   (*The Prelude*, I, 478–89)

'Stopp'd short': yet these lines are about—and supremely evoke—the impossibility of stopping short. There can be no cutting off the sequential, and the verbal sequences themselves tell their tale. Within the first three lines, *and* comes twice (not to return for eight lines). Next, within three lines, *sweeping, spinning,* and *reclining* (all continuing, yet with no such participles recurring thereafter). Next, within three lines, *Stopp'd, Wheel'd,* and *roll'd* (with the 'Stopp'd short' unable to prevent the emergence of such a sequence, and with 'watch'd' waiting to appear three lines later). Last, *and* three times within the single line, embodying the perfect rallentando and diminuendo which chasten the childish expectation that it might be possible to stop short:

> Behind me did they stretch in solemn train
> Feebler and feebler, and I stood and watch'd
> Till all was tranquil as a dreamless sleep.

The pleasure which one takes—like the understanding which one gains—in such an evolution through a dozen lines is itself 'a pure organic pleasure from the lines'. Such verse is a triumphant vindication of the severe judgment which Wordsworth passed on Macpherson's Ossian:

> In nature every thing is distinct, yet nothing defined into absolute independent singleness. In Macpherson's work, it is exactly the reverse; every thing (that is not stolen) is in this manner defined, insulated, dislocated, deadened,—yet nothing distinct. (*Essay, Supplementary to the Preface,* 1815)

It is characteristic of Wordsworth's sturdiness that he wanted to know where he stood. Blank verse was (in Milton's words) to have 'the sense variously drawn out from one verse into another'. The heroic couplet was to practise its natural determinations. Any mongrel verse was more than disapproved of by Wordsworth—it physically and psychically disconcerted him:

> I have indeed, a detestation of couplets running into each other, merely because it is convenient to the writer;—or from affected imitation of our elder poets. Reading such verse produces in me a sensation like that of toiling in a dream, under the night-mair. The Couplet promises rest at agreeable intervals; but here it is never attained—you are mocked and disappointed from paragraph to paragraph. (letter to Hans Busk, 6 July 1819)

Second, there is Wordsworth's understanding of how easily one sense may tyrannize over the others—and in so doing may moreover fail to realise its own fullest potentialities.

> for I had an eye ...
> Which spake perpetual logic to my soul,
> And by an unrelenting agency
> Did bind my feelings, even as in a chain.
> (*The Prelude*, III, 156–67)

The eye and the ear (and not only those two senses) must be reconciled, neither lording it over the other. This too must have as its counterpart and embodiment a literary achievement. Reading should itself be a type of the proper relation of eye to ear; and the poet's lines—the relationships which he creates between the single line and its accommodating passage—must effect such a relationship of eye and ear.

Did the printing press minister to a situation in which literature itself could not but tyrannize through the eye? No, because of the subtly complementary relationship of eye to ear as we read—or rather, as we read such literature as is delicately aware. The fluidity and suppleness of line-endings, especially in true blank verse (such as must always remember the warning 'Blank verse seems to be verse only to the eye'),[10] create an equivocal relationship to the eye; a relationship which creates its own checks and balances. As Hartman says, 'Wordsworth's later thought is constantly busy with the fact that the eye is or should be subdued. . . . He now sees into the life of things not by a defeat of the eye which drives it on, but rather "with an eye made quiet by the power / Of harmony, and the deep power of joy" '.[11]

Since the verse is to epitomise such harmony and balance, it is natural that the word *line* or *lines* should figure so often in Wordsworth's lines, sometimes with a covert metaphorical application to the verse-lines themselves. Pope had used such a self-referring:

> The spider's touch, how exquisitely fine!
> Feels at each thread, and lives along the line.
> (*An Essay on Man*, I, 217–18)

'Line' there is not a mere repetition of 'thread'; by giving us both, Pope ensures our noticing that the verse-line too is evoked, itself to be as exquisitely fine, as feeling, as alive. Wordsworth evokes both the line and the line-ending:

> Dreamlike the blending also of the whole
> Harmonious Landscape, all along the shore
> The boundary lost—the line invisible
> That parts the image from reality;
>
> (Home at Grasmere 574–7)

The boundary is also that which we cross when we pass from one 'line' to another; 'the line invisible' (following the dash—) is also that which separates one line from another, 'invisible' because it is emblematised on the page by the white space, and not, for instance, by the line of a dash. Invisible, but not nonexistent; there is no thing solidly there, no formal punctuation, but there is nevertheless the parting—by means of a significant space, a significant vacancy—of one thing from another. Consider too the self-referring effect created in the skating episode by invoking 'The rapid line of motion'. Or there is the disconcerting mixture of gains and losses—as so often—in the two versions of *The Prelude*, I, 588–93:

1805
even then,

> A Child, I held unconscious intercourse
> With the eternal Beauty, drinking in
> A pure organic pleasure from the lines
> Of curling mist, or from the level plain
> Of waters colour'd by the steady clouds.

1850
even then,

> I held unconscious intercourse with beauty
> Old as creation, drinking in a pure
> Organic pleasure from the silver wreaths
> Of curling mist, or from the level plain
> Of waters coloured by impending clouds.

1850 has the richly proleptic suggestion of 'impending', and it retains the crucial inaugurations of the last two lines, both *Of.* But it weakens the force of the other prepositions, removing *With* from the head of the line and *in* from the end of the line, thereby abolishing the engrossing energy of the enjambment: 'drinking in / A pure organic pleasure'. (The *1850* line-break at 'drinking in a pure / Organic pleasure' is altogether ineffectual.)

But the superiority of *1805* is clearest in the change from 'the lines / Of curling mist' to 'the silver wreaths / Of curling mist'. On the one hand, the austerity of *lines* has been sacrificed to prettiness; on the other, a suggestiveness too has been sacrificed. For the word *lines* unobtrusively related Wordsworth's delight in 'the eternal Beauty' to his own beautiful lines which are here speaking; we were given a sense of what that 'pure organic pleasure' was, by experiencing its literary counterpart, a 'pure organic pleasure' of a literary kind, drinking it in from these very *lines*. It is a bad bargain which trades away both austerity and suggestiveness. Just for a handful of silver wreaths.

It is the placing of *lines* at the end of the line there which should especially alert us. A quiet paradox informs this stanza (added in 1815) of 'I wandered lonely as a cloud':

> Continuous as the stars that shine
> Or twinkle on the milky way,
> They stretched in never-ending line
> Along the margin of a bay:
> Ten thousand saw I . . .

Not literally a 'never-ending' line of daffodils, of course—any more than the line of verse itself is never-ending. Yet the fact that the verse-line is not brought to an end by punctuation, the fact that it opens into unending space, allows the other aspect of the paradox to impinge on us too. The effect of the lines would be quite different if they were repunctuated:

> Continuous as the stars that shine
> And twinkle on the milky way,
> They stretched in never-ending line.
> Along the margin of a bay,
> Ten thousand saw I . . .

Third, there is Wordsworth's insistence that a proper surprise is something serene not crashing: 'a gentle shock of mild surprise' (*The Prelude,* V, 407). Life necessitates transitions, indeed it thrives on them, but a true transition is one which finds its spontaneity and its surprise somewhere other than in violence. Such transitions and transformations can be set by the poet before your very eyes; they can be the transitions and successions by which a line is taken up by a sequence of lines without being impaired, without ceasing to be itself. In Davie's words, 'a little surprise, but a wholly fair one'. The mutuality and reciprocity within the poem itself are witnesses to those mutualities and reciprocities which engaged Wordsworth's mind and heart, and they are to surprise not startle us. The transitions within the poem, from line to line, are to parallel the great transitions to which all life moves. One season gives way to another—gives way, but does not collapse or succumb; the seasons change, but with no sudden or brutal dismissal. 'The seasons came . . .'—and their coming leads naturally to the word 'inobtrusive' (*The Prelude,* II, 307, 316). Or there is the coming of dawn. In what does the superiority of *1850* over *1805* consist in the following example?

1805   But I have been discouraged; gleams of light
      Flash often from the East, then disappear
                (I, 134–5)

1850   That hope hath been discouraged; welcome light
      Dawns from the east, but dawns to disappear

The second line now itself *dawns;* the silent self-referring metaphor then tautens the whole line.

We may therefore wish to apply a word like *passage,* so justly used by Hartman, to the passage of verse itself; everything that Hartman here says has its stylistic counterpart or obligation:

> Change is not destruction, transition is not violence, and the passage from one mode of being to another should resemble the storm at the beginning of 'Resolution and Independence' which passes into the calm, sunny energies of a new day . . .

> [Wordsworth's] aim [is] to render the advent of a new season without defining it into absolute, independent singleness. The passage from one season to another as from one state of being to another is thought of as a gentle transfer of energies. (p. 203)

Such a gentle transfer of energies must be both effected and symbolised in the transfer of energies from one line to the next, in such a *passage.* In Hartman's words, 'transformations can occur without injury': that they can do so is something which the transforming movement of the verse itself must not only state but epitomise.

Lineation in verse creates units which may or may not turn out to be units of sense; the 'flicker of hesitation' (Davie's term) as to what the unit of sense actually is—a flicker resolved when we round the corner into the next line—can create nuances which are central to the poet's enterprise. 'Again and again I must repeat, that the composition of verse', Wordsworth said, 'is infinitely more of an art than men are prepared to believe; and absolute success in it depends upon innumerable minutiae'.[12] Take the conclusion of one of the greatest passages in *The Prelude:*

> in my thoughts
> There was a darkness, call it solitude,
> Or blank desertion, no familiar shapes
> Of hourly objects, images of trees,
> Of sea or sky, no colours of green fields;
> But huge and mighty Forms that do not live
> Like living men mov'd slowly through my mind
> By day and were the trouble of my dreams.
>
>   (I, 420–7)

As we move forward through the lines, it seems that they are asserting, and not just intimating, that the huge and mighty forms do not live; then as we reach the next line, we realise that what may be being said is rather that they live but do not live as men live—or is it that they do not live whereas men do? The ambiguity is not removed by the *1850* punctuation, though the movement within the inaugurating line is thereby changed. Although the ambiguity would still exist if the lines were simply deployed as prose with no change of word-order, the ambiguity would then be less tangible, since there would not be the possibility (created by the line-ending and its nontemporal pause) that the unit of sense is conterminous with the line-unit 'But huge and mighty Forms that do not live'. Redeployed as prose, the following 'Like . . . ' would come too hard upon the heels of 'that do not live', and would hardly permit of much of a 'flicker of hesitation'.

The instance is a famous one, and it is central to Wordsworth, since the question of whether such mighty forms do not live or whether they do indeed live but not as men live (rather as 'unknown modes of being') is one which his poetry never ceased to revolve. Indeed William Empson drew attention to the fugitive suggestiveness of the line-ending at this very point:

> my brain
> Work'd with a dim and undetermin'd sense
> Of unknown modes of being;
>
> (*The Prelude*, I, 418–20)

'There is a suggestion here from the pause at the end of the line that he had not merely "a feeling of" these unknown modes but something like a new "sense" which was partly able to apprehend them—a new *kind* of sensing had appeared in his mind'.[13]

The white space, then, may act somewhat as does a rest in music; it may be a potent absence. One might give a new application to Wordsworth's remark in the Preface to *Lyrical Ballads* that 'To these qualities he [the poet] has added a disposition to be affected more than other men by absent things as if they were present'. Like all poets, Wordsworth creates meanings which take into account those absent senses of a word which his verse is aware of fending off:

> I saw him riding o'er the Desert Sands,
> With the fleet waters of the drowning world
> In chase of him . . .
>
> (*The Prelude*, V, 135–7)

Every reader knows that 'fleet' there means *swift;* yet the pressure within that very line of both 'waters' and 'drowning' is such as to call up that *fleet* (of ships) which the sense positively precludes. That other sense is thereby surmised and then ruled out, so that the total effect of the word resembles *fleet, not—indeed not—fleet.* The adjective 'fleet' would be careless or perverse if it were not positively (rather than forgetfully or wilfully) setting aside the other sense. Such an anti-pun is one form which may be taken by the poet's 'disposition to be affected more than other men by absent things as if they were present'. Or what Wordsworth relatedly called 'The spiritual presences of absent things' (*The Excursion*, IV, 1234).

> and all
> Their hues and forms were by invisible links
> Allied to the affections.
>
> (*The Prelude*, I, 638–40)

There on the page is such an invisible link: off the end of the line. The line-ending can thereby be both a type of and the instrument of all such kindly linkage.

Hartman has used the term *rites de passage*. The crossing from one line to the next must be of particular importance to a poet for whom crossing was so important. We think not only of Wordsworth crossing the Alps, but also of everything which he does with boundaries, and all they meant to him. In James Smith's words:

> He was awake to the notion of the boundary, the imaginary line which sets up place against place, and by crossing which, from having been without London, he would find himself within.

> The very moment that I seem'd to know
> The threshold now is overpass'd . . .
> A weight of Ages did at once descend
> Upon my heart;
> (*The Prelude,* VIII, 699–704)

True boundaries are numinous, and are to be distinguished from man-made categorising; Wordsworth uses the line-ending here to crystallise his contempt:

> Thou are no slave
> Of that false secondary power, by which,
> In weakness, we create distinctions, then
> Deem that our puny boundaries are things

—are *things,* whereas they are only fantasies or fictions?—

> are things
> Which we perceive, and not which we have made.
> (*The Prelude,* II, 220–4)

The critic, then, will need to be alert to that stylistic potentiality, the line-ending, which furnishes a counterpart to such a concern with boundaries. Or with borderers; not just *The Borderers* but much else in Wordsworth, such as the poised and sleeping horse, 'A Borderer dwelling betwixt life and death'. Can there be such suspended animation within a poem? Yes, since the white space at the end of a line is such a suspension, between linguistic life (the words) and linguistic death (*empty* silence). One might apply (with a specific literalness which he did not intend) F. W. Bateson's perceptive remark that for Wordsworth 'the poetry lay *between* the words.'[14] Similarly, John Jones has noted how Wordsworth's solitaries are 'placed at the verge of life', and how his 'lonely buildings' are 'at the extreme of life.'[15] Such a verge, such an extreme, has its stylistic counterpart. It too can be fostered alike by beauty and by fear. On the one hand:

> —Ah! need I say, dear Friend, that to the brim
> My heart was full;
>
> (*The Prelude,* IV, 340–1)

where the brim (itself the brim of the line) is delight, not peril. On the other hand:

> To struggle, to be lost within himself
> In trepidation, from the blank abyss
> To look with bodily eyes, and be consoled.
>
> (*The Prelude,* VI, 469–71, 1850)

—where the sequence which leads up to *abyss* (which at the end of the line opens an abyss) is fearful, so that 'and be consoled' comes with the force of providential surprise.

The metaphorical or mimetic possibilities are many, and Wordsworth is fertile and various. He may take as the defining term the line itself, rather than the ensuing space; and next do the opposite:

> Even as a shepherd on a promontory,
> Who, lacking occupation, looks far forth
> Into the endless sea . . .
>
> (*The Prelude,* III, 546–8)

The line itself functions as a promontory, with the self-referring word concluding it and with the punctuation circumscribing it. Then the next line reverses the implications, with 'looks far forth' having to look forth across the space represented by the white space. The change from verse to prose would be the abolition of the implicit metaphorical enacting: 'looks far forth into the endless sea' lacks a dimension of enacting which operates in

> looks far forth
> Into the endless sea . . .

Forth has one kind of relationship to its ensuing space; *promontory* has another. A third is represented by all those words which signify those great presences which are potent yet invisible: air, sky, space, wind, breath, echo, silence. Wordsworth finds a metaphorical dimension in relating them to that presence on the page which can be potent though invisible: the white space.[16] He therefore often places them at the ends of lines; we cannot see air or sky or space any more than we can see anything but absence at the end of the verse-line:

> From the great Nature that exists in works
> Of mighty Poets. Visionary Power
> Attends upon the motions of the winds
> Embodied in the mystery of words.
>
> (*The Prelude*, V, 618–21)

The varieties of visionary power are analogous, and more than analogous; there is an effect of mysterious rhyming, with *works, winds,* and *words* ending three of the lines. And *winds* meets the invisible.

With such thoughts in mind, we may remember the best lines in *The Borderers:*

> Action is transitory—a step, a blow,
> The motion of a muscle—this way or that—
> 'Tis done, and in the after-vacancy
> We wonder at ourselves like men betrayed:
> Suffering is permanent, obscure and dark,
> And shares the nature of infinity.
>
> (act 3)

How superb is the match of sense and substance in the only line which has no concluding punctuation.

> 'Tis done, and in the after-vacancy

and there the vacancy looms, an intersection of time and the timeless, a miniature counterpart to the 'spots of time'. Of the ten instances of *vacancy* in the *Concordance,* six come at the end of the line. [17]

> What terror doth it strike into the mind
> To think of one, blind and alone, advancing

> Straight toward some precipice's airy brink!
> But, timely warned, *He* would have stayed his steps,
> Protected, say enlightened, by his ear;
> And on the very edge of vacancy
> Not more endangered than a man whose eye
> Beholds the gulf beneath.
>
> (*The Excursion*, VII, 491–8)

The line-endings (and would that this were more often the case in *The Excursion*) are wonderfully exploited:

> To think of one, blind and alone, advancing

(—advancing into space)

> Straight toward some precipice's airy brink!

(—the airy brink at the airy brink)

> But, timely warned, *He* would have stayed his steps,

(—with the comma staying the steps)

> And on the very edge of vacancy

—with the vacancy opening before us. All this is woven through a relationship of eye to ear which is itself a lesson in 'how to read'—protected, say enlightened, by our ears. Such verse superbly practises what Coleridge superbly preached:

> The reader should be carried forward, not merely or chiefly by the mechanical impulse of curiosity, or by a restless desire to arrive at the final solution; but by the pleasurable activity of mind excited by the attractions of the journey itself. Like the motion of a serpent, which the Egyptians made the emblem of intellectual power; or like the path of sound through the air; at every step he pauses and half recedes, and from the retrogressive movement collects the force which again carries him forward. (*Biographia Literaria*, ch. 14)

The metaphorical words may refer to the line itself or to the space itself; or they may refer to what the line-ending precipitates.

> Blew mimic hootings to the silent owls,
> That they might answer him; and they would shout
> Across the watery vale, and shout again,
> Responsive to his call, with quivering peals,
> And long halloos and screams, and echoes loud,
> Redoubled and redoubled, concourse wild
> Of jocund din; and, when a lengthened pause
> Of silence came and baffled his best skill,
> Then sometimes, in that silence while he hung
> Listening, a gentle shock of mild surprise
> Has carried far into his heart the voice
> Of mountain torrents; or the visible scene
> Would enter unawares into his mind,
> With all its solemn imagery, its rocks,
> Its woods, and that uncertain heaven, received
> Into the bosom of the steady lake.
>
> (*The Prelude,* V, 373–88, *1850*)

1805 had its *pause* in the middle of the line ('That pauses of deep silence mock'd his skill'); *1850* lengthens the pause—but also removes it from simple clock-time—not only by adding the adjective 'lengthened' but by setting *pause* at the end of the line:

> and, when a lengthened pause

The *Concordance* shows how often Wordsworth places the word 'pause' so that it pauses at the brink of the line. How often, too, he places his indispensable word 'hung' or 'hang' there:

> Then sometimes, in that silence while he hung

—and there is the silence before us, and he and we hang upon the brink of it. A dozen lines later, there is a literal counterpart which conveys its different sense of suspension:

> Fair is the spot, most beautiful the vale
> Where he was born; the grassy churchyard hangs
> Upon a slope above the village school,

There can be no doubt as to how much of Wordsworth's deepest concerns depended from, hung from, some such way of speaking. The inquiry into the nature of the Imagination which Wordsworth pursues in his Preface to *Poems*, 1815, begins with three instances which depend upon *hangs*—from Virgil, Shakespeare, and Milton: 'Here is the full strength of the imagination involved in the word *hangs*'.[18] Stephen Prickett[19] has drawn attention to 'the basic question why, for both Wordsworth and Coleridge, the most typical feature of these moments of insight is not the feeling of the Imagination at work in perception, but of its *suspension*'. The poetry itself delights in such suspensions:[20]

> Oh! when I have hung
> Above the raven's nest, by knots of grass
> And half-inch fissures in the slippery rock
> But ill sustain'd, and almost, as it seem'd,
> Suspended by the blast which blew amain,
> Shouldering the naked crag; Oh! at that time,
> While on the perilous ridge I hung alone,
> (*The Prelude*, I, 341–7)[21]

There is a variety of dispositions there for the crucial words *hung, Suspended,* and *hung,* and the dispositions answer to varieties of purpose. But the effect of the line-ending can be seen if we think about that last line:

> While on the perilous ridge I hung alone,

It is not Wordsworth's intention at this point (the tone has changed within the lines) to convey only peril; he seeks to convey also exultation, an extraordinary nonchalance of security, and even (banal but newly important, like much of his substance) the knowledge that the young Wordsworth did not in fact fall off. The line, therefore, although it speaks of *perilous* and *ridge* and *hung,* does not put any of them where they could create a frisson; each of them is safely *within* the line, not at its extremities, and the word *hung* has a significantly different effect from that which it had six lines before. Compare these four different drapings of the words, the last three bogus:

(1)   While on the perilous ridge I hung alone,
(2)   Shouldering the crag; while on the perilous
       Ridge,
(3)   Shouldering
       The naked crag; while on the perilous ridge
       I hung alone,
(4)   Shouldering
       The crag, while on the perilous ridge I hung
       Alone,

Granted, the wording cannot stay the same, and the rhythms are altogether different; but we will not have a comprehensive feeling for just what is being conveyed by

> While on the perilous ridge I hung alone,

unless we also sense how unprecipitously the line-ending is there being used, and how easily Wordsworth could have had it otherwise if he had wished.

Last of the important words which can act as a hinge for the line-ending—and different in kind from the others—is the word *end* itself. This too Wordsworth frequently deploys at the end of a line. Just as the word 'beginning' finds itself charged with paradox when we hear at the end of a poem 'In my end is my beginning', so the word *end* acts upon us differently according not only to the context but also to its placing within those units which may not be units of sense—those units which constitute poetry but not prose, and which make of poetry a medium which is more totally and persistently involved in effecting something through its recurrent sense of an ending.[22] Poetry is involved, more than prose, in persistently stopping and starting—and yet it must not be a thing of stops and starts.

Once again metaphors and puns may be effected through the placing within the line. As with the bird's-nesting:

> Though mean
> My object, and inglorious, yet the end
> Was not ignoble.
>   (*The Prelude*, I, 339–41)

There the strong sense—'the aim'—is tempered, and saved from pomposity, by the play effected through the smaller sense of 'end'. Something more like a pun emerges here:

> Ah me! that all
> The terrors, all the early miseries,
> Regrets, vexations, lassitudes, that all
> The thoughts and feelings which have been infus'd
> Into my mind, should ever have made up
> The calm existence that is mine when I
> Am worthy of myself! Praise to the end!
>
> (*The Prelude*, I, 355–61)

The effect of the disposition within the line ('end' at the end)[23] is to encourage us to take 'Praise to the end!' to mean 'Unending praise'. But the turn to the next line discloses a different asseveration:

> Praise to the end!
> Thanks likewise for the means!

The result there is a severe variety of wit. But Wordsworth can elicit quite different tones, as in the touching disposition of 'in the end' (at the end of the line but not, importantly not, at the end of the verse-paragraph) within some of the most touching lines he ever wrote:[24]

> Not in Utopia, subterraneous Fields,
> Or some secreted Island, Heaven knows where,
> But in the very world which is the world
> Of all of us, the place in which, in the end,
> We find our happiness, or not at all.
>
> (*The Prelude*, X, 724–8)

Within the sequence there is a delicate contrast of two kinds of line-ending.

> But in the very world which is the world

—this (in the trice before it turns before our very ears and eyes into ' . . . which is the world Of all of us') suggests the utter intransigence, as near as Wordsworth might ever get to impatience, of a tautology: with its weighty spaced insistence 'the world which is the world'. (The absence of any punctuation makes it the more appropriate that a modern vulgarism expressing something of the same feelings might be 'the world which is the world—*period.*') Then the next line deploys its ending quite differently: ending with 'in the end', and with the concluding (though not fully concluding) comma of a line which has three deliberating commas.

Yet the metaphorical possibilities of the line-ending are not limited to any particular set of words, though they may most often inhere there.

> But deadening admonitions will succeed

—we have at that stage no way of excluding from consideration the possibility that we are on the way to ' . . . will succeed in damping the spirits, etc.' It is only when we round the corner that we find the neutral sense of *succeed:*

> > will succeed
> And the whole beauteous Fabric seems to lack
> Foundation,
> > > (*The Prelude*, I, 225–7)

Of the more dispiriting possibility which momentarily supervened ('will succeed in doing something unfortunate'), we might remark:

> > What might have been is an abstraction
> > Remaining a perpetual possibility
> > Only in a world of speculation.
> > > (*Burnt Norton*)

But it does remain that. Then after this faintly ambiguous line-ending, the next line hinges upon a line-ending which is free of ambiguity but which is beautifully mimetic:

> And the whole beauteous Fabric seems to lack

—waiting, we pass through a spot of time

> Foundation

—at which the foundation is found; the necessary continuance is founded. A weirdly serene enlisting of similar feelings occurs in the pregnant brevity which tells of the death of the young Wordsworth's parents:

> The props of my affections were remov'd,
> And yet the building stood, as if sustain'd
> By its own spirit!
> *(The Prelude,* II, 294–6)

—where the sustaining is invisible but active, is indeed spiritual, and is evoked by the invisible activity of the space.

A comparable mystery is evoked by the extraordinary line-ending (an enjambment which takes all the time in the world despite its necessity for proceeding apace):

> and I would stand,
> Beneath some rock, listening to sounds that are
> The ghostly language of the ancient earth,
> *(The Prelude,* II, 326–8)

It is not just that the sounds are the ghostly language of the ancient earth, though that is pregnantly mysterious enough; the basic mystery is that they exist at all, that they *are:*

> Beneath some rock, listening to sounds that are

—no other poet performs such miracles with the verb to be.

Such suggestions are transitory, but not the less telling for that. Geoffrey Hartman praises surmises, and it is one function of line-endings to be so delicately fertile of surmises: 'They revive in us the capacity for the virtual, a trembling of the imagined on the brink of the real'. That brink can be the brink of the line-ending. Again, a perceptive comment by Herbert Lindenberger[25] could be complemented by a consideration of the stylistic minutiae which effect and reflect what he describes:

> One can discern a certain 'brinkmanship' in which Wordsworth engages, whereby he leads the reader to the edge of the abyss, only to reveal the saving hand of a higher power. His image of the boy virtually hanging from the cliff is, I think, emblematic of this habit.

What then is it which itself emblematises this emblem?

> Oh! at that time,
> While on the perilous ridge I hung alone,
> With what strange utterance did the loud dry wind
> Blow through my ears! the sky seem'd not a sky
> Of earth, and with what motion mov'd the clouds!
>
> (*The Prelude*, I, 346–50)

Again the felicities of space, with *wind* opening into vacancy; and with

> the sky seem'd not a sky

—it did not seem to be a sky at all, with this effect drawing strength from the way in which *sky* is brought to the very edge, up against that free space which is as invisible as the sky or the wind but as existent and active. Then the sense is evolved and dissolved, and Wordsworth is seen to have been about to say something both more confined and less confined than that it didn't seem to be a sky at all:

> the sky seem'd not a sky
> Of earth, and with what motion mov'd the clouds!

We cannot doubt the translatable sense: that the sky did not seem to be the sky which goes with our Earth. Yet there is—at the same time as we feel the Wordsworthian sublimity that inaugurates yet another of its great lines with *Of*—something audacious to the point of apparent wilfulness about such a use of the preposition. 'A sky of earth': it cannot but sound as if the sky might be made of earth. It is not just the ambiguity of *Of* which does this, but the ambiguity of *earth*, by which although the contrast with sky does in one direction insist that earth means the Earth, another implicit contrast with sky (its airiness) suggests the sense of the element earth, the least airy of the elements. Any competent creative-writing course would at once have deleted 'seem'd not a sky / Of earth', and urged the aspiring poet to think what he was about. But Wordsworth was, as so often, about strange things. The extraordinary vision glimpsed here, of a calm vertigo, is one which delights in calling up a suggestion which it then has the power to exorcise: we are to entertain the phantasmal un-imaginability of a sky of earth—to entertain it, and then with a wise relief to cleave to the other sense. Far-fetched? But less so than the supposition

that Wordsworth simply did not notice how strangely misleading his wording could be or simply was unable to think of a less misleading way of
putting it.

'A trembling of the imagined on the brink of the real': it is often at
the brink that we shall see it happening.

> My own voice cheer'd me, and, far more, the mind's

—what this leads us to expect is something like ' . . . and, far more, the
mind's own voice'. What we then meet is significantly like and unlike that.

> My own voice cheer'd me, and, far more, the mind's
> Internal echo of the imperfect sound;
> > (*The Prelude*, I, 64–5)

The effect of the surmised sense is to make us consider the second line as
in some sense a definition. What would it have meant to speak of the
mind's own voice? For the mind's own voice, we are being given to understand, is in fact 'the mind's / Internal echo of the imperfect sound'.
Another instance:

> The Poet, gentle creature as he is,
> Hath, like the Lover, his unruly times;
> His fits when he is neither sick nor well,
> Though no distress be near him but his own

—no distress but his own distress?—such is the expectation. Once again
it is both met and modified.

> Though no distress be near him but his own
> Unmanageable thoughts.
> > (*The Prelude*, I, 145–9)

For if we ask what the poet's 'own distress' would have been, we then find
it defined for us in a way which both sets the poet among the rest of
humanity in that it *is* a form of distress, and yet distinguishes him from
most of humanity in that it is a specific form of distress: 'his own / Un-
manageable thoughts'. Such is the form that the poet's own distress would
take; the line-ending has been used to effect an exploratory definition
which is half-riddling; and there is very little poetry as great as Words-

worth's which does not in some way tap, however subterraneously, the resources of the riddle.

Surmises are doubts, but they can be happy ones. As in the childhood pleasures of the river Derwent:

> Was it for this
> That one, the fairest of all Rivers, lov'd

—the pressure of 'fairest' is such as to make it at least possible (I should say probable) that 'lov'd' will prove to be an epithet for the river: 'the fairest of all Rivers, lov'd by us all with a love deeper than etc.' Indeed, within twenty lines we are told of the river (and the final word is well placed): 'He was a Playmate whom we dearly lov'd.' Yet the verse-sentence evolves otherwise:

> Was it for this
> That one, the fairest of all Rivers, lov'd
> To blend his murmurs with my Nurse's song,
> (*The Prelude*, I, 271–3)

Yet the momentary uncertainty, that trembling of the imagined on the brink of the real, is itself a pointer to the lines' meaning. For it is of the nature of the word *lov'd* that it should evince reciprocity, just as it is of the nature of the pathetic fallacy (the river 'lov'd to blend his murmurs') that it should succeed in speaking the truth when it reflects feelings that are truly existent. It is because the child loved the river (as the line was at first intimating) that it may be said that the river 'lov'd / To blend his murmurs with my Nurse's song'. All this is blended there in Wordsworth's song.

There is an even more piercingly charming instance a few lines later:

> For this, didst Thou,
> O Derwent! travelling over the green Plains
> Near my 'sweet Birthplace', didst thou, beauteous Stream
> Make ceaseless music through the night and day
> Which with its steady cadence, tempering
> Our human waywardness, compos'd my thoughts

—the expectations created by 'music' and 'cadence' urge us to take 'composed' as *fashioned* or *created*. But the sequence chooses another emphasis:

> compos'd my thoughts
> To more than infant softness,
> *(The Prelude,* I, 276–82)

—at which we realise that the river did not so much compose his thoughts as compose them *to* serenity. But the momentary doubt (which would disappear in the immediate succession of prose: 'compos'd my thoughts to . . .') precipitates the pun: it points to what was for Wordsworth the essential relationship between *composition* and *composure.* Just as 'music' and 'cadence' lead mostly toward the sense of *composition,* so 'steady' and 'tempering' lead mostly toward the sense of *composure.* Wordsworth's point is the concurrence. It is, in the profoundest sense, composure (not disturbance) which is creative, which composes. (There is an analogous delicacy of doubt in the phrase 'make ceaseless music', where we are happily uncertain whether the river makes music as composer or as performer.) As John Jones says,

> It remained a cardinal principle with him that only a happy man can write good poetry; and he attributed Coleridge's failure as a poet to his unhappiness, because of which 'he could not afford to suffer with those whom he saw suffer'.[26]

The fluidity of water and of air was for Wordsworth a type of the perfect interrelationship. In some lines which are at once importantly like and importantly unlike Milton, he exults in the multifariousness of creation:

> O'er all that leaps, and runs, and shouts, and sings,
> Or beats the gladsome air, o'er all that glides
> Beneath the wave, yea, in the wave itself
> And mighty depth of waters.
> *(The Prelude,* II, 425–8)

In these lines everything turns upon what is indeed the turn: the word *glides* at the end of the line. It beautifully takes up the preceding 'air'— and then with the turn into the next line we discover that *glides* is about movement through the water, not through the air. (Again the immediateness of prose would destroy this tiny suspension: 'that glides beneath the wave'.) The word *glides,* placed where it is, compacts the two elements without crowding them; it interfuses them, like a beautiful evocation in Wordsworth's *Guide to the Lakes:*

and could almost have imagined that his boat was suspended in an element as pure as air, or rather that the air and water were one.[27]

A supreme instance of such delicacy of doubt happens also to place *hung* where Wordsworth most cared for it and with it:

> the moon to me was dear;
> For I would dream away my purposes,
> Standing to look upon her while she hung
> Midway between the hills, as if she knew

—as if she knew how much we loved her, how much we gazed and worshipped her?

> as if she knew
> No other region; but belong'd to thee,
> Yea, appertain'd by a peculiar right
> To thee and thy grey huts, my darling Vale!
> (*The Prelude*, II, 196–202)

—and we find, with a gentle shock of mild surprise, that *knew* was not as in *savoir* but as in *connaître*. Upon the brink of the real, there trembled our imagining that the moon *knew;* the attribution of the pathetic fallacy has seldom been made with such pathos, and the rescinding of the fallacy has seldom been made with such gentleness.

Such stylistic reaching before and after might be brought into relation with Walter Pater's words on Wordsworth's sense of past and future:

> He had pondered deeply, for instance, on those strange reminiscences and forebodings, which seem to make our lives stretch before and behind us, beyond where we can see or touch anything, or trace the lines of connexion.[28]

Trace the lines, yes.

My final instance can be one where the power of Wordsworth's prepositions allies itself to the sane suggestiveness of his line-ending:

> How goodly, how exceeding fair, how pure
> From all reproach is yon etherial vault,
> And this deep Vale, its earthly counterpart,

By which and under which we are enclosed
To breathe in peace;

(*Home at Grasmere* 640–4)

'By which and under which': the distinction has the scrupulous assurance and authority of Wordsworth at his finest—the poetry's distinction is in its distinctions, at once firm and serene. Then 'enclosed' is not really enclosed at all, since although it brings the line to an end it opens directly into that free space which is a 'counterpart' of all free space:

By which and under which we are enclosed

We have only to make this line the end of its verse-sentence to find the word *enclosed* acting upon us quite differently:

By which and under which we are enclosed.

Too total an enclosing, this would then preclude our breathing in peace; would induce just that claustrophobia, that sense of being pinioned, which Wordsworth eschews—the vault of heaven, after all, is such that though it does indeed enclose us, it does so without coercion and with total freedom and airiness. The sense of an ending is perfectly taken up within the sense of a blending. At which point there dawns upon us the calm splendour of the ambiguity of 'breathe in peace'. Does it mean breathe *in peace* or *breathe in* peace? Both. Under the vault of heaven we can breathe *in peace* because what we *breathe in* is peace. The two meanings co-exist with perfect 'inobtrusive sympathies'; no strain, no pressure, but an interfusion which is limpidly and lucidly at ease. John Jones's useful phrase about 'Wordsworth's busy prepositions' would do less than justice to this instance, which is so active and yet so unbusy.

Such poetry both meets and makes high demands. In particular it asks that we take our time: in poetry such as Wordsworth's there is in the first place nothing more important that we should take. In such a spirit we may recall Wordsworth's anger: 'These people in the senseless hurry of their idle lives do not *read* books, they merely snatch a glance at them that they may talk about them.'[29] The obverse of his anger at such haste of pseudo-reading is his praise for the chastening dignity of the carver's slow art, at work upon a funeral inscription which is committed to reticence:

The very form and substance of the monument which has received the inscription, and the appearance of the letters, testifying with what a slow and laborious hand they must have been engraven, might seem to reproach the author who had given way upon this occasion to transports of mind, or to quick turns of conflicting passion.[30]

The twentieth century is even more open to 'senseless hurry' than was the nineteenth century. Wordsworth urges us to take his time.

Notes

1. W. J. B. Owen, *Wordsworth as Critic* (1969), pp. 17–20.

2. In an interview with D. S. Carne-Ross, *Delos*, i (1968).

3. Introduction to a translation of Valéry's *Art of Poetry* (1958), p. xvi.

4. See my review of John Sparrow's *Visible Words* (1969), in *Essays in Criticism*, xx (1970). Geoffrey N. Leech's *A Linguistic Guide to English Poetry* (1969) has some good instances of the effects created by lineation.

5. 'Mr. Eliot and Milton', *The Common Pursuit* (1952), p. 17.

6. 'Syntax and Music in *Paradise Lost*', in *The Living Milton*, ed. Frank Kermode (1960), p. 73.

7. John Jones is invaluable here; see in particular pp. 32, 33, 47, 68, 84, and 85 of *The Egotistical Sublime* (1954).

8. See *Poetical Works*, ed. E. de Selincourt and H. Darbishire, v (1949), 339.

9. *Scrutiny*, vii (1938), 53. A related point is excellently made by Jonathan Wordsworth (*The Music of Humanity*, 1969, p. 139); he quotes 'The Ruined Cottage' 379–80:

> She did not look at me. Her voice was low,
> Her body was subdued;

and he remarks that 'The end-stop after "low" allows Wordsworth the effect, without the triteness, of a single line with heavy caesura: "Her voice was low,   her body was subdued" '.

10. Johnson's *Life of Milton*.

11. *Wordsworth's Poetry 1787–1814* (1964), p. 114.

12. Letter to William Rowan Hamilton, 22 November 1831.

13. 'Sense in *The Prelude*', *The Structure of Complex Words* (1951), p. 290. Empson's observation that the word *sense* comes very often at the end of the line is one to which I owe a great deal.

14. *Wordsworth: A Re-Interpretation* (1954), p. 38.

15. *The Egotistical sublime*, pp. 67, 103. Donald Wesling's chapter title 'Images of

Exposure' might also be applied in such a way (*Wordsworth and the Adequacy of Landscape*, 1970).

16. John Jones has said: 'Breath is also closely associated with urgent spiritual presence. Thus he describes the thought of an absent person as being like "an *unseen* companionship, a breath" ' (*The Egotistical Sublime*, p. 99; much of pp. 96–104 has its bearing on my argument). I should also wish to apply David Ferry's remark: 'It is especially moving that one of the great representatives of our human powers of articulation should be himself a lover of silence' (*The Limits of Mortality*, 1959, p. 15).

17. A related, but significantly different, effect is achieved by surmising a vacancy which is to be crossed before—instead of after—the word 'vacancy':

> so wide appears
> The vacancy between me and those days,
> (*The Prelude*, II, 28–9)

—'so wide appears': and there it appears

18. Milton's image of the fleet which 'Hangs in the clouds' had figured in a notable letter by Wordsworth to Sir George Beaumont, 28 August 1811.

19. *Wordsworth and Coleridge: The Poetry of Growth* (1970), pp. 141–2.

20. Wordsworth introduced more of them in *1850*. 'In my thoughts / There was a darkness' became 'o'er my thoughts / There hung a darkness' (I, 420–1; I, 393–4). 'The Moon stood naked' became 'The moon hung naked' (XIII, 41; XIV, 40).

21. Donald Wesling speaks finely of the effect of *hung* here: 'it achieves the almost visceral quality of danger at the end of an enjambing line' (*Wordsworth and the Adequacy of Landscape*, p. 38; see also p. 43).

22. Geoffrey Hartman has some characteristically brilliant and arcane thoughts on beginnings and endings in his essay 'The Voice of the Shuttle', *Review of Metaphysics*, xxiii (1969). Reprinted in his *Beyond Formalism* (1970).

23. As again seven lines later.

24. The problem of tone in Wordsworth is brought home by Donald Wesling's hearing in these lines a 'jocular seriousness' (*Wordsworth and the Adequacy of Landscape*, p. 6). Nor can I agree with Mr. Wesling (p. 26) that in 'Tintern Abbey' the blank-verse lines 'in every way deny closure and pause'—not in *every* way, since this would deny the possibility of interplay between the way in which the line does indeed end and the way in which it doesn't.

25. *On Wordsworth's Prelude* (1963), p. 222.

26. *The Egotistical Sublime*, p. 113.

27. Quoted by Herbert Lindenberger, *On Wordsworth's Prelude*, p. 82.

28. 'Wordsworth' (1874), *Appreciations* (1889). Pater's words might be related to

Wordsworth's mild but piercing puns on *prospect;* most notably in 'The Old Cumberland Beggar': 'one little span of earth / Is all his prospect'. (See too *The Prelude,* II, 371 and III, 229.)

29. Letter to Lady Beaumont, 21 May 1807.

30. 'Essays upon Epitaphs, I' (1810); *The Prose Works of William Wordsworth,* ed. W. J. B. Owen and Jane Worthington Smyser (1974), ii 60.

Revision as Form

Wordsworth's Drowned Man

SUSAN WOLFSON

◆ ◆ ◆

> Scattering thus
> In passion many a desultory sound
> I deemed that I had adequately cloathed
> Meanings at which I ha[rd]ly hinted thoughts
> And forms of which I scarcely had produced
> A monument and an arbitrary sign
>
> that considerate and laborious work
> In That patience which admitting no neglect
> By that slow creation {which} imparts to speach
> Outline & substance even till it has give[n]
> A function kindred to organic power
> The vital spirit of a perfect form
> resting not till. . . .
> —Wordsworth, DC MS. 33 (1798–99)

> I had forms distinct
> To steady me: these thoughts did oft revolve
> About some centre palpable which at once
> Incited them to motion and control'd.
> —Wordsworth, *The Prelude* 1805, book 8

> do you simply mean, that such thoughts as arise in the pro-
> gress of composition should be expressed in the first words
> that offer themselves, as being likely to be most energetic and
> natural? If so, this is not a rule to be followed without cautious
> exceptions. My first expressions I often find detestable; and it
> is frequently true of second words as of second thoughts, that
> they are the best.
> —Wordsworth to R. P. Gillies, 22 December, 1814
> (*Letters MY*)

you know what importance I attach to following strictly the
last Copy of the text of an Author.
> —Wordsworth to Alexander Dyce, 19 April, 1830
>
> (*Letters LY*)

Won't almost any theory bear revision?
> —Frost, "The White-Tailed Hornet"

The Textual Authority of Forms

It is rather early on in his autobiographical poem, newly extended by 1805
to thirteen books, that Wordsworth confesses one of its motivations: a hope

> that with a frame of outward life,
> I might endue, might fix in a visible home
> Some portion of those phantoms of conceit
> That had been floating loose about so long,
> And to such Beings temperately deal forth
> The many feelings that oppress'd my heart. (I, 129–34)[1]

But a tendency to revision—Wordsworth's primary labor with this text
across decades nearly coincident with his adult life—makes the hope all
too prone to disruption in the play of an imagination in which floating
and fixing compete for priority. Despite an intent to form a work that, in
the words of its last book would show "in the end / All gratulant if rightly
understood" (XIII, 384–5 / XIV, 388–9), years of revision subverted the rhetoric of *if* from its temporal promise into a perpetually conditional desire.
Even as an illusion of mastery propels revision, the revisions work otherwise: if some fix the phantoms more securely, others often unfix the text
with new uncertainties, new baffles to gratulant understanding. The process is not always additive but often contrary, dispersing authority across
time and unseating any one moment as the limit of meaning.[2]
  This process has another perverse productivity, its generation of debates
about textual authority and its trouble to any formalist criticism depending
on a unified, discrete, finished, stable textual object. No phenomenon more

radically resists (or predicts the challenges to) these notions than Wordsworth's revisionary practices with the poem eventually titled (not by him)
The Prelude. What kind of form do its plural texts, none published in Wordsworth's lifetime, define? What kind of formalist criticism is adequate to this
formation and the whole business of genetic criticism on which it bears?
In one long-standing tradition, revisions are read teleologically: they clarify
an original intent and refine its "final" expression, each stage conveying
the discipline and progress of a poet's mind. This evolutionary model is
not the only one however, and *The Prelude*—perhaps more than any
nineteenth-century text—poses a strong resistance to it. For many, there
is a devolutionary tale: the revisions seem less to signify improvement than
a hardening sensibility, the story of decline, default, and anticlimax that
gets told about the career as a whole; correspondingly, earlier and earliest
versions gain praise for their vitality and fidelity to the best "Wordsworth."
Their recovery is the rationale of Cornell's expensive and elaborate editions:
"Wordsworth's practice of leaving his poems unpublished for years after
their completion, and his lifelong habit of revision . . . have obscured the
original, often the best, versions of his work."[3]

This massive project is the consequence and archival detailing of a critical event in 1926: Ernest de Selincourt's unveiling of an 1805 text and his
introduction of it in terms that, despite preliminary gestures toward a
balanced appraisal of respective strengths and defects, wound up granting
it creative priority. Although his preface ceded some improvements to the
1850 text—it "is a better composition"; its "weak phrases are strengthened,
and its whole texture is more closely knit" in a way that "often gives form
and outline to a thought before but vaguely suggested" (lvii)—he gave
several demonstrations of "later deterioration" (lx–lxiii), and he concluded
by boldly naming "the poet of the years 1798–1805" as "the authentic
Wordsworth" lxxiii). He first promoted the 1805 version in a parallel text
edition that wasn't quite parallel: it appeared on the left side, as if it were
the base text for 1850 variants. With this advance, de Selincourt then issued
the 1805 text as an independent poem in 1933. His editions had considerable
influence. Not only did other parallel-text editions follow, but the 1805
text gained such prestige that it became the standard for quotation and
critical reference.[4] The evolutionary rubric of revision was being displaced
(albeit not without controversy) by an archaeological excavation of original
genius. By the 1970s, the case was settled for many. Geoffrey Hartman was
describing *The Prelude* as a self-corrupting text, "the freshness of earlier
versions . . . dimmed by scruples and qualifications, by revisions that usually

overlay rather than deepen insight" (*Wordsworth's Poetry* xvii). "Moving backward to 1805 we find a distinct improvement," Herbert Lindenberger said more conclusively in 1984 (Gaull 3).

This backward movement was extended by the Norton Critical Edition, which in 1979 not only gave parallel texts of 1805 and 1850 (left to right) but included a "Two-Part" poem of 1798–99 that it promoted, stylistically and pedagogically, for the "small compass" of its extraordinary writing.[5] The formalism in such praise is revealing. Echoing de Selincourt's view that "Books I and II . . . form one vital and self-contained whole" (xlvii), Jonathan Wordsworth and Stephen Gill, two of the Norton editors, called it "a separate and internally coherent form" ("Two-Part *Prelude* of 1798–99" 503). J. Wordsworth admired the "simpler and more concentrated form" of its recollections ("Two-Part *Prelude* of 1799" 570), and J. R. MacGillivray observed "a much more unified theme and a much stronger sense of formal structure" compared to later texts (236). The poem that New Criticism had avoided thus returned in acceptable New Critical form. Meanwhile, Mark Reed was editing *The Thirteen-Book "Prelude"* for Cornell, with decidedly post-modern effects. His edition not only places the principal manuscripts for the 1805 text amidst a swirl of related ones but constructs yet another "principal new manuscript" (2:5), the C-Stage revision of 1818–20 (DC MS. 82). Designating this as a manuscript "stage" that is "incomplete, often unreliable," Reed avoids any claim that it has "achieved a practically finished form" (2:6), presenting it merely—but dauntingly—as more evidence in the unfolding story of the poem's composition.[6] However one is inclined to take its information, the C-Stage text thickens the field to be negotiated.

From de Selincourt's unveiling there was no recovery, and controversies over textual authority and authenticity of poetic vision erupted and persisted, agitated by wider discussions of the theory and principles of textual editing.[7] Advocates of the 1850 text, invoking the credit usually accorded latest versions and revisions, argued for its authority as "a finished and free-standing product" under the control of a "supervising idea," and they cited the aesthetic refinements: its "tightened . . . style," "improved . . . diction," increased "clarity and precision," and more coherent "dramatic effects."[8] Advocates of the 1805 text admired the power and more authentic tidings of its "struggle toward definition" (Lindenberger, *On Wordsworth's "Prelude"* 298); and some even preferred the elemental energy of the earliest drafts. Yet, ultimately, neither career narratives nor editorial ideology are adequate to the full compositional history. Despite what Wordsworth himself optimistically described as his "theme / Single, and of determin'd bounds" (I, 669–70/641–2), its several distinct but interrelated textual forms, as Jack Stillinger remarks, leave open to question whether revisions are in the business of "clarifying [an] original idea" or of "expressing a different idea" (*Multiple* 93). *The Prelude* defies description by a single authorized text. In the eighth decade of debate about which version represents the true "Wordsworth," the terms have become as repetitive as they are irresolvable.[9] And they seem beside the point, for the poem's history cannot be undone.

More productive approaches have turned from the polemical privileging of one text or another, to respond instead to what is conceded by the Norton Critical Edition's naming, on both its cover and title page, of "Authoritative Texts"—namely, the very *large* compass of the poem's composition and the challenge that this poses to theories of textual authority. If the New Critical practice was to slight "variants" in the belief that "the existence and the exhibition of such genetic vestiges is not intrinsic to the confrontation of our minds with the poem" (Wimsatt, "What to Say" 231), later critics, as well as editors, have included such vestiges and versions. Stillinger and Reiman (despite the latter's scholarly and aesthetic preference for the 1850) have elaborated proposals by James Thorpe and others to advocate new principles for representing works such as *The Prelude*. Arguing that to privilege a text is only to state a preference, Stillinger urges "the legitimacy and interest . . . of *all* the versions" (*Multiple* 94). Reiman supports this plurality for historicist principles as well. Resisting such speculative constructions as Owen's admittedly "eclectic" text of the fourteen-book poem (which, whatever its merits, has no discrete textual or historical existence), Reiman urges editorial "versioning," that is, making available "enough different *primary* textual documents and states of major texts" to enable comparisons—a project critical for works involving "two or more radically differing versions that exhibit quite distinct ideologies, aesthetic perspectives, or rhetorical strategies" ("Versioning" 169). All of us now welcome two *King Lears* and two endings to *Great Expectations*,[10] and Romanticists have long accepted more than one version of Coleridge's *Rime*.[11] First prompted by Jerome McGann and David Simpson, we've also renewed attention to "La Belle Dame sans Mercy," the ballad by Keats that Hunt published in the *Indicator*, with important differences from the letter-draft version titled "La Belle Dame sans Merci" that editors have canonized. We also have two texts of *Frankenstein*, 1818 and 1831.[12] The Norton Critical *Prelude* and the cross-referenced Cornell editions do no more than formalize a multi-textual fact and facilitate intertextual attention. Whether one revels in or regrets the resources, there is no revoking their existence and no

profit in resisting their challenge.[13] Wordsworthian revision, as both an
activity of reflection and as a mode of composition, requires an account
of poetic authority and poetic form adequate to its plural texts.

A decentered *Prelude* may even court description as a Barthesian "text,"
a methodological field and *"an activity of production."*[14] Yet such productivity
does not necessarily entail "the death of the author" and the corresponding
"birth of the reader." If we recast Barthes' famous story for *The Prelude,* we
discover a *re*birth, by reading, of a different kind of author. Barthes radically
democratizes the text, canceling meaning from the domain of authorial
intention or historical possibility and deeding it over to the reader's play.
But insofar as Wordsworth's autobiographical situation interplays reading
with writing, it prefigures this dissemination, and his revisionary text often
intuits it. As poetic activity recollects, reviews, interprets, and reinterprets
its phantoms of conceit, poetic composition produces revision as the enactment as well as the report of these processes. Scanning the surfaces and
depths of time past, the "considerate and laborious work" of writing returns Wordsworth to manuscripts past, to reperuse the surfaces and gaps
of their texts.[15] Manuscripts as well as memories constitute his past, and
textual revision reduplicates, perpetuates, and enters into recollection. In
this involute, revision is not just compositional; it is the very trope of
autobiography, a resistance, in events large and small, to arresting and
fixing phantoms of conceit in a final frame of autobiographical argument.

In this respect, to read the network of Wordsworth's texts is to extend
his activity as reader in the network of recollection. Formalist criticism, if
it is to be relevant, has to enter into this network and follow its temporal
process. As a local site for testing this possibility, I take the textual array,
or a text in array, of a drowning in Esthwaite's Lake, a recollection from
the poet's boyhood. To summarize the events: Roving alone along the
lakeside near a new home, Wordsworth noticed a heap of garments on the
opposite shore and assumed that they belonged to a swimmer; evening
fell, the garments remained; the next day, he watched as the lake was
dragged and the corpse of a man recovered. Here are the principal versions:[16]

THE TWO-PART *PRELUDE,* 1798–99 (ED. PARRISH); *FIRST PART:* MS. V7ᵛ–8ʳ

> Ere I had seen
> Eight summers (and 'twas in the very week
> When I was first transplanted to thy vale   260
> Beloved Hawkshead! when thy paths, thy shores

And brooks were like a dream of novelty
To my half-infant mind) I chanced to cross
One of those open fields which, shaped like ears)
Make green peninsulas on Esthwaite's lake   265
Twilight was coming on, yet through the gloom
I saw distinctly on the opposite shore
Beneath a tree and close by the lake side
A heap of garments as if left by one
Who there was bathing: half an hour I watched   270
And no one owned them: meanwhile the calm lake
Grew dark with all the shadows on its breast
And now and then a leaping fish disturb'd
The breathless stillness. The succeeding day
There came a company, & in their boat   275
Sounded with iron hooks and with long poles
At length the dead man 'mid that beauteous scene
Of trees, and hills, and water bolt upright
Rose with his ghastly face. I might advert
To numerous accidents in flood, or field   280
Quarry or moor, or 'mid the winter snows
Distresses and disasters, tragic facts
Of rural history that impressed my mind
With images, to which in following years
Far other feelings were attached; with forms   285
That yet exist with independent life
And, like their archetypes, know no decay.
    There are in our existence spots of time
Which with distinct pre-eminence retain
A fructifying virtue, whence, depressed   290
By trivial occupations and the round
Of ordinary intercourse, our minds,
(Especially the imaginati ve power)
Are nourished, and invisibly repaired.
Such moments chiefly seem to have their date   295
In our first childhood. I remember well . . .

THE PRELUDE, 1805, BOOK V:AB-STAGE (ED. MARK REED)

        Well do I call to mind the very week,   450
    When I was first entrusted to the care

Of that sweet Valley; when its paths, its shores,
And brooks, were like a dream of novelty
To my half infant thoughts; that very week
While I was roving up and down alone,   455
Seeking I knew not what, I chanced to cross
One of those open fields, which, shaped like ears,
Make green peninsulas on Esthwaite's Lake.
Twilight was coming on; yet through the gloom,
I saw distinctly on the opposite Shore   460
A heap of garments; left, as I suppos'd,
By one who there was bathing: long I watch'd,
But no one own'd them: meanwhile, the calm Lake
Grew dark, with all the shadows on its breast,
And, now and then, a fish, unleaping, snapp'd   465
The breathless stillness. The succeeding day,
(Those unclaim'd garments telling a plain Tale)
Went there a Company, and, in their Boat,
Sounded with grappling-irons, and long poles.
At length, the dead Man, 'mid that beauteous scene   470
Of trees, and hills, and water, bolt upright
Rose with his ghastly face; a spectre-shape
Of terror even! and yet no vulgar fear,
Young as I was, a Child not nine years old,
Possess'd me; for my inner eye had seen   475
Such sights before, among the shining streams
Of Fairy Land, the Forests of Romance:
Thence came a spirit, hallowing what I saw
With decoration and ideal grace;
A dignity, a smoothness, like the works   480
Of Grecian Art, and purest Poesy.
          I had a precious treasure at that time,
A little, yellow canvass-cover'd Book,
A slender abstract of the Arabian Tales . . .

THE THIRTEEN-BOOK *PRELUDE,* 1805, *BOOK V:* C-STAGE READING TEXT
(ED. MARK REED)

          Well do I call to mind the very week,
When I was first entrusted to the care
Of that sweet Valley; when its paths, its shores,   445

And brooks, were like a dream of novelty
To my half infant thoughts; that very week
While I was roving up and down alone,
Seeking I knew not what, I chanced to cross
One of those open fields, which, shaped like ears,   450
Make green peninsulas on Esthwaite's Lake.
Twilight was coming on; yet through the gloom,
Appeared distinctly on the opposite Shore
A heap of garments; left, as I suppos'd,
By one who there was bathing: long I watch'd,   455
But no one own'd them: meanwhile, the calm Lake
Grew dark, with all the shadows on its breast,
And, now and then, a fish upleaping, snapp'd
The breathless stillness. The succeeding day,
Those unclaimed garments drew an anxious crowd   460
Of friends and neighbours to the fatal spot.
In passive expectation on the shore
These stood, while others sounded, from a Boat,
The deep—with grappling irons and long poles.
At length, the dead Man, 'mid that beauteous scene   465
Of trees, and hills, and water, bolt upright
Rose with his ghastly face; a spectre-shape
Of terror even! and yet no vulgar fear,
Young as I was, a Child not nine years old,
Possess'd me; for my inner eye had seen   470
Such sights before, among the shining streams
Of Fairy Land, the Forests of Romance:
Thence came a spirit, hallowing what I saw
With decoration and ideal grace;
A dignity, a smoothness, like the works   475
Of Grecian Art, and purest Poesy.
              I had a precious treasure at that time,
A little, yellow canvass-cover'd Book,
A slender abstract of the Arabian Tales . . .

THE PRELUDE, 1850, *BOOK FIFTH:* W.J.B. OWEN'S READING TEXT
(BASE TEXT MS. D)

    Well do I call to mind the very week
When I was first entrusted to the care

Of that sweet Valley; when its paths, its shores,   430
And brooks were like a dream of novelty
To my half-infant thoughts,—that very week,
While I was roving up and down alone,
Seeking I knew not what, I chanced to cross
One of those open fields, which, shaped like ears,   435
Make green peninsulas on Esthwaite's lake.
Twilight was coming on, yet, through the gloom,
Appeared distinctly on the opposite shore.
A heap of garments, as if left by One
Who might have there been bathing. Long I watched,   440
But no one owned them; meanwhile, the calm Lake
Grew dark, with all the shadows on its breast,
And, now and then, a fish upleaping, snapped
The breathless stillness. The succeeding day,
Those unclaimed garments, telling a plain tale,   445
Drew to the spot an anxious Crowd; some looked
In passive expectation from the shore,
While from a boat others hung o'er the deep,
Sounding with grappling irons and long poles.
At last, the dead Man, 'mid that beauteous scene   450
Of trees & hills & water, bolt upright
Rose with his ghastly face: a spectre shape
Of terror, yet no soul-debasing fear,
Young as I was, a Child not nine years old,
Possessed me; for my inner eye had seen   455
Such sights before, among the shining streams
Of fairey land, the forests of romance;
Their spirit hallowed the sad spectacle
With decoration and ideal grace;
A dignity, a smoothness, like the works   460
Of Grecian Art, and purest Poesy.
    A precious treasure I had long possessed,
A little, yellow, canvas-covered book,
A slender abstract of the Arabian tales . . .

I'll briefly indicate the range of forms shaping this map of revisions by
noting two features—one small and unrevised, one big and extensively so.
For the first: Wordsworth seems to have wanted to keep within the form
of a single poetic line his abrupt juxtaposition of the twilight vigil and the

next day's search: "The breathless stillness. The succeeding day" (MS. V 7ᵛ: 274; C:459; V, 466 / 444).[17] Using the same syntax and number of syllables on either side of the period, and crossing it with an iamb ("ness. The"), he joins one scene to the next through the form of his poetic line, rather than a verbal narrative. This poetic form implies the agency of the boy's privately tensed perception in producing the next day's public search— and more: it requires us to fill in the blanks in a manner analogous to the boy's intuition.

Wordsworth's continuing confidence in this local form contrasts with his emphatic "re-vision" of how to form this episode in his story of a poet's mind. And with this revision comes a host of related alterations: tinkerings with syntax and punctuation, recastings of metaphor and invocation, expansions or elisions of narrative detail, as well as important rearrangements of the preliminary context. The effort to secure "perfect form" is never secure from the pressure of "second thoughts." All these reworkings, in both the text and context, involve uncertainties about the story of the poem as a whole, for some revisions support, while others contradict, or even subvert its plot. Writing as an autobiographer, Wordsworth summons this memory into textual recollection with a powerful sense of import; but writing in poetic form acquires its own subversive agency, bearing information that eludes rhetorical mastery and thwarts exact imaginative supervision. In the rest of this chapter, I investigate what is at stake in this revisionary contest and the various poetic formations it affects: the contexts that situate the episode of the drowning; its immediate frames of introduction and ensuing evaluation; and the text of the episode itself.

Form and Context

That Wordsworth would revise this episode is half predicted by its multiple indeterminacies. Each version suspends its narration between premonition and surprise: its very site is likened to "a dream of novelty," seemingly new but latent in the boy's mind. With a similar finesse, Wordsworth represents the events as *chanced* (not claiming, as elsewhere, that he was "led" or "guided"), but also mitigates this impression by noting that the lake peninsulas were "shaped like ears," as if with the attention described in the next day's business—the search party's "sounding" of the lake.[18] In between these faintly sensory registers, the boy's own focus "through the gloom" on an object that appears "distinctly" to sight, a "heap of garments," conveys a probing in the direction of a narrative, his guess that someone was "bathing." The persistently "unclaimed garments" extend this initial narrative attention, generating what Willard Sperry calls a "quickened subjectivity" (27)—both in the boy and, by force of Wordsworth's power of telling, in the poem's reader. The only revision he seems to have made in MS. V (save punctuation) occurs at this point: he first wrote "still lake" (7ᵛ: 271) then made the adjective *calm*. This prevents a repetition by "breathless stillness" a few lines on but also adds a resonance: *calm* bodes *still* with a paradoxical hint of superficial illusion. Implied is another, fatally breathless stillness in the lake's "breathless stillness." The only interruption is the occasional "leaping fish." Like the ear-y peninsulas, this may also be a chance detail; but in the play of ensuing events, it gets invested with an aspect of prefiguration, a sign of "the dead man" who will rise "bolt upright" from the lake's surface. Wordsworth's definite article, *the,* designates something already known and identified.

His finesse with these details—at once tuned to imply the outcome and implied to have been produced by the boy's perspicuous imagination— affiliates this episode with the poem's larger questions about retrospective self-reading: to what degree are the events "determined by various narrative and discursive requirements"?—as Jonathan Culler phrases the issue in his analysis "of a certain self-deconstructive force in narrative and the theory of narrative" (*Pursuit* 186–7). Or, as Wordsworth himself admits,

> I cannot say what portion is in truth
> The naked recollection of that time,
> And what may rather have been call'd to life
> By after-meditation.
>   (III, 646–50/III, 613–16)

Confessing the perplexity that Culler analyzes and that de Man sees as endemic to autobiography,[19] Wordsworth plays it out in shifts of interpretation, ones registering noticeably in his several contextualizations of the events at Esthwaite's Lake.

In 1799, the narrative emerges in a train of recollected boyhood adventures prompted by the mysteriously charged, intention-laden question that launches the autobiography: "Was it for this" (MS. V 2ʳ). Though the pronominal referents are opaque, the metrical emphases, the syntax, as well as the literary antecedents evoked by the rhetoric, all announce a crisis in reckoning, a sense that the present is incommensurate with the promise of the past.[20] The recollections that follow are summoned to close this gap by demonstrating and "tend[ing] ... / To the same point, the growth of mental power / And love of Nature's works" (7ᵛ: 256–8). But even as the autobiographer advances this "argument," he finds his writing arrested by "such effects as cannot here / Be regularly classed" (255–6). It is under this sign of resistance to the dominant naturalizing scheme that the story of the drowning is hailed into the verse. The apostrophe "Beloved Hawkshead!" (261) tropes the rupture, for its turn away (*apostrephein: to turn away*)— in this case, from argument to recollection—is only the first of several uncertain, rhetorically tensed turns of verse. Why this rhetoric attracts Wordsworth at this moment is illuminated by Culler's fine essay on the trope. Apostrophe, he argues, often interrupts a temporal or argumentative progression, to call attention to the presence of writing. This interruption matters in Wordsworth's call to Hawkshead, for by summoning past affection for a place against the uncertain trammelings of a present argument, he attempts, in Culler's words, to remove "the opposition between presence and absence from empirical time" and locate it "in a discursive time," producing thereby "a play of presence and absence governed not by time but by poetic power." Culler is not thinking of Wordsworth (whom he sees characteristically refusing apostrophe in favor of lyrical forms that work "synecdochially or allegorically," acquiring significance like a narrative [e.g., "lyrical ballads"]). But Mary Jacobus applies Culler's terms to *The Prelude* to show how its processes are driven by a tension between "narrative time" (its story) and "discursive time" (the compositional present in which apostrophe plays): "Regarded as a digressive form, a sort of interruption, excess, or redundancy, apostrophe ... becomes the signal instance of the rupture of the temporal scheme of memory by the time of writing"—the force and signature of "a radical discontinuity."[21]

Such rupture looms in another turn of the recollective verse, one allied linguistically and conceptually to apostrophe: advertency. This possibility appears as the episode subsides into the autobiographer's musing that he "might advert / To numerous accidents ... / ... tragic facts / Of rural history that impressed" his boyish mind (MS. V8ʳ 279–83). Might, but does not. He speaks instead of "images" and "forms" that "yet exist with independent life, / And know no decay" (284–7) and then a theory about "spots of time" that "retain / A fructifying virtue" by which the mind is "nourished, and invisibly repaired" (288–94). These terms, echoing the introduction of this episode as yet another event in "the growth of mental power / And love of Nature's works" (257–8), seem to secure this interpretation. But in elaborating this frame, Wordsworth reverts to deathly facts of personal (if not rural) history. The "spots of time" that follow concern himself at age five stumbling on a mouldered gibbet mast where a murderer was hung (8ᵛ: 307–13), and at age thirteen impatiently waiting for his father's horses to fetch him and his brothers home from school for the Christmas holidays, during which time this father died, leaving his sons orphans (8ᵛ–9ʳ).²² If his frame of argument is the growth of mental power, this frame of figures is its rejected shadow, a sequence of forms in the mind which retains the information, signs, and characters of death. As Wordsworth sets the death at the Lake as a text for the mind's life and growth, the mind's "imaginative power" (8ʳ: 293) seems, ghoulishly, to require new deaths to sustain the "independent life" of his poem. This is a fatal link that Wordsworth's revisions labor to undo.

His principal reworkings reconceive context and commentary to sever the story of the drowning from these deathly affinities. In the "Five-Book" version planned and abandoned in 1804, he puts the drowning in book 4 and situates the "spots of time" at the end of 5, to follow the ascent of Mount Snowdon and to participate thus in the poem's concluding claims and promises. In the 1850 and 1850 texts, these spots are further distanced, to books 11 and 12, respectively.²³ With their repetitions thus attenuated, Wordsworth reframes the story of the drowning and revises his reading of its import. From 1805 on, it is set in book 5, installed in a tract about the education of children by the wise spirits of Nature and the nurture of their imagination by books. Where the 1799 text multiplies its death, the new context translates the literal corpse into a literary figure, tempering and derealizing its life in the mind by assimilating its impression to forms of reading.

This is not so much a revision as an emergence, for a literary gloss was latent in the poet's proposed advertence in 1799 to other "distresses and disasters, tragic facts / Of rural history," terms that textualize events into literary categories and genres. Book 5's revision takes this textualizing in earnest and goes further, shifting the genre from tragedy to romance, the idealizing discourse of "purest poesy." Its verse immediately moves into a recollection of an actual book in the genre, a potently exotic "abstract of the Arabian Tales." Substituting for the memory of a father's death that follows soon after the account of the drowning in the 1799 poem, this recollection seems even to restore such loss. In the 1799 text, the memory of returning home to the father's house at the holidays is also the memory of his death. In book 5, the recollection of the Arabian Tales opens a scene of paternal presence and plenty:

> when to my Father's House
> Returning at the holidays, I found

That golden store of books which I had left,
Open to my enjoyment once again
What heart was mine!

(V, 501–5/479–83)

The capitals of "Father's House," following the lightly satirical drama of a "covenant" with a friend to realize the "promise scarcely earthly" of possessing "this Book" and of their religious preserving in this vow "spite of all temptation" (491–8 / 470–7), even cast this return, with some gentle wit, into the paradigm of a spiritual resurrection.

That the method of book 5 so visibly excludes what the 1799 sequence intensifies helps us appreciate Jonathan Wordsworth's spirited case for the "much more concentrated power" effected by the "much smaller scope" of the earlier poem ("Two-Part *Prelude* of 1799" 568). Yet the more capacious text of book 5 gains another kind of power in its new affiliations. While Wordsworth's claims that the child who reads "doth reap / One precious gain, that he forgets himself" (368–9 / 347–8), other passages of book 5, in reviving the specter of death without any protective intercession, show that nothing is ever really forgotten. If the boy who saw the dead man had seen such sights before in his books, Wordsworth's books of autobiography incorporate this sight with a difference. Far from hallowing the corpse with "decoration and ideal grace," their contexts return the information of death in analogous images, figures, and rhetorical events. One is the chronologically later but textually earlier recollection of his encounter as a young man with the "Stiff . . . upright . . . / . . . ghastly" figure of a discharged soldier (IV, 407–11 / 393–6), an episode whose position near the close of book 4 makes it a shady neighbor of the lake's corpse (they may even have cohabited in book 4 of the "Five-Book" poem).[24]

I'll return to the bearing of this nearby figure on Wordsworth's self-construction as a reader and writer of tales; for now, I want to note how this passage, by its resonance and contiguity, forms part of an extended framing for the text of the drowned man, retaining the disturbances that the poet denies to the boy's book-hallowed view of the corpse. Book 5 itself, moreover, begins with a meditation on death and the perishability of books, the repository of "all the meditations of mankind" (37 / 38). Not only does this initial frame reverse the boy's translation of death into books, but book 5 repeatedly implicates books with death. A book inspires a dream of an Arab frantic to save two books from destruction by universal deluge—one of which, the symbolic book of poetry, scarcely tempers the knowledge of death but prophesies it. The poet's ensuing diatribes against book-ridden education and the book-corrupted child prodigy evoke the spiritual death of the children of the earth forecast by the dream. And his reflection on his own boyhood reading conducts to a sense that its books are now "dead in [his] eyes" (574 / 553). Book 5 also contains two of the dead: the poet's mother; and another lake side figure, the Winander Boy.[25] And, after the drowning of Wordsworth's brother John at sea in February 1805, book 5, though never noting this death, always bears it as a referential contingency in its recollection of a drowning.

Despite the determined assignment of the drowned man to book 5, then, the new contexts echo old information. Amidst these returns is one particularly complicated tangle of revision having to do with Wordsworth's varying reports of his age at the time of the drowning. Each revision makes it later and thus more proximate to a major crisis—his mother's death and his consequent removal from the vale of his early years to the vale of the Hawkshead Grammar School.[26] The actual drowning occurred in June 1779, a month after he entered this school (Norton Critical 8, nn. 9 and 1), two months after his ninth birthday, and so on the cusp of his *tenth* summer—a year and three months after his mother's death in March 1778. In the 1799 text, Wordsworth dates the drowning "Ere I had seen / *Eight* summers"—that is, at the start of summer 1777 (his eighth) and several months *before* his mother died. In this aspect, the memory of the drowned man usurps and replaces the memory of her death, or, in the retrospect of twenty years, figures as its obscure anticipation. Then, in book 5, Wordsworth says he was "not *nine* years old"—dating the drowning after his eighth birthday in April 1778, and thus just a few months after his mother's death. That this calendar is still a year ahead of the actual drowning shows the autobiographer refiguring the tragic facts of rural history into a fiction that assists his own tragedies into oblique representation.

Wordsworth's figurative reconstruction writes what Freud calls a "screen memory," one that blocks and conceals another memory but retains "mnemic residues" that signal its latency—such as the shifting dates in Wordsworth's records above, or, as we shall see, some recurrent imagery.[27] This screening function, both a concealment and a cryptic signifying of such concealment, is evident in the way that the deeper memory, of the mother's death, presses more visibly into the verse several hundred lines on in the 1799 text, in another report of loss and searching:

> For now a trouble came into my mind
> From   causes. I was left alone
> Seeking this visible world, nor knowing why

> The props of my affections were remov'd
> And yet the building stood as if sustain'd
> By its own spirit. All that I beheld
> Was dear to me and from this cause it c[am]e
> That now to Nature's finer influxes
> My mind lay open
>
> (MS. V 18ʳ: 320–9)

The contemporaneous MS. U fills the blank space with *obscure* (Parrish ed. 299n.), and by 1805 it becomes *unknown* (2.292 / 278); but the original blank signifies all on its own as a graphic screen of desertion.[28] In the texts of 1805 and 1850, Wordsworth places this report in book 2, so that when the episode of the drowning is told, the images and figures seem already invested by it. Distanced before or after, the record of trouble in these lines shimmers within the account of the drowning, evoking the lost mother as a repressed referent for the sudden, but obscurely anticipated, death in the lake. In the 1799 text, for instance, the apostrophe that summons the memory is one that more specifically opens the verse to Nature's influx: " 'twas in the very week / When I was first transplanted to thy vale / Beloved Hawkshead! . . . thy paths, thy shores" (V 7ᵛ: 259–61). The address projects a sentience and, as *beloved* suggests, affection. Book 5 relinquishes this claim, but it also deepens the suggestion of latent presence by expanding the boy's tracing of the vale: where the 1799 text moves directly from the poet's apostrophe to the boy's chance crossing of the peninsula, the revision interpolates two lines—"that very week / While I was roving up and down alone, / Seeking I knew not what" (454–6 / 432–4)—that affiliate his actions, in both verbal echo and historical particularity, to the era of the solitary, obscurely intentional, motions of "Seeking this visible world, nor knowing why."

One of the most revealing traces of these affiliations in all three texts is the faintly maternal figure of the lake that draws the boy and claims the man: "the shadows on its breast." In this thoroughly Wordsworthian signature, Wordsworth even considered writing *her* for *its*.[29] In the aggregate of book 5, this figuration of a ghostly mother in the scenario of boyhood seeking bears the fatal trajectory of the episode that precedes it, about the Boy of Winander who internalized "the visible scene . . . ⌉ . . . receiv'd / Into the bosom of the steady Lake" and, as if answering its summons, "died / In childhood" (409–15/386–92). The "spots of time" that follow in 1799 likewise focus, first obscurely, then directly, on a memory of a parent's death. Each episode records feelings of abandonment and a confrontation with deathly signs. A boy disjoined from his "guide" by "mischance" stumbles onto a scene of death, and an older boy, anxiously awaiting his father's horses, will return to school an orphan. It is suggestive of an obscurely motivated perplexity in the moment of composition that the first recollection, like the account of the drowning, enmeshes Wordsworth in a confusion of historical references. As the Norton Critical notes (9 n. 8), his account conflates a recent hanging of a murderer at Penrith with a hanging a hundred years earlier at Hawkshead, of a man who poisoned his wife. This conflation traces a logic analogous to that of the screen memory, in which another death at Penrith, Wordsworth's mother's, lurks beneath the recollection of another death at Hawkshead, the drowning. The depths exposed in these episodes suggest succinctly but forcefully why *The Prelude* needs to be read as a process of several texts, revisions, and contesting representations.

If the framing of the drowning in book 5 detaches it from the original text of graveyard plots and their shades of parental deaths, the contents of book 5 retrieve the information—sometimes as a suppressed referent, sometimes a legible one.[30] Sometimes, even, as a direct reference: this is the only place in his poem where Wordsworth cites his mother, doing so in a composite of her death and his grievance: "she who was the heart / And hinge of all our learnings and our loves; / She left us destitute" (257–9 / 259–61). The Boy of Winander passage plays a part in this grievance. Lines added to its text in book 5 describe his grave as forgotten by the social presence in whose "silent neighbourhood" it abides (428/406)—a presence whose gendering as female and maternal is only partly conventional:

> Even now, methinks, I have before my sight
> That self-same Village Church; I see her sit,
> (The throned Lady spoken of erewhile)
> On her green hill; forgetful of this Boy
> Who slumbers at her feet.
>
> (423–7 / 401–4)

Her forgetfulness contrasts his work of remembrance, the voice that says over and over, "Well do I call to mind." These hints of severed or forgetful supervision resist the argument of favored and fostered growth that the autobiography is at pains to develop, a strain aggravated by the original autobiographical status of this Boy and his location in the scene of the drowning: the "green / Peninsulas of Esthwaite" (MS. JJ S^r). The draft alternates its temporal scheme between past and present, absence and presence—and along with this, shifts its rhetoric between elegiac narrative and urgent apostrophe. It begins with a third-person figure and a nonspecific, legendary past, as if to situate this as a text of another time and another person. At the same time, its past imperfect tenses imply an abiding mythic presence, and the rhetoric of apostrophe means to summon a conversational presence:

> There was a boy ye knew him well, ye rocks
> And islands of Winander & ye green
> Peninsulas of Esthwaite many a time
> > When the stars began
> To move along the edges of the hills
> Rising or setting would he stand alone
> Beneath the trees or by the glimmering
> > lakes
> And through his fingers woven in one
> > close knot
> Blow mimic hoot[ings] to the silent owls
> And bid them answer him.
> > (MS. JJ Sʳ: Parrish ed., 86–7)

As these suggestive but uncertainly tensed orientations of rhetoric and temporality shift suddenly into the first person, the legendary account becomes historically specific:

> > And they
> > > would shout
> Across the watry vale & shout again
> Responsive to *my* call
> > (my italics)

With this first-person reference, the account turns into a chapter of autobiographical history, implicitly past and closed.

This self-reference haunts the version of these lines published in the 1800 *Lyrical Ballads,* which not only explicitly closes the Boy's (now third-person) history with the news that he "died" but allows the poet's contemplation of his grave to suggest a kind of death for the living at the end of boyhood. When this tale enters book 5, the contiguous reference to the drowning at Esthwaite deepens the autobiographical implication, displaced into third person and distorted in its dating as it is. While the final line of the poem in the 1800 *Lyrical Ballads* says that its Boy "died when he was ten years old" (32), this information shifts to "*ere* he was ten years old" by 1805 (*LB* 140, my italics), also the term of 1805's book 5 ("ere he was full ten years old" [415])—died, that is, at the same age that the young Wordsworth actually discovered the drowning. This too-suggestive historical affinity perhaps accounts for Wordsworth's loosening of it in his revisions of 1818–20, which now have the Boy die "ere he was full twelve years old" (C 5: 408; cf. 1850: V, 392), two years older than the boy who actually discovers the maternally shadowed death in the Lake, and at least two years older than his textual representations.

Wordsworth's ambivalent affiliations of the Winander Boy's death with his grieving for and grievance against his mother weave into larger ambiguities in book 5 on issues of supervision: by mothers, by Nature, by tutors, and by books. In the verse that joins the elegy for the mother to the Winander Boy, both figures are tendered as examples of education without books. But the coda to the account of the Boy evokes a "race of real children" (436 / 413, italicizing *real*) taught by books as well as nature:

> Though doing wrong, and suffering, and full oft
> Bending beneath our life's mysterious weight
> Of pain and fear; yet still in happiness
> Not yielding to the happiest upon earth.
> Simplicity in habit, truth in speech,
> Be these the daily strengtheners of their minds!
> May books and nature be their early joy!
> And knowledge, rightly honor'd with that name,
> Knowledge not purchas'd with the loss of power!
> Well do I call to mind the very week ...
> (441–50 / 419–28)

The book-mediated recollection of the drowning that ensues, however, severely tests this economy of knowledge "not purchas'd with the loss of power," for in its knowledge, nature becomes a place of "pain and fear," and books are forced into the role of antidote, even agents of denial of what Nature teaches. Hence, when the poet recollects his childhood library, blessing the authors as "Forgers of lawless Tales ... / ... in league" with forces able to "make our wish our power, our thought a deed, / An empire, a possession" (548–53 / 526–31), the illicit gain is precisely that of desire over nature, of textual power over natural deed.

The language Wordsworth uses in this praise is set deliberately against the institutional power and supervision of those "who have the art / To manage books" (373–4):

> the Tutors of our Youth,
> The Guides, the Wardens of our faculties,
> And Stewards of our labour, watchful men
> And skilful in the usury of time,
> Sages, who in their prescience would controul
> All accidents, and to the very road
> Which they have fashion'd, would confine us down,
> Like engines, when will they be taught
> That in the unreasoning progress of the world
> A wiser Spirit is at work for us,
> A better eye than theirs, most prodigal
> Of blessings, and most studious of our good
> Even in what seems our most unfruitful hours?
> There was a Boy, ye knew him well, ye Cliffs
> And Islands of Winander!
>
> (376–90 / 355–67)

This diatribe against the book-masters of the educational establishment points to a strange suppression of historical fact in Wordsworth's account of the drowning: the victim was a schoolmaster, not only undone by an accident of natural power, but undone in the last "ghastly" lesson he thus figures by the overlay of the boy's books.[31]

This quasi-judgment notwithstanding, Wordsworth is not categorically opposed to all instruction, for a hundred lines before he had praised his mother's faith that God-given "instincts" bear "his great correction and controul" (274–5 / 276–7). And in fashioning his own book, he values both the prescience and the road-building that he denounces in the Tutors: his sense of purpose strengthens when he can say, as he does at the end of his book 1, "The road lies plain before me; 'tis a theme / Single, and of determin'd bounds" (669–70 / 641–2). At the same time, however, more than a few accidents happen on this road, including the double accident (of event and discovery) at Esthwaite's Lake. And throughout, the poem's most powerful moments of imagination, from earliest drafts to late revisions, are triggered by recollections that defeat control by imagination and containment by poetic form: moments of shock, mischance, chance, and surprise that "plant, for immortality, images of sound and sight, in the

celestial soil of the Imagination," and yet threaten the possibility of coherent self-knowledge.[32]

Forms with Advertence

In the 1799 text, the recollection of the drowning inhabits a framework of
argument that is nothing if not equivocal. Just before turning to it, Wordsworth stands back to survey the contours of his verse thus far:

> It were a song
> Venial, and such as if I rightly judge
> I might protract unblamed but I perceive
> That much is overlooked, and we should ill
> Attain our object if from delicate fears
> Of breaking in upon the unity
> Of this my argument I should omit
> To speak of such effects as cannot here
> Be regularly classed, yet tend no less
> To the same point, the growth of mental power
> And love of Nature's works.
>
> Ere I had seen
> Eight summers (and 'twas in the very week
> When I was first transplanted to thy vale
> Beloved Hawkshead! . . .)
>
> (MS. V 7ᵛ: 248–61)

Although the "point" emerges at the end of the protracted sentence that
concludes the prefatory paragraph, its path is tortuous. On the one side is
Wordsworth's attraction to subjects that, in the regularity with which their
effects may be classed, promise to protract the song happily underway; on
the other, an uncertainty about sustaining unity of argument in this way.
Although he says that the former attraction is merely "venial" and its
impulse might be "unblamed," both adjectives court the judgments they
would dispel. *Unblamed* raises the question of blame, and *venial* refines its
degrees, indicating an excusable but not an innocent action: a venial sin,
while less than a mortal one, is still a sin; hence Iago's cynical description
as a "venial slip" an error whose appearance courts more scandal than it
may warrant (*Othello* 4.1.9). Wordsworth's "venial" means to evoke the
opening of book 9 of *Paradise Lost,* where Milton elegizes the freedom with

which "God or Angel Guest" used to permit man "Venial discourse un-blam'd" (I–5). Yet where Milton is speaking about errant speculation, Wordsworth means something almost opposite: the argument whose unity is a delicately guarded artifice of omission is the discourse to be blamed; genuine integrity must risk disruption. And the sentence that poses this issue also enacts it, for its syntax is repeatedly self-interrupting. Much "is overlooked" in both contradictory senses of the verb.

The story of the drowning thus enters the verse of 1799 in perplexed alignments, classed with effects that resist the unity of argument, yet leagued with an argument nonetheless: "the growth of mental power / And love of Nature's works." This equivocation recurs right after the climax of the narration, the revelation of the dead man's "ghastly face." Without missing an iamb, Wordsworth writes:

> I might advert
> To numerous accidents in flood, or field
> Quarry or moor, or 'mid the winter snows
> Distresses and disasters, tragic facts
> Of rural history that impressed my mind
> (MS. V 8^r: 279–83)

"I might advert" recalls "I might protract unblamed": though both *mights* are being resisted, they are both described in detail—a rhetoric that blurs the distinction of attraction and denial. And the very category of proposed reference above aggravates the category crisis, for "numerous accidents" names both a common denominator and uncommon events.

These uncertainties about formal unity inflect an even more precise sense of *numerous:* "numerous verse" is blank verse, the form alternately praised as liberty or suspected of abetting errancy, or at least overflow, of imagination. Wordsworth's reference to "numerous verse" early on in book 5 is leagued with extravagant songs in "native prose" (201/202). The allusion is to Milton's description of Adam and Eve's praise of "Thir Maker, in fit strains pronounct or sung / Unmediated": "prompt eloquence / Flow'd from thir lips, in Prose or numerous Verse" (V, 148–50). It is critical, however, that such numerous verse find fit strains by its inspiration and occasion, for without such ground, numbers may turn wayward. No less an arbiter than Dr. Johnson is divided on the question. About Young's wildly popular *Night Thoughts,* he suggests that its "wilderness of thought in which the fertility of fancy scatters flowers of every hue and of every odour" makes it "one of the few poems in which blank verse could not be changed for rhyme but with disadvantage. The wild diffusion of the sentiments and the digressive sallies of imagination would have been compressed and restrained by confinement to rhyme" ("Young" 395). Yet he worries that the "exemption which blank verse affords from the necessity of closing the sense with the couplet, betrays luxuriant and active minds into such self-indulgence that they pile image upon image, ornament upon ornament, and are not easily persuaded to close the sense at all"—and his own mimetically discursive expansion dramatizes the case ("Akenside" 417).

That Wordsworth would accrete "numerous" verse by "distresses and disasters" is a further complication, for as he was working on the 1799 text, he was also taking a stand against poetry exploiting such matter. His half-advertence to "numerous accidents in flood, or field / Quarry or moor" is an implicit self-measuring, by force both of overt echo and a weirdly accidental homonym (another "anti-pun")[33] of *moor* and *Moor* that summons Othello, an autobiographer whose repertoire in this genre of the tale beguiles Desdemona and turns a suspicious Venetian court into rapt and sympathetic listeners. Prompted (like Wordsworth) to give "the story of [his] life, / From year to year.../... from my boyish days / To the very moment" of its telling, Othello spins tales of "most disastrous chances, / Of moving accidents by flood and field" (1.3.129–35).[34] Wordsworth's affinity with such discourse is ambivalent. In the Preface to *Lyrical Ballads* he disdains "craving for extraordinary incident" as a degradation of literary taste (*LB* 746), and in the late 1790s he enlists more than a few of his narrators to the resistance. The poet of *The Ruined Cottage* promises "a common tale / By moving accidents uncharactered" (MS. D 50ᵛ: 231–2); the poet of "Hart-Leap Well" declares, "the moving accident is not my trade" (97); and the poet of *Michael* offers a story "ungarnish'd with events" (19). Yet the 1790s also accumulate a Wordsworthian inventory that patently trades on the appeal so disdained: *Adventures on Salisbury Plain, The Borderers, The Somersetshire Tragedy,* "The Three Graves," and "The Thorn."[35]

Wordsworth masters this advertence in his 1799 text by subjecting the imaginative productivity of all such accidents to a larger frame that, in effect, imposes regular classification. The "growth of mental power" is to be known and owned to the extent that the immediate emotional affect of these distresses can be shorn off, drained away, and disowned through time: all such tragic facts, the poet insists, "impressed my mind / With images, to which in following years / Far other feelings were attached" (MS. V 8ʳ: 283–5). This plot not only revises, but re-verses the original impression: landscapes of death and loss yield to "forms / That yet exist with independent life / And, like their archetypes, know no decay" (285–

7). Yet even as numerous accidents are reduced to this common denominator, the productivity of verse evokes the feelings that its argument would discard. If the argument is that the mind's forms and images "know no decay," as if by independent agency, the word *decay* has a counteragency that evokes the corpses—drowned man, murdered wife, executed murderer, dead father, all. What the mind's images know, with another form of "independent life," is that they can "know not" their original information of death.[36] And it is this not-knowing that the poetic forms of these images oddly contest and subvert.

Even what they contain may be no more knowable, if "spots of time"— the theme of the ensuing verse paragraph of the 1799 text—is the interpretive template. The odd discontinuity by which original impressions are alienated from their historical origins and allied with "other feelings" is read through a scheme, at once spatial and temporal, of invisible relations becoming legible over time. But its master-trope, "spots of time," contests this narrative, for a spot is self-contained, autonomous, and independent, however partitive *of* may be. In one conclusion tested for the first part, subsequently discarded in favor of a scheme in which latent contents are later "called . . . forth / To impregnate and to elevate the mind" (MS. V 10ᵛ: 425–6), Wordsworth even wondered whether to describe "those recollect hours that have the charm / Of visionary things" as "islands in the unnavigable depth / Of our departed time" (MS JJ Qᵛ).[37] And even here, he is uncertain whether to say *visible* or *visionary, thoughts* or *things:* are these recollections substantial and accessible or phantasmic and lost? If, like a "spot of time," an island is connected to a deep, invisible stratum, Wordsworth's adjectives, *unnavigable* and *departed,* interdict approach even to what is visible. In the landscape of memory as well as in the composition of verse, a "spot of time" may be less a radiant center for the growth of the mind than a site akin to what Freud describes as "the dream's navel, the spot where it reaches down into the unknown. The dream-thoughts to which we are led by interpretation cannot, from the nature of things, have any definite endings; they are bound to branch out in every direction into the intricate net-work of our world of thought" (5: 525).

Forms in Revision

Wordsworth's forms of revision involve the literal sense of seeing again and differently. His chief substantive revision to the text of the drowning, drawing on the concern of book 5 with books, is a new reading of its place in the mind. Canceling the advertence proposed in 1799 to other "tragic facts" of life, he recruits its latent literariness to a turn to the salutary effects of childhood reading—the memory, indeed the education, of which, he claims, yields images that superimpose themselves, as if by independent agency, on the sight of the corpse. No sooner does he report the sensational resurrection of "the dead Man" from the lake "bolt upright/ . . . with his ghastly face; a spectre-shape / Of terror even!" (470–3/450–3) than he disclaims its terror for the boy—insisting that "no vulgar fear" (1805 and MS. C), then "no soul-degrading fear," and finally, "no soul-debasing fear" (1850)

> Possess'd me; for my inner eye had seen
> Such sights before, among the shining streams
> Of Fairy Land, the Forests of Romance:
> Thence came a spirit, hallowing what I saw
> With decoration and ideal grace;
> A dignity, a smoothness, like the works
> Of Grecian Art, and purest Poesy.
>
> (475–81 / 455–61)

Imagination displaces death and death is redeemed by imagination. While the work of artifice stirs in the 1799 text (it is cast as a tale—"Ere I had seen / Eight summers"—and affiliated with literary genres: tragedy, history, as well as Othello's repertoire), the emphatic revision is the effect ascribed to it. In 1799, the narrative associations are to tragedy, and despite the repair to an argument about "spots of time," other deaths and disasters crowd into composition. In book 5, it is an incongruously "beauteous scene" that signals and even prefigures advertence: the images and even the syntax of "the dead Man, 'mid that beauteous scene / Of trees, and hills, and water" are repeated in "Such sights . . . among the shining streams / Of Fairy Land, the Forests of Romance." The transposition of *scene* and *sights* in these sites helps the slide from one to the other. Wordsworth uses the aesthetic term *scene* to refer to phenomenal sight and makes *sights* refer both to this and—punning on the "scene" of the outer eye— to what had been "seen" before by the "inner eye" of book-informed memory. Coleridge, always the desynonymizer, objected to this inclination to use *scene* (he is thinking of the similarly punning phrase "the visible scene," from "There was a Boy") "without some clear reference, proper or metaphorical, to the theatre"; even this usage, he protests, is too "equivocal" in evoking both "scenery" and a unit of dramatic action (*Biographia*

2: 103). But equivocation is exactly what Wordsworth is after in the "beauteous scene" of the drowning; the word predicts an improper (super)-imposition of artifice.

The translation of sight into scenery emerges in every version from a train of prior specular events: in 1799, "Ere I had seen / Eight summers," "I saw distinctly," "half an hour I watched" (V 7^v: 258–9, 267, 270); in 1805, "I saw distinctly," "long I watch'd" (460–2); in 1850, "Long I watched," "some looked / In passive expectation" (440, 446–7). The revisions develop the readerly aspect of such visual attention. In the 1799 text, the heap of garments evokes a tentative surmise that is like reading—"as if left by one / Who there was bathing" (269–70). Book 5 makes this scene a text: "Those unclaim'd garments, telling a plain Tale" (467 / 445). This tale—denoted with a capital *T* in 1805 and promoted from the parentheses in 1850— gains a further charge in book 5 from the earlier figure of books as "garments" shed at death by "the immortal being" (22–3 / 23–4). The episode of the drowning literalizes the trope: the heap of unclaimed garments is read as if a book, and its tale is of its status as the posthumous remnant of an absent body.[38] This bookishness takes another turn when the body appears from the lake, for the boy reads it back into books. The 1850 booking of this body goes further yet, for the corpse is not merely hallowed with a "decoration and ideal grace" bestowed by books but, in a revision of 1805's "what I saw" (478), it becomes a "sad spectacle" (458)—a term that gives what was "seen" a literary staging, its "spectre shape" converted, with etymologic affinity, into an aesthetic "spectacle."

The aesthetic melioration applied by revision exposes the strain of its construction, however, not only in view of the intertextual evidence, but even in its own too obvious labors, as if these were a reaction formation of protesting too much. Stillinger is not alone in judging Wordsworth's summary "explanation" so "lame" that the poet might have been better off resisting the impulse "to interpret or theorize" (*Selected Poems* 551–2). Wordsworth's gloss looks "tack[ed] on" to David Perkins, though he is interested in the tacking as a sign of the poet's "need to reassure himself": "the very violence of [his] fears may be what compels [him] to assert that the incident could be blunted, the fears managed" (*Quest* 17). "No vulgar fear" and "no soul-debasing fear," like "unblam'd," display what they disclaim, bearing a "paradoxical power to create as a shimmering mirage lying over their explicit assertions the presence of what they deny," as Hillis Miller writes about the rhetoric of Wordsworth's praise of London from Westminster Bridge ("Still Heart" 306). The textual productivity of Wordsworth's revisions is such that even what he denies may become more explicit. Where the 1799 text, for instance, gives the corpse a "ghastly face" (279), book 5 elaborates the image with terms of impression and effect: it is "a spectre-shape / Of terror even!" (472–3 / 452–3). The contradiction between the sensationalism of this report and the disclaimer of "vulgar fear" may account for the slight tempering in the 1850 text, where the excited insistence of *even!* is dropped and the more rigorously supervisory phrase, "soul-debasing," takes up the adjectival space. But the full text of these cancellations and revisions shows the degree to which, within the would-be purified aesthetic control applied by the rubric of book 5, Wordsworth's writing finds its inspiration by contending with sensations that simultaneously urge formal control and resist its sway. His revisionary text typically works less to refine and stabilize an original intention than to enact a revisionary dialectic of confrontation and containment.

Not only does this dialectic attenuate the authority of the gloss for the corpse, but the textual field of the longer poem bears other, darker glosses—for example, the episode of the discharged soldier that closes book 4, which echoes within the episode of the drowning in more than few chords.[39] The half-dead soldier is not only another specter shape of terror in the mind of the autobiographer; he is also another dark double for both the boy of immunized imagination and the autobiographer he would become. Recalling a figure seemingly left behind in the 1798–99 text, he speaks as a kind of English Othello grown old and impotent, unable to trade in the moving accident, despite an ample repertoire. His is a "strange half-absence . . . / . . . as of one / Remembering the importance of his theme / But feeling it no longer" (475–8 / 442–5)—a figure weirdly akin to the child prodigy of book 5, so dulled by his education that "fear itself, / Natural or supernatural alike, / Unless it leap upon him in a dream, / Touches him not" (315–18/308–11), or the self-forgetting boy reader (368–9 / 347–8), or the romance-shielded boy at the lake.

Such insulation is not just numbing; it may also, as Wordsworth knows, engender illusions and delusions, a romancing of personal and social upheaval.[40] The boy's easy conscription of the corpse into the literature of "Fairy Land" and "Romance" is refigured in the man's later description of the French patriot Beaupuy, who maintained his composure during the the Revolution's convulsions by casting their historical immediacy into idealizing and meliorative literary genres:

> He thro' the events
> Of that great change wander'd in perfect faith,
> As through a Book, an old Romance or Tale

Of Fairy, or some dream of actions wrought
Behind the summer clouds.

                                    (IX, 305–9/298–302)

If Wordsworth's own initial enthusiasm for Revolutionary France showed
the "attraction of a Country in Romance," with "Reason" itself a "prime
Enchanter" (X, 696–9 / XI, 112–15), the equivocal bearing of his lines above
wonders about such enchantments. While he voices no overt judgment of
the strategies one uses to survive war, the notation of wandering, by dint
of literary tradition (Dante, Spenser, Milton), courts reading as a figure of
potential error. The two analogies for this wandering recognize the extremity of the translation. Not only does Beaupuy's eye refigure the world
as a book—the very books that the boy of Hawkshead calls on to mediate
his lone image of death—but it seems to half-create that world in the
second analogy's vocabulary of displacement and insubstantiality: "dream,"
"wrought," "summer clouds."

By far the most attractive literary model is the one to which book 5
turns right after the melioration of the drowned man: the Arabian Tales.
A repetition links the book-hallowed corpse to this Romance: the reciprocal of the claim in the 1850 text that no fear "possessed" the boy (455)
is the recollection of a book he "possessed" (462). Yet Wordsworth's account
of his boyhood romance with this book destabilizes the framework that
summons it by evoking a proliferation beyond the control of any one
imagination. The "slender abstract" of the Tales, in the unknown and
unowned volumes it signifies, bodes uncontainable possibilities; it is "but a
block / Hewn from a mighty quarry" (487–8 / 467), more like nature than
art, a primer of something ever more about to be.[41] Whatever the boy is
able to possess is not enough to make him lord and master of the whole.
The teller of the Tales, Scheherazade, evokes such desire and frustration
with the very structure of her narratives, for as their frame reveals, her
task is to keep the Sultan on the stretch of curiosity in order to prevent
him from executing her at dawn. The narrative expansions propelled by
her forms of suspense recall the mode from which Wordsworth has never
quite adverted: the moving accident, her stock in trade as well as Othello's.
But Scheherazade's is a moving accident with a saving difference, for if her
tales are as seductive as Othello's, she reverses his fate. Othello adeptly
fashions himself as a figure of romance adventure, but he is also undone
by others' plots. Scheherazade loves wisely and well: the Sultan not only
releases her from the sentence of death, but has her tales written down

and published throughout the realm—the highest earthly hope of any author, any poet.

But does her success come to terms with death, as Wordsworth demands of his own writing? Or does it merely forestall considerations of it? Wordsworth's struggle with this question of aesthetic agency often sets his revisions against themselves, its denials paired with greater emphases on what they deny, its forms and antiforms spurring each other on. Some revisions elaborate signs of control over the specter of death. If the 1799 text situates the boy as one "transplanted to" Hawkshead, in book 5 he is "entrusted to the care / Of that sweet Valley"—a rewriting with several important elements. The new phrase of conveyance, "entrusted to the care," smoothes out *transplanted,* which bodes disruption as well as purpose. Its dative projects responsive attention and nurturing, a world in which "chance" wanderings are more protected than they might seem; and the new capital of "Valley" inscribes this mythopoesis.[42] "*That* sweet Valley," referring to the valley of the Boy of Winander's privileged childhood, implicitly confers on the boy of Hawkshead the same prodigal blessings and wise supervision. Yet within this more secure framing, other revisions imply a random eventfulness and give fuller play to the boy's anxiety. Canceled are the personification and second-person address that in the 1799 text projected sensate receptivity; instead, there are signs of otherness—"its . . . its"—that imply an inaccessibility, even to autobiographical retrospection. Under these signs, there is also a fuller staging of the boy's restlessness. In the 1799 text, the valley is said to impress his "mind," that object "fram'd" by "Invisible workmansh[ip]" (MS. V I^v); in the revision, there is an active agency of "thoughts" and motions to suggest their pressure—the boy's "roving up and down alone, / Seeking I knew not what" (455–6 / 433–4). This new map of "up and down" also bears a linguistic anticipation of the signs, events, and aftermath of the drowning that it eventually discovers. In 1799, the Lake's surface is broken by a "leaping fish"; book 5 changes the adjective to "*up*leaping," visibly prefiguring the rising of the dead man "bolt upright" (465, 471 / 443, 451). The C-stage revisions of 1818–20 extend this grid with the detail of the boat party sounding the "deep" (464), and the 1850 text elaborates it even further with the boat's searchers looking "o'er the deep" and the poet's claim that no "Soul-*debasing* fear" possessed the boy (448, 453).

This new verbal texture conveys a deeper sense of the mystery and anxiety that book 5 would legislate into textual control. Even the "heap of garments," though endowed with a more legibly bookish function, is more enigmatic in each revision. The 1799 text writes this object into the sort of prosaic map we recognize in other of Wordsworth's spot-obsessed poems—"on the opposite shore / Beneath a tree and close by the lake side"; and the conjecture, "as if left by one / Who there was bathing," is voiced as a casual guess anyone might make (7^v: 267–70). The 1805 text drops the prepositional grid and expands the act of noticing to "left, as I suppos'd" (461)—the "I" stressing individual attention. The C text then increases the tension both by giving more signifying agency to the heap and less certainty to the boy's surmise. Instead of the previous syntax of subject and object, "I saw distinctly ... / A heap of garments," we read "appeared distinctly ... / A heap," with the predicate preceding the subject (453–4; cf. 1850: 438–9). Not only does this produce the frisson of action before agent, but the syntax lets *appeared* signify ambiguously: it implies "appeared to my sight"; but it also has a suggestive glint of independent emergence and beckoning.

Wordsworth applies a shift in verbal mood in the 1850 text to enhance this semiotic uncertainty: "as if left by One / Who *might have* there been bathing" (439–40). Although the *as if* of 1799 returns, the newly tenuous *might have* prevents any matter-of-fact deduction: one might have been bathing or might have abandoned his clothes and sought the Lake for another reason. The hesitation is subtle, but portent enough to invite conjecture and align this effect with other revisions that dilate the interval of the boy's anxiety. Where the 1799 text records only a chronometric "half an hour I watched / And no one owned them" (7^v: 270–1), book 5 writes, in a strained act of attention, "long I watch'd," that expands the shimmer of implication and heightens its tension by substituting *but* for the merely sequential *and* (462–3 / 440–1). The new term of subjective measure, *long,* furthermore, initiates a train of echoes in the "long poles" that the search party uses and their success "at length," each repetition investing the boy's initial vigil with a sign of prophetic apprehension.

The double effect of these revisions, extending the inscriptions of anxiety within a seemingly more secure frame of interpretation, is also at work in the report of the events of the succeeding day, as the boy's twilight anxiety is translated into a public search. The communal gathering stages the issue of context in the recollection itself, with the revisions again destabilizing the formal charge of context as containment. On the one hand, a group of adults in the light of day vindicates the boy's lone, twilight uncertainties with a matter of plain public fact, defining a chapter of rural history rather than of mere individual trauma. This sense is conveyed by the rather flat notations of the 1799 and 1805 texts—"There came a company" (7^v: 275) and "Went there a Company" (468)—and it is enhanced in the 1850 text by the erasure of 1805's subjective registers for the boy's initial attention: "I saw" and "I suppos'd" (460–1, the first canceled in C). But if Wordsworth uses this company to frame the boy's misgivings with common knowledge, his revision of other textual elements magnifies the initial mystery of agency, even more emphatically in C and the 1850 text. He now endows the garments with a magnetic power that multiples their force on the boy the evening before: in C, they "drew an anxious crowd / Of friends and neighbours to the fatal spot" (460–1); and in 1850, a suspenseful under-statement names the fatality: the garments "drew to the spot an anxious Crowd" (446). Rewriting 1805's merely reportorial "Company" as an "anx-ious Crowd," moreover, gives the boy's apprehensions a communal register. As early as his revision of MS. A, Wordsworth is staging a shared anxiety (the crowd "lookd awhile . . . searched the deep"), and he elaborates it in subsequent drafts:

> In anxious expectation on the shore
> These stood, while those were busy
> (rev. WW, C stage; Reed 2:625)

> In passive expectation on the shore
> These stood, while others sounded
> (C: 462–3)

> some looked
> In passive expectation from the shore,
> While from a boat others hung o'er the deep,
> Sounding with grappling irons and long poles.
> (1850: 446–9)

The Norton Critical editors say that these last lines "place the solitary experience recorded in *1799* and *1805* in an untypically social context" (177 n. 3), but this isn't quite right: both *1799* and *1805* bring a company to the Lake. What is striking is that the social context operates less to counter and contain the boy's anxieties than to multiply and expand them. Those gazing from the shore in passive expectation reprise his watch the evening before and prefigure, in their distance, the way he will compose the scene into a sad spectacle. Those who "hung o'er the deep" probe actively, trying to penetrate the surface reflections of a "beauteous scene." With darker tension, they repeat the story of the Winander Boy, who when he "some-times, in . . . silence . . . hung / Listening," received "a gentle shock of mild surprize" (1850: 383–4) amid his own scene, named variously but resonantly in book 5 as a "beauteous . . . spot" or a "fair . . . Spot" in the vale (1805: 416; C: 409; 1850: 393). The language of the 1850 text also returns its o'er-hanging probers of the deep to the seemingly distanced text of "spots of time." When Wordsworth writes that the garments "drew to the spot an anxious Crowd," his replacement of the simply indicative *there* of the 1799 and 1805 with *the spot* retrieves the episode's original associations with 1799's death-haunted "spots of time"; his phrase is "the fatal spot" in C (461). And, although its elements are configured differently, some of the language of the first spot of time, "a *bottom* where in former times / a murderer . . . was *hung* / In *irons*" (8ᵛ: 308–10, my italics), carries further verbal echoes to reaffiliate these sundered texts.

A more immediate textual affiliate, one about textuality itself, is drawn in by the language that Wordsworth uses in the 1850 text to describe the probers of Esthwaite's Lake. This is the epic simile of his previous book (or the same, in the fleeting five-book poem), launched to image the perplexed epistemology of writing and reading autobiography:

> As one who hangs down-bending from the side
> Of a slow-moving boat, upon the breast
> Of a still water, solacing himself
> With such discoveries as his eye can make,
> Beneath him, in the bottom of the deep,
> Sees many beauteous sights, weeds, fishes, flowers,
> Grots, pebbles, roots of trees, and fancies more;
> Yet often is perplexed, and cannot part
> The shadow from the substance, rocks and sky,
> Mountains and clouds reflected in the depth
> Of the clear flood, from things which there abide
> In their true Dwelling: now is crossed by gleam
> Of his own image, by sun-beam now,
> And wavering motions, sent he knows not whence,
> Impediments that make his task more sweet—
> Such pleasant office have we long pursued,
> Incumbent o'er the surface of past time
> (1850: IV, 256–74)

Not only do readers here preview the metaphors, even the very words, sounded in the text of the drowning—"the breast / Of a still water," its "shadows," its "beauteous sights"—but they find themselves situated in relation to these, drawn into lake-scanning and the analogized reading of "past time" by an inclusive "we" (273). A casual grammatical perplexity— "and fancies more" (262)—even presents them with an analogous phenomenology. In the train of nouns, "fancies more" appears as the summary term for "beauteous sights" and their extended discovery. But it also disrupts the chain of substantive sights by recasting all as "fancies"—projections of the eye's delights, even its whims. This disruption is abetted by a double grammar that lets "fancies more" seem part of a compound predicate, "Sees many beauteous sights . . . and fancies more," a syntax in which the eye first sees and then more than half-creates what it perceives.[43]

This perplexed epistemology, a pleasant office here, is not just recalled by the text-saturated imagery of the lakescape from which the dead man emerges a few hundred lines on; it is re-created by the form of the poem, in which this extended juxtaposition produces a memory of reading this passage about reading. The "surface of past time" becomes in this reverberation a simultaneous figure for the experiential object of the poet's consciousness, for the textualized past of his recollective processing, for the textual past of his writing—and, not the least, for his and our reading of it. When we see the lake-reading of book 4 repeated in the text of the far less pleasant office of corpse-pursuit of book 5, the information of the two passages plays into and implicates them with one another. In the poem's forward trajectory, the poetics of autobiography as an uncertain scanning of the surfaces and depths of past time re-emerges, refigured, as a rediscovery of death in, and by, nature. In the text of retrospect, this recollected discovery exposes its affiliation to the motive of autobiographical writing itself.

There is another kind of death that is always impending in autobiography: the fact that its text escapes revision only when its writer dies. Wordsworth intuits this end of revision in lines first drafted in 1804, as he was expanding his autobiography. Its textual site has to do with a frustrated imagination in the Alps—a set of pages that also contains his first effort to reframe the recollection of the drowning with the reference to books.[44] The lines in question turn meta-revisionary as they produce an epic simile describing the entry of a traveller (one of the poem's master-tropes for its autobiographer) into a cavern whose visual field, a ferment of "Shapes and Forms and Tendencies to Shape," achieves the stability and perfection of a "written book" only as it is drained of life. Here is the form of this simile in 1805, when Wordsworth moved it to book 8:

> As when a traveller hath from open day
> With torches pass'd into some Vault of Earth,

· · ·

He looks and sees the Cavern spread and grow,
Widening itself on all sides, sees, or thinks
He sees, erelong, the roof above his head,
Which instantly unsettles and recedes
Substance and shadow, light and darkness, all
Commingled, making up a Canopy
Of Shapes and Forms, and Tendencies to Shape,
That shift and vanish, change and interchange
Like Spectres, ferment quiet, and sublime;
Which, after a short space, works less and less
Till every effort, every motion gone,
The scene before him lies in perfect view,
Exposed and lifeless, as a written book.

(1805: 8.711–27; cf. WW 26^r–27^v
[Reed 2:255–7]; 1850: 560–76)

Once a specter shape is given a definite form and is turned into a simulacrum of a literary artifact, the life of the subjective eye and I, produced by motion and ferment, dies. Long before de Man articulated the negativity behind language, Wordsworth staged as much in passages such as this: mastery is death.[45]

But as the flux of his revisions demonstrates, mastery is also an illusion that inevitably dissolves into the ferment against which it asserts itself, and revision—that ceaseless play of shifts and vanishing, changes and interchanges—coincides with life, the energy that postpones death and quickens the mind, and writing, with a hope for limitless adventure. Let this traveller "pause a while, and look again," Wordsworth writes,

And a new quickening shall succeed, at first
Beginning timidly, then creeping fast
Through all which he beholds: the senseless mass
In its projections, wrinkles, cavities,
Through all its surface, with all colours streaming,
Like a magician's airy pageant, parts,
Unites, embodying every where some pressure
Or image, recognis'd or new, some type
Or picture of the world; forests and lakes

· · ·

A Spectacle to which there is no end.

(1805: 728–41)

Drawn into this perpetual pressure toward newness is the image of the drowned man, its sad spectacle seemingly lodged in the safe house of books, but with another look, revealed to play within the mind in an endless spectacle of reading and rereading (and here the placement of "end" at the end of the line and verse paragraph opens, by visual pun, into the space of the page).

Wordsworth's revision of forms yields a form of revision in *The Prelude* that, in effect, theorizes form *as* revision. If revision sustains the illusion of formal stability, it also persists in postponing that achievement as each review of the hoped-for "perfect view" disrupts the possibility of closure. Revision is thus an endless opening of poetic form, not simply because any vision is open to numerous, potentially infinite interpretations and organizations, but because each review discovers within itself new motions and forms of reading. The drowned man, dead as he is in the boy's eyes, gains a life in Wordsworth's autobiography that the pursuit of his second death— the corpse's abstraction into the corpus of art and purest poesy—at once suppresses and sustains. The only name Wordsworth himself ever gave his poem, inscribed on the title page of its 1805 drafts, refers to an unfixed future where there will be time yet for another revision: "Poem / title not yet fixed upon / by / William Wordsworth / Addressed to / S. T. Coleridge."[46]

Notes

1. Unless otherwise stated, quotations are of the 1805 "AB-Stage" (based on MSS. A and B [DC MSS. 52 and 53]), in Mark Reed's *Thirteen-Book "Prelude"*; "DC" refers to the Dove Cottage archive in Grasmere. When there are two citations, these refer to AB and the comparable passage in the fourteen-book text in W. J. B. Owen's edition, based on MS. D (DC MS. 124) rather than the 1850 first edition. For fuller remarks on my choice of texts, see n. 16, below.

2. *The Prelude* occupies more than twenty manuscripts: for a census and description, see Norton Critical Edition 507–26; Stillinger provides a helpful tour of the compositional and publication history (*Multiple* 74–7). The manuscripts gather to three principal stages: the "two-part" poem of 1798–99 (JJ [DC MS. 19], RV [DC MS. 21], V [DC MS. 22], U [DC MS. 23], etc.); the thirteen-book poem of 1805 (chiefly A and B, but also W [DC MS. 38] and WW (DC MS. 43]); and the fourteen-book poem of the 1830s (D and E) that yielded the base text for the 1850 publication. Reed's edition gives a full account of the manuscripts from 1799 up to D and constructs a "C-Stage revision of 1818–1820" from base A (DC MS. 82). Jonathan Wordsworth, noting the poet's remark in early 1804 that he is "engaged in a

Poem on my own earlier life which will take five parts or books to complete" (*Letters EY* 436), has speculated (in the absence of any fair-copy manuscript, but with reference to W) about the probable shape and contents of a five-book poem from early 1804, one that he likes for old-fashioned formalist reasons: it "is the most formally rounded of the *Preludes*" ("The Five-Book *Prelude*" 20; summarized in the Norton Critical 516–17). For reservations about some elements of this specu-lative reconstruction, see Robin Jarvis's essay.

3. I quote from the statement at the front of every volume of the Cornell Wordsworth, by the general editor, Stephen M. Parrish, who elaborates the case for attention to earlier versions and multiple intentions in his essay in TEXT. The Cornell project has issued three editions of *The Prelude: "The Prelude," 1798–1799,* ed. Parrish; *The Fourteen-Book "Prelude,"* ed. Owen, and *The Thirteen-Book "Prelude,"* ed. Reed—every *Prelude,* that is, except the publication of 1850, *The Prelude, or Growth of a Poet's Mind: An Autobiographical Poem.* Advocates of the 1850 publication claim that this is the final text authorized by Wordsworth, but as Owen and other editors report, there are questions of accuracy raised chiefly, but not exclusively, by the readings of its two prior manuscripts, D and E (DC MSS. 124 and 145).

4. For citations, see Stillinger, *Multiple* 80. Major parallel-text editions include de Selincourt-Darbishire (1959): J. C. Maxwell's handy paperback *The Prelude: A Par-allel Text* (1971), and the Norton Critical (1979), again in a much-reissued, handy paperback.

5. The conveniently "small compass" of the 1798–99 poem made it, for a while and problematically, a pedagogical favorite: for practical reasons, it was the only version printed "in its entirety" in the 3rd and 4th editions of *The Norton Anthology of English Literature* (1974, 2:196–218; and 1979, 2:231–55, respectively)—an event that in 1974, as Jonathan Arac ("Wordsworth's Revisions") wittily observed, made it "the most extensively circulated new poem published that year, perhaps even of recent decades"; in the 5th edition, it is discussed in a headnote, but dropped as a text.

6. "Wordsworth's C-stage revisions . . . did not culminate in a fair-copy recen-sion, approved by the poet, of a new state of the poem," Reed cautions; "he did not review [the] often obviously imperfect copy . . . attentively; and this stage of revision was not finally finished off, but was simply dropped. No C-stage text of the poem survives with authority equivalent to that of the approved recensions MSS. A, B, D, and E." Even so, Reed urges the claims of this text in any investi-gation of the poem's development: it represents "a distinctive stage . . . which de-serves study in its own right, and neither its extent nor its individuality has been sufficiently recognized" (1: 81–2).

7. As Stillinger summarizes the issues: "Until fairly recently, all editorial the-ories . . . were based on a concept of . . . 'realizing'—approximating, recovering, (re)constructing—the author's intentions," usually equated with the *"final"* inten-

tion (*Multiple* 195). During the nineteenth century and for the first half of the twentieth, credit thus gathered to the latest version—either the last publication in an author's lifetime or the last text prepared under his or her supervision. In the 1950s, W. W. Greg and Fredson Bowers, questioning the degree of such supervision after the first edition, argued for the greater authority of the first published edition or a fair-copy base-text manuscript. The initial essays in this polemic were Greg's "Rationale" (1950) and Bowers' "Current Theories" (1950). Yet this reversion proved as controversial as the paradigm it meant to correct, not only because of its rationale but also because the whole issue of intention and authority was getting theorized. New Criticism opened the gates by formulating the "intentional fallacy" (denying statements of intention absolute authority over interpretation), and subsequent theories pressed further against authorial intention as a presence and court of appeal. For discussion of these issues and a relevant bibliography, see Stillinger's "Implications for Theory" (*Multiple,* esp. 194–202; 243–4).

8. The first set of remarks is by M. H. Abrams (*Natural Supernaturalism* 76) and the second by Donald H. Reiman, in a review for *Studies in Romanticism* (rpt. *Romantic Texts* 153–4).

9. For those unfamiliar with the terms: the keynote is de Selincourt's comparison, in his original introduction (rpt. in Darbishire's revised edition [lvii–lxxiv] and in Gill's new edition [xix–xxxviii]; some points, with a bias toward 1805, are elaborated in Norton Critical 522–3). Helen Darbishire's Clark Lectures (1949), though conceding some technical improvements (121), "deplored" the revisions "which overlay and obscure" and "often mar the poetry" of earlier expression (123), especially in the effort "to explain, to rationalize, to moralize" (133). The controversy climaxed, or anticlimaxed, in the "The Great *Prelude* Debate" at the 1984 Wordsworth Summer Conference, published in *The Wordsworth Circle* 17, ed. Marilyn Gaull. This debate reprises the themes, with some novel twists: Norman Fruman argues for the stylistic superiority of the 1805 text, and Robert Barth claims that the 1850 text does not so much impose alien religious piety as amplify a religious dimension already strong in the 1805 text. For a recent, but largely familiar, polemic against the principles of the Cornell series as well as the notion of Wordsworthian multi-text, see Zachary Leader, who insists on editorial and textual fidelity to "Wordsworth's explicit instructions" (his latest revisions), granting them "the rights of literary and material property" guaranteed in copyright law (677).

10. Stephen Orgel's "What is a text?" studies various problems of bibliography in Renaissance texts. Steven Urkowitz offers an important case for the 1608 first quarto and the 1623 first folio versions of *King Lear* as equivalent, "alternative texts created by a revising author" (5) rather than as partial keys through which one might divine a missing original. And George Bernard Shaw insisted on printing

the original and the revised endings of *Great Expectations* in the edition that he supervised in 1937.

11. *The Rime of the Ancyent Marinere, In Seven Parts,* antiqued and unglossed, appeared anonymously at the head of the 1798 *Lyrical Ballads: The Ancient Mariner. A Poet's Reverie,* less antiqued, with some revision, and still anonymous, held a less privileged position in 1800; in 1802 and 1805, the subtitle was dropped and further revisions applied; *The Rime of the Ancient Mariner,* revised, with marginal gloss and a new epigraph, was issued with Coleridge's name in *Sibylline Leaves* in 1817. In 1961, Royal A. Gettmann published a parallel-text edition of the 1798 and 1834 poems; for readings of the implications of this textual multiplicity, see Frances Ferguson ("Coleridge and the Deluded Reader"), Anne K. Mellor (*English Romantic Irony* 137–50), myself ("The Language of Interpretation" 24–31), and Martin Wallen (unaware of this previous critical work). Stillinger offers an interesting tour through the multiple versions of this and several other of Coleridge's canonical poems, with the intriguing proposal "that Coleridge changed his texts at least partly in order to create the very instability that would make his poems and their meanings elusive"; the "conspicuous featuring of his poetry's instability" implies that his poems were "always in progress" and suggests "that the perfect poem was a chimera and that authority itself was therefore a fiction" ("Multiple Versions" 38 and 146; see *Coleridge and Textual Instability*).

12. For discussions of the texts of "La Belle Dame," see McGann on the *Indicator* text ("Keats and the Historical Method," esp. 31–42), and Simpson (*Irony and Authority* 14–23), who praises Douglas Bush (206 n. 27) for giving both versions equal representation in *Selected Poems and Letters* (199–202). For the two texts of *Frankenstein,* see the editions of D. L. Macdonald and Kathleen Scherf, and James Rieger. These print the 1818 text with the substantive variants of 1831. Rieger also supplies intermediary revisions, and advocates the merits of the 1818 text; for a rebuttal of his argument and a reassessment of the evidence, see Mellor' *Mary Shelley* (58–69) and "Choosing a Text." What is still wanting, as Mellor laments, is a parallel-text edition.

13. As Nigel Wood remarks, "the need for a unitary performance" obscures the fact "that there is enough evidence to suppose that there were several 'final intentions' " (8). In a brisk and shrewd reply to Jeffrey Baker's alarm that "the principles on which the Norton Edition is based [its aesthetic and ideological prejudice toward the earlier texts] constitute a danger for English studies" for failing to "see an object as in itself it really is" (86), Robert Young remarks that not only is the claim to objectivity itself an interested position (an "interpretation") but that Baker's singular *it* is a misrepresentation: "to see *The Prelude* as it really is is to see that it is not one poem at all but several poems—1799, 1805, 1850, and all the intermediate versions and stages as well"; in view of these "different forms,"

the critic's project should not be one of debating relative merits, "but rather the exploration of the complex and subtle intertextual relations and differences among the different poems. Instead of asking which is best, we should be asking what does this multiplicity mean, and what are its effects?" (87). The essay from which this chapter evolved ("The Illusion of Mastery") is one such asking, as are my reviews of Owen's and Reed's editions (in *The Wordsworth Circle* and *Review,* respectively). Others who have analyzed revision, textual authority, and *The Prelude* include Peter J. Manning ("Reading Wordsworth's Revision"), Theresa M. Kelley ("Economics of the Heart"), William H. Galperin (*Revision and Authority*), and Jack Stillinger ("Multiple Consciousness in Wordsworth's *Prelude,*" in *Multiple*).

14. My references to Barthes "theory of the text" and its enfranchisement of reading are drawn from "Theory of the Text" (esp. 36–37, 39, 42–43), "From Work to Text" (esp. 157 [his italics], 159, 161–62), and "The Death of the Author" (esp. 147–48). Nigel Wood's introduction proposes the usefulness of Barthesian models for theorizing how a reader might address the plurality of *The Prelude* (4).

15. The quotation is from DC MS. 33: 49 (*Prelude 1798–1799* 163). Theorizing a textualized subjectivity that also refers to the writer as historical subject, Tilottama Rajan helpfully describes a "discourse of subjectivity," in which, say, the author of *The Prelude* "does not simply represent himself but also puts himself under erasure in the gap between his self-representations." This yields "two complementary movements": "the act of introjection by which a character in a text is claimed as autobiographical and the act of projection which involves the 'I' in a process of self-reflection and specularisation" ("Coleridge" 61–62).

16. One has to have base-texts for reference. I use ones that retain accidentals or note, rather than leave unrecorded ("silent"), any emendations (accidental variants involve elements of spelling, punctuation, or capitals; substantive variants involve matters of wording, sequence, and so forth affecting sense—though it is clear that some accidentals, such as capitals, have substantive bearing). The Norton Critical's collation of several texts and manuscript drafts is handy and affordable, and probably the most widely read; but since the "punctuation in the printed texts of *1799* and *1805*" is "editorial" and silent (511)—including some significant capitals—the text is not as reliable as Reed's (and even Gill's own). In the episode of the drowning, moreover, Norton persists in reprinting a misleading typographical error at 5.480 (*words* for *works*), despite its editors having been informed of this mistake: MS. A 108[r] clearly shows "works" (see Reed 1:776).

For the "Two-Part" *Prelude* of 1798–99, I follow MS. V (Dorothy Wordsworth's fair copy of 1799), in Parrish's edition; the episode of the drowning appears on 7[v]–8[r]; 256–59 (cf. reading text 49–50).

For the 1805 text, I follow Reed's "AB-Stage Reading Text" (based on MS. A, Dorothy Wordsworth's fair copy, and MS. B, Mary Wordsworth's duplicate). Reed's edition has photographs of A; the episode of the drowning appears on 107^r–109^r (1: 774–76) and is transcribed and interpreted in 2:624–6.

For the "C-Stage revision," largely a collation of the corrections made on A through 1818–20, I follow Reed's "Reading Text" in vol. 2.

For the fourteen-book poem, I follow Owen's edition. He uses MS. D as his base text and so rejects the normal determination of the authoritative copy text for published works—in the case of *The Prelude,* a census of the first edition of 1850 and its base-text, the latest authorial manuscript, E. Although Reiman urges the credit of E as the manuscript "which Wordsworth approved before his death" (*Romantic Texts* 153), Owen queries the extent of supervision, because both it and the 1850 publication, he and others note, introduce several alterations of substantives and accidentals that were not clearly authorized by Wordsworth and perhaps reflect the interference of his executors. Owen's is thus an "eclectic" construction, favoring D (written by Mary Wordsworth in 1832 and revised at the end of the decade) and referring to E and *1850* only when their substantive readings patently supersede those of D. Owen believes that this construction corresponds to what "Wordsworth would have approved for his final version of the poem" (11); for a fuller account of his work, see his introduction or, more briefly, my review in *The Wordsworth Circle.* The 1850 publication, of course, has historical validity as the form in which the poem was read in the nineteenth century.

17. Only an 1804 draft tries out and then rejects a narrative transition: "Soon as I reached home / I to our little household of the sight / Made casual mention"; see MS. W 31^v (Reed 1:388 and 2:280).

18. In attending to the aural hint of *ears* and *sounding,* I share Hartman sense of "strange currents of symbols, half formulated symmetries" (*Wordsworth's Poetry* 232) over Cynthia Chase's claim that the language of this episode (contrasting the way words elsewhere in book 5 "resonate with symbolic meaning or imaginative significance") conspicuously effaces "figurative meaning," evincing a "spare literalness" (15): "The principal quality of ears, their power of hearing, is without relevance, the word's usage here referring only to the accidental fact of their shape. The principal meaning of *sound,* its power of resounding, has no pertinence in this usage of the verb that borrows not its sense but only its letters" (20). It is true that the local name for one peninsula was Strickland-ears—fancifully derived, Wordsworth suggests in his *Tour* of the Lakes, from "the form & the manner in which it is attached to the shore" (*Prose* 2:337; noted by Owen 105). It seems to me, however, not only that Wordsworth has taken advantage of this contingency but that Chase's very sorting of literal from accidental shows the power of semiotic ghosts. Christopher Ricks calls such effects "anti-puns," ghostly demarcations that the sense of the statement "positively precludes" but that the "pressure" of contiguous words calls up. Referring to Preface to *Lyrical Ballads,* Ricks proposes that the anti-pun "is

one form which may be taken by the poet's 'disposition to be affected more than other men by absent things as if they were present' " (*Force* 99–100).

19. "We assume that life *produces* the autobiography as an act produces its consequences, but can we not suggest . . . that the autobiographical project may itself produce and determine the life and that whatever the writer *does* is in fact governed by the technical demands of self-portraiture? . . . Does the referent determine the figure, or is it the other way round: is the illusion of reference not a correlation of the structure of the figure, that is to say no longer clearly and simply a referent at all but something more akin to a fiction which then, however, in its own turn, acquires a degree of referential productivity?" (de Man, "Autobiography as Defacement" 69): See also Tilottama Rajan: once "facts" enter a poem, their status as ground for "the meaning of the text" succumbs to the force of "their own figurative constitution" ("Displacing" 472).

20. For my fuller discussion of *The Prelude* in terms of its foundation of questions, see *Questioning Presence* ("The Interrogative Origins of Autobiography" [131–50]), and "Answering Questions and Questioning Answers: The Interrogative Project of *The Prelude*." The formula of this specific question, with antecedents in Virgil, Ariosto, Milton, Thomson, Pope (and its inevitable parody in Byron) works as an allusion to other such questioners in similar crises. The Norton Critical refers to "correspondence in *TLS* April–September 1975" detailing these antecedents (1 n. 2); Jonathan Wordsworth gives the Miltonic formula fuller consideration in *Borders* (36–37, 420 n. 3), and John A. Hodgson attends to the "allusively evocative" character of this question in a specific rhetorical tradition, concentrating on Virgilian instances and resonances.

21. Culler, "Apostrophe" 149–50; Jacobus, "Apostrophe and Lyric Voice" 171–2. Applying another phase of Culler's argument, Jacobus argues that Wordsworth exploits apostrophe throughout *The Prelude* (especially at such key moments as the "glad preamble") as "a form of self-constituting self-address": "The question of the poet's vocation, translated into invocation, becomes the question of poetic voice" (172).

22. Wordsworth's discussion of "spots of time" and the attendant memories appear first in 18A (DC MS. 16, which precedes the base-texts for the 1798–99 poem, MSS. U and V; see Parish 20–21). Norton's house style both indents and puts spaces between verse paragraphs—a format that distorts the closer association of the episode of the drowning and the spots of time passage in Wordsworth's manuscript, where there is indentation only (see Parrish 258–9).

23. II:258–389 and 12:208–335. In this position, the passage is invested with a dramatic function that enhances its claims. Following the books about Wordsworth's imaginative impairment by the specter shapes of Terror in France, the passage on "spots of time"—both as a tale of early memories transformed by later

feelings and as an early text recalled in the poem's later stages of composition—enacts what it describes, as the poet repairs to earlier texts and times to inspire and sustain his present writing.

24. According to Jonathan Wordsworth, book 4 of the five-book poem contained much of the material that would appear in books 4 and 5 of the 1805 text: the dawn dedication, the discharged soldier, the meditation on the perishability of human works and of books in particular, the complaints about modern systems of education and the monstrosity of the child prodigy, the Winander Boy, and the general recollection of the poet's boyhood reading ("Five-Book" 10–15). Jarvis agrees that the drowned man and the discharged soldier were part of its fourth book and thinks that there is a "reasonable ground" for supposing that the Arab dream was intended for the five-book poem, too (but not enough for positing "There Was a Boy" as part of it) (539). For details of the compositional history of 1850's book 5 and relevant manuscripts, see Reed 1:11–39.

25. See Hartman's brief but resonant meditation on the affinity of this passage to that of the drowned man (*Wordsworth's Poetry* 232).

26. Editors feel compelled to "correct" Wordsworth: see de Selincourt-Darbishire (516, note on line 308) and the Norton Critical (8 n. 9).

27. I owe this reading of the drowning as a "screen memory" for the death of the mother to Richard Onorato's illuminating analyses (252, and a related reference on 208). See Freud 15: 200–1 and 23:74.

28. The death of the mother as the suppressed referent of these lines is proposed both by the editors of *The Norton Anthology of English Literature* (4th ed. 2:251 n. 3) and Onorato: the child's seeking the visible world is directed toward finding "a substitute for the mother, upon which many of the dependent needs endangered by her loss could be projected" (148).

29. See Reed 2:624. Coleridge was the first to read the signature of "the bosom of the steady lake": coming on it in MS. JJ (the basis for "There was a Boy" in the 1800 *Lyrical Ballads*), he wrote to Wordsworth, "I should have recognised [the image] any where; and had I met these lines running wild in the deserts of Arabia, I should have instantly screamed out 'Wordsworth!' " (10 December, 1798; *Letters* 1: 452–3).

30. The dynamic of "suppression and retrieval" is illuminated by Theresa Kelley in "The Economics of the Heart," a study of Wordsworth's ambivalent confrontations with the sublime in the revisionary aesthetics of the "spots of time" passage in the three major texts of *The Prelude*. Kelley applies these terms to the drowned-man episode in her paper "Wordsworth's Figural Interventions," some of which appears in *Wordsworth's Revisionary Aesthetics* 93–95.

31. For the historical information, see Norton Critical (176 n. 4) and Maxwell (548 n): "T. W. Thompson, *Wordsworth's Hawkshead* [1970], identifies the drowned man

as 'James Jackson School-Master of Sawrey.'" Chase uses this fact to propose that the account of the drowned man extends the polemic against schoolmasters: "the exemplary educational episode consists in seeing a teacher as a dead man" in a text governed by "the duplicity of a gesture that simultaneously hallows the lost teacher and reinscribes his statuesque disfigurement" (31).

32. The phrase in quotation is from Wordsworth's comment on "There was a Boy" in the Preface to *Poetical Works* (1815), where it is the first of the "Poems of the Imagination." See *Prose* 3:35.

33. See the reference to Ricks, n. 18, above.

34. Norton Critical notes the allusion (8 n. 2). For a subtle exploration of Wordsworth's affinities with Othello, see Manning, "Reading Wordsworth's Revisions."

35. For relevant discussions of this contradiction between ostensible program and imaginative practice, see Averill (147–87) and Jacobus (*Tradition and Experiment* 240–50). As Manning observes, moreover, even the first "spot of time," by recalling a place where a wife-murderer was executed, uncannily traces Othello's story into Wordsworth's own autobiography: the memory has a fitness of detail consonant with "the story of Othello glimpsed in the preceding episode. It is as if the outlines of a plot at first only shadowily glimpsed had been delayed, split off, and had now begun to emerge"; if Othello "can convert his stories of death into tales of love, he also becomes the murderer who kills the wife his tales have won" ("Reading Wordsworth's Revisions" 96, 92).

36. Here, I share the attention to rhetorical figure in Chase's incisive deconstructive reading: "the insistent literalism of *decay*," she argues, "refers back to the decay of the risen corpse. The statement becomes an assertion that forms or images cannot figure (cannot 'know') the literal decay that was a fact. Or, rather, the statement simply displays so conspicuously the 'decay' denied by its syntax that it compels repeated rereading" (25)—a dynamic also observed in Hillis Miller's reading of Wordsworthian negatives in "The Still Heart," cited later in this chapter.

37. See Parrish's text 80–81; Norton Critical 493.

38. Miller notes that in the first usage Wordsworth is transferring the traditional trope of "describing the body as the garment of the soul" to "books" ("The Stone and the Shell" 133). Considering the play of the word *garments* in book 5— first a figure, then a literal fact—Chase takes this "divestment of figurative meaning in the literal recurrence of the noun *garments*" (16) as emblematic of the way book 5 constitutes its text—its operation as context for the drowned man by means of an "atemporal repetition of *wording* from one passage to another, a repetition at once overdetermined and contingent" (23). Andrzej Warminski's essay elaborates the shifty substitutions of this metaphor system and the significance of its analogical slippages.

39. For careful discussions of the parallels between Wordsworth's representa-

tions of the young man's encounter with the soldier and the boy's with the drowned man, see Onorato (252) and Manning ("Reading Wordsworth's Revisions" 98–99).

40. Contemporaneous texts with analogous figures, most notoriously the Pedlar who tells the story of the ruined cottage, yield consequences just as troubling in their aestheticizing of tragedy. Although these texts often ironize this attitude and relativize its authority, Wordsworth's repeated stagings suggest his irresolution. For relevant discussions, see Averill, especially chapters 4 and 7; Manning, "Wordsworth, Margaret, and The Pedlar"; Simpson, *Wordsworth's Historical Imagination;* Michael H. Friedman's study; and chapter 4 of my *Questioning Presence.*

41. Scholars have not been able to identify the "abstract" to the "four large Volume" set of the "Tales" to which Wordsworth refers. Even so, there were several multi-volume editions printed in England and Scotland in the eighteenth century. In 1706, A. Bell of London issued a four-volume edition of "Arabian nights entertainments consisting of one thousand stories, told by the sultaness of the Indies, to divert the sultan from the execution of a bloody vow ... Tr. into French from the Arabian mss. by M. Galland [Antoine Galland] ... and now done into English"; a 7th edition, in twelve volumes, was published in London by J. Osborn and T. Longman in 1728–30; a 14th edition, again in four volumes, was published by T. Longman in London in 1778 (most likely the one to which Wordsworth refers) and reprinted in 1789.

42. The capitalizations are not random accidentals; "What is the reason that our modern Compositors are so unwilling to employ Capital Letters?" Wordsworth complained in 1845 to John Moultrie, whose recent edition of Gray's *Poetical Works* did not reproduce the "substantives ... written in Capital Letters" (*Letters LY* 4:644).

43. Jon Cook's essay (31) helped me think about this grammatical doubleness.

44. An early version of the "Cave" passage appears in MS. WW (26^r–27^v), following lines about the realization that "Alps wer crossd" (26^r) and lines that would evolve into the famous apostrophe to "Imagination": "The vault before him lies / in perfect view / [? revived] [?] / by charm / But let ... / that word must rest / A little while [?Imagination] crosd / me here / Like a[n] unfatherd vapour, & my / verse / Halts in mid course" (27^v–28^r; Reed 2:255–57). The link of these lines to the period of composition in which Wordsworth was experimenting with a new frame for the drowning is revealed by other pages of this manuscript. Earlier in WW appears a sketch for the new coda for the drowning, with the account of the abstract of the Arabian Tales preceding, rather than following, the lines denying fear: the former concludes, "Till by joint saving we could gain our / ends / And make this book our own / But perseverance brought us / enough"; the very next lines on the page are "no vulgar fear / possessed me for my inner eye had seen ..." (see 18^r–18^v; Reed 2:244–5).

45. Words, unlike natural objects, are "engendered by consciousness," de Man

remarks, and he assigns this beginning to a process of negation and difference from nature ("Intentional Structure" 4). Writing thus shifts ambivalently between its immediacy as event and its belatedness as record: "it can be considered both an act and an interpretative process that follows after an act with which it cannot coincide. As such, it both affirms and denies its own nature or specificity" ("Literary History" 152)

46. Photographs of the elaborate title page of MS. B (4ʳ) appear opposite page 1 of the de Selincourt-Darbishire edition, opposite xxxviii of Gill's, and on 1: 1168 of Reed's edition. J. Wordsworth and Gill report that this title also appears on MS. A ("Two-Part" 510), and Reed's edition shows a similar inscription on iii of MS. C; see 1:1217.

References

Abrams, M. H. *Natural Supernaturalism: Tradition and Revolution in Romantic Literature.* New York: Norton, 1971

Arac, Jonathan. "Wordsworth's Revisions and Wordsworthian Revisionism: Genetic Reflections." Paper presented at the MLA Convention, New York, 1981.

Averill, James, H. *Wordsworth and the poetry of Human Suffering.* Ithaca, N.Y.: Cornell University Press, 1980.

Baker, Jeffrey. "Pride and Prejudice." *The Wordsworth Circle* 13 (1982): 79–86.

Barthes, Roland. *Image-Music-Text.* London: Collins, 1977.

Bowers, Fredson. "Current Theories of Copy-Text, with an Illustration from Dryden". *Modern Philology* 48 (1950): 12–20.

Chase, Cynthia. "The Accidents of Disfiguration: Limits to Literal and Figurative Reading of Wordsworth's 'Books' " (1979). In *Decomposing Figures: Rhetorical Readings in the Romantic Tradition,* pp. 13–31. Baltimore: John Hopkins University Press, 1986.

Cook, Jon. "Paul de Man and Imaginative Consolation in *The Prelude.*" In Nigel Wood, ed., *Theory in Practice: "The Prelude."* Philadelphia: Open University Press, 1993, pp. 27–59.

Culler, Jonathan. *The Pursuit of Signs: Semiotics, Literature, Deconstruction.* Ithaca, N.Y.: Cornell University Press, 1981.

Darbishire, Helen. *The Poet Wordsworth: The Clark Lectures, Trinity College, Cambridge, 1949.* Oxford, Clarendon Press, 1950.

de Man, Paul. *The Rhetoric of Romanticism.* New York: Columbia University Press, 1984.

———. *Blindness and Insight: Essays in the Rhetoric of Contemporary Criticism* (1971). 2nd online ed. Minneapolis: University of Minnesota Press, 1983.

Ferguson, Frances. "Coleridge and the Deluded Reader: *The Rime of the Ancient Mariner.*" *Georgia Review* 31 (1977): 617–35.

Friedman, Michael H. *The Making of a Tory Humanist: Wordsworth and the Idea of Community.* New York: Columbia University Press, 1979.

Galperin, William H. *Revision and Authority in Wordsworth: The Interpretation of a Career.* Philadelphia: University of Pennsylvania Press, 1989.

Greg, W. W. "The Rationale of Copy-Text." *Studies in Bibliography* 3 (1950–51): 19–36.

Hartman, Geoffrey H. *Wordsworth's Poetry, 1787–1814.* 1964; New Haven: Yale University Press, 1975.

Hodgson, John A. " 'Was It for This. . . . ?': Wordsworth's Virgilian Questionings." In Kurt Heinzelman, ed., *Romans and Romantics, Texas Studies in Literature and Language* 33 (1991): 125–36.

Jacobus, Mary. "Apostrophe and Lyric Voice in *The Prelude.*" In Patricia Parker and Chaviva Hosek, eds., *Lyric poetry Beyond New Criticism.* Ithaca, N.Y.: Cornell University Press, 1985, 167–81.

———. *Tradition and Experiment in Wordsworth's "Lyrical Ballads" (1798).* Oxford: Clarendon Press, 1981.

Jarvis, Robin. "The Five-Book *Prelude:* A Reconsideration." *Journal of English and Germanic Philology* 80 (1981): 528–51.

Kelley, Theresa M. "The Economics of the Heart: Wordsworth's Sublime and Beautiful." *Romanticism Past and Present* 5 (1981): 15–22.

———. *Wordsworth's Revisionary Aesthetics.* Cambridge.: Cambridge University Press, 1988.

Leader, Zachary. "Wordsworth, Revision, and Personal Identity." *ELH* 60 (1993): 651–83.

Lindenberger, Herbert. *On Wordsworth's "Prelude."* Princeton, N.J.: Princeton University Press, 1963.

Lindenberger, Herbert, Norman Fruman, Robert J. Barth, and Jeffrey Baker. " 'Waiting for the Palfreys': The Great *Prelude* Debate" (1984). *The Wordsworth Circle* 17 (1986): 2–38.

MacGillivray, J. R. "The Three Forms of *The Prelude,* 1798–1805." In Millar MacLure and F. W. Watt, eds., *Essays in English Literature from the Renaissance to the Victorian Age presented to A. S. P. Woodhouse.* Toronto: University of Toronto Press, 1964, 229–44.

Manning, Peter J. "Reading Wordsworth's Revisions: Othello and the Drowned Man" (1983). In *Reading Romantics: Texts and Contexts.* New York: Oxford University Press, 1990, 87–114.

———. "Wordsworth, Margaret, and the Pedlar" (1976). In *Reading Romantics,* 9–34.

McGann, Jerome J. *The Beauty of Inflections: Literary Investigations in Historical Method and Theory.* Oxford: Clarendon Press, 1985.

Maxwell, J. C., ed. *"The Prelude": A Parallel Text.* Middlesex, England: Penguin, 1972.

Mellor, Anne K. *English Romantic Irony.* Cambridge, Mass.: Harvard University Press, 1980.

―――. *Mary Shelley: Her Life, Her Fictions, Her Monsters.* New York: Methuen, 1988.

―――. "Choosing a Text of *Frankenstein* to Teach." In Stephen C. Behrendt, ed., *Approaches to Teaching Shelley's "Frankenstein."* New York: MLA, 1990, 31–37.

Miller, J. Hillis. "The Still Heart: Poetic Form in Wordsworth." *New Literary History* 2 (1971): 295–310.

―――. "The Stone and the Shell: The Problem of Poetic Form in Wordsworth's Dream of the Arab." In *Mouvements premiers: Études critiques offertes à Georges Poulet* Paris: José Corti, 1972, 125–47.

Onorato, Richard. *The Character of the Poet: Wordsworth in "The Prelude."* Princeton, N.J.: Princeton University Press, 1971.

Orgel, Stephen. "What Is a Text?" *Research Opportunities in Renaissance Drama* 24 (1981): 3–6.

Owen, W. J. B., ed. *The Fourteen-Book "Prelude."* Ithaca: Cornell University Press, 1985.

Parrish, Stephen M., ed. *"The Prelude": 1798–1799.* Ithaca: Cornell University Press, 1977.

―――. "The Whig Interpretation of Literature." *Text* 4 (1988): 343–50.

Perkins, David. *The Quest for Permanence: The Symbolism of Wordsworth, Shelley, and Keats.* Cambridge, Mass.: Harvard University Press, 1959.

Rajan, Tilottama. "Displacing Post-Structuralism: Romantic Studies After Paul de Man." *Studies in Romanticism* 24 (1985): 451–74.

―――. "Coleridge, Wordsworth, and the Textual Abject." *The Wordsworth Circle* 24: 2 (Spring 1993): 61–68.

Reiman, Donald H. *Romantic Texts and Contexts.* Columbia: University of Missouri Press, 1988.

Ricks, Christopher. "William Wordsworth: 'A Pure Organic Pleasure from the Lines' " (1971). In *The Force of Poetry.* Oxford and New York: Oxford University Press, 1987, 89–116.

Simpson, David. *Irony and Authority in Romantic Poetry.* London: Macmillan, 1979.

―――. *Wordsworth's Historical Imagination: The Poetry of Displacement.* London: Methuen, 1987.

Sperry, Willard L. *Wordsworth's Anti-Climax.* Cambridge, Mass.: Harvard University Press, 1935.

Stillinger, Jack. *Multiple Authorship and the Myth of Solitary Genius.* New York: Oxford University Press, 1991.

―――. "The Multiple Versions of Coleridge's Poems: How Many Mariners Did Coleridge Write?" *Studies in Romanticism* 31 (1992): 127–46.

————. *Coleridge and Textual Instability: The Multiple Versions of the Major Poems.* New York: Oxford University Press, 1994.

Thorpe, James. *Principles of Textual Criticism.* San Marino, Calif.: Huntington Library, 1972.

Urkowitz, Steven. *Shakespeare's Revision of "King Lear."* Princeton, N.J.: Princeton University Press, 1980.

Wallen, Martin. "Return and Representation: The Revisions of 'The Ancient Mariner.' " *The Wordsworth Circle* 17 (1986): 148–55.

Warminski, Andrzej. "Facing Language: Wordsworth's First Poetic Spirits." In Kenneth R. Johnston, Gilbert Chaitin, Karen Hanson, and Herbert Marks, eds. *Romantic Revolutions: Criticism and Theory.* Bloomington: Indiana University Press, 1990, 26–49.

Wolfson, Susan. "The Language of Interpretation in Romantic Poetry: 'A Strong Working of the Mind.' " In Arden Reed, ed. *Romanticism and Language.* Ithaca: Cornell University Press, 1984, 22–49.

————. "Answering Questions and Questioning Answers: The Interrogative Project of *The Prelude.*" In Nigel Wood, ed., *Theory in Practice: "The Prelude,"* pp. 124–65.

————. *The Questioning Presence: Wordsworth, Keats, and the Interrogative Mode in Romantic Poetry.* Ithaca, N.Y.: Cornell University Press, 1986.

Wood, Nigel. *Theory in Practice: "The Prelude."* Philadelphia: Open University Press, 1993.

Wordsworth, Jonathan, and Stephen Gill. "The Two-Part *Prelude* of 798–99." *Journal of English and Germanic Philology* 72 (1973): 503–25.

Wordsworth, Jonathan. *William Wordsworth: The Borders of Vision.* Oxford: Clarendon Press, 1982.

Young, Robert. "A Reply to 'Prelude and Prejudice,' by Jeffrey Baker." *The Wordsworth Circle* 13 (1982): 87–88.

'Dithyrambic Fervour'

The Lyric Voice of The Prelude

MARY JACOBUS

◆　◆　◆

L OOKING BACK TO the excitement with which *The Prelude* had begun—a mood later described as one of 'distraction and intense desire'
(XIII, 374)—book 7 starts by recalling the 'dithyrambic fervour' of the
opening book. Named here as the 'glad preamble', these introductory lines
are recollected in terms both of the natural Sublime and of the Sublime
of poetry itself:

> Five years are vanished since I first poured out,
> Saluted by that animating breeze
> Which met me issuing from the city's walls,
> A glad preamble to this verse. I sang
> Aloud in dithyrambic fervour, deep
> But short-lived uproar, like a torrent sent
> Out of the bowels of a bursting cloud
> Down Scawfell or Blencathara's rugged sides,
> A waterspout from heaven.
>
> *(Prel,* VII, 1–9)[1]

Wordsworth's 'torrent sent | Out of the bowels of a bursting cloud' is
more than just a means of naturalizing the landscape of poetic inspira-

tion—though it is that too; as in the waters of the Wye, 'rolling from their mountain-springs | With a soft inland murmur' ('Tintern Abbey', ll. 3–4), we recognize the source of a poetic Helicon. But as Geoffrey Hartman puts it, Wordsworth's 'narrative can almost be said to begin with "an Ode, in passion utter'd" ' (V, 97).[2] Although he does not enlarge on this connection between the 'glad preamble' and the apocalyptic blast heard in the shell of book 5, his allusion to the ode—both form and 'passion'—is worth pursuing. The torrent of eloquence poured out here has quite specific associations with the sublime and (by popular misconception) 'irregular' ode, certainly the highest form of lyric poetry for the eighteenth century, and the one in which the poet was also thought to speak most directly in his own voice.[3] Translating Horace's praise of Pindar in one of his own *Pindarique Odes*, Cowley had written:

> *Pindars unnavigable Song*
> Like a swoln *Flood* from some steep *Mountain* pours along
>   The *Ocean* meets with such a *Voice*
> From his enlarged *Mouth,* as drowns the *Oceans* noise.
> So *Pindar* does new *Words* and *Figures* roul
> Down his impetuous *Dithyrambic Tide* . . . [4]

As Cowley notes, the '*Dithyrambic Tide*' of Pindaric eloquence is a risky one to navigate: 'For which reason, I term his Song *Unnavigable;* for it is able to drown any *Head* that is not strong built and well *ballasted*.'[5] Voice not only drowns the ocean's noise, but threatens to drown the reader too, and perhaps even the writer himself. Keeping one's head above water may even mean shutting one's ears. The traditional metaphor of a river for poetic eloquence—here, a torrent of words—might make one want to look again at Wordsworth's contrasting invocation to the River Derwent in book 1 of *The Prelude*. The stream that 'loved | To blend his murmurs with my nurse's song' (I, 272–3) makes 'ceaseless music'; but unlike the torrential waterspout of the 'glad preamble'—a rush of intense but short-lived inspiration—its 'steady cadence' both 'composes' the infant's thoughts and, in another sense, the entire poem. Did Wordsworth, perhaps, find his own dithyrambic tide unnavigable, preferring to emphasize not the voice of the Sublime but the voice of nature?

There are good reasons for his retreat from the Sublime. Cowley goes on to observe of Pindar's dithyrambics that they were '*Hymns* made in honour of *Bacchus* . . . a bold, free, enthusiastical kind of Poetry, as of men inspired by *Bacchus,* that is *Half-Drunk*'; hence the two Greek proverbs he cites, 'You are mad as a *Dithyrambique Poet*' and 'There are no *Dithyrambiques* made by drinking water' (an Attic version, presumably, of 'You can't make an omelette without breaking eggs').⁶ Remembering himself as a young poet in the throes of composition, Wordsworth speaks of hushing his voice and 'composing' his gait so that passers-by would not suppose him mad ('crazed in brain', *Prel.* IV, 116–20); 'kindled with the stir, | The fermentation and the vernal heat | Of poesy' (IV, 93–5), he too is like one half-drunk—just as chanting his favourite poets, when a boy, had brought fancies 'More bright than madness or the dreams of wine' (V, 592). At Cambridge, youthful intoxication took the form of getting drunk in Milton's rooms. Apostrophe and libation blend in a heady brew: 'O temperate bard!',

> I to thee
> Poured out libations, to thy memory drank
> Within my private thoughts, till my brain reeled,
> Never so clouded by the fumes of wine
> Before that hour, or since.
> (*Prel.* III, 303–7)

Drinking to Milton's memory takes on an aspect at once sublime and Bacchic—inebriated with his poetry while disrespectful of Milton's own temperance. Milton himself comes to mind in this context not only as the bard of temperance but as the poet most obsessed with the terror of Bacchic orgies. His own apostrophe to Urania at the start of book 7 of *Paradise Lost*—clearly in Wordsworth's mind as he wrote his opening to book 7 of *The Prelude*—invokes protection against just such a Comus-like crew of drunken revellers:

> But drive far off the barbarous dissonance
> Of Bacchus and his revellers, the race
> Of that wild rout that tore the Thracian bard
> In Rhodope, where woods and rocks had ears
> To rapture, till the savage clamour drowned
> Both harp and voice . . .
> (*Paradise Lost,* VII, 32–7)

Wordsworth could praise Milton for 'a voice whose sound was like the sea' ('Milton', l. 1)—a voice, presumably, in which all others would be lost; but Milton's own anxiety was that his voice would be drowned by savage clamour and the poet dismembered, Orpheus-like, by hordes of Thracian women under the influence of their Bacchic cult. Wordsworth himself had translated this part of the Orpheus and Eurydice story from Virgil's *Georgic* 4 in 1788, and it is hard to imagine that the legend can have been absent from his mind either at the time of the original literary orgy in Milton's rooms, or later, when recollected in *The Prelude*:

> Him, mourning still, the savage maenads found
> And strew'd his mangled limbs the plain around;
> His head was from its neck of marble torn
> And down the Oeagrian Hebrus slowly born.[7]

The figure used by Cowley of the Pindaric Sublime ('it is able to drown any *Head* that is not strong built and well *ballasted*') coincides with the traditional figure of the poet's voice being drowned by barbarous dissonance, and his severed head borne down the flood. Both appear to be articulations of the dread that poetic individuality might be lost—whether by being subsumed into the Sublime or by being dispersed into the meaningless multiplicity of 'clamour'. The Orphic fantasy might be said to involve for Wordsworth, as for Milton, the threat that discomposing Bacchic dithyrambs, or possession by the voices of others, would lead to the individual poet's dismemberment.

One safeguard against such imaginary dismemberment is provided by the compensating fantasy of fully naturalized Orphic song. As Frances Ferguson aptly writes, the dying head gives nature a speaking voice ('Ah! poor Eurydice, it feebly cried, | Eurydice, the moaning banks replied').[8] For her, the echoic structure is that of epitaph itself; but one might also see in it the Wordsworthian desire to appropriate the speaking voice of nature in an attempt to render his own imperishable. Drowned neither by the voice of the Sublime—Milton's voice—nor by the clamour of all the other voices by which the poet risks being possessed, the voice of nature permits a loss of individuality which is at once safe and unifying. In nature, the poet can take refuge against dismemberment. Hailing *The Prelude* in 'To William Wordsworth', Coleridge calls it 'An Orphic song', 'A song divine of high and passionate thoughts | To their own music chaunted' (ll. 45–7. He clearly has in mind the ethical severity and high seriousness of the Orphic tradition (a 'Theme hard as high! . . . Of Duty, chosen Laws controlling choice', l. 44), to which Wordsworth himself alludes when outlining his poetic aspirations early in book 1:

> I yearn towards some philosophic song
> Of truth that cherishes our daily life,
> With meditations passionate from deep
> Recesses in man's heart, immortal verse
> Thoughtfully fitted to the Orphean lyre.
> But from this awful burthen I full soon
> Take refuge . . .
>
> (I, 230–6)

Orphism too has its problems. As Wordsworth well knew, the phrase 'Orphean lyre' occurs at the start of *Paradise Lost,* book 3, just before Milton undertakes to sing of Heaven and immediately after his perilous but successful descent into Hell ('With other notes than to the Orphean lyre | I sung of Chaos . . .', *Paradise Lost,* III, 17–8). Milton may simply be making a doctrinaire point (his notes are other than Orphean because Christian, not pagan);[9] but there is also the possibility that his notes are not Orphic because he—unlike Orpheus—has successfully completed his mission. The 'awful burthen' would have been for Wordsworth not just that of living up to Milton's Christianized 'song', but that of assuming his strength; this is the same 'load of Immortality' which Keats too found burdensome when taking up his own poetic mission.[10]

A fragment written in the copy of *Paradise Lost* which belonged to Wordsworth at Cambridge refers to the Miltonic altar kindled on Religion's holy hill as having the power to elicit not only 'Airs of high melody from solemn harp | And voice of Angel in accordance sweet' but, also the voice of the Sublime:

> Anon the trump of God, with dreadful blast
> Rock'd all the mountain; on their flashing clouds
> The silent cherubs trembled . . . [11]

'Undismayed | Stood the blind prophet.' But could Wordsworth stand likewise undismayed before this dreadful blast? If we seem to be in the familiar terrain of the belated poet's anxiety about his apparently indestructible precursor, this is no more than saying that Wordsworth, while appearing to differ (and to defer), can only repeat. Milton's own invocation to Urania at the start of book 7, after all, had voiced the embattled and solitary poet's fears about his survival, and, in particular, fears about the adequacy of his poetic performance. Wordsworth, too, at the start of his book 7—about to re-enter the city and encounter its discomposing influences—invokes his personal sources of protection, a choir of redbreasts and, in place of Urania's heavenly light, a humble glow-worm. These earth-born voices and sources of illumination surely have the special function of disarming the threat of the Sublime which Milton's invocation had brought uncomfortably close. Although, looking back from the end of *The Prelude*, Wordsworth can see himself as having been spurred on by the reproaches of book 1 to take flight on his own account ('Anon I rose | As if on wings . . . ', XIII, 377–8), in his case it is a flight 'Attempered to the sorrows of the earth' (XIII, 383). In the anxious confrontation with Milton, Wordsworth evades the dangers of the Sublime by making earth, rather than Heaven or Chaos, his chosen sphere. Humanizing his epic—giving it a less elevated lyric voice—simultaneously protects the poet from Milton and from apocalypse, proving to be his most secure guarantee of survival.

If the poet's urgent need to constitute himself as a poet leads him to the dithyrambic fervour of the 'glad preamble', self-preservation throws him back on naturalized Orphic song. On one hand the dismembering voices of the past, or Bacchic possession; on the other, the re-membering continuities of the Derwent, murmurings which assimilate the poet's voice to nature and so preserve it. The ode-like, inspirational passion of the 'glad preamble' ultimately 'vex[es] its own creation' (*Prel.* I, 47), its redundant energy disrupting the flow of river and memory. By contrast, the fiction of a poetry that originates in nature, like the voice of the Derwent, ensures continuity while providing a safely trans-subjective voice into which the poet's own can be merged. Wordsworth's claim is not simply that nature speaks through him, but that he speaks with nature's voice. The characteristic alternations in *The Prelude*—between the uproarious waterspout and the murmuring stream, inspiration and reflection, invocation and narrative—become a sign of this tension between poetic self-assertion and self-immersion. Wordsworth's final sleight of hand may well be that of divesting himself of the Sublime while investing his poetic voice in nature. The Romantic counterpart to Milton's successful flight from Chaos to Heaven is the self-immersing Bard of Gray's 'Pindaric Ode' who 'spoke, and headlong from the mountain's height | Deep in the roaring tide . . . plunged to endless night' ('The Bard', ll. 143–4)—an ostensibly suicidal loss of individual identity which at once destroys the poet's voice and vests nature with those qualities which have proved dangerous to it. As we see in book 8, this leaves the poet free to take refuge in pastoral, the address of one poet-shepherd to another. If the ode is the Sublime (and therefore dangerous) form of the lyric, then apostrophe could be said to be the figure which most completely characterizes the sublimity of the ode. *The Prelude* begins apostrophically but ends by addressing the living—Dorothy and Coleridge—in a way designed to assimilate the poet to a safer pastoral community. It is this formal progression that most clearly marks the concession made by a poet whose lyric voice survives finally at the price of seeming to renounce the Sublime altogether. Paradoxically, only by making the torrential and uproarious voice of inspiration that of nature itself can Wordsworth sustain a voice of his own.

Invoking Apostrophe

> *Apostrophe*! we thus address
> More things than I should care to guess.
> Apostrophe! I did invoke
> Your figure even as I spoke.[12]

Apostrophe, as Jonathan Culler has observed, is an embarrassment. Regularly ignored by writers on the ode, it might be seen 'as the figure of all that is most radical, embarrassing, pretentious, and mystificatory in the lyric'.[13] Critics turn away from it as it turns away from the discourse in which it is embedded; *apo-strophe*—literally, a turning away, the abrupt transition which, as Cowley puts it in his 1656 Preface, takes the Pindaric ode out of 'the common Roads, and ordinary Tracks of *Poesie* . . . The digressions are many, and sudden, and sometimes long, according to the fashion of all *Lyriques,* and of *Pindar* above all men living.'[14] Regarded as a digressive form, a sort of interruption, excess, or redundance, apostrophe in *The Prelude* becomes the signal instance of the rupture of the temporal scheme of memory by the time of writing. Wordsworth's 'two consciousnesses' (*Prel.* II, 32) can then be seen as a division, not simply between me-now and me-then, but between discursive time and narrative time—a radical discontinuity which ruptures the illusion of sequentiality and insists, embarrassingly, on self-presence and voice; insists too that invocation itself may be more important than what is invoked. 'Apostrophe! I did invoke | Your figure even as I spoke' is a poet's joke that accurately mimes the bringing into being of the poet's voice by way of what it addresses. If apostrophe's characteristic function is to invoke the Muse, it is also, ultimately, a form of self-constituting self-address that says: 'to my soul I say "I recognise thy glory" ' (VI, 531–2). The question of the poet's vocation, translated into invocation, becomes the question of poetic voice. Like imagination in book

4, voice halts the poet in his tracks, privileging self-address over narrating the past. The opening apostrophe of the 'glad preamble' may constitute Wordsworth as a poet, but, in doing so, it loses hold of his subject; there is always this incompatibility between the lyric voice of *The Prelude* and its much-desired, 'distracting' epic progress—an incompatibility which typically presents itself as a problem of redundancy. Voice usurps on the ceaselessly murmuring Derwent, making the poet himself the interrupter of his poem.

The 'glad preamble' initiates not only *The Prelude,* but the problem of its composition. The erratic progress to which the opening lines of book 7 allude (' 'twas not long | Ere the interrupted strain broke forth once more . . . then stopped for years', VII, 9–11) may be nothing other than the symptom of Wordsworth's anxiety about writing a long poem. A 'distraction' (in another sense) from *The Recluse, The Prelude* could easily seem a series of fragments, parts instead of a whole. Only in book 8, looking back from a completed poem, can Wordsworth retrospectively see the image of a longed-for completeness in the stream that has been traced from darkness (XIII, 172–84). Meanwhile, the distinct phases of the poem's composition evoked by the opening lines of book 7 present themselves, disturbingly, as fragmentation rather than composition. One recalls the 'fragment' inscribed in Wordsworth's undergraduate copy of *Paradise Lost*—itself a formal tribute to the hopelessness engendered in a beginning poet by the shadow of an epic precursor. Perhaps the 'glad preamble' should in the last resort be read not simply as a dramatization of Wordsworth's anxiety about his poetic undertaking or as a record of the fluctuations of inspiration but rather as a propitiatory gesture that frees the poet from the 'burden of [his] own unnatural self' and, in doing so, from the burdensome past of poetry. *The Prelude*'s opening apostrophe to the breeze would then become an image of liberation which, though predicated on the novelty of self-presence to one 'not used to make | A present joy the matter of [his] song' (I, 55–6), is directed ultimately at sloughing off his poetic precursors or consciousness of the past:

> O welcome messenger! O welcome friend!
> A captive greets thee, coming from a house
> Of bondage, from yon city's walls set free,
> A prison where he hath been long immured.
> Now I am free, enfranchised and at large,
> May fix my habitation where I will.
>   .   .   .   .

> ...I breathe again—
> Trances of thought and mountings of the mind
> Come fast upon me. It is shaken off,
> As by a miraculous gift 'tis shaken off,
> That burden of my own unnatural self...
>
> (*Prel* I, 5–10, 19–23)[15]

The poet's breathing and the breeze are at once the breath of pure, unconstructed sound ('O' or voice) and a prison break, an escape from the confines of memory and self-consciousness. In the same way, apostrophe itself breaks off from the demands of narrative as a moment of lyric redundance or inspired escape. The 'vital breeze' becomes 'A tempest, a redundant energy, | Vexing its own creation' (I, 46–7), just as in the opening lines of book 7 the grove 'tossing its dark boughs in sun and wind— | Spreads through me a commotion like its own' (VII, 51–2). This tempest or commotion is not exactly a 'corresponding mild creative breeze' (I, 43), more a vexation or a kind of uneasiness.[16] The effect is that of voice itself, perceived as an interruption of the past from the present.

Wordsworth comments of the 'glad preamble', 'My own voice cheared me, and, far more, the mind's | Internal echo of the imperfect sound' (I, 64–5). The appeal to voice might usually be thought of as having the function of making the self whole. Whereas writing disperses, voice unifies, providing the illusion of single origin and temporal unity (no 'two consciousnesses' here). Yet, in this instance, Wordsworth writes of a doubling effect whereby the sound of his own voice has an internal echo, and one which, unlike echo as usually figured, perfects rather than incompletely repeating 'the imperfect sound'; it is voice here that functions like echo, since speech is imagined as secondary in its attempt to represent the silence of self-present meaning in consciousness. At this point it seems worth digressing to consider some of the more problematic aspects of the Romantic conception of voice. A small book by Francis Berry, *Poetry and the Physical Voice* (1962), brings to light the hidden implications of Wordsworth's position. Like Wordsworth, Berry appears to insist on the primacy of voice over writing (seeing the letter as a mere representation of sound), and his book laments the debasing of language as a mere means of communication, or 'instrument'. Yet this distinction between language as instrument and the poetic use of language as 'agent' proves oddly difficult to sustain. As Wordsworth had been, Berry, too, is anxious to restore to poetic voice the musicality which he believes once to have been synonymous with poetry itself. Yet even Wordsworth no longer insists on 'feigning that [his] works were composed to the music of the harp or lyre', happily substituting 'nothing more than an animated or impassioned recitation'.[17] Berry's terms—pitch, duration, volume, timbre, and so on—thus emphasize the sound of vocal 'music' to a degree never risked by Wordsworth himself. But, in doing so, they uncover the underlying myth of the voice of which Wordsworth's is a less extreme version; that is, the myth of the 'inner ear' (not a kind of memory but a kind of hearing), which leads us to suppose, according to Berry, that though 'modern poets compose silently . . . in composing they record what they are inwardly experiencing as vocal sound, usually their own voices however idealized . . . we could say they record the double experiences of hearing *and* saying';[18] this is what Wordsworth had called 'the mind's internal echo of the imperfect sound', likewise surrendering to an auditory myth of self-presence. But there follows for Berry an altogether less composing notion, that of the poet as 'a person obsessed, scored and spoored by vocal linguistic sound—'or, put another way, he is *possessed* by vocal sound as a man was said to be possessed by devils'.[19] What it amounts to is that voice, instead of bringing reassurance by guaranteeing the existence of a unified consciousness ('my own voice cheared me'), can equally take on the demonic aspect of possession. Whose are the voices the poet hears? Not necessarily his own, after all.

In the light of such demonic vocalism, Berry's notion of an individuated voice breaks down. His insistence that the attentive or 'listening' reader can recover or reconstruct the unique and authentic voices of, say, Tennyson, Milton, or—presumably—Wordsworth on the evidence of 'the printed signs on the page', is revealed as a fiction. Calling the self into being through apostrophe becomes rather a matter of calling another into being; perhaps an 'authorial' voice, but, equally, the variety of haunting, threatening, nightmarish, or apocalyptic voices heard throughout *The Prelude* in 'the voice | Of mountain-echoes' (I, 389–90), or in 'Black drizzling crags that spake . . . As if a voice were in them' (VI, 563–4), or the 'voice that cried | To the whole city, "Sleep no more!" ' (X, 76–7), or in a shell that broadcasts 'voices more than all the winds'—the voice of 'a god, yea many gods' (V, 107–8). The voice is always a doubling of self, and more often a multiplication or alienation. Berry's view of poetic language as agent, then, turns out to be characterized not by the individuality of the writer but by something closer to the supernatural—the gift of tongues or hearing voices ('he is *possessed* by vocal sound'). Conceived as a man more vocal than other men, the poet becomes an echo chamber for all those voices heard while boat-stealing, descending the Vale of Gondo, unable to sleep in Paris after the September Massacres, or in the Arab dream.

They speak through him, so that far from attesting to unity of origin or a stable identity, voice comes to imply all the destabilizing multiplicity of plural (or ancestral) voices—much as the composing 'voice' of the Derwent can become the discomposing voice of inspired poetry, 'the voice | Which roars along the bed of Jewish song', or the Miltonic 'trumpet-tones of harmony that shake | Our shores in England' (V, 203–4, 206–7). Given these transformations, Wordsworth's quest turns out not to be for an individual voice so much as for one that is transcendentally unified.

The apostrophic moments in book 1 of *The Prelude* are, typically, callings into being of supernatural powers:

> Wisdom and spirit of the universe,
> Thou soul that art the eternity of thought,
> That giv'st to forms and images a breath
> And everlasting motion . . .
>
> (I, 427–31)

> Ye presences of Nature, in the sky
> Or on the earth, ye visions of the hills
> And souls of lonely places . . .
>
> (I, 490–2)

Wordsworth's invocations to the Muse summon up spirits, presences, souls—the supernatural machinery of an unexorcized nature, arising in the same breath as winds, hills, solitude. If Shelley demands of the wind, 'Be thou me, impetuous one!', Wordsworth could be said to ask of nature to give his voice whatever haunts and denatures landscape; whatever puts the individual origin of voice most in question. The Aeolian fantasy so beloved of Romantic poets, after all, is nothing more or less than the wish for the trans-subjective instrumentality which Berry would repress if he could, but fails ultimately to exorcize. Wordsworth's apostrophes to breezes, brooks, and groves, in which he wishes for himself 'a music and a voice | Harmonious as your own' (XI, 20–1), are the equivalent of asking to be played on too. The distinction which Wordsworth himself would have endorsed, between language as instrument (or, as he calls it himself, 'counter-spirit')[20] and language as agent, falls away to leave only breezes or breathings through the poet, 'obedient as a lute | That waits upon the touches of the wind' (III, 137–8). Subsumed into transcendental nature, the poet's voice becomes orphic rather than bacchic, banishing rough music with the myth of natural harmony. Nature steps in to de-demonize voice, turning possession into Aeolianism and sanctifying vocalism as 'Eolian visitations' (i. 104). Instead of the voice of the poet, we have the voice of poetry—that is, nature. In order to achieve this status for his poetry, Wordsworth has to eschew the very fiction of individual voice which is central to Romantic conceptions of the poet. The transcendental defends against possession, but it also takes away the poet's most distinctive and sought-after personal property, the voice that differentiates him from his predecessors, and from Milton in particular. That, perhaps, may be the trade-off—since not to be either Milton or unlike Milton has the effect of losing the Miltonic voice as well as one's own in the impersonally oceanic voice of nature, thereby drowning the ventriloquizing voices of the past in 'A waterspout from heaven' (vii. 9).

The Sound of Nature

What is involved for Wordsworth in sound itself? And what is the relation of voice to writing? The aftermath of the 'glad preamble' turns out to be largely one of discouragement: 'the harp | Was soon defrauded' (I, 104–5), and the hope of fixing 'in a visible home . . . those phantoms of conceit, | That had been floating loose about so long' (I, 129–31) was not to be fulfilled. The disembodied 'phantoms of conceit' remain unrepresented, perhaps unrepresentable. A fragment from the *Peter Bell* MS, possibly an early attempt at an introduction to the two-part *Prelude,* had explored the problem of representation in terms directly relevant to the random vocalizings of the 'glad preamble':

>   nor had my voice
> Been silent—oftentimes had I burst forth
> In verse which with a strong and random light
> Touching an object in its prominent parts
> Created a memorial which to me
> Was all sufficient, and, to my own mind
> Recalling the whole picture, seemed to speak
> An universal language. Scattering thus
> In passion many a desultory sound,
> I deemed that I had adequately cloathed
> Meanings at which I hardly hinted, thoughts
> And forms of which I scarcely had produced
> A monument and arbitrary sign.[21]

Bursting forth in verse becomes the equivalent of a private mnemonic; 'to my *own* mind | Recalling the whole picture', the voice only '*seemed* to speak | An universal language'. Writing to Godwin in 1800, Coleridge had asked, 'Is *thinking* impossible without arbitrary signs? &—how far is the word "arbitrary" a misnomer?' If Coleridge seems to want to destroy 'the old antithesis of *Words & Things,* elevating . . . words into Things, & living Things too',[22] Wordsworth seems to be suggesting that at best—'scarcely', or 'scarcely even'—poetry can produce 'A monument and arbitrary sign' for thought; and, at worst, make only desultory sounds. This is the Aeolian fantasy demystified, and along with it there collapses the entire Romantic fallacy of spontaneous lyric utterance, whether heard or overhead. In another fragment, Wordsworth alludes to 'slow creation' imparting 'to speach | Outline and substance'.[23] This sounds like fixing phantoms of conceit in a visible home, or writing poetry. It is as if representation only begins at the point where Aeolianism—the fiction of unmediated expression—is eschewed; or perhaps, Wordsworth seems to imply, thinking can begin only where the monuments and arbitrary signs of language take over from sound (pure voice or breath) and speech (pure presence). In any event, it is clear that writing, the permanent record of thought, involves both the muting of voice—a kind of deafness—and the death of presence.

No wonder Aeolianism pervades *The Prelude;* it is Wordsworth's defence against that inability to hear oneself think (or speak) involved in writing itself. Going back to the opening of book 7, we find Wordsworth experiencing 'Something that fits me for the poet's task' in the infectious 'commotion' of his favourite grove, 'Now tossing its dark boughs in sun and wind' (VII, 50–3). Presumably both grove and poet make a composing noise much like the one that is wasted on the deaf Dalesman, though not on his peaceful grave, memorialized in Wordsworth's final 'Essay upon Epitaphs':

> And yon tall Pine-tree, whose composing sound
> Was wasted on the good Man's living ear,
> Hath now its own peculiar sanctity;
> And at the touch of every wandering breeze
> Murmurs not idly o'er his peaceful grave.[24]

The Dalesman's epitaph is 'A monument and arbitrary sign' masquerading as the sound of murmuring trees, alias the composing sound of the poet's own voice (Wordsworth loved to compose aloud in a grove of trees, and may well have done so, murmurously, in the grove near Dove Cottage whose commotion he records at the start of book 7). Why does the pine tree murmur 'not idly'? Is it because the entire epitaph, though ostensibly commemorating a man for whom the mountain vale was soundless and the storm-tossed landscape 'silent as a picture'—for whom all voices save those of books were unheard—actually celebrates the poet's own aural imagination as a means of denying the soundlessness of writing? The poet himself, Wordsworth implies, is not only murmurous but has inward ears that can hear; this is what makes him a poet. Imagined sound becomes a way to repress or deny writing and undo the privation of deafness or death. If a monument marks the site of a grave, voice—'Breathings for incommunicable powers' (III, 188)—gives evidence of the poet's enduring life. For the poet, Wordsworth argues covertly, there can be no such thing as silence, but only, as in the Dalesman's epitaph, 'audible seclusions'. The soundless world of the Dalesman's solitude and death is one that speaks to him. So much so that in *The Prelude* a moment of visionary seeing is as likely as not to be one of hearing, an attempt to communicate 'what e'er there is of power in sound | To breathe an elevated mood':

> I would stand
> Beneath some rock, listening to sounds that are
> The ghostly language of the ancient earth,
> Or make their dim abode in distant winds.
> Thence did I drink the visionary power.
>
> (*Prel.* II, 324–30)

Visionary power—'by form | or image unprofaned'—is blindness, not insight; the heightened sense of hearing makes language into something ghostly, non-referential, ancient, and without origin, like the homeless voice of waters in the Snowdon episode.[25] Along with Francis Berry, Wordsworth wants to believe that the poet hears voices as well as speaking with tongues; but what he most desires to hear are the unheard sighings of breathings that writing ('arbitrary signs') must repress. This is the other side of babble, or Babel, the non-linguistic murmur of a composing voice that may be the poet's as he saunters 'like a river murmuring' (*Prel.* IV, 110) or, equally, invoked as that of the Derwent ('O Derwent, murmuring stream,' V, 509), but is above all that of a unified poetic presence that has no need of discourse.

Wordsworth's definitive statement of the ear's power occurs in his 'musical' ode, 'On the Power of Sound' (1828). As the preposterous 'argument' puts it, 'The Ear addressed, as occupied by a spiritual functionary, in communion with sounds, individual, or combined in studied harmony'.[26] The ode is all apostrophe, all voice, all ear:

> a Spirit aerial
> Informs the cell of Hearing, dark and blind;
> Intricate labyrinth, more dread for thought
> To enter than oracular cave . . .
>
> (ll. 3–6)

The ear becomes the prime organ of vision, making audible 'Ye Voices, and ye Shadows | And Images of voice' (ll. 33–4). The poem's function is both to invoke Spirit (ear) and Muse (voice); or 'the mind's | Internal echo of the imperfect sound'. As John Hollander's account of the poem has shown, the ear is a place of echo and reverberation, sounding and resounding, a cave, a 'strict passage', a maze, a temple, a vault, a hollow place where music is made as well as heard.[27] Like the shell, whether a poeticism for the lute or the Romanticized sea shell, it is both sounded on and sounds, combining the Orphean properties of a stringed instrument and the Dionysian properties of a wind instrument.[28] In effect, it is nothing less than the ear of God. Wordsworth's originary myth of the voice ('A Voice to Light gave Being', l. 209) is also apocalyptic: 'A Voice shall . . . sweep away life's visionary stir' (ll. 211–12). Compare the dual functions of music and harmony in *The Prelude,* one to build up, the other to destroy; though 'The mind of man is framed even like the breath | And harmony of music' (*Prel.* I, 351–2), the shell's 'loud prophetic blast of harmony' (V, 96) in the Arab dream announces the end of the world, and the Sublime of revolutionary terror is accompanied by 'Wild blasts of music' (X, 419). Music can both frame and unframe, compose and shake, like the voice of Milton ('Those trumpet-tones of harmony that shake | Our shores', V, 206–7). Wordsworth's unstated argument in 'On the Power of Sound' reconciles this dual aspect of harmony, claiming that even after earth is dust and the heavens dissolved, 'her stay | Is in the WORD, that shall not pass away' (ll. 223–4). His ode is the optimistic, orthodox Christian sequel to the Arab dream, revised not to foretell 'Destruction to the children of the earth' (*Prel.* V, 98) but rather to prophesy salvation of and through the Word. As the type of the divine fiat, poetry itself is guaranteed survival—the consolatory message unavailable to the Arab or the dreamer in book 5 of *The Prelude*—by means of its transformation into the transcendental, imperishable 'WORD'. Poetic utterance now promises 'to finish doubt and dim foreseeing' ('On the Power of Sound', ll. 211), dependent no longer on 'books' (the materiality of stone or shell), but on the special harmony of Christian assurance or faith in life—and therefore faith in hearing—beyond death. This is a word that can continue to hear itself and be heard, even after the apocalypse.

The guaranteeing of poetry as 'WORD' (voice transcendentalized as the Logos) in 'On the Power of Sound' reveals one function of sound, and particularly of voice, in *The Prelude.* What the deaf Dalesman can 'hear' are the immortal voices of the poets, secured against 'imperfection and decay':

> Song of the muses, sage historic tale
> Science severe, or word of holy writ
> Announcing immortality and joy
> To the assembled spirits of the just,
> From imperfection and decay secure.[29]

After the death of the poet, there still remains immortal verse. In lines like these, Wordsworth uses silent reading to free poetry from the monumentality and arbitrary signs of death. Disembodied sound—'The ghostly language of the ancient earth'—comes to be the archetype of poetry. In this light, the 'glad preamble' might be seen not only as a means of calling both poet and voice into being, but also as a way to fantasize their transcendence of material representation. In MS *A* of 'On the Power of Sound', Wordsworth had wondered what skill 'Shall bind these wanderers thro' loose air | In the precious chains of sight . . . ' (ll. 169–74 app. crit.), much as in *The Prelude* he had hoped vainly 'that with a frame of outward life' he might 'fix in a visible home . . . those phantoms of conceit, | That had been floating loose about so long' (I, 128–31). How are we to read Wordsworth's self-proclaimed failure to fix or bind the insubstantial (and hence imperishable) 'phantoms of conceit'? The longing 'To brace myself to some determined aim' (I, 124) is synonymous in *The Prelude* with the epic enterprise itself, yet the poem finally evades even this enterprise by substituting the 'WORD'—lasting, but inaudible except to the mind—for an epic theme. It is left celebrating the spirit or 'voice' of poetry instead of the form. Like the cuckoo, 'No bird, but an invisible thing, | A voice, a mystery' ('To the Cuckoo', ll. 15–16), poet as well as poem becomes unavailable, 'disposse[d] . . . almost of a corporeal existence'.[30] An extended personal lyric, *The Prelude* is redeemed from time and death by the unheard voice of the poet, or, as Wordsworth calls it, 'Imagination', its declared subject. The entire poem becomes an apostrophe or 'prelude' designed to constitute the poet and to permit Wordsworth himself to join the ranks of Homer, the great thunderer, of the Bible, Milton, and even the ballad, as Voice rather than voice, Poetry rather than individual poet: that is, the Voice of Poetry, which resounds not only in the ears of the living but in the ears of the deaf.

'Hear I Not a Voice from Thee . . . ?'

Gray's 'Bard' sacrifices the individual poet so that his poetry may survive to prophesy the extinction of his oppressors. 'The torrent's awful voice' (l. 24) in which the individual is immersed becomes another name for the chorus of slaughtered poets who foretell the downfall of Edward and the rise of the Tudors. The association of Gray's Pindaric ode with Snowdon gives a specifically poetic dimension to 'the homeless voice of waters' which Wordsworth hears from the top of Mount Snowdon in the final book of *The Prelude*:

> from the shore
> At distance not the third part of a mile
> Was a blue chasm, a fracture in the vapour,
> A deep and gloomy breathing-place, through which
> Mounted the roar of waters, torrents, streams
> Innumerable, roaring with one voice.
> The universal spectacle throughout
> Was shaped for admiration and delight,
> Grand in itself alone, but in that breach
> Through which the homeless voice of waters rose,
> That dark deep thoroughfare, had Nature lodged
> The soul, the imagination of the whole.
>
> (*Prel.* XIII, 54–65)

Here again, sight is less profound than sound, as though visionary depths could only be plumbed by the ear; even in the *Descriptive Sketches* prototype for the passage, Wordsworth had rhymed 'sound' and 'profound'.[31] Significantly, too, Wordsworth's source for the original *Descriptive Sketches* passage, a stanza from Beattie's *Minstrel* (1771), had merely contained 'the voice of mirth'; torrential and perhaps ancestral voices are Wordsworth's addition.[32] One might see Wordsworth himself as having lodged in this 'deep dark thoroughfare' not only the soul of nature, 'the imagination of the whole', but the soul of the Sublime—the voices of past poets, and also the dithyrambic fervour of the 'glad preamble', transferred here to nature as a means of protecting him from its self-destructive potential. Once the Sublime becomes the voice of nature, not his own, the poet can withdraw to a place of greater safety, no longer exposed to the dreadful blast of apocalyptic revelation liable to strike Milton's altar in its high place. This place of safety is the sheltered valley of pastoral, Theocritan pastoral in particular, where the poet competes not with the dead but, more in the spirit of shepherdly friendship, with the living. If Wordsworth effects the preservation of poetry by handing the Sublime over to nature in the Snowdon passage, he effects the preservation of the poet by transforming his voice into that of Coleridge's shepherd friend—local, personal, and particular.

The function of *The Prelude*'s apostrophes is to constitute the voice of the poet: the function of its addresses to Coleridge (and to some extent, Dorothy) is to save it by domesticating it. The punctuating addresses to Coleridge ('O friend') throughout *The Prelude* have served to comment on the poem's progress, or to signal pauses and regressions; but, toward the end of the poem, they take on much greater importance, occurring with special concentration and effect at the end of book 10 and in the second half of book 13. In book 10, they become almost a kind of self-locution, a guarantee of the ability to address oneself—to self-commune or 'regulate' oneself; Dorothy, we are told, 'Maintained for me a saving intercourse | With my true self' and 'preserved me still | A poet' (X, 914–15, 918–19) while Coleridge (inaccurately, since the period of his influence was yet to come) is retrospectively credited with having lent 'a living help | To *regulate* my soul' (X, 906–7; my italics) at the time of Wordsworth's supposed post-Revolutionary crisis. By the end of book 10, Wordsworth can represent the entire *Prelude* as having been written, not out of self-reproach, still less out of epic ambition, but for Coleridge's sympathetic ear ('A story destined for thy ear', X, 946), addressed to him in his restorative Sicilian exile:

> Oh, wrap him in your shades, ye giant woods,
> On Etna's side, and thou, O flowery vale
> Of Enna, is there not some nook of thine
> From the first playtime of the infant earth
> Kept sacred to restorative delight?
>
> (*Prel* X, 1001–5)

Sicily may be a lamentable example of the decay of an ancient classical civilization, but, as the *locus amoenus* of pastoral poetry, it is also—imaginatively at least—an idyllic refuge from the dark post-revolutionary times which Wordsworth has been recalling, and from the state of Europe in the time-present of the poem's writing (1804), with England now the only stronghold of resistance against Napoleon. Most of all, it is the island of the Theocritan idyll, of shepherds devoted to the Muse and engaged in companionable rivalry with one another. This is the context in which Coleridge becomes most clearly a talisman for poetic preservation, whether his own or Wordsworth's. The idyll to which Wordsworth specifically alludes in book 10, the seventh, belongs, appropriately enough, to the genre of the *propemptikon* (prayer for safe voyage), and contains as one of its two chief shepherd singers the goatherd Lycidas. Though Coleridge was literally *en voyage* at this moment in the poem's composition, the allusion to idyll 7 suggests that Wordsworth, at least by association, would have had in mind the tragic fate of Milton's Lycidas and that of the Orphic poet generally.[33]

In Theocritus's poem, Lycidas sings of the special preservation of Comates, a goatherd who was shut up in a chest by his master for over-zealously sacrificing his flock to the Muse. This is the story Wordsworth retells in book 10: 'And, O Theocritus',

> not unmoved,
> When thinking on my own beloved friend,
> I hear thee tell how bees with honey fed
> Divine Comates, by his tyrant lord
> Within a chest imprisoned impiously—
> How with their honey from the fields they came
> And fed him there, alive, from month to month,
> Because the goatherd, blessed man, had lips
> Wet with the Muse's nectar.
>
> (*Prel.* X, 1019–26)[34]

Ostensibly an image of Coleridge's restoration to health by Sicily's most famous product, Mount Hybla honey, the story of Comates narrates the poet's salvation by natural powers in reward for his dedication to poetry. It also provides a pastoralized version of Milton's succouring by Urania at the start of *Paradise Lost,* book 7, in the time of his blindness and personal danger ('On evil days though fallen, and evil tongues; | In darkness; and with dangers compassed round', VII, 26–7). So traditional was this the idyll of friendship—Lycidas implores fair weather for the sea-crossing undertaken by his beloved friend, Ageanax—that Tennyson, in one of the earliest composed lyrics of *In Memoriam,* can echo it with his wish for a calm passage for Hallam's remains ('Fair ship, that from the Italian shore | Sailest the placid ocean-plains . . . ', st. 9). For Wordsworth, as for Tennyson, it would obviously have recalled Neptune's plea in 'Lycidas' that the winds were calm and the Nereids at play at the time of the shipwreck, drawing into *The Prelude*'s own field of allusion the fear that the poet's life and work would be cut short by the Orphean fate that consists of the triumph of barbarism over human wisdom and art. This is the fate with which the postrevolutionary crisis had seemed to threaten Wordsworth himself, and, later, Europe in its entirety, as well as the personal anxiety attending Coleridge's Sicilian sojourn.

Wordsworth reverts to the theme of poetic friendship and rivalry celebrated by Theocritus's seventh idyll in his closing book. Here the idyllic scene recalled is that of the Quantocks, the two shepherds are Wordsworth and Coleridge, and the date is 1798, 'That summer when on Quantock's grassy hills | Far ranging' (XIII, 393–4) they composed 'The Idiot Boy' and 'The Ancient Mariner'. Remembering 'times . . . wherein we first | Together wandered in wild poesy', Wordsworth writes of the intervening years as 'Times of much sorrow, of a private grief | Keen and enduring' (XIII, 413–17). The note of elegy is sounded clearly for both himself and Coleridge. But the comparatively anonymous public lyricism of the Theocritan pastoral inhibits direct expression of private grief; the address 'To William Wordsworth', not the ode 'Dejection', is the poem with which Coleridge fittingly responds to hearing *The Prelude* read aloud.[35] At this stage in *The Prelude,* Dorothy and Coleridge are invoked as calming agencies on the passionately dithyrambic poet of the earlier books—she as the 'Child of my parents, sister of my soul' who has tempered the Sublime ('which as Milton sings | Hath terror in it') by decking with flowers 'A rock with torrents roaring' and breathing the pastoral influence of a 'gentler spring' (XIII, 211–46); Coleridge as the 'most loving soul' who has provided 'mild | Interposition, closelier gathering thoughts | Of man and his concerns', thereby chastening, stemming, and balancing (Wordsworth's terms) 'the deep enthusiastic joy, | The rapture of the hallelujah' (XIII, 246–68). Marking as they do the transition in book 13 from the celebration of the Sublime of nature and imagination in the Snowdon episode to the human supports of sister and fellow poet, the two long addresses to Dorothy and to Coleridge also place firmly in the past the dithyrambic fervour of the 'glad preamble' ('The deep enthusiastic joy, | The rapture . . . '). Redundant energy has been channelled into making the poet whole; each of these supporting figures mirror an aspect of Wordsworth's salvaged poetic identity, serving to reflect back on him the chastened, stemmed, and balanced qualities necessary if he is to confront, not the Sublime, but mortality:

'Oh, yet a few short years of useful life, | And all will be complete—thy race be run ... ' (XIII, 428–9). By providing a remembering image of his own subjectivity, the addresses to Dorothy and especially to Coleridge allow Wordsworth finally to claim the stable basis on which to prophesy:

> powers so far confirmed, and such
> My knowledge, as to make me capable
> Of building up a work that should endure.
> (*Prel.* XIII, 277–9)

Ostensibly, Coleridge's greatly increased role at the end of *The Prelude* is important both to redefine the entire poem as 'this gift | Which I for thee design' (XIII, 411–12), and as the justification for its writing; by him at least it will be felt 'that the history of a poet's mind | Is labour not unworthy of regard' (XIII, 408–9). But the underlying importance of Wordsworth's imaginary colloquy with Coleridge lies in the function of the address itself. In speaking to another, the poet hears himself speak with a unity of sound and voice that comes to stand for consciousness itself. Or, to put it another way, to have an imaginary auditor is to fantasize the reproduction of one's speech in another without external mediation or deferral, and so to create the illusion of mastery over the process of signification.[36] Hence the new-found prophetic confidence at the close of book 13: 'United helpers forward of a day | Of firmer trust, joint labourers in the work ... *we to them will speak* | A lasting inspiration' (XIII, 438–9, 442–3; my italics). As 'Prophets of Nature', Wordsworth and Coleridge are self-duplicating; poetic comradeship comes to stand for the simultaneity of speaking and being heard, prophecy and efficacy. Hence, too, the fantasy that Wordsworth now sees as having animated the entire poem, that of an instantly elevating dialogue with himself, the inner colloquy through which he at once knows and makes himself a poet:

> Call back to mind
> The mood in which this poem was begun,
> O friend—the termination of my course
> Is nearer now, much nearer, yet even then
> In that distraction and intense desire
> I said unto the life which I had lived,
> 'Where art thou? Hear I not a voice from thee
> Which 'tis reproach to hear?' Anon I rose
> As if on wings, and saw beneath me stretched

Vast prospect of the world which I had been,
And was; and hence this song, which like a lark
I have protracted . . .

(*Prel.* XIII, 370–81)

Hearing his own voice makes the poet airborne, calling into play images of soaring height, epic prospect, and unlimited power. This is self-possession, the sublime self-mastery which makes prophecy possible. The exchange between the voice of the life and the voice of the poet who has lived it—between 'the world which I had been | And was' and the language of his desire—brings *The Prelude* into being as a lyrical dialogue between past and present, between the discourse of memory and the discourse of poetic aspiration. If the lyric voice, as some would have it, is not so much heard as overheard, overhearing creates the doubling through which self-recognition or self-audition can occur. The lyric voice of *The Prelude* is the fiction of the poet talking to himself; the entire poem becomes a self-constituting apostrophe, a 'glad preamble' or necessary interruption to its own beginning which only comes to an end when the poet assumes his prophetic mission, and only becomes prophetic when it finally succeeds in obliterating the unheard or deafening 'voice' of writing with the transcendent, disembodied song of a bird: 'No bird, but an invisible thing, | A voice, a mystery' ('To the Cuckoo', ll. 15–16).

Notes

1. These lines maintain the fiction that *Prel.* I, 1–54, the 'glad preamble', were the first lines to be written.

2. 'Words, Wish, Worth: Wordsworth', in H. Bloom (ed.), *Deconstruction and Criticism* (London, 1979), 190.

3. See N. Maclean, 'From Action to Image: Theories of the Lyric in the Eighteenth Century', *Critics and Criticism Ancient and Modern,* ed. R. S. Crane (Chicago, 1952), 409. See also, for a sustained discussion of the ode, P. H. Fry, *The Poet's Calling in the English Ode* (New Haven and London, 1980).

4. *The English Writings of Abraham Cowley,* ed. A. R. Waller (2 vols.; Cambridge, 1905), i. 178. Cf. also Gray's 'Progress of Poesy: A Pindaric Ode', where 'the rich stream of music winds along' from Helicon to precipice: 'Now rolling down the steep amain, | Headlong, impetuous, see it pour' (ll. 7, 10–11).

5. *The English Writings of Abraham Cowley,* ed. Waller, i. 180.

6. Ibid. 180.

7. *Poetical Works of William Wordsworth,* ed. Ernest de Selincourt and Helen Darbishire. 5 vols. Oxford: Clarendon Press, 1941–49 (PW), i. 285, ll. 71–4. For the date, see Reed, *Wordsworth: The Chronology of the Early Years, 1770–1799,* p. 21.

8. *PW* i. 285, ll. 77–8. See F. Ferguson, *Wordsworth: Language as Counter-Spirit* (New Haven and London, 1977), 163–5.

9. Compare elegy 6, where Diodati's poetry is associated with Bacchus and Milton's own with the *Nativity Ode,* or Christianizing of pagan myth.

10. *The Letters of John Keats,* ed. H. E. Rollins (2 vols.; Cambridge, Mass., 1958), i. 370.

11. *PW,* v. 362, ll. 6–10. For the date, see Reed, *Wordsworth: The Chronology of the Early Years, 1770–1799,* p. 21.

12. J. Hollander, *Rhyme's Reason: A Guide to English Verse* (New Haven and London, 1981), 48.

13. 'Apostrophe', *Diacritics, 7* (Winter 1977), 60.

14. *The English Writings of Abraham Cowley,* ed. Waller, i. 11.

15. The omitted passage contains Wordsworth's famous allusion to the concluding lines of *Paradise Lost* ('The world was all before them, where to choose | Their place of rest, and Providence their guide', XII, 643–7). See Chandler, *Wordsworth's Second Nature,* pp. 188–99, for a discussion of the opening of *The Prelude,* book 1, in relation to Wordsworth's attempt to free himself from the culturally determined choices (and voices) of the past.

16. Cf Wordsworth's apostrophic reaction to the news of Robespierre's death ('Come now, ye golden times . . . ') where the traveller is 'interrupted by uneasy bursts | Of exultation' (*Prel* X, 541, 557–8).

17. 1815 'Preface', *Prose Works,* iii. 29.

18. F. Berry, *Poetry and the Physical Voice* (London, 1962), 34. Cf. Derrida's paraphrase of this myth of the voice in 'The Voice that Keeps Silence', *Speech and Phenomena,* trans. D. B. Allison (Evanston, 1973), 77: 'When I speak, it belongs to the phenomenological essence of the operation that *I hear myself . . . at the same time* that I speak. The signifier . . . is in absolute proximity to me. The living act . . . which animates the body of the signifier . . . seems not to separate itself from itself, from its own self-presence.'

19. Berry, *Poetry and the Physical Voice,* pp. 36, 7.

20. 'Essays upon Epitaphs', iii; *Prose Works,* ii. 85.

21. *Prel.,* p. 495, fragment (*a*), ll. 1–13. The passage is also discussed by J. Wordsworth, 'As With the Silence of the Thought', in L. Lipking (ed.), *High Romantic Argument: Essays for M. H. Abrams* (Ithaca, N.Y. and London, 1981), 58–64.

22. *Collected Letters of Samuel Taylor Coleridge,* ed. Griggs, i. 625–6.

23. *Prel.,* p. 495, fragment (*b*), ll. 3–4.

24. 'Essays upon Epitaphs', III; *Prose Works,* ii, 96 (*Excursion,* vii. 477–81). Cf. P. de

Man on the Deaf Dalesman's epitaph, 'Autobiography as De-Facement', *The Rhetoric of Romanticism,* pp. 72–4.

25. Cf also the 'breath-like sound, | A respiration short and quick' (*Prel.* IV, 175–6), which Wordsworth in his solitary musings often mistook for the panting of his dog.

26. *PW* ii. 323.

27. See the extended discussion in Hollander's 'Wordsworth and the Music of Sound', in G. Hartman (ed.), *New Perspectives on Coleridge and Wordsworth* (New York and London, 1972), 67–79.

28. See J. Hollander, "Images of Voice: Music and Sound in Romantic Poetry', Churchill College Overseas Fellowship Lecture, V (Cambridge, 1970), 12.

29. *Prose Works,* ii. 95 (*Excursion,* vii. 450–4).

30. 1815 'Preface', *Prose Works,* iii. 32.

31. 'Loud thro' that midway gulf ascending, sound | Unnumber'd streams with hollow roar profound', *Descriptive Sketches,* ed. Birdsall, 1793: ll. 504–5.

32. See J. Beattie, *The Minstrel* (London, 1771), p. 1, st. 23.

33. Theocritus's idyll is, of course, one of a number of possible sources for Milton's choice of name for Edward King.

34. Cf. Theocritus, idyll 7, ll. 78–83.

35. See T. G. Rosenmeyer, *The Green Cabinet: Theocritus and the European Pastoral Lyric* (Berkeley, 1969), 62–4.

36. As Jacques Derrida puts it: 'To speak to someone is doubtless to hear oneself speak, to be heard by oneself; but, at the same time, if one is heard by another, to speak is to make him *repeat immediately* in himself the hearing-oneself-speak in the very form in which I effectuated it. . . . The possibility of reproduction . . . *gives itself out* as the phenomenon of a mastery or limitless power over the signifier.' (*Speech and Phenomena,* trans. Allison, p. 80).

'A Strong Confusion'

Coleridge's Presence in The Prelude

LUCY NEWLYN

◆　◆　◆

COLERIDGE'S PRESENCE in *The Prelude* is deceptive, even at first sight. As an account of Wordsworth's life, the poem does not come up to date, and is concerned with experiences the two poets never shared. Again and again, however, their friendship is introduced as part of the unfolding story:

> O friend, we had not seen thee at that time,
> And yet a power is on me and a strong
> Confusion, and I seem to plant thee there.
> (*1805*, VI, 246–8)

Misremembrance is deliberate, and factual narrative gets left behind.[1] Coleridge, treated in this way, becomes a continuous being, permanently absorbed into a life that is not his own:

> But thou art with us, with us in the past,
> The present, with us in the times to come . . .
> (*1805*, VI, 251–2)

The knowing self-deception here is typical, and alerts us to further and deeper problems. Not only is there the obvious contradiction between *The Prelude*'s design and Coleridge's role; there is also a struggle between Wordsworth's personal quest and the wish to pay homage to his friend. 'Points have we all of us within our souls', he writes, 'where all stand single' (*1805*, VI, 186–7). In its various stages, *The Prelude* is a record of 'singleness'. It finds in childhood memories the origins of imaginative power; and it explains special privilege, not (as with *The Pedlar*) in the context of the 'One Life', but in private Wordsworthian terms. On more wishful and idealizing levels, however, it still remains the 'Poem to Coleridge': a tribute to his powers, and a memorial to the vanished Alfoxden relationship. The result is poetry of a peculiarly divided kind: on the one hand logically moving toward assertions of self-sufficiency and independence; on the other withdrawing guiltily, as though the quest for origins can be valid only if shared, and life without Coleridge would be unthinkable.

Complicating matters further, there is the fact that *The Prelude* really ought to be *The Recluse*. Wordsworth's obligation to Coleridge (who had foisted the scheme on him in spring 1798) means that he should be writing a public poem, a philosophical poem, a poem of redemption for mankind. What he finds himself writing, instead, is something that looks by comparison both limited and self-involved. Different kinds of excuse are offered: 'I am not yet ready to write that poem; let this one stand in its stead'; 'this poem is a preparation for writing the other one; is indeed part of it'. But the best excuse is no excuse at all; it is a plea: 'this is not the poem you expect, I know, but it is a *better* poem, and one more appropriate to me. You, Coleridge, of all people, can appreciate its importance.' These, however, are strategies for dealing with a problem that refuses to go away. Wordsworth's triumph in *The Prelude* rests not just on his inability to write *The Recluse,* but on his refusal to do so. And if he succeeds in asserting his independence, he must accept the guilt involved. I want in this chapter to look at the various complications to which this guilt gives rise. And I want to argue that there are, in effect, two Coleridges in *The Prelude*: one mythologized beyond recognition, and needed by Wordsworth to support the values of his past; the other more flawed and human, but used by him merely as a foil. On the conflict between these two figures, the formal addresses turn. I hope, by looking at them in detail, to establish that *The Prelude*—disguised by Wordsworth as a 'joint labour', to pay homage to his friend—is in fact a solitary quest, to which friendship itself is finally irrelevant.

The reference to *Frost at Midnight,* in the opening of the Two-Part Poem, claims companionship and support for a journey into the past:

> For this didst thou,
> O Derwent, travelling over the green plains
> Near my 'sweet birthplace', didst thou, beauteous stream,
> Make ceaseless music through the night and day . . . ?
>
> (*1799,* I, 6–9)

Coleridge's priority, in discussing the imaginative function of childhood memory, is firmly established in the tribute-paying quotation. But there is an irony implied, of which both poets would have been aware. Wordsworth is attempting to imply similarity, where it is difference that is most apparent. *Frost at Midnight* had turned on the contrast between Wordsworthian and Coleridgean childhoods. The memory of his 'sweet birthplace' and of church-bells ringing 'all the hot fair-day' had been Coleridge's nearest approximation to a spot of time, and his only imaginative release, when 'pent mid cloisters dim' in the 'great City'. It was a fragile, isolated memory, of an entirely nostalgic kind.[2] Wordsworth's recollection of the Derwent has more power. The music it made was ceaseless, through both night and day; it also singled him out, and remained with him throughout boyhood. Difference, then, is accentuated by friendly quotation. *The Prelude* begins with Coleridge's childhood being quietly trumped.

When, at the end of part 1, Wordsworth attempts to justify having written over four hundred lines about himself, he does so in terms of *The Recluse.* Referring back to the question—'Was it for this . . . ?'—with which, in October, he had begun writing, he claims that his movement into the past had been intended as a self-reproach. The assertion, perfectly designed to persuade Coleridge, is prefaced, first by a guilty acknowledgement that the past is tempting in its own terms (*1799,* I, 443–6)—and, second, by an expression of confidence in Coleridge's approval that is full of unease (ll. 447–9). When it comes, the poet's justification in terms of *The Recluse* seems less than entirely honest:

> Meanwhile my hope has been that I might fetch
> Reproaches from my former years, whose power
> May spur me on, in manhood now mature,
> To honourable toil.
>
> (ll. 450–3)

It is only in the last resort, and with a great deal of uncertainty, that he comes to define the purpose of his writing in its own terms. 'Yet should it be | That this is but an impotent desire', he writes, quoting himself, at his most vulnerable, in *Tintern Abbey*,[3] then continues, with another echo:

> . . . need I dread from thee
> Harsh judgements if I am so loth to quit
> Those recollected hours that have the charm
> Of visionary things . . .
>
> (ll. 458–61)

At the back of his mind are the 'rash judgements' and the 'sneers of selfish men' which, only months before, had made up the 'dreary intercourse' of daily life' (*Tintern Abbey,* 130, 132), and which now, the echo might suggest, Wordsworth fears in his friend. *The Recluse,* planned jointly the previous spring, has become his sole responsibility. Can so private an enterprise as *The Prelude* be justified at all? The unconfidence with which part 2 begins would suggest that Wordsworth's own answer to this question was 'no'. There is no scope, here, for considering the two false starts of *1799* in which, openly apprehensive, he longs for the cheering voice of his friend.[4] I want to turn instead to the lines leading into the famous passage about the Infant Babe. Here, more than anywhere in part 1, Wordsworth begins his double dealings with Coleridge:

> Who knows the individual hour in which
> His habits were first sown even as a seed?
> Who that shall point as with a wand, and say
> 'This portion of the river of my mind
> Came from yon fountain'?
>
> (*1799*, II, 245–9)

The distinction between habits 'sown' in childhood and those planted at a later stage is strategically blurred; and it is Coleridge who, as a prophet of 'unity', presides over the poet's rearranging of time:

> Thou, my friend, art one
> More deeply read in thy own thoughts, no slave
> Of that false secondary power by which
> In weakness we create distinctions, then
> Believe our puny boundaries are things

> Which we perceive, and not which we have made.
> To thee, unblinded by these outward shews,
> The unity of all has been revealed ...
>
> (1799, II, 249–56)

It might at first seem, as Jonathan Wordsworth has claimed, that a contrast is being made between Coleridge's 'unified vision' and 'a tendency in the poet himself to categorize, impose distinctions'.[5] But as the passage continues, Wordsworth too moves into a higher sphere, counting himself, *with* Coleridge, as one of the elect:

> And thou wilt doubt with me, less aptly skilled
> Than many are to class the cabinet
> Of their sensations, and in voluble phrase
> Run through the history and birth of each
> As of a single independent thing.
>
> (1799, II, 257–61)

The 'unity of all' which is said to have been 'revealed' to his friend is not merely an envious reference to Unitarianism, though Wordsworth would no doubt value the stability that such faith implies. His choice of language is highly strategic: on the one hand, it suggests to Coleridge that the 'One Life' remains his ideal. On the other, it justifies his quest for personal, secular origins by defining unity in broader terms. 'Hard task', he writes, quoting not just Raphael in book 5, but Adam in book 8, of *Paradise Lost*:

> Hard task to analyse a soul, in which
> Not only general habits and desires,
> But each most obvious and particular thought—
> Not in a mystical and idle sense,
> But in the words of reason deeply weighed—
> Hath no beginning.
>
> (1799, II, 262–7)

Adam had been faced with genuine problems: 'For man to tell how human life began | Is hard; for who himself beginning knew?' (*PL*, VIII, 250–1); Wordsworth is only rhetorically unsure of what he is doing.[6] Miltonic authority corroborates his claim that there can be no beginnings, only the search for them; and this, in its turn, gives stature to his quest. Despite the apparent contrasts with which the passage opens, Wordsworth succeeds

in using Coleridge to support himself. 'The unity of all', he implies, will
be 'revealed' as *The Prelude* unfolds.

Having obtained Coleridge's approval for the study of origins, Wordsworth turns to a subject on which Coleridge rarely touches—the relationship between mother and child (*1799*, II, 267 ff.). With the ending of
Frost at Midnight in mind, he describes the earliest stages of imaginative life,
at once taking his friend into account, and radically modifying his views.
Unity had been 'revealed' to Coleridge—and, within the poem, to his son
Hartley—by God. Wordsworth sees it emerging as an aspect of maternal
love that the child instinctively absorbs (ll. 274–80). The patriarchal world
of *Frost at Midnight*—in which Hartley had wandered about, reading God's
(and his father's) sign-language—has been replaced by a Wordsworthian
universe, in which the mother counts above all else. Instead of 'A motion
and a spirit, that impels | All thinking things, all objects of all thought'
(*Tintern Abbey*, 101–2), there now exists, for the child, 'A virtue which ir-
radiates and exalts | All objects through all intercourse of sense' (*1799*, II,
289–90). Leavis saw the echo, but treated it as though the process of replacement were a matter of course.[7] In effect what has taken place is a
much more aggressive usurpation. Immediately following the reference to
Coleridge as prophet of unity, the passage as a whole corrects any impression of envy we may have received. Paying tribute to his friend gives
Wordsworth the right to go one better: deference is followed by an assertive
rewriting of Coleridge's terms.

As he brings the 1799 *Prelude* to its climax, with an account of his ad-
olescent growth, Wordsworth moves easily back again, as though no contradiction were involved,[8] into the language of the 'One Life':

> From Nature and her overflowing soul
> I had received so much that all my thoughts
> Were steeped in feeling.
>
> (*1799*, II, 446–8)

That he had felt such things as a boy (and in the Pedlar's terms) is palpably
untrue. But in any case the passage is deliberately misleading. It suggests
that his belief in the 'One Life' (already, by *Tintern Abbey*, diminished and
uncertain) lasts through to the present day. And if that can survive, so
too can *The Recluse*. Lines 479–96 are a lengthy, versified quotation from
Coleridge's letter to Wordsworth of September 1799.[9] They evoke, in a
language which is strongly echoic, 'indifference', 'apathy', 'selfishness dis-

guised in gentle names', and 'sneers | On visionary minds'. But they suggest that triumph over 'dereliction and dismay' is possible, through the 'never-failing principle of joy' (l. 495). Despite moving on, in *The Prelude,* to something distinctly his own, Wordsworth manages to present himself as the poet of *The Recluse.*

Rounding off the Two-Part *Prelude,* as the poets go their separate ways,[10] he wishes to ensure that values they have had in common should be seen to survive. The drama played out in his final address is one, therefore, of difference triumphed over by sameness, and continuity insuring against change:

> Thou, my friend, wast reared
> In the great city, 'mid far other scenes,
> But we by different roads at length have gained
> The self-same bourne.
>
> (ll. 496–9)

Part 1 had opened with a quotation from *Frost at Midnight,* and fittingly that is how part 2 ends. As before, Wordsworth is claiming his friend's support for the quest he has begun; but he seems more than usually aware of the paradox implied. As he conflates Coleridge's lament for a wasted childhood—'For I was rear'd | In the great city, pent mid cloisters dim'—with his celebration of Hartley's different future—'thou shalt learn far other lore, | And in far other scenes!' (*Frost at Midnight,* 56–7; 55–6)—Wordsworth seems at once to be admitting, and rhetorically attempting to conceal, his own unease. The same ambivalence is present in the violent terms used to describe what Coleridge is *not* feeling: 'And from this cause to thee | I speak unapprehensive of contempt, | The insinuated scoff of coward tongues' (*1799,* II, 499–501). Language intended to exorcize the poet's fears allows their presence to be felt. An unsympathetic (even hostile) Coleridge hovers behind the image of him that Wordsworth is trying to present. And in the poem's climax there is the same gap between statement and underlying awareness:

> thou art one
> The most intense of Nature's worshippers,
> In many things my brother, chiefly here
> In this my deep devotion.
>
> (*1799,* II, 506–9)

On a surface reading the two poets are brothers, fellow worshippers, alike in all things. Beneath, there is unease, growing difference, and the sense of loss.

A short time before writing this farewell, very probably on the actual day of Coleridge's departure (via Sockburn) for London, Wordsworth had composed as a separate effusion what was later to become the 'glad preamble' to *1805*.[11] The two passages grow out of the same event, but are not alike. While the one anxiously seeks Coleridge's support, and regrets his departure, the other is full of exhilaration:

> O there is blessing in this gentle breeze,
> That blows from the green fields and from the clouds
> And from the sky; it beats against my cheek,
> And seems half conscious of the joy it gives.
>
> (*1805*, I, 1–4)

At Goslar, working on the Two-Part *Prelude*, Wordsworth had jotted down a series of fragments, expressing the same exalted state of mind.[12] At first sight it is surprising that he should recall and draw on them now. In doing so, however, he links not just two moods that happen to resemble each other, but two moments at which, in the absence of Coleridge, his creativity is suddenly released.[13] Significantly enough, it is not until January 1804, when Coleridge is once again setting out on a journey, that Wordsworth begins his next real burst of activity on *The Prelude* book 3. Read to Coleridge, 'in the highest & outermost of Grasmere'[14.] the moving farewell lines of *1799* must have taken on a new appropriateness: in 'Fare thee well: | Health and the quiet of a healthful mind | Attend thee' (*1799*, II, 509–11). But as before, Coleridge's departure brings out in Wordsworth a sense of confidence and inner power:

> And here, O friend, have I retraced my life
> Up to an eminence, and told a tale
> Of matters which not falsely I may call
> The glory of my youth. Of genius, power,
> Creation, and divinity itself,
> I have been speaking, for my theme has been
> What passed within me.
>
> (*1805*, III, 168–74)

The loftiness reminds one of the 'Prospectus' of *The Recluse*.[15] But affinities with the 'Preamble' are also there. Wordsworth celebrates a divinity within himself that re-moulds, and in some respects actually discards, Milton's scheme in *Paradise Lost*:

> Not of outward things
> Done visibly for other minds—words, signs,
> Symbols or actions—but of my own heart
> Have I been speaking, and my youthful mind.
> (*1805*, III, 174–7)

He feels no need, when making his biggest claims, to disguise his singleness. The proof of divinity lies in 'the glory of [his] youth', and this neither Milton nor Coleridge can share:

> Points have we all of us within our souls
> Where all stand single; this I feel, and make
> Breathings for incommunicable powers.
> (*1805*, III, 186–8)

As the passage continues, however, apprehensiveness creeps in. Wordsworth feels the need to generalize—'Yet each man is a memory to himself' (I. 189)—and to include all men in his own sense of achievement: 'There's not a man | That lives who hath not had his god-like hours' (II. 191–2). The claim for universality is moving, and gives the reader a sense of divinity matching the poet's own. But an overemphatic quality in his language registers unease. Coleridge, by way of compensation for having been excluded, is given in the next paragraph the status of Wordsworth's guide:

> A traveller I am,
> And all my tale is of myself—even so—
> So be it, if the pure in heart delight
> To follow me, and thou, O honored friend,
> Who in my thoughts art ever at my side,
> Uphold as heretofore my fainting steps.
> (*1805*, III, 195–201)

This is a collusive way of sustaining friendship, while at the same time defining a quite private self.

The longest and most emotional of Wordsworth's addresses to Coleridge occurs half way through book 6. It begins, as this chapter did, with the poet's reordering of his past:

> O friend, we had not seen thee at that time,
> And yet a power is on me and a strong
> Confusion, and I seem to plant thee there.
>
>   (*1805*, VI, 246–8)

As the passage continues, the purpose of misremembrance becomes clear. Wordsworth, believing his friend already to have left the country, faces the loss and release his departure brings. Resigning himself to separation, he seems also to reassure himself of the deeper bonds that will continue, despite everything, to grow:

> But thou art with us, with us in the past,
> The present, with us in the times to come.
> There is no grief, no sorrow, no despair,
> No languor, no dejection, no dismay,
> No absence scarcely can there be, for those
> Who love as we do.
>
>   (*1805*, VI, 251–6)

The poetry moves one for its underlying pathos, which emerges because of (not despite) the absoluteness of the claims. Wordsworth seems almost to chant his words—'There is no grief, no sorrow, no despair'—as though they made up a spell to keep such feelings away. 'I too have been a wanderer', he continues, moving into a reaffirmation in which the closing lines of the Goslar *Prelude* are distinctly recalled:

> but, alas,
> How different is the fate of different men,
> Though twins almost in genius and in mind.
> Unknown unto each other, yea, and breathing
> As if in different elements, we were framed
> To bend at last to the same discipline,
> Predestined, if two beings ever were,
> To seek the same delights, and have one health,
> One happiness.
>
>   (*1805*, VI, 261–9)

There is evident strain in the notion that two such radically different minds should come together. The words 'framed', 'bend', and 'discipline' all suggest coercion (or at least constriction) whereas the phrase 'breathing | As if in different elements' gives a sense of freedom and natural growth. What the poetry describes is not the reconciliation of opposites, but the temporary binding together of forces that will pull apart. Drawing on a whole sequence of poems in which Coleridge had evolved the myth of his exile from country life, the passage moves deeper and deeper into a world of blatant and unchangeable contrasts:

> Of rivers, fields,
> And groves, I speak to thee, my friend—to thee
> Who, yet a liveried schoolboy in the depths
> Of the huge city, on the leaded roof
> Of that wide edifice, thy home and school,
> Wast used to lie and gaze upon the clouds
> Moving in heaven, or haply, tired of this,
> To shut thine eyes and by internal light
> See trees, and meadows, and thy native stream
> Far distant—thus beheld from year to year
> Of thy long exile.
>
> (*1805*, VI, 274–84)

Coleridge is meant to become the type of a majestic intellect, carrying with him the freedom and space of his origins, who can mentally inhabit the country despite being 'in city pent'. But Wordsworth's sense of his own privilege gives to his quotations from Coleridge's poems—and to his collusion in the myth they represent—an edge of condescension:

> oh, it is a pang that calls
> For utterance, to think how small a change
> Of circumstances might to thee have spared
> A world of pain, ripened ten thousand hopes
> For ever withered.
>
> (*1805*, VI, 292–6)

His belief that he might have protected Coleridge from 'a world of pain'— might, to pick up the Miltonic echo, have prevented his fall[16]—depends upon an assumption of innate superiority. When, at the end of the passage, he attempts to explain, it is in largely moral terms: 'maturer age | And temperature less willing to be moved'; 'calmer habits and more steady voice' (VI, 321–3). But in fact a different kind of explanation has already

emerged, in the highly ambiguous portrait which occupies the intervening
lines:

> I have thought
> Of thee, thy learning, gorgeous eloquence,
> And all the strength and plumage of thy youth,
> Thy subtle speculations, toils abstruse
> Among the schoolmen, and Platonic forms
> Of wild ideal pageantry, shaped out
> From things well-matched, or ill, and words for things—
> The self-created sustenance of a mind
> Debarred from Nature's living images,
> Compelled to be a life unto itself,
> And unrelentingly possessed by thirst
> Of greatness, love, and beauty.
>
> (*1805*, VI, 305–16)

Wordsworth is emphasizing, as he had done earlier on, the power of Coleridge's 'internal light', which seems at once enviable and frightening—like
the loneliness of the leechgatherer, as he 'paces the weary moors contin-
ually', or the solipsism of the Arab Quixote, 'crazed | By love, and feeling,
and internal thought | Protracted among endless solitudes' (*1805*, V, 144–6).
It is surprising, in a book that takes the Coleridgean imagination as its
central subject, to find lines so negative in their implications. What Wordsworth fears might result from Coleridge's imaginative power is the surrender of literal reality—and the loss, therefore, of a capacity to distinguish
between words and things.[17] He sees, side by side, the potential for inner
vastness and the danger of falseness or anarchy. Occupying a central position in this book, Coleridge becomes—like Burns and Chatterton before
him—at once an example, and a warning, of what the mind can do.

The address comes to its close in a way that points up the duality of
Coleridge's role. First, Wordsworth expresses the belief that he could 'with
an influence benign have soothed | Or chased away the airy wretchedness
| That battened on [his] youth.' (II. 324–6) Then, as if to withdraw the
vulnerable picture of Coleridge he has painted, he transforms him into
myth:

> But thou hast trod,
> In watchful meditation thou hast trod,
> *A march of glory, which doth put to shame*

These vain regrets; health suffers in thee, else
Such grief for thee would be the weakest thought
That ever harboured in the breast of man.
                    (*1805*, VI, 326–31; my italics)

In the background, but unmistakeably, one hears the rhythms and language of *Samson Agonistes*: '[His] race of glory run, and race of shame' (I. 597). In a passage that is intended not only to bless Coleridge but to glorify him, the echo has a jarring effect. It recalls, of course, the mood of dejection in which Coleridge had last echoed the same passage, and it highlights the ambiguity of Coleridge's status.[18] On one level, he is a hero with the capacity of a God; on the other, he is a human being whose health and vision are frail. The grandeur of his potential accentuates an underlying pathos, just as the extremity of Wordsworth's myth-making reveals the need to compensate for what is flawed.

A short passage in book 8 brings out the contrasts already implied: 'With an eye so rich as mine was', Wordsworth writes, with a confidence that is surprisingly unselfconscious,

                        I had forms distinct
To steady me. These thoughts did oft revolve
About some centre palpable, which at once
Incited them to motion and controlled...
                    (*1805*, VIII, 594; 597–600)

'Whatsoever shape the fit might take,' he continues, as though talking about madness,[19]

            And whencesoever it might come, I still
            At all times had a real solid world
            Of images about me, did not pine
            As one in cities bred might do—as thou,
            Beloved friend, hast told me that thou didst,
            Great spirit as thou art—in endless dreams
            Of sickness, disjoining, joining things,
            Without the light of knowledge.
                    (*1805*, VIII, 601–10)

Symbolic opposition is taken to its extreme, as Wordsworth emphasizes (more strongly than at any other time) an unbridgeable gulf between the poets' ways of seeing. The 'grand and lovely region' in which he had grown up becomes at once the embodiment in his eyes of all that Coleridge had missed; the cause of his sense of privilege; and a justification for the superiority with which he addresses his friend. The city, on the other hand— at one time a 'pasteboard symbol' for 'the unintelligible, the wholly random' element in man's experience[20]—becomes more specifically a setting against which to see the potential anarchy of Coleridge's mind. 'Debarred from Nature's living images' and 'Compelled to be a life unto [him]self', Coleridge occupies an insubstantial and chaotic world, over which he has no control: 'in endless dreams | Of sickness, disjoining, joining things, | Without the light of knowledge.'

Interestingly, the clearest link that exists between these lines from book 8 and the great central address of book 6 is their common dependence upon Milton. Adam, in book 5 of *Paradise Lost,* has a theory about dreams:

> know that in the soul
> Are many lesser faculties that serve
> Reason as chief; among these fancy next
> Her office holds; of all external things,
> Which the five watchful senses represent,
> She forms imaginations, airy shapes,
> Which reason joining or disjoining, frames
> All what we affirm or what deny, and call
> Our knowledge or opinion; then retires
> Into her private cell when nature rests.
> Oft in her absence mimic fancy wakes
> To imitate her; but misjoining shapes,
> Wild work produces oft, and most in dreams,
> Ill matching words and deeds long past or late.
>
> (*PL,* V, 100–13)

In book 6, Wordsworth's echoing of the phrase 'ill matching words and deeds' in 'things well-matched or ill, and words for things' had drawn attention to the anarchic potential of Coleridge's thought. The echo in book 8 has the same implications. Conflating two separate Miltonic phrases—'joining or disjoining' as applied to reason, 'misjoining' as applied to 'mimic fancy'—Wordsworth suggests that a 'counter-spirit' is at work in Coleridge's imagination, 'disjoining, joining things, | Without the light of knowledge.' Just as fancy takes over, in Adam's view, when reason retires, so the counter-spirit triumphs when palpable reality falls away. The 'light

of knowledge' is, by implication, a faculty akin to reason, which Wordsworth possesses—steadied and controlled, as he is, by distinct forms—but
which Coleridge must do without. Milton's presence within the language
not only sharpens the poet's meaning, it pinpoints an underlying aggression.

If the Coleridge of books 6 and 8 acts essentially as a foil, his role is
different in book 10. On this occasion the poet sees him in a redemptive
capacity: sharing in man's fallen nature, and shouldering the burden of his
guilt, but triumphing, none the less, over the degeneracy that surrounds
him. The address begins, significantly, at the nadir of book 10. Describing
his own immediately post-Godwinian phase in 1796, Wordsworth presents
his earlier self as someone very like the 'disjoining, joining' Coleridge of
book 8:

> Thus I fared,
> Dragging all passions, notions, shapes of faith,
> Like culprits to the bar . . .
> *now believing,*
> *Now disbelieving, endlessly perplexed*
> With impulse, motive, right and wrong . . .
> (*1805,* X, 888–90, 892–4; my italics)

Rhythmic echo, and subtle verbal reminiscence, connect the moral anarchy of a confused Godwinian reason not only with the 'mimic fancy' of
Adam's dreams, but with the dangerous solipsism imaged in the city-
dweller's life. And just when Wordsworth is at his most nearly Coleridgean—'Sick, wearied out with contrarieties', yielding up 'moral questions in despair'—it is Coleridge himself who comes to the rescue:

> Ah, then it was
> That thou, most precious friend, about this time
> First known to me, didst lend a living help
> To regulate my soul.
> (*1805,* X, 904–7)

Wordsworth is guilty, here, of 'Planting [his] snowdrops among winter
snows'[21]—or (to follow his metaphor through, into its later context) of
'seem[ing] to plant' Coleridge where he has no right to be. [22] As the editor
of the Norton text points out, the two friends 'corresponded at times' after
they met in 1795, and 'can have exerted no great influence upon each

other until June 1797'.[23] But by including his friend at his life's most vulnerable point, Wordsworth suggests that he was (and continues to be) indispensable—almost as much the redeemer as Dorothy, who 'Maintained for [him] a saving intercourse | With [his] true self' (*1805*, X, 914–5). That the inaccuracy is intentional cannot be denied: the phrase 'about this time' is sneakily vague. But there is not, here, the same detachment of self-knowledge that one finds in book 6, where Wordsworth reflects on the wishfulness of memories reconstructed:

> Through this retrospect
> Of my own college life, I still have had
> Thy after-sojourn in the self-same place
> Present before my eyes, have played with times
> (I speak of private business of the thought)
> And accidents as children do with cards,
> Or as a man, who, when his house is built,
> A frame locked up in wood and stone, doth still
> In impotence of mind by his fireside
> Rebuild it to his liking.
>
> (*1805*, VI, 296–305)

In both passages, one poet acts as saviour to the other, and in both cases this involves a rewriting of the past. Where book 6 is concerned, Wordsworth (like Lamb) 'detecting the fallacy, will not part with the wish' (Marrs, i. 265). In book 8, strategy can barely be distinguished from self-deception.

Closeness—called into question by books 6 and 8—has been reconstructed, and Wordsworth moves on a stage in the process of transforming his friend. As he contrasts his own visit to France in 1790—when the Revolution had just begun, and when his optimism was at its height—with the very different circumstances of Coleridge's visit to Sicily, he seems to be begging his friend to demonstrate the continuity of their shared beliefs (*1805*, X, 954–65). There is in his portrayal of Coleridge, living 'among the basest and the lowest fallen | Of all the race of men' (ll. 947–8), an underlying fear of his being contaminated, rather than improved.[24] But countering this anxiety is the Miltonic hope—already expressed in *Tintern Abbey* and *1799* part 2—that, like Wordsworth, he will triumph

> though fallen on evil days,
> On evil days though fallen, and evil tongues...
> (*PL*, VII, 25–6)

Tacitly, Coleridge becomes a mirror image of the poet himself, capable, in times of 'dereliction and dismay', of retaining

> A more than Roman confidence, a faith
> That fails not, in all sorrow [his] support,
> The blessing of [his] life . . .
>
> (*1799*, II, 489–91)

and capable, therefore, of transforming the world around:

> Thy consolation shall be there, and time
> And Nature shall before thee spread in store
> Imperishable thoughts, the place itself
> Be conscious of thy presence, and the dull
> Sirocco air of its degeneracy
> Turn as thou mov'st into a healthful breeze
> To cherish and invigorate thy frame.
>
> (*1805*, X, 970–6)

What, though, is to be the basis of Coleridge's faith? It is clear that the poet's own is formed by mountains; but Coleridge, 'Debarred from Nature's living images', is surely less well-placed? Who is to say that, left to its own devices, and in a setting which exactly parallels the barrenness of the city, his imagination will not become anarchic? Forced into a role not his own, he is being used rather obviously by the poet, to re-create early hopes. 'Carrying a heart more ripe | For all divine enjoyment' (l. 598), he stands in for an older Wordsworth, who feels himself to have matured, and whose earlier values must be preserved:

> Our prayers have been accepted: thou wilt stand
> Not as an exile but a visitant
> On Etna's top; by pastoral Arethuse—
> Or if that fountain be indeed no more,
> Then near some other spring which by the name
> Thou gratulatest, willingly deceived—
> Shalt linger as a gladsome votary,
> And not a captive pining for his home.
>
> (*1805*, X, 1031–8)

The closing line reminds one for a moment of the real Coleridge who is concealed behind the myth: a Coleridge who, whether in the city or abroad, felt himself to be exiled, and whose own 'home'—as Wordsworth knew too well—was a mockery of that word. But it is against the poet's will that this reminder comes. The address ends, as it had begun, with self-deception, and with a trust in Coleridge's happiness that is out of keeping with the portrait's most imaginative lines:

> A lonely wanderer art gone, by pain
> Compelled and sickness, at this latter day,
> This heavy time of change for all mankind.[25]

Wordsworth not only passes a fiction on himself; he asks his friend also to be willingly deceived.

The 'Climbing of Snowdon', structurally and symbolically Wordsworth's climactic spot of time, demonstrates the nature of imaginative power: a power which is described in evidently Coleridgean terms, but which (if one takes the chronology of *The Prelude* into account) is said to precede Coleridge's influence. The address which ends book 12, then, is needed to prepare the way for this climax, and to introduce its implications. 'Dearest friend, | Forgive me', Wordsworth writes, in tones that are formal, apologetic, distanced:

> Forgive me if I say that I, who long
> Had harboured reverentially a thought
> That poets, even as prophets, each with each
> Connected in a mighty scheme of truth,
> Have each for his peculiar dower a sense
> By which he is enabled to perceive
> Something unseen before—forgive me, friend,
> If I, the meanest of this band; had hope
> That unto me had also been vouchsafed
> An influx, that in some sort I possessed
> A privilege, and that a work of mine,
> Proceeding from the depth of untaught things,
> Enduring and creative, might become
> A power like one of Nature's.
>
> (*1805*, XII, 298–312)

The aspiration itself is moving; but the mock-humility, exaggerated and misplaced, registers unease. Coleridge, it seems, must be apologized to because Wordsworth is ambitious. But is this because the poet regards his friend as being higher up the ladder than himself, or because he assumes he's not up to competing? Curiously, the language seems to hold out both alternatives, the extremity of the self-abasement (where else would Wordsworth dream of calling himself 'the meanest of the band'?) at once rating Coleridge at an absurdly high level, and implying that he is altogether excluded.

As though to confirm this ambiguity, the address continues with a definition of the poet's creative power that seems barely to take his friend into account. Bypassing seven years of intimacy, influence, and exchange, Wordsworth returns to the most complex of his pre-Coleridgean poems (*1805*, XII, 312 ff.). *Salisbury Plain* comes to stand not just for an exalted state of mind, but for a particular quality of Wordsworth's poetic imagination. He sees it as the origin of his greatness—the poem, above all others, on which he would base his claim to have created 'a power like one of Nature's.'—and he sees it, moreover, in completely un-Coleridgean terms:

> The voice of spears was heard, the rattling spear
> Shaken by arms of mighty bone, in strength
> Long mouldered, of barbaric majesty.
> I called upon the darkness, and it took—
> A midnight darkness seemed to come and take—
> All objects from my sight; and lo, again
> The desart visible by dismal flames!
> It is the sacrificial altar, fed
> With living men—how deep the groans!—the voice
> Of those in the gigantic wicker thrills
> Throughout the region far and near, pervades
> The monumental hillocks, and the pomp
> Is for both worlds, the living and the dead.
>
> (*1805*, XII, 324–36)

It is a passage that links back, in atmosphere, language, and meaning, with the Boat-Stealing episode in *1799*, part 1:

> In my thoughts
> There was a darkness—call it solitude,
> Or blank desertion—no familiar shapes
> Of hourly objects, images of trees,
> Of sea or sky, no colours of green fields,

> But huge and mighty forms that do not live
> Like living men moved slowly through my mind
> By day, and were the trouble of my dreams.
>
> (*1799*, I, 122–9)

Wordsworth is making of the Salisbury Plain experience a 'spot of time'—moving it back, through the years, so that it takes on the qualities of childhood trauma, and belongs to a pre-Coleridgean past. With a sort of apologetic readiness, however, he accepts Coleridge's different (and in some ways opposite) valuation:

> Nor is it, friend, unknown to thee; at least—
> Thyself delighted—thou for my delight
> Hast said, perusing some imperfect verse
> Which in that lonesome journey was composed,
> That also I must then have exercised
> Upon the vulgar forms of present things
> And actual world of our familiar days,
> A higher power—have caught from them a tone,
> An image, and a character, by books
> Not hitherto reflected.
>
> (*1805*, XII, 356–65)

Having chosen *Salisbury Plain*, out of all his poems, to represent his claim to greatness, and having made this claim in un-Coleridgean terms, he then uses Coleridge's words to congratulate himself.[26] At first, he makes a show of modesty to hide it: 'Call we this | But a persuasion taken up by thee | In friendship' (*1805*, XII, 365–7). Confidence returns, however, and book 12 ends with the poet having it both ways—defining his private sense of power, but appropriating Coleridge's view of him as well:

> in life's everyday appearances
> I seemed about this period to have sight
> Of a new world—a world, too, that was fit
> To be transmitted and made visible
> To other eyes, as having for its base
> That whence our dignity originates,
> That which both gives it being, and maintains
> A balance, an ennobling interchange
> Of action from within and from without:

> The excellence, pure spirit, and best power,
> Both of the object seen, and eye that sees.
>
> > (*1805*, XII, 369–79)

In effect, what Wordsworth manages to suggest is that before even meeting Coleridge his poetry had reached its height and that, by further implication, he had evolved already his belief in imagination's transforming power. The arrangement of time, as on so many occasions in *The Prelude*, has an unacknowledged purpose. In this instance it is the displacement of Coleridge, which prepares one for book 13.

There is no scope in this chapter for discussing the Coleridgean implications of the 'Climbing of Snowdon', which are in any case sufficiently well known.[27] My concern here is with the more ambiguous areas of relationship that emerge in the passage immediately following it, and with various strategies the poet uses in rounding off his poem. It is in book 13 that Wordsworth allows the two extremes of his mythologizing process to meet. Here, therefore, we are presented with a final Janus-like image of his friend.

Wordsworth's commentary on the Snowdon episode (the last and greatest of his 'spots of time') concerns itself with the potential not just of ordinary human imagination, but of the creative power that 'higher minds' possess:

> They from their native selves can send abroad
> Like transformation, for themselves create
> A like existence, and whene'er it is
> Created for them, catch it by an instinct.
>
> > (*1805*, XIII, 93–6)

No definition of a 'higher mind' is offered, but from the exalted language it is clear that what Wordsworth has in mind is a visionary company of poets—'each with each │ Connected in a mighty scheme of truth'—to which he himself aspires:

> Such minds are truly from the Deity,
> For they are powers; and hence the highest bliss
> That can be known is theirs—the consciousness
> Of whom they are, habitually infused
> Through every image, and through every thought,
> And all impressions . . .
>
> > (*1805*, XIII, 106–11)

It is the strength of his aspiration that causes Wordsworth, at this climactic moment in *The Prelude,* to examine his credentials, and to find himself (as one might expect) rather more than 'the meanest of the band'. He bases his claim to be a 'power' on the inviolable strength of his character, and the integrity of his imagination: 'I never in the quest of right and wrong', he solemnly declares,

> Did tamper with myself from private aims;
> Nor was in any of my hopes the dupe
> Of selfish passions; nor did willfully
> Yield ever to mean cares and low pursuits;
> But rather did with jealousy shrink back
> From every combination that might aid
> The tendency, too potent in itself,
> Of habit to enslave the mind . . .
>
> (*1805,* XIII, 131–9)

It is primarily to education—his 'early intercourse | In presence of sublime and lovely forms' (XIII, 145–6)—that this integrity can be ascribed, and there is the strongest of implications that without it imagination could not have thrived. Where, then, does Coleridge stand? What is *his* chance, with so different a childhood to look back on, of being one of the 'higher minds'? And where does Wordsworth place him, as he brings *The Prelude* to an end?

Love has its place in the poet's scheme of things—

> From love, for here
> Do we begin and end, all grandeur comes,
> All truth and beauty—from pervading love—
> That gone, we are as dust.
>
> (*1805,* XIII, 149–52)

—and one might expect this at least to represent common ground; especially when the definition that Wordsworth offers is so self-consciously Coleridgean. 'Thou calls't this love', he writes of sentimental attachments,

> And so it is, but there is higher love
> Than this, a love that comes into the heart
> With awe and a diffusive sentiment.
> Thy love is human merely: this proceeds
> More from the brooding soul, and is divine.
>
> (*1805,* XIII, 161–5)

But not even the 'brooding soul' image—intended, perhaps, as a gesture of inclusion[28]—can reverse the significance of the preceding lines. Coleridgean terms may be adopted, and Coleridgean values shared, but the essence of Coleridge the man is somehow left on one side. Wordsworth is unable, for whatever reason, to regard him as an exemplar of imaginative strength. He assembles a visionary company around himself, but carefully ignores his friend.

One might be tempted to think of this process as wholly unconscious, but there is manuscript evidence proving the reverse. In its original form— as part of the Five-Book *Prelude*—the passage quoted above was followed immediately by lines in which, as a note in the *Norton Prelude* puts it, 'Wordsworth turned to consider the factors which in practice conspired to thwart ... "divine" love'.[29] These lines—originally intended to lead into the 'spots of time' (which formed the climax of the Five-Book poem)—survive in *MS W,* and leave us in no doubt as to Wordsworth's meaning. The factors he writes about seem at first to be universal: 'petty duties and degrading cares' on a mundane level; 'Labour and penury, disease and grief' on a more threatening scale. But as he continues, one particularly thwarting situation looms largest in his thoughts: 'vexing strife | At home', he writes,

> and want of pleasure and repose,
> And all that eats away the genial spirits,
> May be fit matter for another song ...
>
> (ll. 8–10)

No one reading this passage can fail to connect it with Coleridge. They will hear, in the phrase 'genial spirits', a clear echo of those famous lines from *Dejection,* which are themselves a double quotation from *Tintern Abbey* and *Samson Agonistes:*

> My genial spirits fail—
> And what can these avail
> To lift the smothering weight from off my breast?
>
> (*Letter to Sara,* 44–6)[30]

But they will also recognize a more general reference to Coleridge's domestic predicament: what he painfully calls, in the *Letter to Sara,* 'those habitual Ills | That wear out Life, | When two unequal Minds | Meet in one House, & two discordant Wills' (ll. 243–5).

Our attention is drawn in this passage, clearly and unmistakeably, to the destruction of Coleridge's imaginative potential. Factors which conspire (in a general and external sense) to thwart 'divine' love have given place to more insidious forces that 'eat away' the spirits from within. Joy, love, imagination—all seen as vital to the moral strength Wordsworth claims as his own—disappear under the pressure of 'vexing strife | At home'. We are given, in this process, the strongest possible reasons for Coleridge's disqualification from the band of 'higher minds': reasons, furthermore, which seem so unambiguous in their application that Wordsworth is forced to edit them out of the poem before going on.

The Five-Book *Prelude,* intended originally as the poem Coleridge would take with him on his travels, may never have reached its final shape. Wordsworth decided at a late stage to set the last book aside for future use and to split the fourth one in two, thus creating *1805,* books 4 and 5. During the first half of March 1804, Coleridge was sent five books of a longer *Prelude* of which Wordsworth himself did not at this moment know the probable length. No convincing explanation has yet been offered for the sudden shelving of a poem which must have been very nearly complete,[31] and it is interesting to speculate whether he abandoned the Five-Book poem because the drafts in *MS W* had taken him into a discussion of Coleridge's inadequacy that was wholly inappropriate. A letter written in March 1804 suggests that he still needs Coleridge, almost desperately, in order to think himself capable of writing *The Recluse*:

> I am very anxious to have your notes . . . I cannot say how much importance I attach to this, if it should please God that I survive you, I should reproach myself for ever in writing the work if I had neglected to procure this help. (*EY,* 452)

But he has muddled himself through, in the poetry itself, to seeing his friend as unworthy. The conflict of attitudes is familiar, and in various ways representative of *The Prelude* as a whole; but it amounts in this case to something like a crisis.

A year later, when he makes his second attempt—this time with a poem of thirteen books—to construct an ending, Wordsworth is feeling more honest:

> Imagination having been our theme,
> So also hath that intellectual love,
> For they are each in each, and cannot stand
> Dividually. Here must thou be, O man,

> Strength to thyself—no helper hast thou here—
> Here keepest thou thy individual state:
> No other can divide with thee this work,
> No secondary hand can intervene
> To fashion this ability. 'Tis thine,
> The prime and vital principle is thine
> In the recesses of thy nature, far
> From any reach of outward fellowship,
> Else 'tis not thine at all.
>
> (*1805*, XIII, 185–97)

On two different levels, the passage brings into the open attitudes that have been previously implied. Seen as a continued address to Coleridge, it offers some kind of excuse for the poet's abandonment of his friend—for if the capacity for 'intellectual love' comes from within, and cannot be acquired, then Coleridge is truly beyond redemption. Seen, on the other hand, as a dialogue within himself, the passage faces up to a loneliness and self-sufficiency that are present throughout *The Prelude*, but which the poet is very frequently at pains to deny. One is reminded, in the solemn and emphatic repetitions—'No other can divide with thee this work, | No secondary hand can intervene | To fashion this ability'—of the lines in *Home at Grasmere* which most impressively define Wordsworth's aloofness:

> Possessions have I, wholly, solely mine,
> Something within which yet is shared by none—
> Not even the nearest to me and most dear . . .
>
> (*MS B*, 897–9; Darlington, 94)

The stress on a principle which exists 'in the recesses' of man's nature—'far | From any reach of outward fellowship'—is one that gives Wordsworth the maximum possible independence from Coleridge. It is an independence that allows for the possibility of continuing with *The Recluse*, but that acknowledges (for the first and last time) the inappropriateness of expecting to be helped. Having, a year earlier, brought himself by mistake to a confrontation with Coleridge's inadequacy, Wordsworth now accepts the obvious implications.

But not for long. As he moves into the second part of book 13, he becomes worried by the implied withdrawal, and looks anxiously round for a role to give his friend. This, after all, is the 'Poem to Coleridge': a role must be found. It is not difficult to fit his sister into his final scheme of things:

> thy breath,
> Dear sister, was a kind of gentler spring
> That went before my steps.
>
> (*1805*, XIII, 244–6)

But when Coleridge is given the same status as Dorothy, the old unease returns:

> O most loving soul,
> Placed on this earth to love and understand,
> And from thy presence shed the light of love,
> Shall I be mute ere thou be spoken of?
> Thy gentle spirit to my heart of hearts
> Did also find its way . . .
>
> (*1805*, XIII, 248–53)

It is not that one cannot value, or find credible, the impulse behind these emotional and moving lines. It is just that the myth-making process is being asked to do too much. The Coleridge who, again and again in *The Prelude*, has been seen as a solipsistic figure, shut out from the light of knowledge, his imagination feeding solely on itself, is transformed here into an emblem of outgoing love. We are asked to forget a whole sequence of extremely powerful images:

> Thou, my friend, art one
> More deeply read in thy own thoughts . . .
>
> (*1799*, II, 249–50)

> But yet more often living with thyself,
> And for thyself . . .
>
> (*1799*, II, 512–13)

> The self-created sustenance of a mind
> Debarred from Nature's living images,
> Compelled to be a life unto itself . . .
>
> (*1805*, VI, 312–14)

> in endless dreams
> Of sickness, disjoining, joining things,
> Without the light of knowledge.
>
> (*1805*, VIII, 608–10)

> A lonely wanderer art gone, by pain
> Compelled and sickness ...
>
> (*1805,* X, 983–4)

And not only to forget *them*; but to cancel out any of the more critical attitudes to Coleridge which have emerged, overtly or by implication, earlier in the poem. The reluctant admission, in *MS W,* of Coleridge's inadequacy, and the honest facing up to independence earlier in book 13, are both discarded. 'Placed on this earth to love and understand', Coleridge takes on, once again, the redemptive status he had been given in book 10. Alongside Dorothy, he becomes the poet's saviour, leading him on, from the 'deep enthusiastic joy' of his early responses to a perception of

> the life
> Of all things and the mighty unity
> In all which we behold, and feel, and are ...
>
> (*1805,* XIII, 253–5)

It is a fiction based entirely on need, and it prepares the way for Wordsworth's final address to his friend. 'When thou dost to that summer turn thy thoughts', he writes, retreating nostalgically into Alfoxden and the summer of 1798:

> When thou dost to that summer turn thy thoughts,
> And hast before thee all which then we were,
> To thee, in memory of that happiness,
> It will be known—by thee at least, my friend,
> Felt—that the history of a poet's mind
> Is labour not unworthy of regard:
> To thee the work shall justify itself.
>
> (*1805,* XIII, 404–10)

Wordsworth's mood, in May 1805, as he writes these lines, is one of acute anxiety. With Coleridge expected back from Malta at any time, he is asking himself whether *The Prelude* will be well received, whether his neglect of *The Recluse* will count against him, whether—in any terms—the work can 'justify itself'. The Coleridge whom he sets up as judge of these questions is not the man who left for the Mediterranean, or the one who will return the following August, sadly changed. He is a figure at once creative and sympathetic, belonging to the now distant past.

Behind Wordsworth's evocation of 1797–98 as a 'golden age' lie the threatening memories of a collaborative period when the two writers had not always agreed. Neither *Christabel* nor *The Ancient Mariner* can be mentioned in this context without unease; and—for different reasons—*The Idiot Boy* and *The Thorn* are scarcely more tactful. Wordsworth's references at this climactic moment imply perhaps the hope that he can subdue painful associations. The self-mockery of the allusions to *The Thorn* and *The Idiot Boy* is there to balance the tacit aggression in his treatment of Coleridge; and the hope is that all poems belonging to the 'golden age' will take on the same colouring, pass unpainfully into myth.

Just as the past must be carefully treated, so as neither to reveal the disparities it contained, nor to reflect back the disagreements that have since emerged, so the present must seem of a piece with what has gone before. Under the pressure of 'a private grief | Keen and enduring' (ll. 416–17)—the grief occasioned by the death of his brother, John—Wordsworth anticipates the moment when, in remembrance of the Alfoxden days, he will read aloud his 'Poem to Coleridge':

> a comfort now, a hope,
> One of the dearest which this life can give,
> Is mine: that thou art near, and wilt be soon
> Restored to us in renovated health—
> When, after the first mingling of our tears,
> 'Mong other consolations, we may find
> Some pleasure from this offering of my love.
> (*1805,* XIII, 421–7)

The words 'some pleasure' are not mere self-deprecation. No more than in October 1799—'I long to see what you have been doing. O let it be the tailpiece of "The Recluse!" for of nothing but "The Recluse" can I hear patiently' (Griggs, i. 538)—can it be guaranteed that Coleridge the taskmaster will be mollified by an offering of love. It is for this reason that the poet is heard at this moment talking anxiously to himself:

> Oh, yet a few short years of useful life,
> And all will be complete—thy race be run,
> Thy monument of glory will be raised.
> (ll. 428–30)

Once more in Wordsworth's mind is the passage from *Samson Agonistes* to which he and Coleridge have turned so often[32]:

> So much I feel my genial spirits droop,
> My hopes all flat, nature within me seems
> In all her functions weary of herself...

only this time it is the final lines of Milton's sentence that matter most:

> My race of glory run, and race of shame,
> And I shall shortly be with them that rest.
>   (ll. 594–6; 597–8)

Useful life—life that might achieve the writing of *The Recluse*—is dwindling. The poet's race of glory may prove a race of shame. 'Then, though too weak to tread the ways of truth', he goes on,

> This age fall back to old idolatry,
> Though men return to servitude as fast
> As the tide ebbs, to ignominy and shame
> By nations sink together, we shall still
> Find solace in the knowledge which we have,
> Blessed with true happiness if we may be
> United helpers forward of a day
> Of firmer trust, joint labourers in the work—
> Should Providence such grace to us vouchsafe—
> Of their redemption, surely yet to come.
>   (ll. 431–41)

In December 1799 Wordsworth had brought the Two-Part *Prelude* to a close by maintaining his 'more than Roman confidence' in the face of

> indifference and apathy
> And wicked exultation, when good men
> On every side fall off...
> To selfishness...
>   (II, 480–3)

Now, he contemplates whole nations sinking together 'to ignominy and shame',[33] and yet is able—apparently—to think in terms not just of personal confidence but of the redemption of mankind. He and Coleridge, who before were merely brothers in a deep private devotion to Nature, are now 'joint labourers' in a work ordained by Providence. Biblical allusion reinforces the redemptive claims, as Wordsworth (identifying himself, by implication, with St. Paul) quotes Philippians 4:3: 'And I intreat thee also, true yoke-fellow, help those women which laboured with me in the gospel, with Clement also, and with other my fellow-labourers, whose names *are* in the book of life'.[34]

The tentativeness of Wordsworth's language might anyhow lead us to see anxiety beneath his claims;[35] but beyond the allusions to *1799*, there is an echo even more disquieting. 'I've join'd us', says Rivers to Mortimer in the central scene of *The Borderers*,

> by a chain of adamant;
> Henceforth we are fellow-labourers—to enlarge
> The intellectual empire of mankind.
>
> (IV. ii: 187–9)

Biblical allusion in this context had been ironic, for it is Pauline assumptions that Rivers overturns. In *The Prelude* no irony is intended, but while conscious biblical parallel pulls in one direction, unconscious self-echo pulls in the other. Wordsworth and Coleridge too are to enlarge the empire of intellect—

> Prophets of nature, we to them will speak
> A lasting inspiration *sanctified*
> *By reason and by truth . . .*
> Instruct them how *the mind of man* becomes
> A thousand times more beautiful than the earth
> On which he dwells . . .
>
> (XIII, 442–4; 446–7; my italics)

One obvious effect of the echoes is to undermine confidence. As *The Borderers* reminds us, schemes built on the perfectibility of mankind can be misguided, or go badly wrong. More damaging, however, is the implication for the poets' relationship. Rivers binds Mortimer with a chain of adamant by causing him to repeat the crime he has himself committed. There is no way that Wordsworth can be thought of as doing the same to Coleridge; but may not an echo be called to mind by a situation in reverse? Much of the resentment and aggression seen in *The Prelude* invocations stems from the oppressive sense that a task is yet to be completed, an obligation waits to be fulfilled. Coleridge has bound his friend by making him the poet of *The Recluse*.[36] It is indeed a chain of adamant: one that leaves Wordsworth dominated by guilt almost to the end of his life. And it places him, too, in a strange and unreal relation to his tormentor.

Notes

Abbreviations used in text and notes:

Baker: Jeffrey Baker. *Time and Mind in Wordsworth's Poetry.* Michigan, 1980.

Borders of Vision: Jonathan Wordsworth. *William Wordsworth: The Borders of Vision.* Oxford, 1982.

Darlington: Beth Darlington, ed. *Home at Grasmere.* Ithaca, N.Y., 1977.

Griggs: E. L. Griggs, ed. *Collected Letters of Samuel Taylor Coleridge.* 6 vols. Oxford, 1956–71.

Lindenberger: Herbert Lindenberger. *On Wordsworth's 'Prelude'.* Princeton, 1963.

Marrs: Edwin J. Marrs, ed. *The Letters of Charles and Mary Anne Lamb.* 3 vols. Ithaca, N.Y., 1975–78.

Onorato: R. J. Onorato. *The Character of the Poet: Wordsworth in 'The Prelude'.* Princeton, 1971.

PL: Paradise Lost, The Poems of John Milton, ed. John Carey and Alastair Fowler. Longman Annotated Poets. London, 1968.

Prose Works: The Prose Works of William Wordsworth, ed. W. J. B. Owen and Jane Worthington Smyser. 3 vols. Oxford, 1974.

1. For a brief discussion of Wordsworth's deviation from actual chronology in *The Prelude*, see Lindenberger, 170; and for an explanation of the more disconcerting aspects of confused time, see Baker, 41–5.

2. See *Frost at Midnight*, 23–43.

3. For a discussion of the unconfidence implied by the line 'If this | Be but a vain belief' (*Tintern Abbey*, 50–1), see in Lucy Newlyn, *Coleridge, Wordsworth, and the Language of Allusion*, chapter 2.

4. Both belong to c. May 1799, and are quoted in full in the notes to the Norton edition, pp. 13–14.

5. See Jonathan Wordsworth, 'The Two-Part *Prelude* of 1799', *Norton Prelude*, 575.

6. Compare the artful inadequacy of words at *1799*, I, 320–2: 'I should need | Colours and words that are unknown to man | To paint the visionary dreariness.' Lindenberger, 51–61, discusses the rhetorical strategy of wordlessness under the heading 'The struggle toward definition'.

7. See *Revaluation: Tradition and Development in English Poetry* (1936), 160.

8. See chapter 5, Newlyn, *Coleridge, Wordsworth, and the Language of Allusion,* for an explanation of the poet's indiscriminateness in this respect.

9. See Griggs, i, 527.

10. Literally, as well as metaphorically. In November 1799 Coleridge went to London to become a journalist.

11. See *Norton Prelude,* 30, n. 6.

12. See *Norton Prelude,* 494.

13. Wordsworth and Coleridge had completely different responses to being separated. In Germany, during the winter of 1798–9. Wordsworth moved into his greatest creative period to date. Coleridge, on the other hand, was crippled by absence (not just from the Wordsworths, but from England) and his two important poems of this period—*Hexameters* and *Lines Written at Elbingerode*—are expressions of loneliness and exclusion.

14. Coleridge *Notebooks,* i. 1801 (4 January 1804).

15. Compare the most daring of his out-Miltonings:

> Jehovah, with his thunder, and the quire
> Of shouting angels and the empyreal throne—
> I pass them unalarmed.
>
> (Darlington, 102)

16. Wordsworth's allusion is to *PL,* IX, 11.

17. It is a danger he takes seriously—as one sees for instance in his comments on 'Ossian' in the *Essay Supplementary to the Preface*: 'In nature every thing is distinct, yet nothing defined into absolute independent singleness. In MacPherson's work, it is exactly the reverse; every thing (that is not stolen) is in this manner defined, insulated, dislocated, deadened,—yet nothing distinct. It will always be so when words are substituted for things (*Prose Works,* iii. 77). The passage, both in its content and its phrasing, seems to echo Coleridge's distinction between Hebrew and Greek poetry.

18. See the *Letter to Sara,* 44.

19. For an assessment of the extent to which Wordsworth was afraid of madness, see John Beer, *Wordsworth in Time* (1979), 24. And for my own earlier criticism of Dr Beer's argument, which I should now like to modify, see *Review of English Studies* New Series, 32, 126, 230–1.

20. John Jones, *The Egotistical Sublime* (1954), 100.

21. *1799,* J, 446.

22. *1805,* VI, 248.

23. *Norton Prelude,* 408.

24. There is even, as one reads this ambiguous line, the strong implication that

Coleridge too has undergone a fall: 'A story destined for thy ear, who now, |
Among the basest and the lowest fallen | Of all the race of men, dost make abode
(ll. 946–8).

25. Lindenberger, 19–20, points to the impersonal pity of this passage, and links
it with Thomson's address to Lyttleton (*Spring*, 904–14).

26. The response here attributed to Coleridge is analogous to his comment in
Biographia. The similarity of the two critical positions does not persuade one that
they represent Coleridge's original response, which was primarily political. It does,
however, suggest that at some stage in the relationship he may have made a
remark of this kind. Unless, that is, one is to take it that *The Prelude* puts words
into his mouth, and the comment in *Biographia* is a confirming form of quotation.

27. See *Borders of Vision*, 308–39.

28. See the dove image of the *Letter to Sara*, which has its own private allusive
history.

29. *Norton Prelude*, 468. The passage is printed in full in *MS. Drafts and Fragments*,
3(b) (*Norton Prelude*, 499–500).

30. For Wordsworth's and Coleridge's very different allusions to the same
phrase from Milton's *Samson Agonistes*, and the reason for them, see Newlyn, *Coleridge,
Wordsworth, and the Language of Allusion*, chapter 3.

31. See *Norton Prelude*, 517.

32. See above, p. 159, for the presence of these lines in Wordsworth's address
to Coleridge in book Six. Presumably Milton is also at the back of the poet's mind
when he writes in *Intimations*, 'Another race hath been, and other palms are w[on]'
(1: 192).

33. In the background is not just Luke's personal fall in *Michael*—'He in the
dissolute city gave himself | To evil courses: ignominy and shame | Fell on him'
(ll. 453–5)—but the fall of the vainglorious in *Paradise Regained*:

> But why should man seek glory? who of his own
> Hath nothing, and to whom nothing belongs
> But condemnation, ignominy and shame?
>
> (III, 134–6)

34. I am grateful to Wallace Robson for pointing out this echo.

35. Onorato, 8–11, gives a full and perceptive account of the unease Wordsworth feels as he brings *The Prelude* to an end.

36. See Onorato, 90, for Coleridge's creation of Wordsworth as a second and
dependent self.

The Via Naturaliter Negativa

GEOFFREY H. HARTMAN

◆　◆　◆

MANY READERS HAVE FELT that Wordsworth's poetry honors and even worships nature. In this they have the support of Blake, a man so sensitive to any trace of "Natural Religion" that he is said to have blamed some verses of Wordsworth's for a bowel complaint which almost killed him.[1] Scholarship, luckily, tempers the affections, and the majority of readers have emphasized the poet's progression from nature worship or even pantheism to a highly qualified form of natural religion, with increasing awareness of the "ennobling interchange" between mind and nature and a late yielding of primacy to the activity of the mind or the idealizing power of imagination. A very small group, finally, has pointed to the deeply paradoxical character of Wordsworth's dealings with nature and suggested that what he calls imagination may be *intrinsically* opposed to nature. This last and rarest position seems to me closest to the truth, yet I do not feel it conflicts totally with more traditional readings stressing the poet's adherence to nature. It can be shown, via several important episodes of *The Prelude,* that Wordsworth thought nature itself led him beyond nature; and, since this movement of transcendence, related to what mystics have called the negative way, is inherent in life and achieved without violent or ascetic discipline, one can think of it as the progress of a soul which is *naturaliter negativa.*

The Prelude opens with a success immediately followed by a failure. Released from the "vast city" and anticipating a new freedom, the poet pours out a rush of fifty lines: "poetic numbers came / Spontaneously to clothe in priestly robe / A renovated spirit" (I, 51–3).[2] Here is the consecration, the promise of poetry as a sacrament, a gift efficacious beyond the moment. Why should a chance inspiration assume such significance? The reason is that Wordsworth was not used to make "A present joy the matter of a song"; yet here, apparently, is evidence that he may soon become self-creative, or need no more than a "gentle breeze" (the untraditional muse of the epic's opening) to produce a tempest of poetry. "Matins and vespers of harmonious verse!" is the hope held out to him, and having punctually performed matins the poet is content to slacken, to be gradually calmed by the clear autumn afternoon.

He meditates beneath a tree on a great poetic work soon to be begun. The sun sets, and city smoke is "ruralised" by distance. He starts to continue his journey, but now it is clearly time for vespers:

> It was a splendid evening, and my soul
> Once more made trial of her strength, nor lacked
> Aeolian visitations.
>
> (I, 94–6)

An outside splendor challenges the creative mind. Is the poet strong enough to answer it spontaneously, as if he needed only a suggestion, the first chord?

> but the harp
> Was soon defrauded, and the banded host
> Of harmony dispersed in straggling sounds,
> And lastly utter silence! "Be it so;
> Why think of any thing but present good?"
>
> (I, 96–100)

Wordsworth once again sees present good, like present joy, strangely opposed to the quickening of verse. The poetic outburst which he had considered a religious thing ("punctual service high . . . holy services") is now disdained as profane and *servile:*

So, like a home-bound labourer I pursued
My way beneath the mellowing sun, that shed
Mild influence; nor left in me one wish
Again to bend the Sabbath of that time
To a servile yoke.

(I, 101–5)

His reversal of mood is surprisingly complete. One who, at the impassioned outset of his reflections, had been so sure of the freely creative, autonomous nature of his poetic soul that famous passages on the emancipated spirit—from *Paradise Lost* and Exodus³—swell the current of his verse, while he thinks to possess total freedom of choice,

now free,
Free as a bird to settle where I will
(I, 8–9)

that same person now writes of himself, with a slight echo of Gray's *Elegy*:

So, like a home-bound labourer I pursued
My way.

The meaning of the reversal is not immediately clear. It does not deject the poet; it endows him, on the contrary, with a Chaucerian kind of cheer and leisure:

What need of many words?
A pleasant loitering journey, through three days
Continued, brought me to my hermitage.
I spare to tell of what ensued, the life
In common things—the endless store of things.

(I, 105–9)

The form of the reversal is that of a return to nature, at least to its rhythm. For the moment no haste remains, no tempest, no impatience of spirit. It is the mood of the hawthorn shade, of a portion of Wordsworth's Cambridge days, when he laughed with Chaucer and heard him, while birds sang, tell tales of love (III, 278–81).

In the exultant first lines of *The Prelude,* Wordsworth had foreseen the spirit's power to become self-creative. Though fostered by nature it eventually outgrows its dependence, sings and storms at will (I, 33–8). The poet's anticipation of autonomy is probably less a matter of pride than of necessity: he will steal the initiative from nature so as to freely serve or sustain the natural world should its hold on the affections slacken. His poetic power, though admittedly in nature's gift, must perpetuate, like consecration, vital if transitory feelings. Without poetry the supreme moment is nothing.

> Dear Liberty! Yet what would it avail
> But for a gift that consecrates the joy?
> (I, 31–2)

But he is taught that the desire for immediate consecrations is a wrong form of worship. The world demands a devotion less external and willful, a wise passiveness which the creative will may profane. The tempest "vexing its own creation" is replaced by a "mellowing sun, that shed / Mild influence." Nature keeps the initiative. The mind at its most free is still part of a deep mood of weathers.

Wordsworth's failure to consecrate, through verse, the splendid evening is only the last event in this reversal. It begins with the poet placing (so to say) the cart before the horse, Poetry before Nature: "To the open fields I told / A prophecy: poetic numbers came . . ." (I, 50 ff.). He never, of course, forgets the double agency of inward and outward which informs every act of poetry. So his heart's frost is said to be broken by both outer and inner winds (I, 38 ff.).[4] Such reciprocity is at the heart of all his poems. Yet he continually anticipates a movement of transcendence: Nature proposes but the Poet disposes. Just as the breeze engendered in the mind a self-quickening tempest, so poetry, the voice from that tempest, reechoing in the mind whence it came, seems to increase there its perfection (I, 55 ff.). The origin of the whole moves farther from its starting point in the external world. A *personal* agent replaces that of nature: "I paced on . . . down I sate . . . slackening my thoughts by choice" (I, 60 ff.). There is a world of difference between this subtle bravado and the ascendancy of *impersonal* constructions in the final episode: "Be it so; / Why think of any thing but . . . What need of many words? . . . I pursued / My way . . . A pleasant loitering journey . . . brought me to my hermitage."

This change, admittedly, is almost too fine for common language. Syntax becomes a major device but not a consistent one. In the 1850 text, while the poet muses in the green, shady place, certain neoclassical patterns, such as the noble passive combined with synecdoche, create an atmosphere in which personal and impersonal, active and passive, blend strongly:

> Many were the thoughts
> Encouraged and dismissed, till choice was made
> Of a known Vale, whither my feet should turn.
>
> (I, 70–2)

Devices still more subtle come into play. In the passage immediately preceding, Wordsworth describes the quiet autumn afternoon:

> a day
> With silver clouds, and sunshine on the grass,
> And in the sheltered and the sheltering grove
> A perfect stillness.
>
> (I, 67–70)

"Sheltered and sheltering"—typical Wordsworthian verbosity? The redundance, however, does suggest that whatever is happening here happens in more than one place; compare "silver clouds, and sunshine on the grass." The locus doubles, redoubles: that two-fold agency which seems to center on the poet is active all around to the same incremental effect. The grove, sheltered, shelters in turn, and makes "A perfect stillness." The poet, in a sense, is only a single focus to something universally active. He muses on this intensifying stillness, and within him rises a picture, gazing on which with *growing* love "a higher power / Than Fancy" enters to affirm his musings. The reciprocal and incremental movement, mentioned explicitly in I, 31 ff., occurs this time quite unself-consciously, clearly within the setting and through the general influences of Nature.

No wonder, then, that the city, which the poet still strove to shake off in the first lines, appears now not only distant but also "ruralised," taking on the colors of nature, as inclosed by it as the poet's own thought. The last act of the reversal is the episode of the splendid sunset. Wordsworth not only cannot, he *need* not steal the initiative from nature. Her locus is universal, not individual; she acts by expedients deeper than will or thought. Wordsworth's failure intensifies his sense of a principle of generosity in nature. That initial cry of faith, "I cannot miss my way" (I, 18), becomes true, but not because of his own power. The song loses its way.

Wordsworth's first experience is symptomatic of his creative difficulties. One impulse vexes the creative spirit into self-dependence, the other exhibits nature as that spirit's highest object. The poet is driven at the same time from and toward the external world. No sooner has he begun to enjoy his Chaucerian leisure than restiveness breaks in. The "pilgrim," despite "the life / In common things—the endless store of things," cannot rest content with his hermitage's sabbath. Higher hopes, "airy phantasies," clamor for life (I, 114 ff.). The poet's account of his creative difficulties (I, 146–269) documents in full his vacillation between a natural and a more than natural theme, between a Romantic tale and one of "natural heroes," or "a tale from my own heart" and "some philosophic song"—but he adds, swinging back to the more humble, "Of Truth that cherishes our daily life." Is this indeterminacy the end at which nature aims, this curious and never fully clarified restlessness the ultimate confession of his poetry?

It would be hard, in that case, to think of *The Prelude* as describing the "growth of a poet's mind"; for what the first part of book I records is, primarily, Wordsworth's failure to be a visionary or epic poet in the tradition of Spenser and Milton. No poem of epic length or ambition ever started like his. The epic poet begins confidently by stating his subject, boasts a little about the valor of his attempt, and calls on the Muse to help him. Yet Wordsworth's confident opening is deceptive. He starts indeed with a rush of verses which are in fact a kind of self-quotation, because his subject is poetry or the mind which has separated from nature and here celebrates its coming-of-age by generously returning to it. After this one moment of confidence, all is problematic. The song loses its way, the proud opening is followed by an experience of aphasia, and Wordsworth begins the story of the growth of his mind to prove, at least to himself, that nature had intended him to be a poet. Was it for this, he asks, for this timidity or indecision, that nature spent all her care (I, 269 ff.)? Did not nature, by a process of both accommodation and weaning, foster the spirit's autonomy from childhood on? Yet when the spirit tries to seize the initiative, to quicken of itself like Ezekiel's chariot, either nature humbles it or Wordsworth humbles himself before her. "Thus my days," says Wordsworth sadly, "are past / In contradiction; with no skill to part / Vague longing, haply bred by want of power, / From paramount impulse not to be withstood, / A timorous capacity from prudence, / From circumspection, infinite delay" (I, 237–42).

Wordsworth never achieved his philosophic song. *Prelude* and *Excursion* are no more than "ante-chapels" to the "gothic church" of his unfinished work. An unresolved opposition between Imagination and Nature prevents him from becoming a visionary poet. It is a paradox, though not an unfruitful one, that he should scrupulously record nature's workmanship, which prepares the soul for its independence from sense-experience, yet refrain to use that independence out of respect of nature. His greatest verse *still takes its origin* in the memory of given experiences to which he is often pedantically faithful. He adheres, apparently against nature, to natural fact.

There are many who feel that Wordsworth could have been as great a poet as Milton but for this return to nature, this shrinking from visionary subjects. Is Wordsworth afraid of his own imagination? Now we have, in *The Prelude,* an exceptional incident in which the poet comes, as it were, face to face with his imagination. This incident has many points in common with the opening event of *The Prelude*; it also, for example, tells the story of a failure of the mind vis-à-vis the external world. I refer to the poet's crossing of the Alps, in which his adventurous spirit is again rebuffed by nature, though by its strong absence rather than presence. His mind, desperately and un-self-knowingly in search of a nature adequate to deep childhood impressions, finds instead *itself,* and has to acknowledge that nature is no longer its proper subject or home. Despite this recognition, Wordsworth continues to bend back the energy of his mind and of his poem to nature, but not before we have learned the secret behind his fidelity.

Having finished his third year of studies at Cambridge, Wordsworth goes on a walking tour of France and Switzerland. It is the summer of 1790, the French Revolution has achieved its greatest success and acts as a subtle, though, in the following books, increasingly human background to his concern with nature. Setting out to cross the Alps by way of the Simplon Pass, he and a friend are separated from their companions and try to ascend by themselves. After climbing some time and not overtaking anyone, they meet a peasant who tells them they must return to their starting point and follow a stream down instead of further ascending, i.e. they had already, and without knowing it, crossed the Alps. Disappointed, "For still we had hopes that pointed to the clouds," they start downward beset by a "melancholy slackening," which, however, is soon dislodged (VI, 557–91, 616 ff).

This naive event stands, however, within a larger, interdependent series of happenings: an unexpected revelation comes almost immediately (624–40), and the sequence is preceded by a parallel disappointment with the natural world followed by a compensatory vision (523 ff.). In addition to this pattern of blankness and revelation, of the soulless image and the sudden renewed immediacy of nature, we find a strange instance of the past flowing into the present. Wordsworth, after telling the story of his disappointment, is suddenly, in the very moment of composition, over-powered by a feeling of glory to which he gives expression in rapturous, almost self-obscuring lines (VI, 592 ff.). Not until the moment of compo-sition, some fourteen years after the event,[5] does the real reason behind his upward climb and subsequent melancholy slackening strike home; and it strikes so hard that he gives to the power in him, revealed by the extinction of the immediate external motive (his desire to cross the Alps) and by the abyss of intervening years, the explicit name Imagination:

> Imagination—here the Power so called
> Through sad incompetence of human speech,
> That awful Power rose from the mind's abyss
> Like an unfathered vapour that enwraps,
> At once, some lonely traveller. I was lost;
> Halted without an effort to break through;
> But to my conscious soul I now can say—
> "I recognise thy glory." (VI, 592–9)

Thus Wordsworth's failure vis-à-vis nature (or its failure vis-à-vis him) is doubly redeemed. After descending, and passing through a gloomy strait (621 ff.), he encounters a magnificent view. And crossing, one might say, the gloomy gulf of time, his disappointment becomes retrospectively a prophetic instance of that blindness to the external world which is the tragic, pervasive, and necessary condition of the mature poet. His failure of 1790 taught him gently what now (1804) literally *blinds* him: the inde-pendence of imagination from nature.

I cannot miss my way, the poet exults in the opening verses of *The Prelude*. And he cannot, as long as he respects the guidance of nature, which leads him along a gradual via negativa to make his soul more than "a mere pensioner / On outward forms" (VI, 737 f.). It is not easy, however, to "follow Nature." The path, in fact, becomes so circuitous that a poet follows least when he thinks he follows most. For he must cross a strait where the external image is lost yet suddenly revived with more than original immediacy. Thus a gentle breeze, in the first book, calls forth a tempest of verse, but a splendid evening wanes into silence. A magnificent hope, in the sixth book, dies for lack of sensuous food, but fourteen years later the simple memory of failure calls up that hope in a magnificent tempest of verse. When the external stimulus is too clearly present the poet falls mute and corroborates Blake's strongest objection: "Natural Objects always did and now do weaken, deaden, and obliterate Imagination in Me."[6] The poet is forced to discover the autonomy of his imagination, its independence from present joy, from strong outward stimuli—but this discovery, which means a passing of the initiative from nature to imagination, is brought on gradually, mercifully.

Wordsworth does not sustain the encounter with Imagination. His direct cry is broken off, replaced by an impersonal construction—"here the Power." It is not Imagination but his "conscious soul" he addresses directly in the lines that follow. What, in any case, is the soul to do with its extreme recognition? It has glimpsed the height of its freedom. At the end of his apostrophe to Imagination, Wordsworth repeats the idea that the soul is halted by its discovery, as a traveler by a sudden bank of mist. But the simile this time suggests not only a divorce from but also (proleptically) a return to nature on the part of the soul,

> Strong in herself and in beatitude
> That hides her, like the mighty flood of Nile
> Poured from his fount of Abyssinian clouds
> To fertilise the whole Egyptian plain.
>
> (VI, 613–16)

It follows that nature, for Wordsworth, is not an "object" but a presence and a power; a motion and a spirit; not something to be worshiped and consumed, but always a guide leading beyond itself. This guidance starts in earliest childhood. The boy of *Prelude* I is fostered alike by beauty and by fear. Through beauty, nature often makes the boy feel at home, for, as in the Great Ode, his soul is alien to this world. But through fear, nature reminds the boy from where he came, and prepares him, having lost heaven, also to lose nature. The boy of *Prelude* I, who does not yet know he must suffer this loss as well, is warned by nature itself of the solitude to come.

I have suggested elsewhere how the fine skating scene of the first book (425–63), though painted for its own sake, to capture the animal spirits of children spurred by a clear and frosty night, moves from vivid images of immediate life to an absolute calm which foreshadows a deeper and more hidden life.[7] The Negative Way is a gradual one, and the child is weaned by a premonitory game of hide-and-seek in which nature changes its shape from familiar to unfamiliar, or even fails the child. There is a great fear, either in Wordsworth or in nature, of traumatic breaks: *Natura non facit saltus.*

If the child is led by nature to a more deeply meditated understanding of nature, the mature singer who composes *The Prelude* begins with that understanding or even beyond it—with the spontaneously creative spirit. Wordsworth plunges into *medias res,* where the *res* is Poetry, or Nature only insofar as it has guided him to a height whence he must find his own way. But book VI, with which we are immediately concerned, records what is chronologically an intermediate period, in which the first term is neither Nature nor Poetry. It is Imagination in embryo: the mind muted yet also strengthened by the external world's opacities. Though imagination is with Wordsworth on the journey of 1790, nature seems particularly elusive. He goes out to a nature which seems to hide as in the crossing of the Alps.

The first part of this episode is told to illustrate a curious melancholy related to the "presence" of imagination and the "absence" of nature. Like the young Apollo in Keats's *Hyperion,* Wordsworth is strangely dissatisfied with the riches before him, and compelled to seek some other region:

> Where is power?
> Whose hand, whose essence, what divinity
> Makes this alarum in the elements,
> While I here idle listen on the shores
> In fearless yet in aching ignorance?[8]

To this soft or "luxurious" sadness, a more masculine kind is added, which results from a "stern mood" or "underthirst of vigor"; and it is in order to throw light on this further melancholy that Wordsworth tells the incident of his crossing the Alps.

The stern mood to which Wordsworth refers can only be his premonition of spiritual autonomy, of an independence from sense-experience foreshadowed by nature since earliest childhood. It is the 'underground' form of imagination, and *Prelude* II, 315 ff., describes it as "an obscure sense / Of possible sublimity," for which the soul, remembering *how* it felt in exalted moments, but no longer *what* it felt, continually strives to find a new content. The element of obscurity, related to nature's self-concealment, is necessary to the soul's capacity for growth, for it vexes the latter toward self-dependence. Childhood pastures become viewless; the soul cannot easily find the source from which it used to drink the visionary power; and while dim memories of a passionate commerce with external things drive it more than ever to the world, this world makes itself more than ever inscrutable.[9] The travelers' separation from their guides, then that of the road from the stream (VI, 568), and finally their trouble with the peasant's words that have to be "translated," express subtly the soul's desire for a *beyond.* Yet only when poet, brook, and road are once again "fellow-travellers" (VI, 622), and Wordsworth holds to Nature, does that reveal—a Proteus in the grasp of the hero—its prophecy.

This prophecy was originally the second part of the adventure, the delayed vision which compensates for his disappointment (the "Characters of the great Apocalypse," VI, 617–40). In its original sequence, therefore, the episode has only two parts: the first term or moment of natural immediacy is omitted, and we go straight to the second term, the inscrutability of an external image, which leads via the gloomy strait to its renewal. Yet, as if this pattern demanded a substitute third term, Wordsworth's tribute to "Imagination" severs the original temporal sequence, and forestalls nature's renewal of the bodily eye with ecstatic praise of the inner eye.

The apocalypse of the gloomy strait loses by this the character of a *terminal* experience. Nature is again surpassed, for the poet's imagination is called forth, at the time of writing, by the barely scrutable, not by the splendid emotion; by the disappointment, not the fulfillment. This (momentary) displacement of emphasis is the more effective in that the style of VI, 617 ff. and the very characters of the apocalypse, suggest that the hiding places of power cannot be localized in nature.[10] Though the apostrophe to Imagination—the special insight that comes to Wordsworth in 1804—is a real peripety, reversing a meaning already established, it is not unprepared. But it takes the poet many years to realize that nature's "end" is to lead to something "without end," to teach the travelers to transcend nature.

The three parts of this episode, therefore, can help us understand the mind's growth toward independence of immediate external stimuli. The measure of that independence is Imagination, and carries with it a precarious self-consciousness. We see that the mind must pass through a stage where it experiences Imagination as a power separate from Nature, that the poet must come to think and feel as if by his own choice, or from the structure of his mind.[11] Book VI-a (557–91) shows the young poet still dependent on the immediacy of the external world. Imagination frustrates that dependence secretly, yet its blindness toward nature is accompanied by a blindness toward itself. It is only a "mute Influence of the soul, / An Element of nature's inner self" (1805, VIII, 512–13).

Book VI-b (592–616) gives an example of thought or feeling that came from the poet's mind without immediate external excitement. There remains, of course, the memory of VI-a (the disappointment), but this is an internal feeling, not an external image. The poet recognizes at last that the power he has looked for in the outside world is really within and frustrating his search. A shock of recognition then feeds the very blindness toward the external world which helped to produce that shock.

In book VI-c (617–40) the landscape is again an immediate external object of experience. The mind cannot separate in it what it desires to know and what it actually knows. It is a moment of revelation, in which the poet sees not as in a glass, darkly, but face to face. Book VI-c clarifies, therefore, certain details of book VI-a and *seems* to actualize figurative details of book VI-b.[12] The matter-of-fact interplay of quick and lingering movement, of up-and-down perplexities in the ascent (VI, 567 ff.), reappears in larger letters; while the interchanges of light and darkness, of cloud and cloudlessness, of rising like a vapor from the abyss and pouring like a flood from heaven have entered the landscape bodily. The gloomy strait also participates in this actualization. It is revealed as the secret middle term which leads from the barely scrutable presence of nature to its resurrected image. The travelers who move freely with or against the terrain, hurrying upward, pacing downward, perplexed at crossings, are now led narrowly by the pass as if it were their rediscovered guide.

The Prelude, as history of a poet's mind, foresees the time when the "Characters of the great Apocalypse" will be intuited without the medium of nature. The time approaches even as the poet writes, and occasionally cuts across his narrative, the imagination rising up, as in book VI, "Before the eye and progress of my Song" (version of 1805). This phrase, at once conventional and exact, suggests that imagination waylaid the poet on his mental journey. The "eye" of his song, trained on a temporal sequence with the vision in the strait as its final term, is suddenly obscured. He is momentarily forced to deny Nature that magnificence it had shown in the gloomy strait, and to attribute the glory to imagination, whose interposition in the very moment of writing proves it to be a power more independent than nature of time and place, and so a better type "Of first, and last, and midst, and without end" (VI, 640).

We know that book VI-b records something that happened during composition, and that enters the poem as a new biographical event. Wordsworth has just described his disappointment (VI-a) and turns in anticipation to nature's compensatory finale (VI-c). He is about to respect the original temporal sequence, "the eye and progress" of his song. But as he looks forward, in the moment of composition, from blankness toward revelation, a new insight cuts him off from the latter. The original disappointment is seen not as a test, or as a prelude to magnificence, but as a revelation in

itself. It suddenly reveals a power—imagination—that could not be sat-
isfied by anything in nature, however sublime. The song's progress comes
to a halt because the poet is led beyond nature. Unless he can respect the
natural (which includes the temporal) order, his song, at least as narrative,
must cease. Here Imagination, not Nature (as in I, 96 ff.), defeats Poetry.

This conclusion may be verified by comparing the versions of 1805 and
1850. The latter replaces "Before the eye and progress of my Song" with a
more direct metaphorical transposition. Imagination is said to rise from
the mind's abyss "Like an unfathered vapour that enwraps, / At once, some
lonely traveller." The (literal) traveler of 1790 becomes the (mental) traveler at the moment of composition. And though one Shakespearean doublet has disappeared,[13] another implicitly takes its place: does not imagination rise from "the dark backward and abysm of time" (*The Tempest*,
1.2.50)? The result, in any case, is a disorientation of time added to that of
way; an apocalyptic moment in which past and future overtake the present; and the poet, cut off from nature by imagination, is, in an absolute
sense, lonely.

The last stage in the poet's "progress" has been reached. The travelers
of book VI-a had already left behind their native land, the public rejoicing
of France, rivers, hills, and spires; they have separated from their guides,
and finally from the unbridged mountain stream. Now, in 1804, imagination separates the poet from all else: human companionship, the immediate scene, the remembered scene. The end of the via negativa is near.
There is no more "eye and progress"; the invisible progress of book VI-a
(Wordsworth crossing the Alps unknowingly) has revealed itself as a progress independent of visible ends,[14] or engendered by the desire for an
"invisible world"—the substance of things hoped for, the evidence of
things not seen. Wordsworth descants on the Pauline definition of faith:

> in such strength
> Of usurpation, when the light of sense
> Goes out, but with a flash that has revealed
> The invisible world, doth greatness make abode,
> There harbours; whether we be young or old,
> Our destiny, our being's heart and home,
> Is with infinitude, and only there;
> With hope it is, hope that can never die,
> Effort, and expectation, and desire,
> And something evermore about to be.
>
> (VI, 599–608)

Any further possibility of progress for the poet would be that of song itself, of poetry no longer subordinate to the mimetic function, the experience faithfully traced to this height. The poet is a traveler insofar as he must respect nature's past guidance and retrace his route. He did come, after all, to an important instance of bodily vision. The way is the song. But the song often strives to become the way. And when this happens, when the song seems to capture the initiative, in such supreme moments of poetry as book VI-b or even book VI-c, the way is lost. Nature in book VI-c shows "Winds thwarting winds, bewildered and forlorn," as if they too had lost their way. The apocalypse in the gloomy strait depicts a self-thwarting march and counter-march of elements, a divine mockery of the concept of the Single Way.

But in book VI-c, nature still stands over and against the poet; he is still the observer, the eighteenth-century gentleman admiring a new manifestation of the sublime, even if the lo! or mark! is suppressed. He moves haltingly but he moves; and the style of the passage emphasizes continuities. Yet with the imagination athwart there is no movement, no looking before and after. The song itself must be the way, though that of a blinded man, who admits, "I was lost." Imagination, as it shrouds the poet's eye, also shrouds the eye of his song, whose tenor is nature guiding and fostering the power of song.

It is not, therefore, till 1804 that Wordsworth discovers the identity of his hidden guide. Book VI-c was probably composed in 1799, and it implies that Wordsworth, at that time, still thought nature his guide. But now he sees that it was imagination moving him by means of nature, just as Beatrice guided Dante by means of Virgil. It is not nature as such but nature indistinguishably blended with imagination that compels the poet along his Negative Way. Yet, if book VI-b prophesies against the world of sense-experience, Wordsworth's affection and point of view remain unchanged. Though his discovery shakes the foundation of his poem, he returns after a cloudburst of verses to the pedestrian attitude of 1790, when the external world and not imagination seemed to be his guide ("Our journey we renewed, / Led by the stream,"etc.).[15] Moreover, with the exception of book VI-b, imagination does not move the poet directly, but always through the agency of nature. The childhood "Visitings of imaginative power" depicted in books I and XII also appeared in the guise or disguise of nature. Wordsworth's journey as a poet can only continue with eyes, but the imagination experienced as a power distinct from nature opens his eyes by putting them out. Wordsworth, therefore, does not adhere to nature because of natural fact, but despite it and because of human and poetic fact. Imagination is indeed an *awe-full* power.

"And men go about to wonder at the heights of the mountains, and the mighty waves of the sea, and the wide sweep of rivers, and the circuit of the ocean, and the revolution of the stars, but themselves they consider not." Petrarch, opening on the top of Mt. Ventoux his copy of Augustine's *Confessions,* and falling by chance on this passage, is brought back forcefully to self-consciousness: "I closed the book, angry with myself that I should still be admiring earthly things, who might long ago have learned from even the pagan philosophers that nothing is wonderful but the soul, which, when great itself, finds nothing great outside itself."[16]

Wordsworth's experience, like Petrarch's or Augustine's, is a conversion: a turning about of the mind as from one belief to its opposite, and a turning *ad se ipsum.* It is linked to the birth of a sharper self-awareness, and accompanied by apocalyptic feelings. By "apocalyptic" I mean that there is an inner necessity to cast out nature, to extirpate everything apparently external to salvation, everything that might stand between the naked self and God, whatever risk in this to the self.

It is often the "secret top" of a mountain that turns the man about. Mountains, according to the general testimony of the imagination, are fallen heroes: they have giants in or below them. Atlas stares mutely out of Mt. Atlas. The Titans groan under Mt. Aetna. "What can have more the Figure and Mien of a Ruin," asks Burnet, for whom the hills are noble relics of the Flood, "than Crags, and Rocks, and Cliffs?"[17] An old world, a former self, is passed over; a new consciousness is born. Wordsworth's mountains also tell of the passing of an order—their own order, for nature there prophesies its doom. An eternal witness amid eternal decay, it reveals the "Characters of the great Apocalypse." The poet's earliest sketch of Mt. Blanc condenses in one couplet this monitory and prophetic role:

> Six thousand years amid his lonely bounds
> The voice of Ruin, day and night, resounds.[18]

Many years later, after a further visit to the Alps, ancient myth joins personal intuition to give the idea its most explicit form:

> Where mortal never breathed I dare to sit
> Among the interior Alps, gigantic crew,

Who triumphed o'er diluvian power!—and yet
What are they but a wreck and residue,
Whose only business is to perish?—true
To which sad course, these wrinkled Sons of Time
Labour their proper greatness to subdue;
Speaking of death alone, beneath a clime
Where life and rapture flow in plenitude sublime.[19]

It is as if the mountains exhibited, on a monster-scale, the Christian virtue of self-abnegation. Yet all concepts of transcendence imply some such necessity. The revolutionary or apocalyptic mind sees a future so different from the past that the transition must involve violence. The Titans, in Keats's *Hyperion,* are weighed down by the mystery as well as the fact of change. In Christian eschatology the new heaven and earth are separated from our familiar world by a second Deluge: the flood of fire and terror described in the Book of Revelation. There is a necessary violation of nature or of a previous state of being. Yet Wordsworth keeps his faith in the possibility of an unviolent passage from childhood to maturity or even from nature to eternity. He converts nature into a paraclete, *the* paraclete. Perhaps he remembers that though according to Paul "we shall be changed," and in a twinkling, a rape of time, there is the counterbalancing promise that "All shall survive."[20] The divine hiatus, the revolutionary severance of new from old, is never total: the previous order, as if nothing could die absolutely, remains latent, waiting to return.

Wordsworth's explicit subject, however, is not cosmic or societal except in implication. His subject is the growth of the mind, and the question of apocalypse arises therefore in a limited though specific way. The special nature of his theme, his focus on the individual mind, is already a sign of a "general and gregarious advance" in human self-consciousness. Keats says that Wordsworth thinks into the human heart more than Milton does, not because he is the greater poet, but because he is a great poet coming at a later time.[21]

On the matter of apocalypse, there was a bridge between Milton and Wordsworth via the theological concept of the Light of Nature. Wordsworth never refers specifically to it, but we need a joining concept from the area linking nature and personal consciousness. Although I am not primarily concerned with drawing a parallel between the two poets, it might clarify Wordsworth's non-apocalyptic view of how the mind grows. He always, of course, looks at growth from within, and this provides a rather rigid limit to comparison. Wordsworth is still part of the experience he narrates, as many subtle and some startling changes of consciousness reveal; while Milton has divided his subject in advance, and is truly *spectator ab extra,* except where the desire to subsume classical myth allows his imagination an autonomous vigor. But some episodes are directly comparable, and I propose to bring together Adam's personal story of how he woke to his first thoughts, and beyond them to God (*Paradise Lost,* VIII, 253 ff.), and the account, already partially covered, of how nature during the Alpine journey woke in the young poet the sense of his own, separate consciousness. In both episodes the human mind is led from nature to beyond nature.[22]

Milton divides the growth of Adam's mind into clear and easily separated phases. The most significant of these is what is attained by the light of nature and what by supernatural illumination. Adam's apostrophe to the sun,

> Thou Sun, said I, fair Light,
> And thou enlight'n'd Earth, so fresh and gay,
> Ye Hills and Dales, ye Rivers, Woods, and Plains
> And ye that live and move, fair Creatures, tell,
> Tell, if ye saw, how came I thus, how here?
> Not of myself; by some great Maker then,
> In goodness and in power preëminent . . .[23]

shows him instinctively seeking knowledge, recognizing ascending order and reciprocity, recognizing also that there are creatures participating like himself in life and movement. By the light coming from nature and by the light of nature in him he then deduces the existence of an invisible Maker:

> For the invisible things of him from the creation of the world
> are clearly seen, being understood by the things that are made,
> even his eternal power and Godhead.[24]

So far, and no farther, does natural light extend. There is a Maker, he is preeminently good and powerful. Man, without further illumination, thirsts for knowledge and is unrequited:

> While thus I call'd, and stray'd I knew not whither,
> From where I first drew Air, and first beheld
> This happy Light, when answer none return'd,

> On a green shady Bank profuse of Flow'rs
> Pensive I sat me down; there gentle sleep
> First found me.[25]

In that sleep, which separates Adam clearly yet gently from his previous state, God dream-walks him to Eden, and natural light begins to be complemented by supernatural revelation.

But if Milton distinguishes categorically between natural and supernatural, he still allows the former a generous domain. That is why a comparison between him and Wordsworth is fruitful. His respect for the mind's natural powers anticipates that of Wordsworth. Supernatural guidance enters as late as possible, and even then is not inevitably overpowering. It cooperates with natural light in a most gentle way, though it must indeed occasionally extinguish that light, as before Eve's birth, when the *tardemah,* the deep sleep of Genesis 2:21, falls on Adam (a somewhat ominous occurrence which foreshadows the first wounding of man and the later wounding of Creation by the Fall). Even the *tardemah,* however, is not presented by Milton as total loss of sight, for the "Cell of Fancy," the internal sight, survives, and Adam is allowed to see the operation that must at once complete and deplete him.

In fact, each internal as well as external "generation" of Adam is preceded by a merciful sleep allowing the natural being to persist or even strengthen during influx of divine power. There is first the "soundest sleep" from which he wakes into being. He is bathed in a balmy sweat, the birth-dew of existence. That nature willingly cooperates in his birth is shown by the grotesque image of a Sun feeding on the amniotic or generative moisture.[26] This image is, of course, a conceit on evaporation, but the natural view and the visionary exploitation of it coexist and suggest from the outset the more general coexistence (in the unfallen world at least) of natural and supernatural. Instead of waking, moreover, to revelation and in Eden, Adam's reason is allowed to unfold more gradually. Only at its limit, thirsting for what it cannot find, does it call on God, "call'd by thee I come thy Guide." The supernatural does not intervene before the natural is perfected, and responds rather than intervenes.

When it finally appears it is superbly gentle, a "soft oppression." For the sleep by which it comes has its own charitable, paracletic function. Before Adam is allowed to see Eden in actual sight, as before he is allowed to look at Eve, both are anticipated in dream, because the reality is too great to bear without the adumbration of a dream, or because Adam's spirit must be gently raised toward the truth that is to meet him. By these repeated dream-awakenings divine light kindles rather than darkens the natural light in man.

But for a further sleep, and awakening into the darkness of the Fall, Adam's eyes might have been permanently tempered to the divine. Within the limits of sacred story, and the explicit framework of natural and supernatural, Milton approaches Wordsworth's view of a mind led from stage to transcendent stage by a similar monitory gentleness. No rape of the mind is necessary; no wounding of nature or of a previous mode of being. Milton's delicacy, in this matter, is absolute. When Raphael, divine historian, has finished his relation of the first things, Adam is impelled to tell of his own beginning: grateful, excited into reciprocity, desiring to converse longer with the Angel, "now hear mee relate / My story." The response of his mind to the Angel has by contagion some of the charm and energy of the Angel's own—Adam is already "ascending winged."

But Wordsworth cannot, like Milton, go back to a fixed beginning, to prehistory. "How shall I seek the origin?" he asks, knowing that the beginning is already the middle (and muddle) of things. Though deprived of both first term and last, of *arche* and *eschaton,* he still undertakes to trace the history of his mind. To what end? To justify the faith he has in the possibility of his renovation through daily and natural means, or to settle that wavering faith. Nature restored him unapocalyptically in the past; it surely can do so again. The restoration he talks of is identical with being renewed as a poet: it is not dryness of heart that plagues him, but the fear that nature is not enough, that his imagination is essentially apocalyptic and must violate the middle world of common things and loves.

The Alpine journey, as we have seen, contains three distinct reversals. The structure of each is that a disappointment is followed by a compensation. The imagination does not find, and strays like Adam, and is then seemingly completed. Two of the reversals, though having in them an element of surprise, are not violent; and the third, which is violent, and supplants nature as the poet's muse, still somehow returns to nature. For nature remains in Wordsworth's view the best and gentlest guide in the development surpassing her. It is part of the poet's strength that he faithfully records an experience he did not at the time of writing and still does not control. The greatest events of his journey is not book VI-c (the "Characters of the great Apocalypse"), or the parallel bewilderment of time and way near Gravedona (VI, 688–726), but the spectral figure of Imagination cutting him off, fulfilling Nature's prophecy, and revealing the end of his Negative Way.

Besides these reversals there is the tempo of the whole journey. This is often neglected for the striking events that detach themselves only partially from it. Wordsworth generally avoids making his epiphanies into epocha: into decisive turns of personal fate or history. A mythic structure would allow him to do that; Milton even overuses his "firsts" when it comes to a psychological matter: "Then Satan first knew pain" (cf. "there gentle sleep / First found me"). Though Wordsworth must pattern his story and life, he is as apologetic about this as Raphael is for having to relate divine matters in terms intelligible to human sense—whenever possible he assumes a mazy motion which makes *The Prelude* a difficult poem to follow.

The reason for Wordsworth's avoidance of epochal structure is complex and linked probably to his avoidance of myth. For though he is compelled to seek beginnings, the unfolding causes of things, nature itself resists this kind of exactness, as if it diminished her generosities, her power to make anything a new beginning. To excerpt the various epiphanies from Wordsworth's narrative is, in any case, to neglect the pull of the underlying verse that refuses them too great a distinctity of self. Much of the drama, as I now hope to show, is played out on a quietly continuing level; the ordinary events swelling into and absorbing the special insights; the peripeties threatening but finally sustaining the light of nature.

The young travelers of book VI instinctively associate nature with freedom. They believe it has the strength to waken or reawaken man. By glorious chance their destination is a land where human nature seemed born again on account of revolution (339 ff.). Man is again as open as nature itself:

> once, and more than once,
> Unhoused beneath the evening star we saw
> Dances of liberty, and, in late hours
> Of darkness, dances in the open air
> Deftly prolonged.
>
> (369–73)

They are not sidetracked, however, by these public rejoicings. "We held our way" (350), "We glided forward with the flowing stream" (377), "We sailed along" (385), "We pursued our journey" (416)—various clichés and fillers abundant in the topographical literature of the eighteenth century, including Wordsworth's own earlier work, recover life and literal significance. Nature is their principal guide and even the energy which bears them on:

Swift Rhone! thou wert the *wings* on which we cut
A winding passage with majestic ease
Between thy lofty rocks.

(378–80)

Along this southerly route marked out by nature, they are caught up
in a crowd of delegates returning home from the "great spousals"[27] in
Paris. Though Wordsworth and his friend are also "emancipated" (387),
they remain among them like "a lonely pair of strangers" (384). We glimpse
here the encounter of two different types of human freedom. The encounter always keeps below the level of allegory: it is accidental and un-
predictable as all incidents in *The Prelude*. It has, nevertheless, the force of
providence peering through chance, or idea through matter-of-fact.

The first type is the revolutionary. Wordsworth and he are traveling
along the same road and have much in common. Both delight in freedom
and believe man may be regenerated by human or natural power. Their
eye is on this world: the "great spousals" are a political fact, just as the
marriage of heaven and earth, which first emboldened Wordsworth to
think he could be a poet (IV, 323–38; VI, 42–57), is a daily fact. But there
are also important differences. The revolutionaries are journeying home,
merry and sociable: they receive the poet and his friend as Abraham of
old the angels (394 ff.). This world is their home, they have no other. The
poet and his friend, on the other hand, are lonely men, "strangers" or
"angels" whose freedom has connotation of exile. They are obscurely looking for another home: this-worldly perhaps, yet more awe-full, more sublime than what they have seen.

In this respect they do not resemble revolutionaries but pilgrims. The
pilgrim is the second type of human freedom. He travels through this
world as a free man, pushing toward the place nearest heaven. He has no
home properly speaking, no company, only an obscure burden which
drives him from one spot to another. Although there is a "home" toward
which he strives, the way is important and becomes an essential worship.
Wordsworth shares his homelessness, his solitude, his respect for the way.
He has already compared himself to a pilgrim in book 1. His travels here
are also a "pilgrimage" (763); the Alpine region is a "temple" (741); he
aspires, guided by nature, to reach "the point marked out by Heaven"
(753). His use of religious terms seems very sparse, a kind of poetic sea-
soning. Yet when the lonely traveler, many years removed from the young
adventurer of 1790, obtains a sudden glimpse of the soul's home, he bursts
into that descant on the Pauline definition of faith:

> our being's heart and home,
> Is with infinitude, and only there;
> With hope it is, hope that can never die.
>
> (604–6)

Wordsworth cannot be identified with either of these mutually exclusive types. He holds a precarious middle position as a new, emergent type, not unknown by the end of the eighteenth century, but as unstable as the Bedouin-Quixote figure ("Of these was neither, and was both at once") of which he dreams in *Prelude* 5. This radically ambivalent type takes many forms, appearing as Cain, Ahasuerus, Childe Harold, or simply poet-errant. In book 6 he is no more than "wanderer," "traveller." Yet we recognize him by the fact that fugitive and pilgrim, pursuer and pursued are unified in his person.

The Chartreuse, the first significant stop in the Alpine journey, will act as catalyst to divide clearly pilgrim from revolutionary, and to show that Wordsworth is both and neither, that he typifies a new vision, or perhaps by-pass, of the relation between natural and supernatural. Pursuing nature, the poet is actually pursued by nature beyond it. But it seems, for a moment, as if he might be swept along by the revolutionaries: he travels their road and occasionally becomes one of them. This foreshadows *Prelude* IX to XI, where Wordsworth is almost swept away. Yet nature with its intimations of a more private peace and a less ostensive freedom gradually separates the two strangers from the "merry crowd" (386), "blithe host" (387), "bees . . . gaudy and gay as bees" (391), "proud company" (394), "boisterous crew" (413):

> The monastery bells
> Made a sweet jingling in our youthful ears;
> The rapid river flowing without noise,
> And each uprising or receding spire
> Spake with a sense of peace, at intervals
> Touching the heart amid the boisterous crew
> By whom we were encompassed. Taking leave
> Of this glad throng, foot-travellers side by side,
> Measuring our steps in quiet, we pursued
> Our journey.
>
> (408–17)

And, as Wordsworth approaches the Chartreuse, the revolutionaries change proleptically into "riotous men" (425) who expel its religious community and desecrate the spirit of the place. Wordsworth, "by conflicting passions pressed," adopts two voices to argue for the preservation of the Chartreuse without condemning revolutionary zeal.[28]

His view of the monastery is, however, quite unambiguous. He sees it as a stronghold of nature's paracletic function rather than as a Catholic institution. The conquest of nature is here aided by an impulse from nature herself. The monastery's sublime natural setting *bodies forth* the ghostliness of things. But it also *clothes* it, mediating between the "bodily eye" and the "blank abyss" (470), between man's power of vision and his utter nakedness before the apocalyptic vision.[29] There is paradox here, but not ambiguity.

After the Chartreuse a new landscape begins. The positive and privative aspects of nature intermingle more obviously. Every step of the travelers attends on swift interchanges:

> Abroad, how cheeringly the sunshine lay
> Upon the open lawns! Vallombre's groves
> Entering, we fed the soul with darkness; thence
> Issued, and with uplifted eyes beheld,
> In different quarters of the bending sky,
> The cross of Jesus stand erect, as if
> Hands of angelic powers had fixed it there,
> Memorial reverenced by a thousand storms;
> Yet then, from the undiscriminating sweep
> And rage of one State-whirlwind, insecure.
>
> (479–88)

The travelers' pace seems to speed up; the earth changes its images and forms as fast as clouds are changed in heaven (492); and the uphill-downhill motion which culminates in VI-a to VI-c becomes prominent. The friends not only wing or sail along but are birds of prey, a ship on the stretch (498). We feel something of their joy in movement, in variety, and hardly suspect that nature is eluding their expectations. Then she clearly fails them for the first time just before their blind crossing of the Alps.

The failure is quickly redeemed, but it has come and prepares for book VI, 592 and the lines that follow. The very day they look with bounding heart on an "aboriginal vale" they also see Mt. Blanc and grieve:

> To have a soulless image on the eye
> That had usurped upon a living thought
> That never more could be.
>
> (526–8)

When Wordsworth discovers that the mind has no home except with

> . . . something evermore about to be
>
> VI-b, 608)

he sounds the depth of the disparity between Nature and Imagination.

Book VI-b, of course, is the peripety of a traveler many years advanced. His actual progress, to judge by the two epiphanies or compensations given by nature, the first for the blank of Mt. Blanc, the second for his blind crossing of the Alps, is as propaedeutic as Adam's dreams. The first, the poet's sight of the valley of Chamonix (VI, 528–40), still serves to reconcile imagination and nature: it carefully veils the naked vision of transcendent forces. Man is still the measure of this view. The streams of ice are balanced by five rivers broad and vast; small birds and leafy trees flourish in the same atmosphere as soaring eagle; yellow sheaf and haycock, reaper and maiden, live easily among the wilder forces of nature. Winter sports like a lion, but one well-tamed. In the second, as if penultimate view (VI-c), the balance breaks. Now the "dumb cataracts" (530) find voice, become "stationary blasts" (626); there is no well-tamed descent but torrents shooting from the clear blue sky; no warbling but muttering and ravings; no broad, spacious living but winds thwarting winds in the narrow rent; no leisurely, seasonal occupation but giddy interchanges of opposite powers. All this is still "food" (the metaphor occurs in line 723 at the end of another fantastic bewilderment, a vacillation from "fairest, softest, happiest influence" to a night ensnared by witchcraft), but one is no longer certain whence it comes or what in man it feeds. An impassioned envoi to the book finally cautions us not to think the poet a passive recipient here or anywhere in *The Prelude*:

> Not rich one moment to be poor for ever;
> Not prostrate, overborne, as if the mind
> Herself were nothing, a mere pensioner
> On outward forms.
>
> (735–8)

To be more emphatic, the poet then returns to an image found in the opening episode of his poem: that of the external breeze waking an internal tempest, an acceleration which propels the travelers along, as if nature were discovering to them their own powers. Their mind is being raised to nature as at least equal in dignity to it:

> whate'er
> I saw, or heard, or felt, was but a stream
> That flowed into a kindred stream; a gale,
> Confederate with the current of the soul,
> To speed my voyage.
>
> (742–6)

It is clear that in 1790 Wordsworth's soul was already making a "trial of its strength," with poetic numbers as the "banded host" and nature as the objective to be gained. Only in 1804 does Wordsworth realize he mistook his objective. The soul, in book VI-b, is its own objective. It is so sure of its home *away from* nature that it has no need to snatch a "trophy of the sun."[30] But Wordsworth, in truth, is never able to look complacently at the sun. He can never say with Petrarch that "nothing is wonderful but the soul, which, when great itself, finds nothing great outside itself." Even the verse of his decline, however placid in sentiment, is a trial of strength: the failing endeavor to meet with his own light the light once emanating from nature.

The ascent of Snowdon, a great moment in poetry, stands in a place of honor: Wordsworth chooses it as his coda episode for *The Prelude*. Not only is it, as poetry, a true "mounting of the mind"; it is also a culminating evidence that imagination and the light of nature are one. The certainty that there is an imagination in nature analogous to that in man opened to him a "new world." The incident is a difficult one to interpret, not only for us, but for the poet himself; yet he insists that though nature on Snowdon points to imagination, and even thrusts the vision of it on him, what he sees is still a Power like nature's (XIII, 312, XIV, 86 ff.). This time his recognition of imagination *sub specie naturae* does not (as in VI-b) give a mortal shock to nature. The episode is Wordsworth's most astonishing avoidance of apocalypse.

We must not forget, however, that the peripety described in book VI-b followed all others studied in this chapter, if we can trust the extant manuscripts. It is the last of a series of evaded recognitions, a magnificent yet inexorable after-birth. From late January to April 1804, Wordsworth was intensely engaged in work on *The Prelude*; and, under that pressure of composition, came once, and only once, face to face with his imagination. Comparing the mountain experience of book VI with that of book XIV, we obtain a clear picture of a mind finally forced to meet and to recognize its inherently apocalyptic vigor.

The experience again falls into three parts. The travelers ascend and are soon surrounded by mist (XIV-a, 11–39). There follows the vision proper (XIV-b, 39–62), and a meditation arising immediately after it (XIV-c, 63 ff.). The first part, as in the ascent of the Alps, is akin to inscrutability, while the second, a moment of strong bodily sight, could be compared to the "Characters of the great Apocalypse" (VI-c), delayed by the tribute to imagination. This tribute is itself comparable to the last section, a moment of insight which understands the external events as revealing expressly (i.e. in open sight) a power similar to the human imagination. The sequence of events in *Prelude* XIV might therefore be an unscrambling of the order of events in book VI: inscrutability, followed by the immediacy of an external image, then by the interpretation (immediate here, delayed in book VI) of that image as the resemblance of an inner power.

But since book VI-b is *hors de série* we cannot properly talk of unscrambling: the sequence of XIV existed before that of book VI was complete. It is here that we meet a problem peculiar to *The Prelude*. In most poems we need only respect the structural sequence, according to which XIV does indeed come after book VI. But in a poem also autobiography, and in which the act of composition may itself produce a further biographical event, two other sequences may have to be kept in mind. They are the biographical and the compositional order of events.

Notes

1. See *Blake, Coleridge, Wordsworth, Lamb, etc., Being Selections from the Remains of Henry Crabb Robinson,* ed. E. J. Morley (Manchester, 1932), pp. 5 and 15.

2. Throughout this book, quotations from *The Prelude* (unless otherwise stated) are from the 1850 text as printed by De Selincourt and Darbishire in *William Wordsworth, The Prelude* (Oxford, 1959), short-titled *Prelude²*. Charles Moorman has established that there is a pattern to the opening episode, although I will differ from him in my view of the pattern and its meaning. See "Wordsworth's *Prelude: I*, 1–269," *Modern Language Notes* 72 (1957), 416–20. R. D. Havens, *The Mind of a Poet* (Baltimore, 1941), pp. 290 ff., had failed to see any pattern.

3. Emanciapted—but through exile. For the allusions to *Paradise Lost* and Exodus, see *Prelude* I.14 and 16–18.

4. Cf. M. H. Abrams, "The Correspondent Breeze: A Romantic Metaphor," in *English Romantic Poets,* ed. Abrams (Galaxy paperback, New York, 1960), pp. 37–54.

5. That the rising up of imagination occurred as Wordsworth was remembering his disappointment rather than immediately after it (i.e. in 1804, not in 1790) was first pointed out by W. G. Fraser in *Times Literary Supplement* (April 4, 1929), p. 276.

6. Marginalia to Volume I of Wordsworth's *Poems* of 1815. I may venture the opinion that Wordsworth, at the beginning of *The Prelude,* goes back to nature not to increase his chances of sensation but rather to emancipate his mind from immediate external excitements, the "gross and violent stimulants" (1800 Preface to *Lyrical Ballads*) of the city he leaves behind him.

7. *The Unmediated Vision* (New Haven, 1954), pp. 17–20.

8. *Hyperion* III.103–07.

9. Cf. the Intimations Ode; also *Prelude* I.597 ff.

10. Of the four sentences which comprise lines 617–40, the first three alternate the themes of eager and of restrained movement ("melancholy slackening... Downwards we hurried fast... at a slow pace"); and the fourth sentence, without explicit transition, commencing in mid-verse (line 624), rises very gradually and firmly into a development of sixteen lines. These depend on a single verb, an unemphatic "were," held back till the beginning of line 636; the verb thus acts as a pivot that introduces, without shock or simply as the other side of the coin, the falling and interpretative movement. This structure, combined with a skillful interchange throughout of asyndetic and conjunctive phrases, always avoids the sentiment of abrupt illumination for that of a majestic swell fed by innumerable sustaining events, and thereby strengthens our feeling that the vision, though climactic, is neither terminal nor discontinuous.

11. Cf. Preface (1802) to *Lyrical Ballads:* "[The poet] has acquired a greater readiness and power in expressing... especially those thoughts and feelings which, by his own choice, or from the structure of his own mind, arise in him without immediate external excitement."

12. Book VI-c was composed before VI-b, so that while the transference of images goes structurally from VI-b to VI-c, *chronologically* the order is reversed.

13. De Selincourt, *William Wordsworth, The Prelude* (1959), p. 559, calls "Before the eye and progress of my Song" a Shakespearean doublet, which is right except that the texts he refers us to should be *Much Ado about Nothing,* IV.1.238, rather than *King John,* II.1.224.

14. Cf. *The Unmediated Vision,* pp. 129–32.

15. The "return to nature" is anticipated by the last lines of VI-b (lines 613–16).

16. Letter to Francesco Dionigi de' Roberti, April 26, 1336. The end of the quoted passage is an allusion to Seneca, *Epistles* 8.5.

17. Quoted from *The Sacred Theory of the Earth* (1684–89), in Marjorie Nicolson, *Mountain Gloom and Mountain Glory* (New York, 1959), p. 206. Her chs. 5 and 6 on Burnet are especially relevant to the present theme.

18. *Descriptive Sketches* (1793), lines 692–93; see also below, p. 105 f.

19. "Desultory Stanzas," in *Memorials of a Tour on the Continent, 1820* (published 1822).

20. I Corinthians 15:15–54 and Acts 3:21; cf. *The Poetical Works of William Wordsworth,* ed. Ernest de Selincourt and Helen Darbishire 5 vols. (Oxford: Clarendon Press, 1940–49), 5, 337 ("Home at Grasmere," line 743).

21. Letter to John Hamilton Reynolds, May 3, 1818. Yet did not Saint Augustine think into the human heart, at an earlier time?

22. Cf. also Keats' *Hyperion,* the quest of Apollo in Bk. III, which is directly under the influence of *Paradise Lost* VIII.253 ff. "The Imagination may be compared to Adam's dream," Keats says in a letter (to Benjamin Bailey, November 22, 1817), "he awoke and found it truth." Keats was haunted by that Miltonic sequence which incorporates, of course, a structural principle of repetition.

23. *Paradise Lost* VIII.273–79.

24. Romans 1:20, one of the proof-texts for the "light of nature."

25. *Paradise Lost* VIII.283–88.

26. Ibid. 253–56.

27. VI, 389. The marriage of the People and the King, or of the Estates and the King, in the Constitution of July 1790.

28. Legouis, *The Early Life,* has pointed out that if there were soldiers at the monastery at this time they could only have been paying a domiciliary visit and were not expelling anyone. See also Moorman, *Wordsworth,* pp. 136–37.

29. "This substance by which mortal men have clothed,/Humanly clothed, the ghostliness of things / In silence visible and perpetual calm" (MS A², 1808, *Prelude*² p. 198); "which so long / Had bodied forth the ghostliness of things / In silence visible and perpetual calm" (1850, VI.427–29).

30. Hart Crane, "Praise for an Urn."

31. The question as to whether the Snowdon excursion took place in 1791 or 1793 remains unanswered, though much evidence points to the former date. For most matters of chronology I depend on the information provided by De Selincourt and Darbishire in *Prelude*².

32. See his attempts to achieve a precise understanding in the variant texts, *Prelude*², pp. 482 f. and 622 f.

The Prelude and The Recluse

Wordsworth's Long Journey Home

M. H. ABRAMS

◆　◆　◆

IN THE "PROSPECTUS" to his intended masterwork, *The Recluse,*
Wordsworth announces that his "high argument" will be the capacity
of the mind of man, "When wedded to this goodly universe / In love and
holy passion," to transform the world into a paradise which will be "A
simple produce of the common day."[1] He then goes on to pray to the
"prophetic Spirit" that

> if with this
> I mix more lowly matter; with the thing
> Contemplated, describe the Mind and Man
> Contemplating; and who, and what he was—
> The transitory Being that beheld
> This Vision; when and where, and how he lived;—
> Be not this labour useless.

In this way Wordsworth designated and justified the personal narrative
which makes up the opening book of *The Recluse* he called *Home at Grasmere,*
as well as the entire poem that his wife later named *The Prelude.* Wordsworth
described the latter work as a "tributary" and also "as a sort of portico to

the Recluse, part of the same building."[2] The time taken to compose *The Prelude* straddled the writing of the Prospectus, and the completed work was conceived as an integral part of the overall structure whose "design and scope" Wordsworth specified in that poetic manifesto. "The Poem on the growth of your own mind," as Coleridge recalled the plan in 1815, "was as the ground-plat and the Roots, out of which the Recluse was to have sprung up as the Tree"—two distinct works, but forming "one compleat Whole."[3] The role of *The Prelude,* as Wordsworth himself describes his grand design, is to recount the circumstances and mental growth of a "transitory Being," culminating in his achievement of a "Vision" and in the recognition that his mission is to impart the vision in the public and enduring form of an unprecedented kind of poem:

> Possessions have I that are solely mine,
> Something within which yet is shared by none . . .
> I would impart it, I would spread it wide,
> Immortal in the world which is to come.[4]

The Idea of The Prelude

In this era of constant and drastic experimentation with literary materials and forms, it is easy to overlook the radical novelty of *The Prelude* when it was completed in 1805. The poem amply justified Wordsworth's claim to have demonstrated original genius, which he defined as "the introduction of a new element into the intellectual universe" of which the "infallible sign is the widening the sphere of human sensibility."[5]

The Prelude is a fully developed poetic equivalent of two portentous innovations in prose fiction, of which the earliest examples had appeared in Germany only a decade or so before Wordsworth began writing his poem: the *Bildungsroman* (Wordsworth called *The Prelude* a poem on "the growth of my own mind") and the *Künstlerroman* (Wordsworth also spoke of it as "a poem on my own poetical education," and it far surpassed all German examples in the detail with which his "history," as he said, was specifically "of a *Poet's* mind").[6] The whole poem is written as a sustained address to Coleridge—"I speak bare truth / As if alone to thee in private talk" (X, 372–3); Coleridge, however, is an auditor *in absentia,* and the solitary author often supplements this form with an interior monologue, or else carries on an extended colloquy with the landscape in which the interlocutors are "my mind" and "the speaking face of earth and heaven" (V, 11–12).

The construction of *The Prelude* is radically achronological, starting not at the beginning, but at the end—during Wordsworth's walk to "the Vale that I had chosen" (I, 100), which telescopes the circumstances of two or more occasions but refers primarily to his walk to the Vale of Grasmere, that "hermitage" (I, 115) where he has taken up residence at that stage of his life with which the poem concludes.[7] During this walk an outer breeze, "the sweet breath of Heaven," evokes within the poet "a corresponding mild creative breeze," a prophetic *spiritus* or inspiration which assures him of his poetic mission and, though it is fitful, eventually leads to his undertaking *The Prelude* itself; in the course of the poem, at times of imaginative dryness, the revivifying wind recurs in the role of a poetic leitmotif.[8]

Wordsworth does not tell his life as a simple narrative in past time but as the present remembrance of things past, in which forms and sensations "throw back our life" (I, 660–1) and evoke the former self, which coexists with the altered present self in a multiple awareness that Wordsworth calls "two consciousnesses." There is a wide "vacancy" between the I now and the I then,

> Which yet have such self-presence in my mind
> That, sometimes, when I think of them, I seem
> Two consciousnesses, conscious of myself
> And of some other Being.
>
> (II, 27–33)

The poet is aware of the near impossibility of disengaging "the naked recollection of that time" from the intrusions of "after-meditation" (III, 644–8). In a fine and subtle figure for the interdiffusion of the two conciousnesses (IV, 247–64), he describes himself as one bending from a drifting boat on a still water, perplexed to distinguish actual objects at the bottom of the lake from surface reflections of the environing scene, from the tricks and refractions of the water currents, and from his own intrusive but inescapable image (that is, his present awareness). Thus "incumbent o'er the surface of past time" the poet, seeking the elements of continuity between his two disparate selves, conducts a persistent exploration of the nature and significance of memory, of his power to sustain freshness of sensation and his "first creative sensibility" against the deadening effect of habit and analysis, and of manifestations of the enduring and the eternal within the realm of change and time. Only intermittently does the narrative order coincide with the order of actual occurrence. Instead Wordsworth proceeds by sometimes bewildering ellipses, fusions, and as he says, "motions retrograde" in time (IX, 8).

Scholars have long been aware that it is perilous to rely on the factual validity of *The Prelude,* and in consequence Wordsworth has been charged with intellectual uncertainty, artistic ineptitude, bad memory, or even bad faith. The poem has suffered because we know so much about the process of its composition between 1798 and 1805—its evolution from a constituent part to a "tail-piece" to a "portico" of *The Recluse,* and Wordsworth's late decision to add to the beginning and end of the poem the excluded middle: his experiences in London and in France. A work is to be judged, however, as a finished and free-standing product; and in *The Prelude* as it emerged after six years of working and reworking, the major alterations and dis-locations of the events of Wordsworth's life are imposed deliberately, in order that the design inherent in that life, which has become apparent only to his mature awareness, may stand revealed as a principle which was invisibly operative from the beginning. A supervising idea, in other words, controls Wordsworth's account and shapes it into a structure in which the protagonist is put forward as one who has been elected to play a special role in a providential plot. As Wordsworth said in the opening passage, which represents him after he has reached maturity: in response to the quickening outer breeze

> to the open fields I told
> A prophecy: poetic numbers came
> Spontaneously, and cloth'd in priestly robe
> My spirit, thus singled out, as it might seem,
> For holy services.
>
> (I, 59–63)

Hence in this history of a poet's mind the poet is indeed the "transitory Being," William Wordsworth, but he is also the exemplary poet-prophet who has been singled out, in a time "of hopes o'erthrown . . . of dereliction and dismay" (II, 448–57), to bring mankind tidings of comfort and joy; as Wordsworth put it in one version of the Prospectus,

> that my verse may live and be
> Even as a light hung up in heaven to chear
> Mankind in times to come.

The spaciousness of his chosen form allows Wordsworth to introduce some of the clutter and contingency of ordinary experience. In accordance with his controlling idea, however, he selects for extended treatment only those of his actions and experiences which are significant for his evolution toward an inherent end, and organizes his life around an event he regards as the spiritual crisis not of himself only, but of his generation: that shattering of the fierce loyalties and inordinate hopes for mankind which the liberal English—and European—intellectuals had invested in the French Revolution.

> Not in my single self alone I found,
> But in the minds of all ingenuous Youth,
> Change and the subversion from this hour.
>
> (X, 232–4)

The Prelude, correspondingly, is ordered in three stages. There is a process of unified mental development which although at times suspended, remains a continuum; this process is shattered by a crisis of apathy and despair; but the mind then recovers an integrity which, despite admitted losses, is represented as a level higher than the initial unity, in that the mature mind possesses powers, together with an added range, depth, and sensitivity of awareness, which are the products of the critical experiences it has undergone. The discovery of this fact resolves a central problem which has been implicit throughout *The Prelude*—the problem of how to justify the human experience of pain and loss and suffering; he is now able to recognize that his life is "in the end / All gratulant if rightly understood" (XIII, 384–5).

The narrative is punctuated with recurrent illuminations, or "spots of time," and is climaxed by two major revelations. The first of these is Wordsworth's discovery of precisely what he has been born to be and to do. At Cambridge he had reached a stage of life, "an eminence," in which he had felt that he was "a chosen Son" (III, 82 ff., 169), and on a walk home from a dance during a summer dawn he had experienced an illumination that he should be, "else sinning greatly, / A dedicated Spirit" (IV, 343–4); but for what chosen, or to what dedicated, had not been specified. Now, however, the recovery from the crisis of despair after his commitment to the French Revolution comprises the insight that his destiny is not one of engagement with what is blazoned "with the pompous names / Of power and action" in "the stir / And tumult of the world," but one of withdrawal from the world of action so that he may meditate in solitude: his role in life requires not involvement, but detachment.[9] And that role is to be one of the "Poets, even as Prophets," each of whom is endowed with the power "to perceive / Something unseen before," and so to write a new kind of poetry in a new poetic style. "Of these, said I, shall be my Song; of these . . . / Will I record the praises": the ordinary world of lowly, suffering men and of commonplace or trivial things transformed into "a new world . . . fit / To be transmitted," of dignity, love, and heroic grandeur (XII, 220–379). Wordsworth's crisis, then, involved what we now call a crisis of identity, which was resolved in the discovery of "my office upon earth" (X, 921). And since the specification of this office entails the definition, in the twelfth book, of the particular innovations in poetic subjects, style, and values toward which his life had been implicitly oriented, *The Prelude* is a poem that incorporates the discovery of its own *ars poetica*.

His second revelation he achieves on a mountain top. The occasion is the ascent of Mount Snowdon, which Wordsworth, in accordance with his controlling idea, excerpts from its chronological position in his life in 1791, before the crucial experience of France, and describes in the concluding book of *The Prelude*. As he breaks through the cover of clouds the light of the moon "upon the turf / Fell like a flash," and he sees the total scene as "the perfect image of a mighty Mind" in its free and continuously creative reciprocity with its milieu, "Willing to work and to be wrought upon" and so to "create / A like existence" (XIII, 36–119). What has been revealed to Wordsworth in this symbolic landscape is the grand locus of *The Recluse* which he announced in the Prospectus, "The Mind of Man—/ My haunt, and the main region of my song," as well as the "high argument" of that poem, the union between the mind and the external world and the resulting "creation . . . which they with blended might / Accomplish." The event Wordsworth selects for the climactic revelation in *The Prelude,* then, is precisely the moment of the achievement of "this Vision" by "the transitory Being" whose life he had, in the Prospectus, undertaken to describe as an integral part of *The Recluse*.

In the course of *The Prelude* Wordsworth repeatedly drops the clue that his work has been designed to round back to its point of departure. "Not with these began / Our Song, and not with these our Song must end," he had cried after the crisis of France, invoking the "breezes and soft airs" that had blown in the "glad preamble" to his poem (XI, 1 ff. and VII, 1 ff.). As he nears the end of the song, he says that his self-discovery constitutes a religious conclusion ("The rapture of the Hallelujah sent / From all that breathes and is") which is at the same time, as he had planned from the outset, an artistic beginning:

> And now, O Friend; this history is brought
> To its appointed close: the discipline

And consummation of the Poet's mind.
                    . . . we have reach'd
The time (which was our object from the first)
When we may, not presumptuously, I hope,
Suppose my powers so far confirmed, and such
My knowledge, as to make me capable
Of building up a work that should endure.
                              (XIII, 261–78)

That work, of course, is *The Recluse,* for which *The Prelude* was designed to
serve as "portico . . . part of the same building." *The Prelude,* then, is an
involuted poem which is about its own genesis—a prelude to itself. Its
structural end is its own beginning; and its temporal beginning, as I have
pointed out, is Wordsworth's entrance upon the stage of his life at which
it ends. The conclusion goes on to specify the circular shape of the whole.
Wordsworth there asks Coleridge to "Call back to mind / The mood in
which this Poem was begun." At that time,

                                        I rose
As if on wings, and saw beneath me stretch'd
Vast prospect of the world which I had been
And was; and hence this Song, which like a lark
I have protracted. . . .
                              (XIII, 370–81)

This song, describing the prospect of his life which had been made visible
to him at the opening of *The Prelude,* is *The Prelude* whose composition he is
even now concluding. . . .

The Circuitous Journey

It is time to notice that Wordsworth's account of unity achieved, lost, and
regained is held together, as various critics have remarked, by the recurrent
image of a journey: like a number of works by his contemporaries, Wordsworth's "poem on my own poetical education" converts the wayfaring
Christian of the Augustinian spiritual journey into the self-formative traveler of the Romantic educational journey. The poem in fact opens, as
Elizabeth Sewell has said, "with the poet in a prospect of wide landscape
and open sky," on a literal walk which serves as "the great over-all poetic

figure or trope of a journey which he is about to undertake."[10] In the course of this episode the aimless wanderer becomes "as a Pilgrim resolute" who takes "the road that pointed toward the chosen Vale," and at the end of the first book the road translates itself into the metaphorical way of his life's pilgrimage:

> Forthwith shall be brought down
> Through later years the story of my life.
> The road lies plain before me. . . .
>   (1850; I, 91–3, 638–40)

The Prelude is replete with "the Wanderers of the Earth" (XII, 156), and after the period of childhood, its chief episodes are Wordsworth's own wanderings through the English countryside, the Alps, Italy, France, and Wales—literal journeys through actual places which modulate easily into symbolic landscapes traversed by a metaphorical wayfarer. This organizing figure works in two dimensions. In one of these, *The Prelude* represents the life the poet narrates as a self-educative journey, "from stage to stage / Advancing," in which his early development had been "progress on the self-same path," the crisis following the French Revolution had been "a stride at once / Into another region," and the terminus was his achievement of maturity in "the discipline / And consummation of the Poet's mind."[11] In the second application, the poet repeatedly figures his own imaginative enterprise, the act of composing *The Prelude* itself, as a perilous quest through the uncharted regions of his own mind.

At times the vehicle for this latter poetic journey is a voyage at sea, connoting the wanderings of Odysseus in his search for home:

>   What avail'd,
> When Spells forbade the Voyager to land,
> The fragrance which did ever and anon
> Give notice of the Shore? . . .
> My business was upon the barren sea,
> My errand was to sail to other coasts.
>   (XI, 48–56; see I, 35–8)

Elsewhere Wordsworth's implied parallel is to Dante, who "Nell mezzo del cammin di nostra vita" had been granted a visionary journey, with a relay of guides, through hell and the earthly paradise to heaven:

> A Traveller I am,
> And all my Tale is of myself; even so,
> So be it, if the pure in heart delight
> To follow me; and Thou, O honor'd Friend!
> Who in my thoughts art ever at my side,
> Uphold, as heretofore, my fainting steps.
>
> (III, 196–201)

At the beginning of the ninth book, "as a traveller, who has gained the brow / Of some aerial Down" and "is tempted to review / The region left behind him," Wordsworth turns back to his earlier youth, before he moves reluctantly on into the discordant "argument" that begins with his residence in France—"Oh, how much unlike the past!" (1850, IX, 1–22). The eleventh book, narrating the process of Wordsworth's recovery, opens in a parallel to Milton's description of his epic journey back from hell to the realms of light (XI, 1–7; see *Paradise Lost,* III, 13–20). And through all these regions the imagined presence of Coleridge serves both as auditor and guide, heartening the exhausted poet in his pilgrimage and quest:

> Thou wilt not languish here, O Friend, for whom
> I travel in these dim uncertain ways
> Thou wilt assist me as a Pilgrim gone
> In quest of highest truth.
>
> (XI, 390–3)

The last book of *The Prelude,* in symmetry with its first book, also opens with a literal walk which translates itself into a metaphor for the climactic stage both of the journey of life and of the imaginative journey which is the poem itself. This time the walk is not a movement along an open plain but the ascent of a mountain, the traditional place for definitive visions since Moses had climbed Mount Sinai. As in Hegel's contemporary *Phenomenology* the spirit, at the close of its educational journey, recognizes itself in its other, so Wordsworth's mind, confronting nature, discovers itself in its own perfected powers:

> A meditation rose in me that night
> Upon the lonely Mountain . . .
>   and it appear'd to me
> The perfect image of a mighty Mind.

In the earliest stage of its development Wordsworth's "Babe, / Nurs'd in his Mother's arms" had not only acquired "The gravitation and the filial bond . . . that connect him with the world," but had also, as "inmate of this *active* universe," established the beginnings of the reciprocative power by which

> his mind . . .
> Creates, creator and receiver both,
> Working but in alliance with the works
> Which it beholds.—Such, verily, is the first
> Poetic spirit of our human life.
>
> (II, 265–76)

On Mount Snowdon, in an evident parallel and complement to this early passage, his mind recognizes, in that image of itself "which Nature thus / Thrusts forth upon the senses," the same power, which has now developed into "the fulness of its strength." As mist and moonlight transform the natural scene, so higher minds by a similar "Power"

> can send abroad
> Like transformation, for themselves create
> A like existence, and, whene'er it is
> Created for them, catch it by an instinct . . .
> Willing to work and to be wrought upon

by the works they behold. An essential alteration, however, is that the mature poetic mind, whose infant perception had been a state of undifferentiated consciousness, has acquired self-consciousness, and is able to sustain the sense of its own identity as an individuation-in-unison with the objects it perceives. In Wordsworth's terse rendering,

> hence the highest bliss
> That can be known is theirs, the consciousness
> Of whom they are habitually infused
> Through every image, and through every thought,
> And all impressions.
>
> (XIII, 84–111)

I have remarked that *The Prelude* has a circular organization. This circularity of its form, we now see, reflects the circularity of its subject matter.

In the opening passage of *The Prelude* the narrator is confirmed in his vocation as a poet-prophet and, in response to an impulse from the autumnal
wood, chooses as his goal "a known Vale, whither my feet should turn,"
in the assurance "of some work of glory there forthwith to be begun."
"Keen as a Truant or a Fugitive, / But as a Pilgrim resolute," and also (in
a complementary pedestrian metaphor) "like a home-bound labourer," he
then pursued his way until a three days' walk "brought me to my hermitage" (1850; I, 71–80, 90–107). At the end of *The Prelude* Wordsworth,
having taken up his "permanent abode" (XIII, 338) in this hermitage, calls
"back to mind" the occasion of its beginning. But *The Prelude* has a complex
function, for it is designed not only as a poem in itself, but also as a
"portico" to *The Recluse*. The spiritual journey thus circles back at its conclusion to the literal journey with which it had originated; but this beginning at once turns over into the opening book of Wordsworth's "work of
glory," *The Recluse* proper, which describes his way of life in the chosen
vale.[12] Only now does he identify the aspect of the vale which had all along
made it the goal of his tortuous literal, spiritual, and poetic journey. That
goal, as in all the ancient genre of the circuitous pilgrimage of life, is
home—*Home at Grasmere*.

The initial passage of *Home at Grasmere* makes it clear that the place to
which the poet has returned is not his literal home but one which, on his
first overview of the "Vale below" when, solitary, he had chanced across
it as "a roving School-boy," he had recognized to be his spiritual home.
"Perfect was the Spot . . . stirring to the Spirit"; and he had immediately
felt that "here / Must be his Home, this Valley be his World." Throughout
his youth the vale had lingered in memory, "shedding upon joy / A
brighter joy," and now the home of his imagining has become his actual
home (the word reverberates through the opening passage):

> And now 'tis mine, perchance for life, dear Vale,
> Beloved Grasmere (let the Wandering Streams
> Take up, the cloud-capt hills repeat, the Name),
> One of thy lowly Dwellings is my Home.
>   (1–59)

The place in which, "on Nature's invitation" (line 71), Wordsworth's
literal and metaphoric wanderings have terminated is identified, after the
venerable formula of the Christian quest, as a home which is also a recovered paradise. In his Pisgah-sight of it as a schoolboy he had looked
upon it as a "paradise before him" (line 14); and it remains, after he takes

up his abode in it, an "earthly counterpart" of heaven (line 642), which he describes in terms echoing Milton's description of the Garden of Eden, and in which Wordsworth and Dorothy, "A solitary pair" (line 255) are somewhat incongruously the Adam and Eve. The journey to this ultimate stage has taken him through "the realities of life so cold," but this had been a fortunate fall into experience, for "the cost" of what he has lost from the earlier stage of his life is greatly outweighed by "what I keep, have gain'd / Shall gain," so that

> in my day of Childhood I was less
> The mind of Nature, less, take all in all,
> Whatever may be lost, than I am now.

For him, man's ancient dream of felicity has been brought down from a transcendent heaven and located in this very world—

>   the distant thought
> Is fetch'd out of the heaven in which it was.
> The unappropriated bliss hath found
> An owner, and that owner I am he.
> The Lord of this enjoyment is on Earth
> And in my breast.[13]

Here he dwells, therefore, as a second and more fortunate Adam, because unlike his predecessor he possesses an Eden which has been gained:

> The boon is absolute; surpassing grace
> To me hath been vouchsafed; among the bowers
> Of blissful Eden this was neither given,
> Nor could be given, possession of the good
> Which had been sighed for, ancient thought fulfilled
> And dear Imaginations realized
> Up to their highest measure, yea and more.[14]

As in comparable passages in Hölderlin and Novalis (in Blake the parallel is more with Beulah than with the New Jerusalem), all the natural scene becomes alive, human, and feminine, and encloses the poet in an embrace of love:

> Embrace me then, ye Hills, and close me in. . . .
> But I would call thee beautiful, for mild
> And soft, and gay, and beautiful thou art,
> Dear Valley, having in thy face a smile
> Though peaceful, full of gladness.
>
> (ll. 110–7)

And when the solitary pair had first entered this valley together in the winter season, its elements had addressed them as fellow beings:

> "What would ye," said the shower,
> "Wild Wanderers, whither through my dark domain?"
> The sunbeam said, "be happy." When this Vale
> We entered, bright and solemn was the sky
> That faced us with a passionate welcoming,
> And led us to our threshold

—a threshold that in an earlier version of the text had been that of "a home / Within a home, which was to be" (ll. 168–73, and n.).

This terminus of all the poet's journeyings is not only home and paradise, but also a recovered unity and wholeness which he had experienced nowhere else except "as it found its way into my heart / In childhood"; for this "blended holiness of earth and sky" is

> A termination, and a last retreat,
> A Centre, come from wheresoe'er you will,
> A Whole without dependence or defect,
> Made for itself; and happy in itself,
> Perfect Contentment, Unity entire.
>
> (ll. 135–51)

And only here does he find a human community. Man "truly is alone" only in the "vast Metropolis," where he is "doomed / To hold a vacant commerce . . . / With objects wanting life, repelling love," and where "neighbourhood serves rather to divide / Than to unite." In this rural place, however, all is on a human scale, a multeity-in-unity in which individuality is preserved in a society which is a family writ large, and which finds itself thoroughly at home in its natural milieu.

> Society is here
> A true Community, a genuine frame
> Of many into one incorporate. . . .
> One household, under God, for high and low,
> One family, and one mansion. . . .
>   possesors undisturbed
> Of this Recess. . . . their glorious Dwelling-place.
>
>   (ll. 592–624)

The poet's spiritual home, however, remains ineluctably a paradise of this earth, for in the vale man differs "but little from the Man elsewhere" and exhibits the common qualities of "selfishness, and envy, and revenge, . . . / Flattery and double-dealing, strife and wrong" (ll. 347–57). But, he asks, is there not a strain of words that shall be "the acknowledged voice of life," and so speak "of solid good / And real evil" in a higher poetic harmony than that of the unalloyed pastoral fantasy—

> More grateful, more harmonious than the breath,
> The idle breath of softest pipe attuned
> To pastoral fancies?
>
>   (ll. 401–9)

For this poetry of real life he dismisses the poetry of wish-fulfillment, "All Arcadian dreams / All golden fancies of the golden Age" engendered by man's "wish to part / With all remembrance of a jarring world" (ll. 625–32). Confident of "an internal brightness," he assumes "his office" as a mature artist and announces his manifesto: in this "peaceful Vale . . . / A Voice shall speak, and what will be the Theme?" (ll. 660–90, 751–3).

Home at Grasmere concludes with the answer to this question, in the passage Wordsworth later excerpted to serve as the Prospectus to the subject and argument of *The Recluse* and all its related poems. This statement in fact epitomizes, and proclaims as valid for other men, what the poet himself has learned from the long and arduous journey of his life that has just terminated in Grasmere Vale. The subject, he tells us, will incorporate the poetic narrative of that life itself, in the account of "the transitory Being" who had beheld the "Vision" which constituted his poetic credential, and which it was his unique mission to impart. This vision is of "the Mind of Man," through which he will undertake a poetic journey that must ascend higher than Milton's heaven and sink deeper than Milton's hell. Of this audacious poetic enterprise it will be the high argument that we can re-create the experienced world, and that this new world, despite the inescapable fact of evil and anguish—no less evident in the solitude of "fields and groves" than when they are "barricadoed . . . / Within the walls of cities"—will provide a sufficient paradise to which we have immediate access. Here we return to Wordsworth's figure for an imaginative apocalypse that will restore paradise, taken from the vision of the marriage of the Lamb in the biblical Apocalypse and adapted to his naturalistic premises of mind and its relations to nature. Only let a man succeed in restoring his lost integrity, by consummating a marital union between his mind and a nature which, to the sensual in their sleep of death, has become a severed and alien reality, and he shall find "Paradise, and groves Elysian, . . . A simple produce of the common day."

Notes

1. Wordsworth excerpted the verse passage that he called "a kind of Prospectus of the design and scope" of *The Recluse* from the conclusion to *Home at Grasmere* and printed it in his Preface to *The Excursion* (1814). For the manuscript drafts, composed probably between 1800 and 1806, see M. H. Abrams, *Natural Supernaturalism* (New York, 1971), app.

2. To DeQuincey, 6 March 1804, *Letters: The Early Years* (2d ed.; Oxford, 1967), p. 454; to Beaumont, 3 June 1805, p. 594.

3. To Wordsworth, 30 May 1815, *Collected Letters* (Oxford, 1956–9), 4, 573.

4. *Home at Grasmere*, 11. 686–91, preceding the prospectus.

5. "Essay, Supplementary to the Preface of 1815."

6. *Letters: The Early Years*, p. 518, Isabella Fenwick note to "There Was a Boy," and *The Prelude*, XIII, 408. (All references are to *The Prelude* of 1805, unless indicated by the date "1850.")

7. For convincing evidence that the chief prototype of the walk described in the "preamble" to *The Prelude* was Wordsworth's walk to Grasmere, see John Finch, "Wordsworth's Two-Handed Engine," *Bicentenary Wordsworth Studies*, ed. Jonathan Wordsworth (Ithaca, N.Y., 1970). But Wordsworth probably telescoped events from several walks in real life, to make the "preamble" to *The Prelude* a typological change of venue, signifying a new stage in his spiritual history).

8. E.g., VII, 1–56; XI, 1–12.

9. *The Prelude*, XII, 44–76, 112–16. Cf. *Home at Grasmere*, II. 664–752.

10. *The Orphic Voice: Poetry and Natural History* (New Haven, 1960), pp. 338–9.

11. *The Prelude*, XI, 43–4; X, 239–42; XIII, 270–1.

12. As de Selincourt points out (*Wordsworth's Poetical Works*, V, 365), the opening

book of *The Recluse* "is in fact a continuation of his poetical autobiography from the place where *The Prelude* leaves off." This place, as we have seen, is also the place from which *The Prelude* has set out.

13. Lines 60 ff., MS variant, *Poetical Works*, V, 315–16.

14. Lines 103–9. As late as in a poem of 1811 Wordsworth parallels his "Departure from the Vale of Grasmere" to that of a tenant of "Elysian plains" or of "celestial Paradise," whom it might please to absent himself from felicity long enough to take a round trip to a lower realm.

> O pleasant transit, Grasmere! to resign
> Such happy fields, abodes so calm as thine . . .
> Ne'er can the way be irksome or forlorn
> That winds into itself for sweet return.
>
> (*Poetical Works*, III, 64)

The Image of a Mighty Mind (*1805,* Book 13)

JONATHAN WORDSWORTH

◆　◆　◆

> The secret Strength of things
> Which governs thought, and to the infinite dome
> Of heaven is as a law, inhabits thee.
> And what were thou, and earth, and stars, and sea,
> If to the human mind's imaginings
> Silence and solitude were vacancy?
>
> Shelley, *Mont Blanc*

THE CLIMBING OF SNOWDON

It was a summer's night, a close warm night,   10
Wan, dull, and glaring, with a dripping mist
Low-hung and thick that covered all the sky,
Half threatening storm and rain; but on we went
Unchecked, being full of heart and having faith
In our tried pilot. Little could we see,   15
Hemmed round on every side with fog and damp,
And, after ordinary travellers' chat
With our conductor, silently we sunk
Each into commerce with his private thoughts.
Thus did we breast the ascent, and by myself   20
Was nothing either seen or heard the while
Which took me from my musings, save that once
The shepherd's cur did to his own great joy
Unearth a hedgehog in the mountain-crags,
Round which he made a barking turbulent.   25
This small adventure—for even such it seemed

In that wild place and at the dead of night—
Being over and forgotten, on we wound
In silence as before. With forehead bent
Earthward, as if in opposition set   30
Against an enemy, I panted up
With eager pace, and no less eager thoughts.
Thus might we wear perhaps an hour away,
Ascending at loose distance each from each,
And I, as chanced, the foremost of the band—   35
When at my feet the ground appeared to brighten,
And with a step or two seemed brighter still;
Nor had I time to ask the cause of this,
For instantly a light upon the turf
Fell like a flash. I looked about, and lo,   40
The moon stood naked in the heavens at height
Immense above my head, and on the shore
I found myself of a huge sea of mist,
Which meek and silent rested at my feet.
A hundred hills their dusky backs upheaved   45
All over this still ocean, and beyond,
Far, far beyond, the vapours shot themselves
In headlands, tongues, and promontory shapes,
Into the sea, the real sea, that seemed
To dwindle and give up its majesty,   50
Usurped upon as far as sight could reach.
Meanwhile, the moon looked down upon this shew
In single glory, and we stood, the mist
Touching our very feet; and from the shore
At distance not the third part of a mile   55
Was a blue chasm, a fracture in the vapour,
A deep and gloomy breathing-place through which
Mounted the roar of waters, torrents, streams
Innumerable, roaring with one voice.
The universal spectacle throughout   60
Was shaped for admiration and delight,
Grand in itself alone, but in that breach
Through which the homeless voice of waters rose,
That dark deep thoroughfare, had Nature lodged
The soul, the imagination of the whole.   65

A meditation rose in me that night
Upon the lonely mountain when the scene
Had passed away, and it appeared to me
The perfect image of a mighty mind,
Of one that feeds upon infinity,   70
That is exalted by an under-presence,
The sense of God, or whatsoe'er is dim
Or vast in its own being—above all,
One function of such mind had Nature there
Exhibited by putting forth, and that   75
With circumstance most awful and sublime:
That domination which she oftentimes
Exerts upon the outward face of things,
So moulds them, and endues, abstracts, combines,
Or by abrupt and unhabitual influence   80
Doth make one object so impress itself
Upon all others, and pervade them so,
That even the grossest minds must see and hear,
And cannot chuse but feel. The power which these
Acknowledge when thus moved, which Nature thus   85
Thrusts forth upon the senses, is the express
Resemblance—in the fulness of its strength
Made visible—a genuine counterpart
And brother of the glorious faculty
Which higher minds bear with them as their own.   90
(*1805*, XIII, 10–90)

'A meditation rose in me *that* night / Upon the lonely mountain . . . '
(II. 66–7), writes the poet; but the claim should not be taken as a statement
of fact. Wordsworth climbed Snowdon with Robert Jones in the summer
of 1791, and whatever else he was thinking about, it is not likely to have
been the creative imagination. It was only by a gradual process that the
scene came to have its later implications. Wordsworth himself had to learn
to see in Wordsworthian terms. His first attempts at landscape are as far
from the great poetry of *The Prelude* as the dying woman and her babes of
An Evening Walk are from Margaret of *The Ruined Cottage*. In each case the
failure of the early poetry can be blamed on the poet's idiom, but one
suspects that Wordsworth at the age of twenty did not in fact feel very

strongly either about landscape or about suffering—that the development of response brought with it the ability to create an appropriate medium.

Of Wordsworth's immediate impressions on Snowdon nothing is known; but certain deductions can be made from comparing his first account of the scene, in *Descriptive Sketches* of summer 1792, with the stanza of Beattie's *Minstrel* that is his literary source:

1793 DESCRIPTIVE SKETCHES, 492–511

'Tis morn—with gold the verdant mountain glows;
More high, the snowy peaks with hues of rose.
Far stretched beneath the many-tinted hills,
A mighty waste of mist the valley fills,
A solemn sea, whose vales and mountains round
Stand motionless, to awful silence bound.
A gulf of gloomy blue, that opens wide
And bottomless, divides the midway tide;
Like leaning masts of stranded ships appear
The pines that near the coast their summits rear;
Of cabins, woods, and lawns a pleasant shore
Bounds calm and clear the chaos still and hoar.
Loud through that midway gulf ascending, sound
Unnumbered streams with hollow roar profound:
Mounts through the nearer mist the chaunt of birds,
And talking voices, and the low of herds,
The bark of dogs, the drowsy tinkling bell,
And wild-wood mountain lutes of saddest swell.
Think not, suspended from the cliff on high,
He looks below with undelighted eye.

THE MINSTREL, PART 7, ST. 23

And oft the craggy cliff he loved to climb,
When all in mist the world below was lost.
What dreadful pleasure, there to stand sublime,
Like shipwrecked mariner on desert coast,
And view th'enormous waste of vapour, tost
In billows, lengthening to th'horizon round,
Now scooped in gulfs, with mountains now embossed—
And hear the voice of mirth and song rebound,
Flocks, herds, and waterfalls, along the hoar profound![1]

The extent to which the first passage derives from the second is very surprising. Situation and setting, diction and imagery, are contentedly taken over. Resemblances go beyond paraphrase ('mighty waste of mist' / 'enormous waste of vapour') to presumably unconscious repetition of sound ('with hollow roar profound'; 'along the hoar profound'). Even where Wordsworth adds a new detail—the pines on the edge of the mist, for instance—he does so in terms of the earlier poem: 'Like leaning masts of stranded ships appear / The pines that near the coast'; 'Like shipwrecked mariner on desert coast'.

To compose his picturesque scene Wordsworth, one feels, hardly needed to go near a mountain, let alone have a specific occasion in mind. And yet there is one element in his description that does suggest personal experience—the 'gulf of gloomy blue' that is to become the 'deep and gloomy breathing-place' of *The Prelude*. As usual, there is a hint from Beattie ('Now *scooped in gulfs,* with mountains now embossed'), but it is no warrant for the way this particular rift is singled out:

> A mighty waste of mist the valley fills,
> A solemn sea, whose vales and mountains round
> Stand motionless, to awful silence bound.
> A gulf of gloomy blue, that opens wide
> And bottomless, divides the midway tide . . .
> Loud through that midway gulf ascending, sound
> Unnumbered streams with hollow roar profound . . .

It is possible that the 'Unnumbered streams' derive from a passage in James Clarke's *Survey of the Lakes* (1787), which seems to have produced Wordsworth's 'chaunt of birds' and the 'talking voices' that rise through the mist.[2] But if this is so, it is interesting that the poet deliberately contradicted Clarke's central point:

> About half way up the mountain, or not quite so high, you will be above the mist, which lyes thick and white below . . . *the voice of extremely distant waterfalls is heard perfectly distinct, and not one confusing another.* The loud crowing cock at every cottage, joined to the warbling of the smaller-feathered choir, comes with an almost magical sweetness to the ear . . . *every sound is much more distinctly heard than at any other time.* The words of men conversing at two miles distance are perfectly intelligible.[3]

For Clarke, who incidentally quotes Beattie's stanza, every sound is distinct: for Wordsworth the nearer, domestic ones are, but not those heard through the gloomy midway gulf. Wordsworth does not seem to have singled the rift out for any special purpose—it is not yet 'The soul, the imagination of the whole'—but already it is there, set apart from the cabins, woods, and lawns of the 'pleasant shore', its 'hollow roar profound' distinguished from the cosy rural noises.[4]

Wordsworth wrote no landscape poetry, at least as such, for five and a half years between the summer of 1792 and the end of 1797. There are the heightened descriptions that form the backgrounds of *Salisbury Plain* and *The Borderers,* and there is the far more important natural setting of *The Ruined Cottage,* but not until the beginning of 1798 at Alfoxden does the poet go back to writing about his personal response to Nature. Then, prompted by the entry in his sister's *Journal* for 25 January, he composes *A Night-Piece.* Like *The Discharged Soldier,* with which it is closely connected (and *In storm and tempest,* which is perhaps a week or two later), the poem shows Wordsworth's border intuitions in the moment just before his 'obscure sense of possible sublimity' is exchanged for pantheist communion:

> The sky is overspread
> With a close veil of one continuous cloud
> All whitened by the moon, that just appears,
> A dim-seen orb, yet chequers not the ground
> With any shadow—plant, or tower, or tree.
> At last a pleasant instantaneous light
> Startles the musing man whose eyes are bent
> To earth. He looks around, the clouds are split
> Asunder, and above his head he views
> The clear moon and the glory of the heavens.
> There in a black-blue vault she sails along
> Followed by multitudes of stars, that small,
> And bright, and sharp, along the gloomy vault
> Drive as she drives. How fast they wheel away!—
> Yet vanish not. The wind is in the trees;
> But they are silent.[5]

In its details, and in the quality of personal response, the poetry is very close to Dorothy's prose:

> The sky spread over with one continuous cloud, whitened by the light of the moon, which, though her dim shape was seen, did not throw forth so strong a light as to chequer the earth with shadows. At once

the clouds seemed to cleave asunder, and left her in the centre of a black-blue vault. She sailed along, followed by multitudes of stars, small, and bright, and sharp. Their brightness seemed concentrated (half-moon).

A matter of weeks later Wordsworth was to write of the Pedlar's universe of blessedness and joy,

> The clouds were touched,
> And in their silent faces did he read
> Unutterable love . . .
>   (*Pedlar*, 99–101)

but at this point feeling is not yet identified with perception of the One Life. In a sense the landscape is alive, but it is noticeable that Wordsworth's animist description of the moon comes almost verbatim from Dorothy. It was the level of response to Nature, identification with her, that the two shared; though in Wordsworth's greatest poetry it is not much more than the surface.

But, early and indebted as it is, the *Night-Piece* does have certain touches that go beyond Dorothy's sensitive yet limited vision. The penseroso, whose presence is itself a hint of border perceptions, sees not just the clear moon but 'the glory of the heavens'; and though taking over Dorothy's very precise observation of the stars as 'small and bright and sharp', Wordsworth adds the numinous detail of their silence—a silence heightened by the border possibilities of the wind in the trees. Like the nonexistent steps 'Almost as silent as the turf they trod', the stars could not logically make a noise; their silence is an extension of the poetry beyond description and into the mind. As Kenneth Johnston has enviably said,

> The cumulative effect of all these details is to intimate, almost invisibly, the *conjunctive* character of the vision. A man suddenly discovers himself to be standing between heaven and earth, standing, moreover, as a link between them. The traveller does not simply apprehend or suffer this dualism, he *is* the dualism—without him it does not exist. The two spheres are brought together not so much by, as in, man; recognizing his mediate position, he defines his being.[6]

To some extent (as Professor Johnston is aware) this interpretation depends on reading backwards from later accounts of visionary experience. The difference between *A Night-Piece* and the Climbing of Snowdon is that in 1804–5 Wordsworth had fully understood, and was consciously portraying, the border condition which in February 1798, though certainly to be implied from the poetry, had yet to be thought out.[7]

There was presumably nothing in Wordsworth's actual memories of Snowdon in 1791 impressive enough to be useful in building up towards his account of the blue chasm; when looking for additional material he remembered the 'pleasant instantaneous light' seen at Alfoxden, and the *Prelude* lines combine the two quite separate experiences.[8] His purpose as he begins the Climbing of Snowdon is to create in the reader a sense of expectancy, and show in his former self a withdrawal into the state of mind in which the expected surprise can have its fullest effect. The poetry works through a series of contrasts between the poet's situation and what goes on about him. At first he is part of a group, undaunted like the others by the discomfort of the close night and dripping mist, and capable of 'ordinary travellers' chat'; but this normal responsiveness to the outside world is then removed. Surrounded by mist and silence, in commerce only with his own private thoughts, the poet is clearly ready to be startled; but Wordsworth is not yet ready to startle him. At this stage the unearthing of the hedgehog is introduced by way of a deliberate non-adventure, its unimportance emphasized by the grandiloquence of 'barking turbulent' and the levity of Wordsworth's use of 'joy':

> The shepherd's cur did to his own great joy
> Unearth a hedgehog in the mountain-crags,
> Round which he made a barking turbulent.
>
> (II. 23–5)

On the face of it the episode is meant to stress the loneliness and silence in which the dog's hunting could be taken for a 'small adventure', but Wordsworth is also teasing his audience, as he does overtly in *Simon Lee* and *The Idiot Boy,* for having the wrong kind of anticipations.[9] And, as in the earlier 'spots of time', he is mocking his former self. The stolen boat in Patterdale seemed to the child 'an elfin pinnace'; the vision of the Woman on the Hill opens with a knight-errant and his trusty squire ('I mounted, and we rode towards the hills'); and here the poet—now twenty-one, not six—is seen panting up the mountain full of a slightly ridiculous eagerness, and as unaware as the child of what is really to be important. Like the 'fell destroyer' of the Woodcock-snaring, he is bent on conquest, 'as if in opposition set / Against an enemy' (II. 30–1).

There are serious reasons too for playing up the drama of the scene.

The 'pleasant instantaneous light' of *A Night-Piece* in its new context falls 'like a flash'. It is a deliberate use of shock, and carefully prepared for by anticipations that heighten the sense of expectancy without destroying the suddenness:

> at my feet the ground appeared to brighten,
> And with a step or two seemed brighter still;
> Nor had I time to ask the cause of this,
> For instantly a light upon the turf
> Fell like a flash.
>
> (ll. 36–40)

Despite the context one is startled into assuming that something dramatic, even supernatural, is about to happen. It isn't, of course; this is a Wordsworthian adventure. What follows is some of the greatest poetry he ever wrote:

> I looked about, and lo,
> The moon stood naked in the heavens at height
> Immense above my head, and on the shore
> I found myself of a huge sea of mist,
> Which meek and silent rested at my feet.
> A hundred hills their dusky backs upheaved
> All over this still ocean, and beyond,
> Far, far beyond, the vapours shot themselves
> In headlands, tongues, and promontory shapes,
> Into the sea, the real sea, that seemed
> To dwindle and give up its majesty,
> Usurped upon as far as sight could reach.
> Meanwhile, the moon looked down upon this shew
> In single glory, and we stood, the mist
> Touching our very feet...
>
> (ll. 40–54)

Once more we have a landscape that is alive, but its animism is some way from the fairly simple pathetic fallacy of the *Night-Piece* and the moon that sails along followed by attendant multitudes of stars. Nor, of course, should the passage be read in terms of the slightly later Alfoxden poetry of the One Life: 'The clouds were touched ...'. It is not difficult to see how the Snowdon landscape could have been described in these terms. In place of the animism would have been a consciousness of the pervasive, life-giving presence of God; the moon, the mist, and the mind of the onlooking poet would have shared and reflected equally the blessedness of love. But this is 1804 not 1798. Perhaps there is still an element of pathetic fallacy in the moon's looking down upon the shew in single glory, though Wordsworth's identification with her as spectator and solitary gives her a new and positive role.[10] The meek and silent mist has life of quite a different kind. Oddly, though they had all made the standard comparison with the sea, neither Beattie and Clarke, nor Wordsworth himself in *Descriptive Sketches*, had treated the mist as alive. By making this extension in the Climbing of Snowdon, Wordsworth—half-consciously, perhaps—introduce a border potential, creates the sense of latent power that was lacking in the static, pictorial earlier descriptions. The landscape is at rest, but it is the rest of suppressed activity. For the moment all may be still, but the ocean is composed of a hundred hills, 'their dusky backs *upheaved*', of vapours that may again shoot into new 'headlands, tongues, and promontory shapes'. And yet not everything is animated: *hills* and dusky backs are juxtaposed, *headlands* and tongues. The whole situation is fluid. There is a fusion of different states, a possibility of change and interchange that Wordsworth exploits as the figurative sea usurps upon the real.

It is with the blue chasm that one becomes aware of transcendental associations in the landscape of Snowdon. Wordsworth is drawing partly on his own earlier description, partly on recollections of *Kubla Khan,* but the poetry he writes is very different from either:

> and from the shore
> At distance not the third part of a mile
> Was a blue chasm, a fracture in the vapour,
> A deep and gloomy breathing-place through which
> Mounted the roar of waters, torrents, streams
> Innumerable, roaring with one voice.
> The universal spectacle throughout
> Was shaped for admiration and delight,
> Grand in itself alone, but in that breach
> Through which the homeless voice of waters rose,
> That dark deep thoroughfare, had Nature lodged
> The soul, the imagination of the whole.
>
> (ll. 54–65)

The passage falls clearly in two, the casual opening of each half giving special emphasis to the chasm and its implications. There is a sense of Wordsworth building up to his full rhetorical power ('waters, torrents, streams / Innumerable') then deliberately checking himself and lowering the tone ('The universal spectacle throughout . . . ') so as to be sure that he is carrying the reader with him. The poetry is so good that one does not for a moment doubt that some great assertion is being made. And yet, as so often when Wordsworth is writing at his best, there is a disparity between what one takes to be there, and what is actually claimed. Though one may not read it as such, 'The soul, the imagination of the whole' is as clearly metaphor as are the *roaring* streams and the 'dusky backs' *upheaved* in the mist. The 'gulf of gloomy blue' from *Descriptive Sketches* is shown now as the centre of a humanized universe, just as in the Simplon Pass the disparate elements are drawn together by analogy of the features of a face or thoughts in a single mind. But *en route* the analogies make their own claims—and they make them more powerfully for being metaphor rather than simile. Simile must to some extent restrict association, tie it down. However grand the language of the Simplon Pass, however compelling its rhythms, one is conscious that the 'tumult and peace' are merely '*like* workings of one mind', *like* 'The types and symbols of eternity' (VI, 568, 571). The underlying implication can never become dominant, the figurative never entirely displace the real. In the Climbing of Snowdon, by contrast, Nature positively *lodges* 'The soul, the imagination' in the cloud rift, and one takes the statement with an absurd literalness. Indeed one tends to go *beyond* the literal implications of Wordsworth's lines. Despite the controlling presence of Nature, one reacts to the chasm as if it were itself a power at the centre of the landscape.

It may be worth going back to examine the passage quoted in greater detail. Wordsworth's verse has a disarming straight-forwardness. His tones are those of the returned traveller—Bartram, or Barrow, perhaps.[11] The prosaic attention to detail ('not the third part of a mile') and the unexpected harshness of 'fracture', serve to emphasize the chasm's actuality, creating confidence in the narrator's authority at a moment when the poetry is moving away from its basis of fact. Important as it is, the 'deep and gloomy breathing-place' easily passes unnoticed. At the back of his mind Wordsworth seems to have Coleridge's always fanciful, now unfortunately ludicrous, simile of the chasm

> with ceaseless turmoil seething,
> As if this earth in fast thick pants were breathing . . .
> (*Kubla Khan*, 17–18)

But if he is aware of his debt, he has removed all traces of extravagance. So measured are his tones that despite the border adjectives 'deep' and 'gloomy', and the very strong border associations of breath, the 'breathing-place' remains as ordinary, and as physical, as the fracture in the vapour. What is odd is that it should be felt to be so concrete and yet not raise the question—answered easily enough on the level of Coleridge's fantasy—as to who is doing the breathing. *Kubla Khan* is at once more and less evocative: more in that the dream-world it portrays is deliberately exotic, less because the logic and the magic of a dream are dead-ends. On the one side there are 'Ancestral voices prophesying war', on the other is the noise of 'waters, torrents, streams / Innumerable', roaring with one voice that may, or may not, be transcendental. Coleridge's voices are static, caught like the figures on Keats's urn: Wordsworth's roaring streams can develop, expand—their meaning is not restricted. And yet at this point he stands back to make an aesthetic judgement that is straight out of *Kubla Khan*. 'It was a miracle of rare device', Coleridge had written, and Wordsworth catches his tones exactly:

> The universal spectacle throughout
> Was shaped for admiration and delight...
>   (ll. 60–1)

The lines are quite un-Wordsworthian, but in their context oddly impressive. Wordsworth is playing for a moment on his reader's sense of the marvellous. It is not *his* way of looking at landscape, but it adds to the total effect. He does not himself take an uninvolved view (that is left to the moon who looks down upon the 'shew'), but suggests that even for those who did there would be pleasure of a kind. But more important, Wordsworth is enabled to give to the originally rather tenderly described scene a new grandeur and universality; and at the same time to present it as an artifact—something that has been consciously 'shaped'.

The implications of 'breathing-place' had been deliberately passed over, but the shaping power Wordsworth proposes to identify. Before doing so, however, he returns to the blue chasm, emphasizing its centrality, and developing the imagery that has gone before. It is now a 'breach' (which merely takes up the word 'fracture') through which rises 'the *homeless* voice of waters'. The border effect of 'homeless' is important. At a first reading the word seems to be asking sympathy for the voice of waters, but more significant is the fact that where before Wordsworth had stressed the power and actuality of the torrents roaring through the mist, he now shows their sound as mysteriously disembodied. First the 'streams / Innumerable' merge into one noise, lose their separate identity; then this combined voice becomes detached, not only without a home, but by implication without a specific source. It is tempting to present the lines that follow as a complex and highly sophisticated use of paradox: the alternative is that they are a jumble that happens to work. 'Lodged' (stationary, by implication) within the chasm that has become a *thoroughfare,* and in some sense responsible for the voice that is *homeless,* is a power that is both soul and imagination, a part of the landscape and not a part of it, autonomous and yet subordinate. Whatever view one might take of intentionalism, it would be nice to know what Wordsworth meant in all this, and especially what he meant by the introduction of Nature, and the bracketing of soul and imagination.

It may be that as one actually reads the Climbing of Snowdon Nature makes little impression—so much is happening by this stage, and Wordsworth's rhythms are so forceful, that one is carried quickly past. But poetry does not exist solely in its immediate impact. At a closer reading her presence has the deadening effect of forcing out into the open the distinction between symbol and fact. Only if it belongs to God, or Nature, can the soul/imagination have an actual existence. If God (Nature) stands outside, there is no longer the possibility of seeing the landscape in terms of the universal mind. Even the breathing-place becomes overtly metaphor. In restrospect it cannot be the breath of God that rises through the dark deep thoroughfare, because God is seen to be an external shaping force, not an immanent presence. The chasm is deprived at a blow of the transcendental power it has come to possess. It is almost as if Wordsworth was worried that the poetry should come so near to asserting his earlier belief in the One Life, and introduced Nature to give a conventional and acceptable air.

One responds to the terms soul and imagination as radically opposed, as bringing together and momentarily equating the religious principle in man (with the implication of communion with an ultimate power outside the self) and human creativity. Wordsworth was perfectly capable of a slovenly use of language in which no such distinction would be intended. It is disconcerting, for instance, to discover his willingness in the manuscripts to cross out 'heart' and write 'soul', 'soul' and write 'mind', simply to avoid repetition. In this case, however, the equation seems to have been more considered.[12] On a surface level the two words are identified as metaphors stressing the centrality of the cloud-rift; but their connection goes beyond this mere similarity of function. The opposition and reconciliation implied has a history in Wordsworth's poetry that goes back to 1798. In *Tintern Abbey* a distinction is made (and made in the context of a transcendental presence in landscape) between what the mind *perceives* and what it half-*creates* (ll. 107–8). Wordsworth may, as his footnote claims, be thinking of Young's 'And half-create the wond'rous world they see'; but also in the background is his Racedown fragment on the River Derwent;[13] and, much more important, his treatment of perception and imaginative creation in *The Pedlar.* At this earlier period Wordsworth had presented, and presumably believed in, the One Life as fact. His conviction was distantly related (via Coleridge and Joseph Priestley) to quasi-scientific theories about the presence of God in matter; but his own speculations centred not on the form taken by the 'active principle alive / In all things' so much as on the nature of human response. At one stage in *The Pedlar* 'predominance of thought' is offered as a possible means, but for the most part the alternatives, as in *Tintern Abbey,* are straightforward perception on the one hand, and the creative imagination on the other. Wordsworth is fully aware of a logical opposition between the two, and yet seems to feel from the first that the contradiction is unreal. In the Climbing of Snowdon he has chosen to evoke the importance of the blue chasm in terms that imply a complete reconciliation. He is not, of course, talking directly about human perception at all, but his metaphors have the effect of making this extension of theme. At the start merely the description of a particular expedition, the poetry expands to take in an animist landscape, then to evoke the power lying beneath the animation, and finally to imply the kind of response that is taking place.

Wordsworth himself naturally makes no such hard and fast distinctions. As Coleridge wrote in his 1802 letter to Sotheby: 'A poet's *heart and intellect* should be *combined, intimately* combined *and unified,* with the great appearances in Nature' (Griggs, 2:864). The passage is quoted in full, and related to the Climbing of Snowdon, by Herbert Lindenberger in the second of his chapters on 'The Rhetoric of Interaction'. Much of his discussion is admirable, but there is too great an emphasis on deliberateness, method—the poetry makes 'a *radical attempt* to fuse inner and outer', Wordsworth makes '*constant endeavors* to synthesize his concepts and percepts into *dazzlingly new rhetorical formations*'[14]—and too little stress on vision, the way that Wordsworth felt things, saw into their life. Wordsworth *is* a conscious artist, *is* working with materials that he has thought about, but he is certainly *not* achieving his greatest effects through manipulation. The border implications and questionings of response come in sideways with the metaphor because their relevance is intuitively perceived, not part of the poet's considered intention. The greatness of the poetry is quite unmethodical. It can be broken down, named, for critical purposes; but in breaking it down one is seeing how it works, not how it was made. 'Dazzlingly new rhetorical formations' gives a false impression of line and images that derive their power from an instinctive and largely unrationalized union of the poet's heart and intellect with the external world. Coleridge certainly had Wordsworth in mind as he wrote, but he was evoking the nature and grandeur of his creativity, not revealing the tricks of a trade.

'A meditation rose in me *that night* | Upon the lonely mountain', writes Wordsworth. It might have been more accurate to say, as he had done in book 6, 'Imagination . . . here that power | In all the might of its endowments | Came athwart me'; but there were great advantages to be gained from claiming that this central imaginative insight of May 1805 had been his immediate reflection fourteen years before. The moments, of *The Prelude* where Wordsworth steps back to draw conclusions from his experience are not always a success, but here the reader is carried straight through from the narrative (which has itself changed in tone a number of times) into the gloss; and the gloss instead of being flat and expository is composed of poetry that brilliantly takes up the earlier terms and implications:

> A meditation rose in me that night
> Upon the lonely mountain when the scene
> Had passed away, and it appeared to me
> The perfect image of a mighty mind,
> Of one that feeds upon infinity,
> That is exalted by an under-presence,
> The sense of God, or whatsoe'er is dim
> Or vast in its own being . . .
>
> (ll. 66–73)

Though Wordsworth is now explaining things that before had been unstated, the poetry has lost none of its fluidity. The opposition between soul and imagination is beautifully taken up by the last two quoted lines, and in the spatial quality of 'under-presence', 'dim', and 'vast', one responds again to the power of the deep and gloomy breathing-place. But this is not all. The meditation is said to rise *within* the poet, well up of its own accord from those same interior depths from which had 'Mounted the roar of waters, torrents, streams | Innumerable'; and the meditation too is a sense of God, or of the godlike in man, produced by the soul | imagination. Then there are the different, and appropriately different, ways of reading 'it': 'and *it* appeared to me | The perfect image of a mighty mind'. The dominant meaning is no doubt that the cloud-rift images the mind ('image' in the primary sense still of 'picture'), but grammatically 'it' would be expected to refer back to the meditation as subject of the sentence, and that too in this interchange of meanings makes very good sense: the poet's thoughts reflect the mighty mind that is the subject of his poem, show it in the process of feeding upon infinity. Not that the mind is initially taken to *be* the poet's: at first—and again the confusion is useful, enhancing— one assumes that it is God's. It is an amazing piece of poetry, poetry adequate to this climactic moment when the epiphany that Wordsworth has kept back to be a second time his conclusion has to be shown in its relevance to his new, longer, far more complex, poem.

Among the complexities, or the complicating factors, at all stages in the poem has been the presence of Milton. Clear and undoubted echoes take the Climbing of Snowdon back to *Paradise Lost,* book 7—back, that is, to the account of Creation. Mountains that in Milton's poem

> appear
> Emergent, and their broad bare backs upheave
> Into the clouds . . .
>
> (*PL* VII, 285–7)

find themselves in *The Prelude* replaced by hills of mist, whose 'dusky backs upheaved' imply not the achievement of an original creative moment, but the sense of possible future sublimity. The poet and Jones on the edge of the mist recall two earlier figures (one could say two persons, but not in this case, two 'people') who stand similarly on the shore of a sea that is not a sea, and whose role similarly is to impose from through the power of innate creativity. As he writes, Wordsworth surely has at the back of his mind

> The King of Glory, *in his powerful Word*
> *And Spirit,* coming to create new worlds.

'On heavenly ground they stood', Milton had written,

> and from the shore
> They viewed the vast immeasurable abyss
> Outrageous as a sea, dark, wasteful, wild,
> Up from the bottom turned by furious winds
> And surging waves . . .
>
> (*PL* VII, 208–14)

Wordsworth's tones seem at first to be very different—

> and from the shore
> At distance not the third part of a mile
> Was a blue chasm . . .

—and so of course is his immediate purpose, but the 'waters, torrents, streams / Innumerable', though mounting with a single voice, have about them much of the surging energy of Chaos.[15] More surprising perhaps is that there should be affinities between Wordsworth's 'mighty mind', feeding upon the infinity of its own inner turmoil, and Milton's Holy Spirit, brooding dove-like over an external abyss. The mind, however, does not feed directly upon the dim and vast that are the ultimate sources of its strength, it subjects them first to a kind of brooding transformation:

> He had discoursed
> Like one who in the slow and silent works,
> The manifold conclusions of his thought,
> Had brooded till imagination's power
> Condensed them to a passion, whence she drew
> Herself new energies, resistless force.[16]

The condensing of thought to a passion seems closely analogous to the process by which experience becomes intensified into a 'spot of time'. In each case the mind confers upon its inchoate material a sort of pre-formal form, and then draws from its own creation strength that enables the poet consciously to become creative.[17]

The Prelude has been the image of a mighty mind, and the mist on Snowdon is presented as Nature's parallel creation. The landscape is an artifact like the poem itself, and shows in Nature 'a counterpart . . . of the glorious faculty / Which higher minds bear with them as their own'—

> That domination which she oftentimes
> Exerts upon the outward face of things . . .
>   by abrupt and unhabitual influence
> [Making] one object so impress itself
> Upon all others, and pervade them so,
> That even the grossest minds must see and hear,
> And cannot chuse but feel.
>   (XIII, 77–84)

Nature has demonstrated the role and power of the poet (and given him, incidentally, the confidence to insult the rest of us). He is at once her counterpart and her perfect audience, for higher minds

> build up greatest things
> From least suggestions, ever on the watch,
> Willing to work and to be wrought upon.
>   (XIII, 98–100)

It was this process that had been exemplified in the transformation of the statue horse to 'A borderer dwelling betwixt life and death'. Because they are fully imaginative—both perceptive and creative—the Wordsworthian elect

> need not extraordinary calls
> To rouze them—in a world of life they live,
> By sensible impressions not enthralled,
> But quickened, rouzed, and made thereby more fit
> To hold communion with the invisible world.
>   (XIII, 101–5)

'Such minds', Wordsworth concludes, 'are truly from the Deity, / For they are powers' (XIII, 106–7). The poetry of course is saying loudly and clearly, 'for *we* are powers'—'for *I* am a power'—and the egocentricity becomes still more impressive as the poet asks

> Oh, who is he that hath his whole life long
> Preserved, enlarged, this freedom in himself?
>   (XIII, 120–1)

and answers firmly, me.

For the last time in the poem the imagery of the Fall returns, as an older, sadder Wordsworth calls upon the hills and groves to witness that he for one has never colluded:

> Oh, who is he that hath his whole life long
> Preserved, enlarged, this freedom in himself?—
> For this alone is genuine liberty.
> Witness, ye solitudes, where I received
> My earliest visitations (careless then

Of what was given me), and where now I roam,
A meditative, oft a suffering man,
And yet I trust with undiminished powers;
Witness—*whatever falls my better mind,*
Revolving with the accidents of life,
May have sustained—that, howsoe'er misled,
I never in the quest of right or wrong
Did tamper with myself from private aims;
Nor was in any of my hopes the dupe
Of selfish passions; nor did wilfully
Yield ever to mean cares and low pursuits;
But rather did with jealousy shrink back
From every combination that might aid
The tendency, too potent in itself,
Of habit to enslave the mind . . .

The sentence has gone on too long, and for the poet to reach his main point it has to go on longer still—

                    I mean
Oppress it by the laws of vulgar sense,
And substitute a universe of death,
The falsest of all worlds, in place of that
Which is divine and true.
                    (XIII, 120–43)

—but though the writing is slack, what is being said is important. Once more we are told that the Fall that would have mattered has never taken place. On the populous plain of experience the poet had been caught up by Fortune's wheel, 'Revolving with the accidents of life' (and implicitly opposed to the harmonious natural round of Lucy and the skating boy); he had been tempted, and he had been misled; but he had never eaten of the tree of the knowledge of good and evil. M. H. Abrams has suggested that imagination for Wordsworth has the redemptive role of Milton's Christ, but in reading *The Prelude* one is more likely to be reminded of the poet's amazing remark in 1812 to Crabb Robinson: 'I have no need of a Redeemer' (Morley, I, 158).[18] Imagination is the power that has *at all times* enabled him to ward off the universe of death, escape at once the tyranny of the eye and the counter-spirit of language ill used.

Perhaps the achievement of the Climbing of Snowdon is finally that it brings together in a uniquely satisfying way the two aspects of imagination that have been present throughout the poem: the shaping force that is perceived as an external agency, and has been responsible for restorative— one might say, preventive—impressions upon the mind, and the power that is felt to well up from underlying sources within the individual. It is imagination in this second aspect, perfectly imaged in the mounting streams on Snowdon that roar with a single voice, which supports the poet's hope that his own work, 'Proceeding from the depth of untaught things, / Enduring and creative' may 'become / A power like one of Nature's'. Internal depth, an inner vastness where things are 'untaught' because they lie beneath, and beyond, the palimpsest layers of experience, is the guarantee of a mind that is truly 'Of substance and of fabric more divine' (XIII, 452). In its portrayal of an 'under-soul', an 'under-*presence*'—within the landscape, within the mind, within the mind of God—Snowdon enacts the ultimate border possibility. The poetry, and with it the poem as a whole, becomes a creative self-naming, a finite work that is the incarnation of man's highest aspiring, and that lays claim to permanence because it is not different in kind from 'the infinite I AM'.

Almost all these implications are fudged or removed in the text of *1850*. Wordsworth does not merely destroy one of his greatest pieces of poetry, he weakens precisely those aspects which had made it the fitting climax to his poem. To watch him in full retreat is to be reminded of the grandeur of the claims that he no longer dares to make. It is difficult to know whether it is the episode itself, or the gloss, that suffers most in revision. From the moment when the light first falls upon the turf, only half a dozen isolated lines have not been changed for the worse:

> *Nor was time given to ask or learn the cause,*
> For instantly a light upon the turf
> Fell like a flash, *and lo! as I looked up,*
> The Moon *hung* naked *in a firmament*
> *Of azure without cloud, and at my feet*
> *Rested a silent sea of hoary mist.*
> A hundred hills their dusky backs upheaved
> All over this still ocean; and beyond,
> Far, far beyond, *the solid vapours stretched,*
> In headlands, tongues, and promontary shapes,
> *Into the main Atlantic, that appeared*
> To dwindle, and give up *his* majesty,
> Usurped upon as far as sight could reach.

Not so the etherial vault; encroachment none
Was there, nor loss; only the inferior stars
Had disappeared, or shed a fainter light
In the clear presence of the full-orbed Moon,
Who, from her sovereign elevation, gazed
Upon the billowy ocean, as it lay
All meek and silent, save that through a rift—
Not distant from the shore whereon we stood,
A fixed, abysmal, gloomy breathing-place—
Mounted the roar of waters, torrents, streams
Innumerable, roaring with one voice
Heard over earth and sea, and, in that hour,
For so it seems, felt by the starry heavens.
(*1850*, XIV, 37–63; new work in italics)

The last two nebulous, safe, apologetic lines are designed to replace the now too daring implications of the earlier conclusion:

The universal spectacle throughout
Was shaped for admiration and delight,
Grand in itself alone, but in that breach
Through which the homeless voice of waters rose,
That dark deep thoroughfare, had Nature lodged
The soul, the imagination of the whole.
(*1805*, XIII, 60–5)

The cloud-rift could not be removed altogether without recasting the passage, but the voice of its 'waters, torrents, streams innumerable' is no longer permitted either the immediacy of personal experience or the transcendental associations of border poetry. It is diffused 'over earth and sea', heard by no one in particular, and cannot even be said for certain to be 'felt' by the heavens. There has been a new usurpation, in fact. The moon, always enviable to the poet as a fellow solitary ('Meanwhile the moon looked down upon this shew/In single glory') has taken over from the cloud-rift as the central focus of the landscape. It is a cosier moon now, no longer aloof, looking down upon the earth and its concerns as on a 'shew', but seen in conventional terms as queen of the night, full-orbed, and gazing from 'her sovereign elevation' amid attendants ('inferior stars') respectfully dimmed in her presence. Isolation which in *1805* had hinted at the poet's own aloofness, the distance of his vision from a norm, has been replaced by a different kind of distancing, as the poetic moon comes to represent withdrawal into the safety of convention—the world of hoary mist, firmament of azure, etherial vault, and starry heavens.

Elements of the great poetry of *1805* of course remain in Wordsworth's account of the moonscape, offering an intermittent and incongruous power that can no longer be put to a purpose. The gloss, however, is completely rewritten:

> When into air had partially dissolved
> That vision, given to spirits of the night
> And three chance human wanderers, in calm thought
> Reflected, it appeared to me the type
> Of a majestic intellect, its acts
> And its possessions, what it has and craves,
> What in itself it is, and would become.
> There I beheld the emblem of a mind
> That feeds upon infinity, that broods
> Over the dark abyss, intent to hear
> Its voices issuing forth to silent light
> In one continuous stream; a mind sustained
> By recognitions of transcendent power,
> In sense conducting to ideal form,
> In soul of more than mortal privilege.
>
> (*1850*, XIV, 63–77)

The spirits of the night must be among the most intrusive and distracting of all Wordsworth's later additions to *The Prelude*. Presumably they are there for decoration.[19] But though they have no function, they do have an effect. Comparison of *1850* and *1805* shows a dwindling in the poet's own importance that goes along with the playing down of the cloud-rift. The vision on Snowdon is given in the first place to spirits, and then, on a lower level (as the self-abasing tones imply), impartially to the shepherd, the poet, and Jones—the 'three chance human wanderers' through this vale of tears. It is true that it is still the poet who perceives the landscape as an emblem, but the mediation no longer rises in him, linking gloss and landscape in a recollection of the mounting voice of waters:

> A meditation rose in me that night
> Upon the lonely mountain when the scene
> Had passed away, and it appeared to me

> The perfect image of a mighty mind,
> Of one that feeds upon infinity,
> That is exalted by an under-presence,
> The sense of God, or whatsoe'er is dim
> Or vast in its own being.
>
>   (*1805*, XIII, 66–73)

It is not that the Wordsworth of *1850* wishes to cut out the transcendental implications, just that this earlier clarity frightens him. Man is still 'more than anything we know, instinct / With godhead', but he is also 'born / Of dust, and kindred to the worm' (*1850*, VIII, 492–3, 487–8), and must not forget it. And so we get the fudging that will make the great claims less unacceptable. First a sequence of lines nominally presenting the scene as 'the type / Of a majestic intellect', but in fact with no relation to the landscape at all; the poet is simply permitting himself to dwell on irrelevant aspects of the mind that he would like his poetry to conjure up—

>   its acts
> And its possessions, what it has and craves,
> What in itself it is, and would become.

Then, after this buffer has been placed between the original account and any attempt at detailed allegorization, comes a reading of the landscape that needs very careful attention. Few readers probably will notice that the imagery preserved from *1805* is now being viewed from quite another standpoint:

> *There* I beheld the emblem of a mind
> That feeds upon infinity, that broods
> Over the dark abyss, intent to hear
> Its voices issuing forth . . .

Where? What now is the emblem? Not surely the landscape at the poet's feet, centring on the cloud-rift that had been 'The soul, the imagination, of the whole', but the moon, gazing and brooding up above. The 'roar of waters, torrents, streams' that had been an internal voice, welling up from within to speak of inner vastness and infinite possibilities, is now caught by an external listener waiting to be sustained by recognitions of a power beyond the self. It is a very big change.[20]

In their different ways, however, or from their different standpoints, both versions of the Climbing of Snowdon portray the source of the river of imagination. 'We have traced the stream / From darkness', Wordsworth wrote very shortly after composing the gloss in its original form,

> and the very place of birth
> In its blind cavern, whence it faintly heard
> The sound of waters; followed it to light
> And open day, accompanied its course
> Among the ways of Nature, afterwards
> Lost sight of it bewildered and engulphed,
> Then given it greeting as it rose once more
> With strength, reflecting in its solemn breast
> The works of man, and face of human life;
> And lastly, from its progress have we drawn
> The feeling of life endless, the one thought
> By which we live, infinity and God.
>
> (XIII, 172–84)

As countless border images show, there had always been a sense in which Wordsworth lived by the one thought of infinity and God, but in May 1805, when these lines were presumably written, it was true in a different way. Possessed by grief at the death of John two months before, he leads the stream of imagination right through from the *Kubla Khan* caves of the womb to the ocean of Christian rest and reward in which he now so urgently needs to believe. But he is of course hoping too to impose retrospectively a structure on his poem, using the recurrent river image to suggest that imagination has been not just 'the moving soul of [his] long labour', but the subject of a connected narrative. The river of *The Prelude* had flowed along the dreams of the sleeping child in the very opening lines of *1799*, and made its appearance as metaphor a year later, in part 2:

> Who that shall point as with a wand, and say
> 'This portion of the river of my mind
> Came from yon fountain'?
>
> (*1799*, II, 247–9)

It is doubtful whether at the time Wordsworth had intended to develop the image, but it recurs at points in book 3 of *1805*,[21] and early in book 4 there is a set-piece that shows just how aware the poet is of its structural possibilities. The student, returned from his first year at Cambridge, is taking stock among the scenes of his boyhood, and confronts the stream in his landlady's garden—

> that unruly child of mountain birth,
> The froward brook, which, soon as he was boxed
> Within our garden, found himself at once
> As if by trick insidious and unkind,
> Stripped of his voice, and left to dimple down
> Without an effort and without a will
> A channel paved by the hand of man.
> I looked at him and smiled, and smiled again,
> And in the press of twenty thousand thoughts,
> 'Ha', quoth I, 'pretty prisoner, are you there!'
> —And now, reviewing soberly that hour,
> I marvel that a fancy did not flash
> Upon me, and a strong desire, straitway,
> At sight of such an emblem that shewed forth
> So aptly my late course of even days
> And all their smooth enthralment, to pen down
> A satire on myself.
>
> (*1805*, IV, 39–55)

The indulgent personification of the stream alerts us to the fact that Wordsworth is penning down a satire on himself long before he chooses to point it out. In explaining the emblem, however, he is drawing attention not to a particular moment in a cottage-garden, but to a way of looking at his life and his poem.

To the same late period as the book 13 stream of imagination belong almost certainly two river-images inserted in earlier books—the relatively unimportant brook of X, 905 (and implied river of X, 923) and the full-scale apology for his meandering narrative that the poet makes in the opening lines of book 9: 'As oftentimes a river . . . Turns and will measure back his course. . . . ' It is interesting that this last example of retrospective structuring should be clearly influenced by lines from *The Task.* The Derwent at the opening of *1799* links *The Prelude* back via *Tintern Abbey* and the Wye to Coleridge and the Otter, Bowles and the Itchen, Warton and the Loden, Akenside and 'Wensbeck's limpid stream';[22] but as well as these nostalgic revisited rivers there is in the background Coleridge's scheme for *The Brook,* forerunner to *The Recluse,* in which the river was designed specifically to give the cohesion lacking in Cowper. 'I had considered it as a defect', Coleridge writes in *Biographia Literaria,*

> in the admirable poem of the *Task* that the subject which gives the title to the work was not, and indeed could not be, carried on beyond the three or four first pages, and that throughout the poem the connections are frequently awkward, and the transitions abrupt and arbitrary. I sought for a subject that should give equal room and freedom for description, incident and impassioned reflections on men, nature and society, yet supply in itself a natural connection to the parts, and unity to the whole. Such a subject I conceived myself to have found in a stream, traced from its source in the hills among the yellow-red moss . . . to the first cultivated plot of ground . . . to the hamlet, the villages the manufactories and the sea-port. (*BL* X, chap. 10)

We know from the ludicrous 'Spy Nozy' episode that the Wordsworths and Coleridge charted the brook at Alfoxden in the summer of 1797, and there is every reason to think that they discussed the poetic use of a river as a structural device. At different times in his work on *The Prelude* Wordsworth seems to have recollected Coleridge's rather literal-minded scheme, but there was no likelihood of his adapting it consistently to his own very different vision and purposes. The river never achieves any great structural importance; instead it becomes the poet's organic metaphor for form—or metaphor for organic form—just as the wind is his live (reanimated) image for the dead metaphor of inspiration. Metaphors in *The Prelude* proliferate and interconnect: imagination may finally become the stream of Wordsworth's consciousness, but in the full-length poem it rises as 'the mild creative breeze' of the Preamble, and *en route* it has been the 'unfathered vapour' of book 6, the mist on Snowdon. As well as these, a host of minor images evoke or enact imagination's power, few of them one supposes deliberately implanted, but all drawing attention in some small way to the poem's central preoccupation, and all in that sense connective. A characteristic way of thought is itself a structural principle, and it is that much more so if it finds expression in images that recur, and bring to mind their predecessors and their cousins. The truest of Wordsworth's retrospects in *The Prelude* does not seek to present the poem as a sequential narrative at all; an image of still water (water this time that is going nowhere) enables him to muse over the heterogeneous material of his poetry, seen amid distortions of every kind in the hidden depths of memory:

As one who hangs down-bending from the side
Of a slow-moving boat upon the breast
Of a still water, solacing himself
With such discoveries as his eye can make
Beneath him in the bottom of the deeps,
Sees many beauteous sights—weeds, fishes, flowers,
Grots, pebbles, roots of trees—and fancies more,
Yet often is perplexed, and cannot part
The shadow from the substance, rocks and sky,
Mountains and clouds, from that which is indeed
The region, and the things which there abide
In their true dwelling; now is crossed by gleam
Of his own image, by a sunbeam now,
And motions that are sent he knows not whence,
Impediments that make his task more sweet;
Such pleasant office have we long pursued
Incumbent o'er the surface of past time—
With like success.

(IV, 247–64)

On its more obvious level, the passage works superbly. The man looking over the side of his boat is single-mindedly trying to see what is on the bottom; he does not value the products of fancy, and wishes to exclude the reflections of surrounding Nature—rocks and sky, mountains and clouds. His own reflection and the sunbeams are both intrusions, and movements of the boat and water are hindrances (though they make his task more challenging as well as more difficult). But the 'solemn imagery' of Nature 'received / Into the bosom of [a] steady lake' was not irrelevant to Wordsworth. And isn't the whole poem about the gleam of his image, about sunbeams on water, and motions sent one knows not whence? A passage that appears to state the difficulties of getting at objective memory suggests on closer reading that there could be no point in trying. The growth of a poet's mind concerns not just the details of the period that is nominally his subject, but all those elements and experiences of the present and more recent past that confuse or refract them (for the I altering, alters all).

It is no wonder really that Wordsworth did not attempt to sustain a connective image such as Coleridge found to be lacking in *The Task:* he was too like Cowper, and he was too like Coleridge himself.[23] At the center of *The Task* are the speaking voice and the personality of the writer, neither of them forceful or compelling, yet both attractive, and together strong enough to hold attention if we choose to give it. It is a poem of many moods, informative, indignant, satirical, reflective, and merely self-indulgent:

> Not undelightful is an hour to me
> So spent in parlour twilight: such a gloom
> Suits well the thoughtful or unthinking mind,
> The mind contemplative, with some new theme
> Pregnant, or indisposed alike to all.
>
> (*Task,* IV, 277–81)

Wordsworth of course knew Cowper too, and there is an obvious route from *The Task* through *Frost at Midnight* to *Tintern Abbey,* the Two-Part *Prelude,* and on into *1805.* What Coleridge had for his own purposes cut down Wordsworth built up again, but he did so retaining the features that had given new strength to the genre—in fact he made a bond between the two. Normally in the conversation-poem the writer's preoccupation had been foisted on the listener;[24] it is the greatness of *The Prelude* that the poetry is truly part of a relationship, part of a continuing discussion.

From the reference to *Frost at Midnight* in the eighth line of *1799* right through to the euphoric conclusion to *1805*—

> Prophets of Nature, we to them will speak
> A lasting inspiration . . .
>
> (XIII, 442 ff.)

—*The Prelude* is 'The Poem to Coleridge'. Part 1 of *1799* begins in response to Coleridge's pressure to write *The Recluse*; part 2 cannot begin until Coleridge's approval has been gained, and comes to its conclusion in a touching farewell as he leaves for the south, seeking the haunts of men; the five-book *Prelude* is undertaken in January 1804 as a gift for Coleridge to take abroad, and then redeveloped to beguile the poet of heavy thoughts before he even sets sail; the new work on *1805* later in the year begins in a progress-report for the poet's 'Beloved friend'; and in bringing his poem to an end, Wordsworth describes it as 'this offering of my love'. Coleridge is addressed again and again, and though *we* may at times forget his presence, Wordsworth never does. It is he who validates the whole undertaking, often providing the sustaining thought, and always providing the sustaining confidence that 'the discipline / And consummation of the poet's mind' is in truth heroic argument:

> O heavens, how awful is the might of souls,
> And what they do within themselves while yet
> The yoke of earth is new to them . . .
>
> (III, 178–80)

Beneath the *Prelude's* defiance of Milton, and the attempt to impose Miltonic structures on the narrative, lie more personal Falls and fallings-away—Wordsworth's sense that *nothing*

> can bring back the hour
> Of splendour in the grass, of glory in the flower . . . [25]

—and, more important still, the sense that he and Coleridge have in common of a falling-off from the shared idealism and shared certainties of spring 1798.

Coleridge, looking back in the greatest of his conversation-poems, *Dejection* (April 1802), picks up the *Intimations* reference to loss of childhood vision ('There was a time when meadow, grove and stream . . .') and applies it with a pathos that Wordsworth would very well understand to the creative joy that both had felt at Alfoxden:

> Yes, dearest Sara! Yes!
> There *was* a time when tho' my path was rough,
> The joy within me dallied with distress . . .
>
> (*Dejection*, 231–3)

Imagination for Coleridge has been sapped. He can form a concluding reconciliation from Sara's joy, but no longer believe in a regeneration of his own. Wordsworth as he works on the *Preludes* of 1804 and 1805 is just as aware that 'the power / Of harmony and the deep power of joy' will no longer enable him to 'see into the life of things'; but his domestic situation is tranquil, and his creativity for the moment is plainly unimpaired. Finally, though, it is his continuing sense of election that distinguishes his position from Coleridge's. As in *The Leech Gatherer,* he writes to supply both their needs, seeking constantly to find an alternative basis for optimism now that earlier certainties and sources of power seem closed. In a conversation with Coleridge it is naturally to the imagination that he turns most frequently. The thought that had been at the centre of his friend's despair—

> I may not hope from outward forms to win
> The passion and the life, whose fountains are within . . .
>
> O Sara! we receive but what we give,
> And in *our* life alone does Nature live.
>
> (Dejection, 50–1, 296–7)

—is transformed in *1805* to positive assertion. Dominance of mind becomes the criterion of excellence. Imagination has been the moving soul of *their* (the two poets') long labour, and as prophets of Nature they will instruct men

> how the mind of man becomes
> A thousand times more beautiful than the earth
> On which he dwells . . .

The poetry of this great final paragraph (XIII, 428–52) rises to the occasion, but the poet's *bravura* is to be valued chiefly in its poignancy. The millennarian assertions, carried over from the conclusion to *1799,* are hollow now, and if Coleridge could ever have been classed as a 'prophet of Nature', the time is long past. In Wordsworth's grandiloquence, however, one reads the depth and importance of the relationship that has sustained him through his poem.

It is Coleridge's presence that licenses *The Prelude*'s organic form. Sterne and Byron use apparent uncontrol as a structural method. Their voices tell the reader constantly that his formal expectations are being ignored, that they don't give a damn for his views; but their eyes are fixed constantly on audience-reaction. Their act depends on the projection of the writer's personality: they may lay claim to privacy, but if there are moments that are truly revealing, they happen by mistake. Wordsworth, though he too is his own subject, invents himself no character. Some of his voices of course are more public, and there is no doubt that from time to time he composes his gait, and shapes himself

> To give and take a greeting that might save
> [His] name from piteous rumours. . . .
>
> (IV, 118–19)

but he has no wish to be watched, and for the most part he is safe from the constrictions of formal behaviour. He is with a friend who values his monologue as a conversation that may be resumed or dropped at will— a conversation that cannot be formless because it grows out of relationship and preoccupation, and perfectly images the mind that is its subject.[26] Adopting a broadly chronological pattern, but feeling free to measure back his course, and to switch round blocks of poetry that do not in an ordinary sense belong to any single place, Wordsworth dawdles through his work 'like a river, murmuring / And talking to itself' (IV. 110–11). Often the current is slack, the narrative floats into a back-water of self-regard, is sucked into an eddy of irrelevance, but such leisureliness is the condition of the poetry:

> The writer must introduce the truth with such accompaniment as shall imply that he has mounted to the sources of things—penetrated the dark cavern from which the river that murmurs in every one's ear has flowed from generation to generation. (*Prose Works*, II, 78–9)

If Wordsworth had imposed (or been able to impose) a tighter structure on *The Prelude*, it would surely have been restrictive. We should have been left wishing 'The river to have had an ampler range / And freer pace' (III, 509–10).

Notes

1. James Beattie, *The Minstrel*, Book the First (1771), 12.
2. See Z. S. Fink, *The Early Wordsworthian Milieu* (Oxford, 1958), 45–8.
3. *Survey of the Lakes*, 73.
4. Revising *Descriptive Sketches* in 1836 with the Climbing of Snowdon in mind, Wordsworth gave a new importance and mysteriousness to the cloud-rift:

> A single chasm, a gulf of gloomy blue,
> Gapes in the centre of the sea—and through
> That dark mysterious gulf ascending, sound
> Innumerable streams with roar profound.
> (*Oxford Wordsworth*, I, 73, ll. 413–16)

5. *Bicentenary Studies*, 431, ll. 1–16.
6. *New Perspectives*, 24; K. J.'s italics.
7. Professor Johnston rightly points out (*New Perspectives*, 20) that in *Bicentenary*

Studies (1970) I overstated the ordinariness of the experience that takes place, or is implied, in *A Night-Piece.*

8. The fusion may in fact go beyond the mere use of one faithful memory to lead up to another: it could be that the light by which Wordsworth originally saw the mist in 1791 was not the moon, but the sun. He sets off after all in line 3 of the *Prelude* account 'to see the sun / Rise from the top of Snowdon', and the passage quoted from *Descriptive Sketches* begins: '—'Tis morn: with gold the verdant mountain glows'. Alternatively perhaps he replaced the moon by the sun in *Descriptive Sketches* because the scene would more appropriately be viewed in daylight by the 'pastoral Swiss', and returned to what he had actually seen when writing the Climbing of Snowdon.

9. See especially *Simon Lee,* 69–76 and *Idiot Boy,* 322–56.

10. Wordsworth's identification with the moon is more important, and unexpectedly different, in the *1850* text.

11. William Bartram, *Travels Through North and South Carolina* (2nd ed., London, 1794) and John Barrow, *Travels in China* (1804) are among the many travel books that *The Prelude* draws upon in passing. It was a kind of reading, exciting and yet leaving all to the imagination, that Wordsworth and Coleridge both particularly enjoyed.

12. For the alternative view, see Robert Langbaum's bold statement that in *The Prelude* 'the words *soul* and "imagination" are used interchangeably' ('The Evolution of Soul in Wordsworth's Poetry', *PMLA* lxxxii [1967].

13. Found on the verso of the Pierpont Morgan *Description of a Beggar* manuscript, apparently of c. May 1797:

> Yet once again do I behold the forms
> Of these huge mountains, and yet once again,
> Standing beneath these elms, I hear thy voice,
> Beloved Derwent, that peculiar voice
> Heard in the stillness of the evening air,
> *Half heard and half created.*
>
> (*Oxford Wordsworth*, v. 340)

14. *On Wordsworth's 'Prelude'* (Princeton, 1963), 91–2.

15. Wordsworth's image of usurpation, which appears first in the Climbing of Snowdon, seems also to be Miltonic: the moon in *Comus,* 331ff., is 'dammed up. / With black usurping mists'. It is interesting that she should in the same passage be invoked to stoop down her face 'And disinherit Chaos'.

16. From a draft conclusion to *The Ruined Cottage* of spring 1798.

17. The 'spots of time', of course, attach themselves to their involutes, and achieve their power to nourish and invisibly repair the poet's mind and im-

agination, *before* they are submitted to the Word, re-created (or incarnated) as poetry.

18. 'It is apparent, then, that in Wordsworth's sustained myth of mind in its interchange with nature, the imagination plays a role equivalent to that of the Redeemer in Milton's providential plot. For in Milton's theodicy it is the birth, death, and return of the risen Christ to save mankind and to restore a lost paradise which serves to demonstrate the "goodness infinite . . . / That all this good of evil shall produce, / And evil turn to good" ' (M. H. Abrams, *Natural Supernaturalism.* New York: W. W. Norton, 1971, 19. *Henry Crabb Robinson on Books and Their Writers,* ed. Edith J. Morley. 3 vols. London: J. M. Dent, 1938).

19. The spirit-world of 1799, pt. 1, though perhaps no more credible, had at least had a purpose.

20. Compare the sad transformation of the end of Waiting for the Horses, where the seven taut lines of *1805,* XI, 382–8 are replaced by twelve flaccid ones (*1850,* XII, 324–35) in order to blur the claims that had originally been made.

21. In the opening lines, for instance, Cambridge is an eddy that sucks the poet in.

22. See Mary Jacobus' elegant and detailed account, *Tradition and Experiment,* 111–16.

23. Wordsworth does of course use the river as a connective image in the *Duddon Sonnets* of 1820, but, as he points out in the Postscript, the subject in this case is particular rather than general. Despite this he is, or pretends to be, concerned at encroaching upon Coleridge's plans for *The Brook.* There is surely a little mischief in his comment: 'There is a sympathy in streams, "one calleth to another"; and I would gladly believe that *The Brook* will ere long murmur in concert with *The Duddon*' (*Oxford Wordsworth,* III, 503–4).

24. The 'pensive Sara' of *The Eolian Harp,* whose eye at a convenient moment darts'a mild reproof', bidding the poet to stop speculating and 'walk humbly with [his] God' (ll. 49–52); Lamb in *This Lime-Tree Bower,* the truest Londoner of them all, who has allegedly 'pined / And hungered after Nature, many a year / In the great city pent' (ll. 28–30); the cradled Hartley of *Frost at Midnight*; the unresponding Wordsworth of *The Nightingale*; Dorothy in *Tintern Abbey.*

25. *Intimations,* 180–1, in the text of 1807—the original reading had been 'What thought it be past the hour . . . '.

26. 'The organic form . . . is innate; it shapes as it develops itself from within, and the fulness of its development is one and the same with the perfection of its outward form. Such is the life, such the form' (Samuel Taylor Coleridge, *Shakespearean Criticism,* ed. Thomas Middleton Raysor. 2 vols. London: J. M. Dent, 1933, 224).

The Creative Soul

Simplon Pass to Mount Snowdon

WILLIAM A. ULMER

◆ ◆ ◆

B OOK 6 OF *The Prelude*, with its apostrophe to Imagination and journey through the Ravine of Arve, was Wordsworth's first endeavor after deciding to reorganize and expand the five-book *Prelude*. Drafts towards the Simplon crossing and address to Imagination exist in MS WW, and by the end of March 1804 the poet was developing them into a coherent narrative for his sixth book.[1] The Simplon adventure and apostrophe to Imagination were especially important for his reconceived *Prelude*, for these passages permitted Wordsworth a useful framing strategy. The 1805 *Prelude* relegates most of its newly added material to an intermediate position between book 6 and book 13, 13 being the new location of the Snowdon episode: the result is an account of the Fall framed by depictions of imaginative power. Wordsworth could thereby invoke the corruption of creativity by abstruse rationalization and still anchor his poem's darker episodes within a supervening optimism. At the same time book 6 complexly portrays both triumph and failure. Due to its breadth of implication, book 6 "has become one of a handful of paradigms capable by itself of representing the poet's work," Alan Liu justly declares, and matters change little in moving on to the complexities of book 13.[2] With these rich, difficult books, I will restrict my argument to two main points. First, I will argue that Wordsworth's celebrations of imagination clearly presuppose religious values. Second, I will reconsider the narrative logic connecting the apostrophe to Imagination to the Ravine passage, and book 6 as a whole to book 13, in order to argue that the mystical disorientation of book 6 dangerously prefigures the protagonist's subsequent Fall.

As with the Immortality Ode, the religious resonance of book 6 rests on the identity of imagination and soul which Wordsworth posits. That resonance has not always been given its due. In our two most powerful readings of the Simplon crossing, the text's ostensible revelations of transcendence are restaged as revelations of merely an apocalyptic *desire* for transcendence and of an elided historicity scattering political traces in its wake.[3] To these readings, with their displacements of the supernatural as mind and history, can be added Jonathan Wordsworth's respected claim that "the sense of 'something evermore about to be' is infinitely valuable, but not a religious experience" (*Borders of Vision,* 34). Fair enough, one might respond, but it is an experience of imaginative potentiality with manifest religious implications. Wordsworth's Simplon episode draws on a familiar religious *topos.* This *topos* portrayed the soul expanding inwardly to encounter its own infinitude as a result of encountering God's infinitude in a natural prospect—and the succession of Alpine mountains had long provided a preferred prospect. Actually, Wordsworth's book 6 passage may have been prompted by one of Coleridge's early theological reflections:

> But we were not made to find Happiness in the complete gratification of our bodily wants—the mind must enlarge its sphere of activity, and progressive by nature, must never rest content. For this purpose our Almighty Parent hath given us Imagination that stimulates to the attainment of real excellence, by the contemplation of splendid possibilities, that still revivifies the dying motives within us, and fixing our eyes on the glittering Summits that rise one above the other in Alpine endlessness, still urges us up the ascent of Being. . . . The noblest gift of Imagination is the power of discerning the *Cause* in the *Effect* a power which when employed on the works of the Creator elevates and by the variety of its pleasures almost monopolizes the Soul. We see our God everywhere—the Universe in the most literal Sense is his written Language.[4]

The Berkeleyan close occurs elsewhere in Coleridge, but its occurrence here may lie behind Wordsworth's "Characters of the great Apocalyps" (VI, 570). For Coleridge's comments bring together the idea of a verbally inscribed natural world, the motif of unending progression, an Alpine scene, claims of the inadequacy of nature to human aspiration, and the celebration of imagination as the vehicle of spiritual infinitude.

Wordsworth's apostrophe to Imagination certainly contends, with Coleridge, that the liberation of imagination produces a revelation of the soul. Wordsworth begins by addressing "Imagination," describes its visionary eruption, and then, in direct response to the resulting experience of loss and recovery, applauds the glory of his "Soul":

> Imagination!—lifting up itself
> Before the eye and progress of my Song
> Like an unfather'd vapour; here that Power,
> In all the might of its endowments, came
> Athwart me; I was lost as in a cloud,
> Halted without a struggle to break through,
> And now recovering to my Soul I say
> I recognize thy glory; in such strength
> Of usurpation, in such visitings
> Of awful promise, when the light of sense
> Goes out in flashes that have shewn to us
> The invisible world, doth Greatness make abode,
> There harbours whether we be young or old.
>
> (VI, 525–37)

Suspended vertiginously between contending realities, consciousness momentarily loses its way, unable to break through or even struggle effectively against the supernatural power encompassing it. Here the imagination rises "like an unfather'd vapour" because it has no natural origin, no father, and because it encloses the poet in a cloud which nullifies his visual contact with the world, extinguishing the "light of sense." Although placed in the moment of composition in Wordsworth's 1805 text, this nullification still implicates the Alpine setting of Wordsworth's narrative. Losing not merely the "progress" but the "eye" of his song, Wordsworth briefly misplaces his poem's narrative thread *and* natural setting, vicariously losing nature in consequence. So these lines confirm again the importance of the Immortality Ode for Wordsworth's expansion of *The Prelude*. They reclaim for early manhood those "Blank misgivings" which the Ode locates in childhood, and which Wordsworth glossed in remarking, "Many times while going to school have I grasped at a wall or tree to recall myself from this abyss of idealism to the reality" (Fenwick note, *PW* 4: 463). The apostrophe

dramatizes an Ode-like usurpation of time and place, the present moment of composition and the text's natural setting, by the visionary imagination.

This appropriative power illustrates nature's ontological subordination
to spirit. It discloses the existence of supernatural realities and, even here,
implies the soul's immortality. Wordsworth's lines associate "Greatness"
with the "invisible world" conceived as a final "harbour" to which the
voyaging soul returns. This "harbour" will become the soul's "home"—
recall the soul's arrival "From God, who is our home" (Ode, I. 65)—in
the next lines of Wordsworth's meditation:

> Our destiny, our nature, and our home
> Is with infinitude, and only there;
> With hope it is, hope that can never die,
> Effort, and expectation, and desire,
> And something evermore about to be.
> The mind beneath such banners militant
> Thinks not of spoils, or trophies nor of aught
> That may attest its prowess, blest in thoughts
> That are their own perfection and reward,
> Strong in itself, and in the access of joy
> Which hides it like the overflowing Nile.
>
> (VI, 538–48)

These lines prefigure and justify Wordsworth's book 13 assertion that his
story of imaginative progress substantiates "The feeling of life endless, the
one thought / By which we live, Infinity and God" (XIII, 183–4). In book
6 the portrait of imaginative aspiration as the soul's internalization of "infinitude" moves similarly to the soul's endless being, its "hopes that can
never die" and desires "evermore about to be." The closing image of the
Nile, another emanation from a mysterious source, transposes the visionary
scenario the passage began with: here the mind's emergence hides rather
than discloses it. Enacting that return to nature which Geoffrey Hartman
finds so profoundly Wordsworthian, the images reassert seasonal cycles and
natural experience. Those reassertions nonetheless naturalize beatitude.
The blessedness and joy which flow like the Nile are legacies of the imagination's transcendence of nature: they lull apocalypse while remaining
linked to the apocalyptic motif of inundation.

The religious resonance of that motif helps Wordsworth move to the
more overtly religious portrayal of the Arve Ravine:

> The immeasurable height
> Of woods decaying, never to be decay'd,
> The stationary blasts of waterfalls,
> And every where along the hollow rent
> Winds thwarting winds, bewilder'd and forlorn,
> The torrents shooting from the clear blue sky,
> The rocks that mutter'd close upon our ears,
> Black drizzling crags that spake by the way-side
> As if a voice were in them, the sick sight
> And giddy prospect of the raving stream,
> The unfetter'd clouds, and region of the heavens,
> Tumult and peace, the darkness and the light
> Were all like workings of one mind, the features
> Of the same face, blossoms upon one tree,
> Characters of the great Apocalypse,
> The types and symbols of Eternity,
> Of first and last, and midst, and without end.
>
> (VI, 556–72)

Moving from the illimitable to the undecaying, and on to "symbols of Eternity," the lines follow the apostrophe to Imagination in developing from infinitude to eternality. They advance beyond the Ode by staging a Romantic theophany, as book 6 shifts from the gloriously aspiring soul to an all-comprehending Deity. Wordsworth found assistance for this transition, we know, in the tradition of Christian apologetics concerned with geographical manifestations of divine power. His efforts to draw out the religious meaning of the Arve Ravine found independent assistance in Milton and the Bible. For Wordsworth's passage ends by merging Adam and Eve's call "to extol / Him first, him last, him midst, and without end" (*Paradise Lost,* V, 164–6) with a biblical allusion to "the Lord God, who is and who was and who is to come" (Rev. 1: 8).

Wordsworth's naturalized theophany has usually been taken as the terminus of a corrective progression, with the lost poet finding his way morally as well as literally. Properly reoriented, this Wordsworth moves from visionary isolation to natural harmony healed by his understanding "that it is the eternal mind, the face of God, that reconciles the warring features of the landscape" (Jonathan Wordsworth, *Borders of Vision,* 33).[5] This reconstruction of the narrative logic of book 6, however, grants Wordsworth's Arve tableau greater reconciliatory import than in my view it possesses. For this passage, I prefer critics like Alan Bewell and Isobel Armstrong, who consider Wordsworth's representation of the Arve Ravine deeply problematic. Noting the "suffering" of Wordsworthian locales which "have not yet been made habitable," Bewell reads the Arve Ravine as a traumatized landscape struggling toward a humanized articulation it never achieves.[6] Noting its blockage of power, Armstrong reads Wordsworth's passage for its "irreconcilable opposites . . . simultaneous but disjunct," its chaotic combination of violence and paralysis.[7] Such readings seem truer to the disturbing excessiveness of Wordsworth lines. Here nature is self-conflicted— "Winds thwarting winds"—and threatening. It raves and sickens. It dwarfs the human in its immeasurability and assumes an almost hallucinatory quality, with "rocks that mutter'd close upon our ears" and crags that *seem* to speak ("*As if* a voice were in them"). Harmony is the province of beauty; in its main thrust Wordsworth's passage unveils the sublime. His conclusion attains a tenuous unity ("Were all *like* workings of one mind") which lasts barely a moment before lapsing incrementally into discrete plural elements: features, blossoms, characters, types. The Ravine of Arve leaves nothing harmonized. It is less reconciling in affect than it is fearful and disorienting.

Consequently, the apostrophe to Imagination and Arve tableau should be construed less as progressive phases than as complementary perspectives on a single problem. For despite the grand avowals, a problem exists: the temptations of power mistaken as a hallmark of spiritual and political heroism. In *Prelude 6* this is the danger of the apocalyptic. Wordsworth's two visionary climaxes are joined by their respective treatments of apocalypse as an event in consciousness and nature. Both passages disclose appropriative agencies of mind: the power of the poetic imagination to transcend, and perceptually negate, its mundane environment at moments of mystical epiphany; the power of God's "one mind" to suffuse, wreck, and remake the fallen world of nature. One sees the power, but, as Armstrong asks, "where is peace?" (Armstrong, 37). For the religious argument of *The Prelude,* then, it is not that the Arve lines correct the glorious but threatening autonomy of the apostrophe to imagination, for the Arve passage merely translates those threats into another register. Rather, the climbing of Snowdon in book 13 corrects the interrelated errors of book 6.

The appealing visionary power of book 6 facilitates Wordsworth's Fall by extending the seductions of power into the political sphere. For the poet's attraction to power encourages, if not endorsements of violence, then rationalizing equivocations about it. His fascination with power he directly acknowledges. Confessing his temptation to regard the violence of the times as "consummation of the wrath of Heaven" (1: X, 408), Wordsworth remarks,

> So did some portion of that spirit fall
> On me, to uphold me through those evil times,
> And in their rage and dog-day heat I found
> Something to glory in as just and fit,
> And in the order of sublimest laws;
> And even if that were not, amid the awe
> Of unintelligible chastisement,
> I felt a kind of sympathy with power.
>
> (X 409–16)

This sympathy remained tied to controlling moral values, Wordsworth quickly adds (X, 418), but an attraction to power remains implicated in the Fall which organizes *The Prelude* as a crisis autobiography. Wordsworth scholarship has long recognized that *The Prelude* draws an "explicit parallel," in Harold Bloom's phrase, between Wordsworth's "Alpine expedition and the onset of the French Revolution."[8] More recent criticism has lent that parallel detailed illustration. Pointing to the poet's association of Godwin's rationality with Robespierre's politics, for example, Nicholas Roe isolates a sympathy with Jacobin decisiveness latent in Wordsworth revolutionary activism: he isolates the "sympathy with power" that is, which effectively hastened Wordsworth toward his moral and poetic nadir.[9] The political subtext of imaginative apocalypse is an overreaching revolutionary ambition.

If the apostrophe to Imagination and Ravine of Arve sections of book 6, legitimate but incomplete revelations, do not precipitate Wordsworth's crisis, they prepare the ground for it. Wordsworth suggests as much by giving his great Imagination passage a displaced political significance. The "banners militant" of the apostrophe to Imagination strategically glance at Napoleon's addresses to his army and usurping aspirations to cross the Alps.[10] The "flashes" exposing "the invisible world" ironically anticipate "the light of circumstances, flash'd / Upon an independent intellect" in *Prelude* 10 (X, 828–9), phrases borrowed from *The Borderers* to denote the amorality of Godwinian ethical autonomy. In these ways, the language of *Prelude* 6 tacitly connects visionary aspiration with political overreaching, hinting at the hidden violence of even the religious imagination when love fails to master power. Since, for Wordsworth, the Reign of Terror took place because Robespierre's "imagination had slipped the control of love" (Roe,

218), the meditation on Snowdon ends appropriately as a celebration of spiritual love. It is because Wordsworth needs his Snowdon ascent to counterbalance the excesses of his Alpine crossing that book 13 echoes book 6 so often. Moving to Snowdon from the Simplon Pass, we again encounter a mountain, mist which intensifies self-consciousness, an illuminating "flash" and accompanying usurpation ("Usurp'd upon as far as sight could reach"—XIII, 51), and affirmations of both the mind's infinitude and "the invisible world" XIII, 105).

The Snowdon vision stages Wordsworth's grandest affirmation of spiritual and imaginative plenitude. The emphasis on plenitude can seem ill considered, admittedly, because the elisions and dissonances of the Snowdon scene seem so utterly apparent. Their disruptive power only intensifies when the central feature of Wordsworth's mistscape—a "blue chasm" formed by a "fracture" in the vapors—appears to ground presence disconcertingly in absence. The relationship of nature to mind, of the visual features of the scene to the poet's interpretation of them, of the creative mind to the divine Creator, and of the various stages of composition interlayered in the 1805 text, all resist easy Symbolic closure. Yet if the Snowdon prospect virtually solicits deconstructive reflection, such reflection can make the poetry appear more darkly problematic than it is. Certainly I cannot agree with Mary Jacobus that Wordsworth's "troping of metaphor as analogy" in Prelude 13 renders "emptiness . . . the most powerful presence in the Snowdon landscape."[11] Nor can I feel that a supplemental logic ultimately inimical to Wordsworth's celebrations of God, immortality, and love generates any discernible unease in the voice speaking the poem. For the poet himself, the rifts and errancies of the Snowdon passage at most suggest a subliminal recognition of absence—of death as the horizon of loss—as a motive contributing to both poetic endeavor and religious faith.

In proclaiming that faith, Wordsworth begins by invoking the divine. While describing the moonlit mistscape as the "genuine Counterpart" of the human imagination in its interaction with nature, Wordsworth also depicts the imagination's omphalic connection with divinity (XIII, 88–9). That connection occurs through the fracture in the mist. In an especially detailed reading of the Snowdon ascent, W. J. B. Owen argues that Wordsworth's "blue chasm," while suggestive of the unconscious, signifies principally the natural or empirical matrices of consciousness, the flow of "data from various sources—notably the senses."[12] From this perspective, the mind "feeds upon infinity" through its openness to an endless series of sensory impressions. For me, conversely, the darkened sea audible in the distance represents not material but spiritual infinitude. Wordsworth wrote of an "immortal sea" in the Ode, and viewed the ocean as an image of God's "eternal motion" in other poems. Here the distant sea symbolizes supernatural origins, with the mountain scene stationed above it depicting a mind

> that feeds upon infinity,
> That is exalted by an underpresence,
> The sense of God, or whatso'er is dim
> Or vast in its own being.
>
> (XIII, 70–3)

The "blue chasm" (XIII, 56,) through which the voice of many waters surges upward, Wordsworth calls "The Soul, the Imagination of the whole," then, because it allows the mind access to the divine. No locus of absence, it teems with superabundant energies, recalling the upsurging of the sacred waters in "Kubla Khan" even as it adds sound to sight, recalling as well "the mighty world / Of eye and ear" in "Tintern Abbey" (ll. 106–7). Wordsworth's tunnel in the mist can serve as the locus of "the sense of God" and still retain its associations with the unconscious because it is amid the mind's mysterious depths that God's presence survives. As in the Ode, such contact underlies both ordinary human perception and the poet's special ability to express ideas through images—mist serving Wordsworth as an image of visionary power, as in book 6, and moonlight connoting creative illumination.

Wordsworth's concentration on poetic power explains the qualifications of his invocation of the divine. The imagination, he declares, can be uplifted to infinitude through the intimation of God *or* whatever is dim and vast in its own being. Indicating alternatives, Wordsworth acknowledges moments in which "the soul / ... retains an obscure sense / Of possible sublimity" (1805 *Prelude*, II, 334–6) or experiences a sublimity distinct from the religious sublime. It is nonetheless the religious implications of its opening vision that book 13 subsequently develops. Actually, it is not always perfectly clear that the natural spectacle of book 13 symbolizes merely the higher mind of the poet. Nudged by Wordsworth's commentary, readers ultimately take the poetic imagination as the referent of the speaker's vision. Jonathan Wordsworth concedes the accuracy of that inference but still adds, "not that the mind is initially taken to be the poet's: at first— and again the confusion is useful, enhancing—one assumes that it is God's" (*Borders of Vision,* 323). God appeared as an "omniscient Mind" in *Religious Musings,* as specifically a "mighty Mind" in both Young and Milton, as a Mind variously described in numerous eighteenth-century poems. Wordsworth's contemporary readers could hardly have missed the theophanic suggestiveness of a "mighty Mind, / . . . [feeding] upon infinity" or, for that matter, of the Miltonic allusions concentrated in the initial passages of book 13. When Wordsworth's "huge sea of mist" is disrupted as "A hundred hills their dusky backs upheaved / All over this still Ocean" (XIII, 45–6), *The Prelude* conjures up Milton's description of the separation of land and water during the creation:

> Immediately the Mountains huge appear
> Emergent, and their broad backs upheave
> Into the Clouds, their tops ascend the Sky:
> So high as heav'd the tumid Hills, so low
> Down sunk the hollow bottom broad and deep,
> Capacious bed of Waters.
>
> (*Paradise Lost* VII, 285–90)

This Miltonic vision of God's creation will modulate, in the course of book 13, into Wordsworth's vision of the poet's creation: but the poetry which carries us to the imagination begins with God. So the prospect from Snowdon at once replicates the divine Mind in the act of creation and, through the comparison Wordsworth posits, symbolizes that same creative power in the register of the human mind.

Characteristically Wordsworthian, the secularizing gestures of the Snowdon vision are equally profound and incomplete. The mountainous mistscape does not effect outright substitutions, replacing God with the imagination, but connections, substantiating the poet's analogy between divine and human creativity. A commonplace of eighteenth-century aesthetics, that analogy has a long history in both Wordsworth and Coleridge's understanding of imagination. It recalls chapter 13 of the *Biographia Literaria*, where the secondary imagination acts as the hierarchically demoted type of "the infinite I AM." But we also find it in 1798 in "Frost at Midnight" and, as noted previously, in the Blessed Babe passage of the Two-Part *Prelude*, where the child's perceptual orchestrations make him "an agent of the one great mind" (*TPP* II, 301). The Snowdon tableau advances the claims of the Blessed Babe portrait by showing, as Abrams observes, that "the mature poetic mind, whose infant perception had been a state of undifferentiated consciousness, has acquired self-consciousness, and is able to sustain the sense of its own identity" (*NS,* 287). The higher minds of *Prelude* 13 are those fit

To hold communion with the invisible world.
Such minds are truly from the Deity;
For they are Powers; and hence the highest bliss
That can be known is theirs, the consciousness
Of whom they are, habitually infused
Through every image, and through every thought,
And all impressions: hence religion, faith,
And endless occupation for the soul,
Whether discursive or intuitive.

(XIII, 105–13)

Imagination raised to self-consciousness provides understanding not only of the self but also the universe. Here Wordsworth sketches his own theology of the imagination.

For the scene on the mountain's summit inspires a meditation recurrently theological in its reflections and claims. The lines cited above afford only one example of religious discourse, religious argument, in the concluding book of Wordsworth's poem. One aspect of the religious orientation of book 13 is its continual reference to an existing God. Another aspect involves Wordsworth's inference of spiritual immortality—"The feeling of life endless, the one thought / By which we live, Infinity and God" (XIII, 183–4)—from his insight into imagination's link to the divine. The culminating religious revelation of *The Prelude,* however, emerges when Wordsworth identifies imagination and love. Wordsworth praises the passion felt by lovers, but insists,

there is higher love
Than this, a love that comes into the heart
With awe and a diffusive sentiment;
Thy love is human merely; this proceeds
More from the brooding Soul, and is divine.
This love more intellectual cannot be
Without Imagination, which in truth
Is but another name for absolute strength
And clearest insight, amplitude of mind,
And reason in her most exalted mood.
This faculty hath been the moving soul
Of our long labour. . . .
. . . .
Imagination having been our theme,

> So also hath that intellectual love,
> For they are each in each, and cannot stand
> Dividually.
>
> (XIII, 161–72, 185–8)

This spiritual love originates in "the brooding soul" precisely because it both arises and grows imaginatively, emerging from a soul which broods creatively as Milton's God "Dove-like satst brooding on the vast Abyss / And mad'st it pregnant" (*Paradise Lost*, I, 21–2). So the ultimate affirmations of book 13 elaborate on an underlying identification of soul and imagination, alternate names for an excursive creative power which is spiritual love in action.

Framing Wordsworth's Fall, the great visions of *Prelude* 6 and 13 foreground this foundational identification. As Wordsworth discovers "The Soul, the Imagination of the whole" on the summit of Snowdon (XIII, 65), so did his confrontation with Imagination in Book 6 move him to remark similarly that "now recovering to my Soul I say, / I recognise thy glory" (VI, 531–2). In its long form, *The Prelude* pursues a protracted narrative incorporating passages written long before 1804. Such a poem cannot sustain—and *The Prelude* clearly does not sustain—a rigorous terminological consistency or establish an unfailing equation of the terms "soul" and "imagination." Robert Langbaum has even argued the that synonymity of the words "soul" and "imagination" remains entirely casual throughout *The Prelude*.[13] But I must agree with Jonathan Wordsworth's comment on the Snowdon episode:

> One responds to the terms soul and imagination as radically opposed, as bringing together and momentarily equating the religious principle in man (with the implication of communion with an ultimate power outside the self) and human creativity. Wordsworth was perfectly capable of a slovenly use of language in which no such distinction would be intended. It is disconcerting for instance, to discover his willingness to cross out "heart" and write "soul," "soul" and write "mind," simply to avoid repetition. In this case, however, the equation seems to have been more considered. (*Borders of Vision*, 321)

In the poet's most philosophically ambitious passages after 1804, the equation ordinarily seems considered and deliberate. Is it coincidental that Wordsworth, defining the importance of the spots of time in his transition to them, declares that they revealed him "A sensitive and a *creative* Soul"

(XI, 256; italics mine)? First formulated in the Immortality Ode, his association of soul and imagination remains highly traditional.[14] But it justified
Wordsworth's determination to seek spiritual truth in his own poetic experiences, allowing him an existentially authentic faith that could explain
his life.

Sublimity, Beauty, and the Typology
of Redemption

Seduced by sympathy with power into enervating polemics, and then rescued by his understanding of imagination as reciprocal interchange and
spiritual love, the protagonist of the 1805 *Prelude* undergoes moral development from the sublime to the beautiful. The sublime and the beautiful
had been variously conceived, not to say much discussed, by eighteenth-
century theorists. But Wordsworth's understanding of these terms rests
principally on Edmund Burke's famous *Philosophical Enquiry.* "By the sublime," Owen helpfully generalizes, "Burke means things which are large,
imposing, rugged; by the beautiful he means things which are small, delicate, smooth."[15] Burke's analysis touches on both the natural and rhetorical sublime—on landscape and poetic style—and shares his century's interest in the emotional dynamics of a spectator's divergent responses to
the sublime and beautiful. Whereas some earlier theorists construed sublimity as a higher beauty, Burke placed the beautiful and sublime in antithetical relation by associating sublimity with fear and beauty with love.[16]
While "the link between sublimity and terror had been suggested before"—
in not only Burnet but Dennis and Thomson, for example—"Burke was
the first to convert it into a system" (James Boulton, "introduction," lvi).
In the *Philosophical Enquiry,* Wordsworth found an emotional and moral dis-
sociation of the sublime and beautiful answering to his own imaginative
responses to nature.

Wordsworth's conceptual reliance on the categories of the sublime and
beautiful in *The Prelude,* long recognized in Wordsworth studies, begins with
the 1798–1799 text. He invokes sublimity and beauty in part 1 of his poem,
in this case taking his cue from Akenside's glance, in *The Pleasures of Imagination,* at the contrary inclinations of different minds. One kind of person,
Akenside avowed, seeks "The vast alone, the wonderful, the wild" while
"Another sighs for harmony, and grace, / And gentlest beauty."[17] In the
Two-Part *Prelude* Wordsworth similarly stresses his own temperamental affinity with the sublime:

> . . . there are spirits, which, when they would form
> A favored being, from his very dawn
> Of infancy do open out the clouds
> As at the touch of lightning, seeking him
> With gentler visitation; quiet Powers!
> Retired and seldom recognized, yet kind,
> And to the very meanest not unknown;
> With me, though rarely, [in my early days]
> They communed: others too there are who use,
> Yet haply aiming at the self-same end,
> Severer interventions, ministry
> More palpable, and of their school was I.
>
> *(TPP* I, 69–80)

While leading specifically to the stolen boat incident, these lines implicate all the 1798 spots of time, presenting them as episodes in the protagonist's progressive introduction to the sublime. If both spiritual agencies contribute, one wields far greater influence—or so Wordsworth claims initially. But as the 1799 *Prelude* develops from part 1 to part 2, it exchanges visionary disquietude for the predominating love and joy of the Blessed Babe and the One Life. The Pedlar's experiences had carried him too from natural "communion, not from terror free" to "the lesson deep of love" (*MH,* lines 27, 89). Only with the 1805 *Prelude,* however, does Wordsworth dilate upon these structural implications and explicitly correlate a progression from terror to love with the categories of the sublime and the beautiful.

The idea of such a progression is one of the leading claims of Theresa Kelley's study of Wordsworthian aesthetics. "Because the sublime is primitive and incomplete" in Wordsworth, Kelley contends, "it needs the beautiful as its successor."[18] In fact, the notion of a diachronic relationship between sublimity and beauty seems to be the poet's own adaptation of the theories known to him. If Burke's contrast between authoritarian sublimity and domesticated beauty struck Wordsworth in part for "its suggestion of a progress from sublimity to beauty," as Kelley surmises (Kelley, 24), he built upon that suggestion in revising his poetic autobiography beyond five books. In the thirteen-book *Prelude,* the idea of a progression from sublimity to beauty emerges in Wordsworth's use of the Simplon and Snowdon visions to frame his Fall. He presents his Simplon crossing as a disruptive confrontation with the sublime, and the Snowdon revelation as a saving return to the beautiful.

The vision in the Ravine of Arve, I realize, has been interpreted as a reconciliation of power and peace, sublimity and beauty, and it certainly (and quite unavoidably) contains elements of the beautiful within it. In the awesome vision on Snowdon, similarly, nature assumes symbolic form with "circumstance most awful and *sublime*" (XIII, 76; italics mine). But the presence of beauty in an essentially sublime prospect, or of sublimity in a scene ultimately dominated by the beautiful, was theoretically unobjectionable in the context of the *Enquiry*. "If the qualities of the sublime and beautiful are sometimes found united," Burke asked, "does this prove, that they are the same, does it prove, that they are in any way allied, does it prove even that they are not opposite and contradictory?" (*Enquiry*, 124–5)— and the point of these rhetorical questions was not lost on either the Wordsworth of the fragmentary essay on "The Sublime and the Beautiful" or the earlier Wordsworth of *The Prelude*. So power and sublimity merely dominate the passage on the Ravine of Arve, while the ascent of Snowdon, as Kelley writes, "secures the ascendancy of values that belong to the beautiful over those of the sublime."[19] I argued previously that the interaction of mountain, sky, and water in the Arve ravine seems violently majestic, a threatening, superabundantly energized *topos*. The interaction of natural elements on Snowdon finally appears reconciling and reciprocal, the appropriate inspiration for a meditation on spiritual love. The contrary emphases of these Wordsworthian scenes make them each other's antithetical complement. They also permit *The Prelude* to enact a pilgrimage from the sublime to the beautiful in moving formally from book 6 to book 13 (1805).

But we need not argue over the mix of sublimity and beauty in these two framing books. Finally, Wordsworth summarizes his development in terms which make the sublime-to-beautiful progression unmistakable. In book 13 he tells Dorothy,

> And true it is
> That later seasons owed to thee no less;
> For, spite of thy sweet influence and the touch
> Of other kindred hands that open'd out
> The springs of tender thought in infancy;
> And spite of all which singly I had watch'd
> Of elegance, and each minuter charm
> In nature or in life, still to the last,
> Even to the very going out of youth,
> The period which our Story now hath reach'd,
> I too exclusively esteem'd that love,

> And sought that beauty, which, as Milton sings
> Hath terror in it.
>
> (XIII, 214–26)

If Milton sang it, Satan said it, and who was Satan but the first revolutionary? Wordsworth's attraction to the sublime, to sublimity as the manifestation of power, had the Reign of Terror in it. His recovery from the resulting Fall declares itself in his development beyond the turbulence of the sublime to the serenity of the beautiful. So he gratefully informs Dorothy:

> Thou didst soften down
> This over sternness: but for thee, sweet Friend,
> My soul, too reckless of mild grace, had been
> Far longer what by Nature it was framed,
> Longer retain'd its countenance severe,
> A rock with torrents roaring, with the clouds
> Familiar, and a favorite of the Stars:
> But thou didst plant its crevices with flowers,
> Hang it with shrubs that twinkle in the breeze,
> And teach the little birds to build their nests
> And warble in its chambers.
>
> (XIII, 226–36)

Dorothy "beautified" his soul by tempering its isolation and, as connoted by the image of the rock rendered habitable, readying it for domestic life. Wordsworth's celebration of love in book 13 merely raises to self-consciousness the course of his own moral education.

This developmental paradigm implies a particular spiritual history. For the poet's progress from sublimity to beauty refigures Christianity's construction of its own historical development. We have long understood that Wordsworth's recourse to the sublime and beautiful helped to place the events of *The Prelude* in religious perspective. In an influential section of *Natural Supernaturalism* Abrams showed that "behind this familiar eighteenth-century aesthetic dichotomy lay centuries of speculation about the natural world—speculation whose concerns were not aesthetic but theological and moral, and which in fact constituted a systematic theodicy of the landscape" (*NS*, 98). But I would suggest further that the apocalyptic scars borne by the mountains were in Christian tradition the topographical legacies of a specifically Old Testament violence, the sublime testimonials of

Jehovah's awesome power, whether left by the Creation or the Flood. Moreover, the Hebraic associations of the natural sublime were recurrently echoed in critical investigations of the rhetorical sublime. The Old Testament struck many critics as the preeminent example of an imaginative or stylistic sublimity. The eighteenth century recurrently claimed that religious texts had inherent advantages for representation of the sublime. Some commentators on the sublime accordingly privileged Milton; others declared for the sublimity of both the New and Old Testaments. From the time of Longinus, in fact, theorists of the sublime had been consistently impressed, Samuel Holt Monk remarks, "with the abundance of that quality in the Psalms, Job, and the writings of Isaiah."[20] By the time of *The Prelude* Robert Lowth's studies of Hebrew poetry offered the Old Testament as the supreme example of the rhetorical sublime, and the association of sublimity with primitivism championed by Blair secondarily encouraged appreciation of a Hebraic Sublime. "Sublimity," Coleridge could declare, "is Hebrew by birth."[21]

Burke himself had associated sublimity not merely with terror but with the anger of Jehovah and the imagery of the Old Testament. In a culturally characteristic gesture, his analysis of the fear provoked by imaginative responsiveness to divine power reverts to the Old Testament in seeking illustrations, turning to David's cry, "fearfully and wonderfully am I made!" in Psalm 139 as an instance of "divine horror." After nodding to similarly terrified astonishment in Horace and Lucretius, Burke continues on to assert,

> But the scripture alone can supply ideas answerable to the majesty of this subject. In the scripture, wherever God is represented as appearing or speaking, every thing terrible in nature is called up to heighten the awe and solemnity of the divine presence. The psalms, and the prophetical books, are crowded with instances of this kind. (*Enquiry*, 69)

Disavowing theories which attributed the rise of religion to fear and superstition, Burke nevertheless insists that

> dread must necessarily follow the idea of such a power, when it is once excited in the mind. It is on this principle that true religion has, and must have, so large a mixture of salutary fear; and that false religions have generally nothing else but fear to support them. Before the christian religion had, as it were, humanized the idea of divinity, and brought

it somewhat nearer to us, there was very little said of the love of God. (*Enquiry,* 70)

Burke's commentary shows how the ideas of terror, sublimity, and the Old Testament were mutually associated in eighteenth-century aesthetic discourse. But Burke's reference to Christianity redirecting religious experience from fear to love also shows, with great pertinence for Wordsworth, the way in which this constellation of motifs impinged upon traditional conceptions of the history of Christianity.

When engaged with historical problems, eighteenth-century apologists for Christianity ordinarily insisted on the essential unity of the Old and New Testaments. This insistence survived Deist polemics against topological interpretation, as well as the skepticism underlying many Enlightenment studies of comparative mythography, and flourished in the intellectual life of the time. In Wordsworth's day, admittedly, claims for the mutual congruence of the Old and New Testaments were still a hallmark of historical defenses of the Scriptures. It remains true nonetheless, as Ernest Tuveson succinctly observes, that "Christian history tends to be *developmental.*"[22] It certainly proved developmental in its genealogical demotion of Hebrew tradition: from the time of Saint Paul, Tertullian, and Saint Augustine, defenders of Christianity declared Old Testament law the mere childhood, or shadowy type, of the true faith. Fundamental to the belief of any Christian, this subordination of the Old Testament to the New Testament enjoyed a long history in Western civilization, underwrote the logic of typological interpretation, and shaped various intellectual and artistic traditions.[23] Moreover, one common representation of the relationship of Old and New Testament ideas of God involved exactly the notion of a progression from wrathful power to peaceful love.

Allowing for both the mercy of Jehovah and the wrath of the Lamb, this traditional distinction rarely became absolute. It survived its qualification, however, retained its place in several eighteenth-century discourses, and was part of the cultural background available to any poet grappling with spiritual mysteries. So Isaac Watts's "The Law and the Gospel" can make a familiar appeal in beginning,

> "Curst be the man, for ever curst,
> That doth one wilful sin commit;
> Death and damnation for the first,
> Without relief, and infinite."

Thus Sinai roars; and round the earth
Thunder, and fire, and vengeance flings;
But, Jesus, thy dear gasping breath,
And Calvary, say gentler things.[24]

The distinction between a potentially apocalyptic violence—as in Watts's Burnet-like thunder and fire flung round the earth—and gentle love recurs in the "unobtrusive but forceful transition from Old to New Testament conceptions of divine power" which, for David Morris, organizes Smart's "On the Power of the Supreme Being."[25] Blake relies on the same distinction, Morton Paley shows, in depicting the tiger as an "expression of the Wrath of God in the Bible, particularly in the Old Testament," as opposed to the lamb as an expression of Christian gentleness and love.[26] Wordsworth himself, Bewell argues, relies on a similar distinction in dramatizing Peter Bell's conversion.[27]

Eighteenth-century aesthetic discourse on the sublime, with its latent biblical associations, mediates Wordsworth's use of this same developmental paradigm for *The Prelude*. Depicting the sublime in *The Prelude*, Wordsworth evokes an idea commonly connected with divine wrath and Old Testament grandeur, and specifically reconfirms Burke's association of sublimity with terror. When he then places the sublime and beautiful in developmental succession, he constructs a personal history which reiterates Christianity's historical self-representation.[28] The typological progression from Old Testament law to New Testament love serves in itself as a type, writ large in cultural history, of Wordsworth's own development from power to love. These developmental associations merely inflect the poet's story because the psychological realism of *The Prelude* displaces and secularizes them. Yet his "sympathy with power," he confessed in book 10, encouraged him to see "The consummation of the wrath of Heaven" in the spectacle of revolutionary violence, a violence descending "in the order of sublimest laws," and in fulfillment of warnings issued by "the ancient Prophets" (X, 416, 408, 413, 401). At one point, then, *The Prelude* expressly associates violence, sublimity, and the Old Testament. The sublimity of the Ravine of Arve culminated similarly in "Characters of the great Apocalypse" (VI, 570) engraved by the Old Testament God. Moving from Simplon to Snowdon, Wordsworth moves from prophetic violence to moral love. He enhances the suggestion of a development beyond Old Testament misconceptions when he internalizes the promise of redemption after first looking to political violence, Jacobin rather than messianic, to establish the kingdom of God on earth. In all of these ways Wordsworth's moral progress from the sublime to the beautiful in *The Prelude* subtly recapitulates the history of Christianity.

The connections Wordsworth sketches between that history and his own life work two ways. They justify his concentration on personal experience because his experience makes him a representative figure, a spiritual hero whose struggles and victories reflect on every Christian's situation. But if the Christian paradigms underlying *The Prelude* confirm Wordsworth's importance, Wordsworth's personal experiences, as they fall into final form, reconfirm the Christian paradigms they personalize and displace. The very idea of a historically progressive revelation demands that believers look at particular biblical and doctrinal formulations as potentially inessential encumbrances, the vestiges of the transitory cultural traditions through which the Word made its way. Encoded in typological conceptions of the collective progression of the faith, the poet implies, is a pattern which continues to govern individual moral development. Through the typology of redemption in *The Prelude* Wordsworth creates a modern religious myth, a secularized reaffirmation of Christian insights into the way of the soul.

The Prelude and Christianity

The Excursion, Aubrey De Vere thought, announces a theism which finds its necessary complement in revelation, in "that Christianity so zealously asserted in Wordsworth's maturer poetry, and so obviously implied in the whole of it."[29] The related questions with which I will conclude are, does the visionary humanism of *The Prelude* also imply Christianity, and if so are the poem's Christian analogues, images, and allusions intellectually functional or merely ornamental? For readers willing to acknowledge the poetry's preoccupation with religious issues, the final question raised by the 1805 *Prelude* is precisely the question of the text's Christian affiliations.

Wordsworth scholars generally deny that the 1805 *Prelude* invokes Christianity as a significant conceptual background. Most of those denials rest on arguments first presented by Ernest de Selincourt in his great 1926 facing-page edition of the 1805 and 1850 texts; subsequent accounts of the theological differences between these versions of the poem ordinarily just restate de Selincourt's conclusions. For de Selincourt, the 1805 *Prelude* reaffirms "that religious faith which is reflected in all the poet's greatest work" and which, calling it "Hartley transcendentalized by Coleridge," he describes in terms reminiscent of the One Life (*EdS,* lxviii, lxix). In his opinion, Wordsworth's faith underwent no real changes from "Tintern

Abbey" to the thirteen-book *Prelude*. The poet's beliefs were never positively or self-consciously opposed to Christianity, but Christian doctrine interested him little, failing to engage his deepest needs and intuitions. After 1805 Wordsworth "turned more consciously to the Christian faith" (*EdS*, lxx), altering *The Prelude* accordingly. While some of the revisions involve mere "embroidery," others, de Selincourt argued, reveal Wordsworth obscuring his earlier religious views:

> By changes such as these, the last [1850] Book in particular, which is the philosophical conclusion of the whole matter, leaves a totally different impression from that created by the earlier text. The ideas he has introduced are from the brain that wrote *Ecclesiastical Sonnets*; they were entirely alien to his thought and feeling, not only in that youth and early manhood of which *The Prelude* recounts the history, but in that maturer period when it was written; and they have no rightful place in the poem. (*EdS*, lxxiii)

De Selincourt's analysis of the religious changes made in *The Prelude* is finely responsive to the language of the poem and generally persuasive. Wordsworth clearly labored to make the 1805 *Prelude* more recognizably Christian in the decades following its initial composition, and ultimately produced a more conventionally pious poem. Yet de Selincourt's references to "totally different" impressions and "entirely alien" ideas insinuate that the 1805 text contains no Christian associations at all. Although it further encouraged the poet's return to the Anglican Church, even John's drowning, in de Selincourt's judgment, did not prevent the Wordsworth of 1805 from finishing *The Prelude* "in the spirit in which it had been begun, with no sign of wavering from his early faith" (*EdS*, lxxiv).

De Selincourt substantiates these claims by juxtaposing lines from the 1805 and 1850 versions of the poem. As an example of the contrasts he typically points out, we might take the lines,

> I worshipp'd then among the depths of things
> As my soul bade me: . . .
> I felt, and nothing else. . . .
>
> (1805, XI, 234–5, 238)

"Nothing could be more significant," de Selincourt remarks, "than the change" in this passage's 1850 variant:

> Worshipping then among the depths of things
> As piety ordained, ...
> I felt, observed, and pondered. ...
>
>   (XII, 184–5, 188)

The spiritual self-reliance and trust in personal feeling proclaimed in 1805 relent in 1850 to the ordinations of piety and the discipline of observation and thought. Yet can we fairly say that the 1805 text, lacking these solemnities, lacks any recognizably Christian qualities? We need read back only a few lines in the 1805 *Prelude* to find Mary Hutchinson characterized as someone in whom "God delights / ... for her common thoughts / Are piety, her life is blessedness" (XI, 221–3). If thoughtful in its way, Mary's piety appears spontaneous rather then doctrinally ordained. The point remains, however, that her instincts move her to something Wordsworth will approvingly call "piety" even in 1805, and in lines which, mentioning God and blessedness, encourage conventionally religious understanding. Wordsworth's description of Mary then moves immediately to the lines de Selincourt cites, which I will now quote at slightly greater length:

>   I had not at that time
> Liv'd long enough, nor in the least survived
> The first diviner influence of this world
> As it appears to unaccustom'd eyes;
> I worshipp'd then among the depths of things
> As my soul bade me: could I then take part
> In aught but admiration, or be pleased
> With any thing but humbleness and love;
> I felt, and nothing else; I did not judge,
> I never thought of judging, with the gift
> Of all this glory fill'd and satisfied.
>
>   (1805, XI, 230–40)

Since these lines evoke the Immortality Ode, the speaker's reference to his "soul" qualifies as a religious assertion. He also portrays his appreciation of natural beauty as an act of worship, and the beauty itself as a "gift" and a "glory" in which unjaded sensibilities enjoy the world's "diviner influence." As always, Wordsworth's lines avoid doctrine, preferring "the religion in Poetry" to "versified Religion." Their generality notwithstanding, the sentiments are commonplaces of Christian devotional reflection. One can justly ask, then, how profoundly the 1805 text's omission of the phrase "as piety ordained" dissociates it in tone and import from the Christianity de Selincourt discerns in the 1850 version?

In my view, the greater moralism of the 1850 *Prelude* represents merely the rhetorical ossification of Christian affinities scattered everywhere in the religious language of the 1805 poem. Here is another example:

> In the midst stood Man,
> Outwardly, inwardly contemplated,
> As of all visible natures crown, though born
> Of dust, and Kindred to the worm, a Being
> Both in perception and discernment, first
> In every capability of rapture,
> Through the divine effect of power and love,
> As, more than any thing we know, instinct
> With Godhead, and by reason and by will
> Acknowledging dependency sublime.
>
> (1850, VIII, 485–94)

In a Norton Critical Edition note keyed to line 488, Jonathan Wordsworth calls this passage "one of the most extreme of the Christian revisions of *The Prelude*" (*NCP* 301 n. 8). De Selincourt would have doubtless agreed; he too mentions these lines and stresses the orthodoxy of other *Prelude* passages which, like this one, posit contrasts "between the body and the spirit of man" (*EdS,* lxx, lxxi n.1). So how dramatically do the lines differ from their 1805 counterparts?

> Then rose
> Man, inwardly contemplated, and present
> In my own being, to a loftier height;
> As of all visible natures crown; and first
> In capability of feeling what
> Was to be felt; in being rapt away
> By the divine effect of power and love;
> As more than any thing we know, instinct
> With Godhead, and by reason and by will
> Acknowledging dependency sublime.
>
> (VIII, 631–40)

The 1805 lines celebrate emotional susceptibility and ignore humankind's dust-like creatureliness, a biblically resonant image tinged with the humility of Wordsworth's later orthodoxy. But do the resulting differences indicate a revolution in spiritual outlook? Wordsworth's 1805 reflections declare humanity the crown of creation, a biblically resonant image in its own right. The poet then ascribes that preeminence to our rational and emotional recognition of divine power and love—an awareness rendering us "instinct / With Godhead"—and concludes by acknowledging his dependence on God with sincere humility.

One can similarly challenge de Selincourt's contention that "the last Book in particular" undergoes a drastic change in religious orientation in the 1850 version. De Selincourt makes Wordsworth's two descriptions of redemptive love the chief exhibit for this claim:

> thou call'st this love,
> And so it is; but there is a higher love
> Than this, a love that comes into the heart
> With awe and a diffusive sentiment;
> Thy love is human merely; this proceeds
> More from the brooding Soul, and is divine.
>> (1805, XIII, 160–5)

> There linger, listening, gazing with delight
> Impassioned, but delight how pitiable!
> Unless this love by a still higher love
> Be hallowed, love that breathes not without awe;
> Love that adores, but on the knees of prayer,
> By heaven inspired; that frees from chains the soul,
> Bearing in union with the purest, best
> Of earth-born passions, on the wings of praise
> A mutual tribute to the Almighty's Throne.
>> (1850, XIV, 179–87)

With admirable restraint, de Selincourt simply comments that

the change in the text here, with the introduction of a definitely Christian interpretation of the character of that "higher love," is noteworthy, as is the change in the next line of "intellectual" to "spiritual." Wordsworth would not, in 1804–5, have denied that the love was spiritual, but he prefers to emphasize his belief that it is essentially a part of the natural equipment of man as man, and does not depend, as in the later text, upon a definitely Christian faith and attitude to religion. (*EdS,* 628–9)

I entirely agree that the 1850 passage is heavy-handed and impositional. I merely suggest that here too Wordsworth's 1805 meditation depends—if not on a definite—on an *implied* "Christian faith and attitude to religion." The "higher love" Wordsworth praises in 1805, after all, is seemingly not "part of the natural equipment of man as man": the text expressly states that it informs the heart and Soul as a divine legacy. The greater naturalism of the 1805 version hardly renders it unreligious, or divests Wordsworth's references to the "divine" and the "Soul" of their conventionally religious implications, particularly as those references echo within the rhetorical and dramatic context of book 13 as a whole. Obtrusively Christian the 1805 passage certainly is not—but would anyone cite it as evidence of Wordsworth's intellectual rejection of Christian belief? Surely the changes distinguishing the 1805 from the 1850 *Prelude,* even in this worst-case instance, are not substantive enough to warrant the conclusion that Christianity remained "entirely alien" to the poet's moral imagination in 1805.

"We have too often been led," Robert Barth remarks, "to believe that the differences between the 1805 and 1850 versions, in terms of their religious attitudes and values, are greater than they actually are" (Barth, 18). Indeed we have, and the prevalence of the belief is no less instructive than it is welcome, frankly, for my argument. For once de Selincourt demonstrated the religious chasm ostensibly separating the 1805 and 1850 texts, he paved the way for widespread recognition of the Christianity of the 1850 *Prelude* by allowing that recognition to arise in the form of disapproval. So Herbert Lindenberger declares of Wordsworth's "Dust as we are, the immortal Spirit grows / Like harmony in music" (1850, I, 340–1), "this is much too stiff—abstract, formal, too obtrusively Christian for a modernist sensibility."[30] So Harold Bloom writes that the 1850 *Prelude* "manifests an orthodox censor at work, straining to correct a private myth into an approach at Anglican dogma" (Bloom, 141). Lindenberger's and Bloom's admissions of the Christian quality of the 1850 text articulate a position prevalent in Wordsworth studies. Consequently, any demonstration that the religious differences between the 1805 and 1850 texts have been exaggerated, that Wordsworth's texts manifest an overriding similarity of spiritual emphasis and outlook, raises the possibility that the 1805 *Prelude* is itself significantly Christian. The very possibility may make Wordsworthians less quick to concede the 1850 text's Christian aspects, but for the moment I will disallow such backpedaling. *The Prelude* could only become "somewhat more explicitly or assertively [religious] in the 1850 version," Barth writes, "because it was deeply religious from the beginning."[31] The 1805 text lent itself to Christianizing revision, I would add, only because of Christian affinities latent in it from the beginning.

Initially, those affinities are deliberately understated. What Abrams terms the "circuitous" structure of *The Prelude* obliges Wordsworth to unveil only in concluding "a principle which was invisibly operative from the beginning" (*NS,* 76), or which was at first obscurely operative. As a result, one common response to the Christian qualities of Wordsworth's Snowdon meditation, for instance, has been to deplore them as inconsistent with the preceding books of *The Prelude.* The poem's faith in immortality can serve as a case in point. Jonathan Wordsworth annotates Wordsworth's assertion of "life endless" (1805, XIII, 183) as "a reference to the afterlife which emerges very suddenly in the context of the poem as a whole, but which is explained by Wordsworth's urgent need to believe in the survival of his brother John" (*NCP* 468 n. 6). Yet Wordsworth prefigures his book 13 allusion to "life endless" in earlier books. The claim is clearly anticipated, I suggested, in book 6. And additional examples come easily to mind: in book 4 Wordsworth thinks about "How Life pervades the undecaying mind, / How the immortal Soul [creates] with Godlike power" (VI, 155–6); introducing the dream sequence of book 5, he praises the "sovereign Intellect" for diffusing through the human body "A soul divine which we participate, / A deathless spirit" (V, 14–17). The affirmation of immortality in book 13 should seem neither precipitous nor unanticipated. It acts as Wordsworth's more declamatory (and more pointedly theological) reassertion of one of his poem's established convictions.

The immortality lines afford merely one example of how Christian motifs in Wordsworth's Snowdon episode expand upon previous points. The glad preamble leaves the poet "cloth'd in priestly robe" as if intended "For holy services" (1805, I, 61, 63) so that Wordsworth's Romantic self-fashioning can from the beginning look ahead to his prophetic election. In the dawn dedication lines from book 4 he similarly reflects

> My heart was full; I made no vows, but vows
> Were then made for me; bond unknown to me
> Was given, that I should be, else sinning greatly,
> A dedicated Spirit. On I walked
> In blessedness, which even yet remains.
>
> (1805 IV, 334–8)

Here Wordsworth gives his vocational mythmaking a distinctly Christian aspect by allusively restaging the baptismal rite from the Book of Common Prayer.[32] In like manner, Wordsworth's Simplon crossing and apostrophe to Imagination prefigure the religious claims—and the biblical and Miltonic phrasing—of his epiphany on Mount Snowdon. As his poem approaches Snowdon, Wordsworth's language becomes more self-consciously Christian in spiritual ambience. Confessing his intention to celebrate outwardly humble people who honor human nature through their selflessness, he declares in 1805 book 12:

> it shall be my pride
> That I have dared to tread this holy ground,
> Speaking no dream but things oracular,
> Matter not lightly to be heard by those
> Who to the letter of the outward promise
> Do read the invisible soul. . . .
> . . . .
> . . . . This I speak
> In gratitude to God, who feeds our hearts
> For his own service, knoweth, loveth us
> When we are unregarded by the world.
> (XII, 250–5, 274–7)

In lines praising the watchful love of a personal God, Wordsworth accommodates Christ's transvaluation of the lowly and humble to the moral office of poetry. Yet the biblical and Christian sanctions this passage bestows on the poet's labor merely concentrate, for privileged summation, Christian associations subtly woven throughout the 1805 text.

Despite this associative pattern, the religious vision which culminates in the Snowdon episode does not *depend* on biblical revelation or Church doctrine. Wordsworth's vision is his own, anchored in his experience and validated by his exalted conception of humankind's potential for goodness and love. The 1805 *Prelude* is dominated by secular issues and eventuates in an insistent, deeply felt humanism. As book 13 draws to a close, Wordsworth praises Coleridge precisely for helping him humanize his nature worship:

> And so the deep enthusiastic joy,
> The rapture of the Hallelujah sent
> From all that breathes and is, was chasten'd, stemm'd,

And balanced by a Reason which indeed
Is reason, duty and pathetic truth;
And God and Man divided, as they ought,
Between them the great system of the world
Where Man is sphered, and which God animates.

(XIII, 261–8)

But here too, in a passage balancing the moral claims of Man and God, the poet's belief in God finds straightforward expression. By no means the earthbound anthropocentrism of a "*Semi*-atheist," the humanism of even the 1805 *Prelude* is a religious humanism. It is simply not the case that the poem divests its theological paradigms of any significant reference to the divine. Critical accounts of a Wordsworthian humanism separate from spiritual reality—grounded strictly in human consciousness—read tendentiously and slight important essentialist continuities. Certainly one could argue that *The Prelude* anticipates contemporary insistence that the traditional ideas "God" and "Man" are so deeply complicit as to be unthinkable apart—that Wordsworth anticipated recent claims that we cannot have "Man" without "God." Yet we cannot accord Wordsworth's religious affirmations the seriousness they deserve without also crediting his persistent invocations of Christianity.

Like the Immortality Ode, the thirteen-book *Prelude* presents its religious insights not as coincident but as coterminous with the Christian revelation. Without claiming the poem for orthodoxy, one can claim that the Christian suggestiveness of Wordsworth's language remains intellectually pertinent and strategic. Implying that Romantic prophecy and religious tradition are mutually corroborative, Wordsworth positions his spiritual autobiography on the brink of the doctrinally explicit Christianity his text both reinscribes and creatively revises. The question of whether the text's similarity to Christianity outweighs its dissimilarity from Christianity depends, as always, on how one understands "Christianity." For some critics, no doubt, the Christian affinities of the 1805 *Prelude* do not dominate its heterodox aspects sufficiently to allow for an overall endorsement of Christianity. Certainly Wordsworth seems less interested in endorsing than transforming orthodox values. Even so, the metaphorical approximation to Christianity in *The Prelude* remains an intellectually contributive element of Wordsworth's poem, and as such a part of its religious meaning. Summoning up the convictions which define him, the Wordsworth of the 1805 *Prelude* calls upon God with rapture and gratitude, dramatizes a providential order shaping his life, insists that the creativity and immortality of the soul are a divine legacy, and centers his final prophecy on an apotheosis of love—an apotheosis reenacting the progression from Old Testament sublimity to New Testament beauty, and celebrated in language filled with spiritually familiarizing allusions to Christian texts and attitudes. We have grown skilled of late at reading the displacements of Wordsworth's poetry. It should not prove too difficult, I hope, to read the displacement of Christian promise informing Wordsworth's vision of a life "centring all in love, and in the end / All gratulant if rightly understood" (XIII, 384–5).

Wordsworth's dialogue with Christianity in the thirteen-book *Prelude* envisions a faith capable of accommodating modern humanism. As innovative as that vision can appear, Wordsworth's allusions to Christian tradition signify a profound accommodation in their own right. Wordsworth's poetics were modeled, whether consciously or not, on the revaluative traditionalism of the Higher Criticism—and that his intentions as a religious poet were to circumscribe innovation within tradition. The Immortality Ode and the thirteen-book *Prelude* attempt to preserve Christianity by assuming its status as a progressive revelation and prefiguring its future form. For all the liberating energies of Wordsworth's Romantic gospel, it would be a mistake to undervalue his traditionalism, then, or imagine him agreeing in 1805 that his revisionary engagement of Christianity thrust him beyond its pale. The poet who wrote the thirteen-book *Prelude* had renewed his commitment to an Anglican Church associated in his mind with his nation, his family, and his childhood. In recent years critics have argued—one thinks of James Chandler and Kenneth Johnston—that Wordsworth's political viewpoint and imaginative purposes became fundamentally conservative earlier than has often been thought.[33] The Christian affiliations of the 1805 *Prelude* represent the religious dimension of this conservative reorientation.

Notes

Abbreviations used in text and notes:

CWSTC: Samuel Taylor Coleridge, *The Collected Works of Samuel Taylor Coleridge,* Gen. ed. Kathleen Coburn. Bollingen Series 75. Princeton, N.J.: Princeton University Press, 1971–.

EdS: *The Prelude,* ed. Ernest de Selincourt; 2nd ed. rev. Helen Darbishire. Oxford: Clarendon Press, 1959.

MH: Jonathan Wordsworth, *The Music of Humanity.* New York: Harper and Row, 1969.

NCP: William Wordsworth, *The Prelude: 1799, 1805, 1850.* Ed. Jonathan Wordsworth, M. H. Abrams, and Stephen Gill. Norton Critical Edition. New York: Norton, 1979.

NS: M. H. Abrams, *Natural Supernaturalism: Tradition and Revolution in Romantic Literature.* New York: Norton, 1971.

PW: The Poetical Works of William Wordsworth. Ed. Ernest de Selincourt and Helen Darbishire. 5 vols. Oxford: Clarendon Press, 1940–49.

TPP: William Wordsworth, *The Prelude, 1798–1799.* Ed. Stephen Parrish. The Cornell Wordsworth. Ithaca N.Y.: Cornell University Press, 1977.

1. See MS WW 28^r–28^v (1805 *Prelude* 2.257–8). Jonathan Wordsworth mentions these drafts and notes that composition on book 6 was underway by late March in "Five-Book *Prelude*" (4, 24). Here too, incidentally, Coleridge's remained a central presence, with Wordsworth using book 6 to engage and revise the notion of sublimity propounded in Coleridge's "Chamouny; The Hour Before Sun-Rise. A Hymn," as Keith G. Thomas adroitly shows in his "Coleridge, Wordsworth, and the New Historicism: 'Chamouny; The Hour before Sun-Rise. A Hymn' and Book 6 of *The Prelude*," in *Studies in Romanticism* 33 (1994): 81–117.

2. Alan Liu, *Wordsworth: The Sense of History* (Stanford: Stanford University Press, 1989), 4.

3. Geoffrey Hartman, *Wordsworth's Poetry 1787–1814* (1964; New Haven: Yale University Press, 1971), 39–69; Liu, 3–31.

4. Coleridge, "Fragment of Theological Lecture," *Lectures 1795 On Politics and Religion,* ed. Lewis Patton and Peter Mann, *CWSTC* 1 (Princeton: Princeton University Press, 1971), 337–9. Although Wordsworth may have been most familiar with Akenside's development of this motif, see Albert O. Wlecke's discussion of John Baillie, author of *An Essay on the Sublime,* and Edward Young, in *Wordsworth and the Sublime* (Berkeley: University of California Press, 1973), 57–9.

5. Jonathan Wordsworth, *William Wordsworth: The Borders of Vision* (New York: Oxford University Press, 1982).

6. Alan Bewell, *Wordsworth and the Enlightenment* (New Haven: Yale University Press, 1989), 272–3.

7. Isabel Armstrong, "Wordsworth's Complexity: Repetition and Doubled Syntax in *The Prelude* Book VI," *Oxford Literary Review* (1981): 38. Also see her similar comments on 27–8, 37–41.

8. Harold Bloom, *The Visionary Company: A Reading of English Romantic Poetry,* rev. and enl. ed. (Ithaca: Cornell University Press, 1971), 151.

9. Nicholas Roe, *Wordsworth and Coleridge: The Radical Years* (Oxford: Clarendon Press, 1988), 219–23.

10. Liu, 23–31. While I concede the Napoleonic palimpsest Liu discovers in Wordsworth's lines, I also argue that the poet's language refers more directly to the Church Militant. Certainly we should recall with Michael Walzer that "the 'militancy' of the church and the spiritual warfare of godly men were ancient Christian themes" (*The Revolution of the Saints: A Study in the Origins of Radical Politics* [Cambridge: Harvard University Press, 1965], 278); and note, as William Haller writes, that Christian moral dedication found perhaps its supreme image in the "soldier who, having been pressed to serve under the banners of the spirit, must enact faithfully his part in the unceasing war of the spiritual against the carnal man" (*The Rise of Puritanism or, The Way to the New Jerusalem as Set Forth in the Pulpit and Press From Thomas Cartwright to John Lilburne and John Milton, 1570–1643* [New York: Columbia University Press, 1938], 142). Wordsworth invokes this widely disseminated iconographic tradition to suggest that the transcendental imagination can circumvent the disjunction of the Church Militant and the Church Triumphal, the soul's struggle against worldliness producing a visionary triumph ordinarily unavailable in life.

11. Mary Jacobus, *Romanticism, Writing and Sexual Difference* (Oxford: Clarendon Press, 1989), 268, 269. Deconstructive analysis of the Snowdon passage might begin with the decentering noticed by John Hodgson, who points out that "in relation to the land on which Wordsworth is standing, the mist appears as a sea," while "in relation to 'the real Sea' . . . the mist appears as land" (*Wordsworth's Philosophical Poetry, 1797–1814* [Lincoln: University of Nebraska Press, 1980], 114), so that the mist functions figurally as a Derridean frame or supplement.

12. W. J. B. Owen, "The Perfect Image of a Mighty Mind," *Wordsworth Circle* 10 (1979): 8.

13. Robert Langbaum, "The Evolution of Soul in Wordsworth's Poetry," in *The Modern Spirit: Essays on the Continuity of Nineteenth and Twentieth Century Literature* (Oxford: Oxford University Press, 1970), 18–36.

14. See, for instance, Abrams' discussion of "The Poem as Heterocosm" in *The Mirror and the Lamp: Romantic Theory and the Critical Tradition* (1953; New York: Norton, 1958), 272–85.

15. Owen, "The Sublime and the Beautiful in *The Prelude*," 4 (1973): 67. This article helped establish not only Wordsworth's dependence upon notions of sublimity and beauty in *The Prelude* but his specific debts to Burke. I cite *A Philosophical Enquiry into the Origin of our Ideas of the Sublime and Beautiful,* ed. with an introduction by James T. Boulton (Notre Dame: University of Notre Dame Press, 1958). For Wordsworth's debts to Thomas Burnet, also significant, see Abrams (*NS,* 99–107).

16. Even after the ascendancy of the *Enquiry* in eighteenth-century England,

Marjorie Hope Nicolson cautions: "sometimes the Sublime was a 'dreadful' Beauty—the creation of a God of Power; sometimes it was a 'higher' Beauty—the reflection of a God of Benignity," in *Mountain Gloom and Mountain Glory: The Development of the Aesthetics of the Infinite* (Ithaca: Cornell University Press, 1959), 324–5.

17. Akenside, *The Pleasures of Imagination* (3.546–50) in *The Poetical Works of Mark Akenside,* ed. Robin Dix (Madison: Fairleigh Dickinson University Press, 1996).

18. Theresa Kelley, *Wordsworth's Revisionary Aesthetics* (Cambridge: Cambridge University Press, 1988), 18. Although the statement I cite pertains specifically to the geological argument of Wordsworth's *Guide through the District of the Lakes,* Kelley finds the same "aesthetic progress in the [spectator's] mind" in Wordsworth's fragmentary essay "The Sublime and the Beautiful," and argues, in fact, that "Wordsworth repeatedly describes sublimity and beauty as successive, then competing categories," and that "beauty's capacity to supplant the sublime is the critical point in Wordsworth's aesthetics" (Kelley 8, 3, 42). Bewell also discusses Wordsworth's idea of the sublime-to-beautiful progression in the mind's responsiveness to nature (Bewell, 140). For the poet's understanding of a "primitive sublime and secondary beautiful" in the context of the geological theory of his day, see John Wyatt, *Wordsworth and the Geologists,* Cambridge Studies in Romanticism 16 (Cambridge: Cambridge University Press, 1995), 44–51.

19. Kelley, 130. Kelley contends, however, that "the Ravine of Arve passage is less indebted to the sublime than it is to the beautiful for its figuration" (Kelley, 10). Those interested should consult her argument that in *Prelude* 6 Wordsworth's beautiful figures successfully contain or domesticate the sublime (Kelley, 105–7).

20. Samuel Holt Monk, *The Sublime: A Study of Critical Theories in Eighteenth Century England* (1935; Ann Arbor: University of Michigan Press, 1960), 79.

21. Coleridge's 25 July 1832 Table Talk entry, cited from *Coleridge's Miscellaneous Criticism,* ed. Thomas M. Raysor (Cambridge: Harvard University Press, 1936), 412.

22. Ernest Tuveson, *Millennium and Utopia: A Study in the Background of the Idea of Progress* (Berkeley: University of California Press, 1949), 6.

23. Erich Auerbach summarizes the development of typological theories of exegesis in his essay "Figura," in *Scenes from the Drama of European Literature* (Gloucester, Mass.: Peter Smith, 1973), 11–76. For the endurance of typological paradigms in eighteenth-century literature, see Thomas R. Preston, "From Typology to Literature," *The Eighteenth Century: Theory and Interpretation* 23 (1982): 181–94; and Paul J. Korshin, *Typologies in England, 1650–1800* (Princeton: Princeton University Press, 1982), which even argues that the natural imagery of *Prelude* 6 is typologically organized (Korshin, 98–99).

24. Watts, "The Law and the Gospel" (ll. 1–8); cited from *The Poetical Works of Isaac Watts and Henry Kirke White* (Boston: Houghton, Mifflin, n.d.), 87–8.

25. David Morris, *The Religious Sublime: Christian Poetry and Critical Tradition in Eighteenth-Century England* (Lexington: University of Kentucky Press, 1972), 128. Morris

usefully emphasizes how frequently passages of Old Testament sublimity—as in Warton's impressive "The dread Jehovah comes," his version of Isaiah 13—were topics of biblical paraphrase in eighteenth-century British poetry.

26. Morton Paley, "Tyger of Wrath," *PMLA* 81 (1966): 542. Through its breadth of citation, Paley's article brilliantly reconstructs the late eighteenth-century cultural ambience in which the Old Testament, sublimity, and terror could seem mutually analogous facets of a single prophetic vision.

27. Bewell's commentary on *Peter Bell* anticipates my account of *The Prelude* by correlating Peter's progress beyond superstitious fear with an anthropological progression "in which fear and ignorance are a necessary part of the development of religious ideas," and in which the poem's third part, "as quite literally a 'gospel of nature,' can thus stand to the violent 'world of death' from which Peter has emerged in the same manner as New Testament love stands to Old Testament prophecy" (Bewell, 123, 141).

28. This historical transition, unsurprisingly, was commonly invoked to explain the moral development of the individual Christian: in a sermon "On the Discoveries of Faith," Wesley wrote, for instance, that "even one who has gone thus far in religion, who obeys God out of fear, is not in any wise to be despised, seeing 'the fear of the Lord is the beginning of wisdom.' Nevertheless he should be exhorted not to stop there. . . . Exhort him to press on by all possible means, till he passes 'from faith to faith'; from the faith of a *servant* to the faith of a *son*; from the spirit of bondage unto fear, to the spirit of childlike love," in *The Works of John Wesley,* vol. 4: *Sermons, 115–51,* ed. Albert C. Outler and others (Nashville: Abingdon Press, 1984—), 35. Abrams' well-known discussion of Christian internalizations of historical paradigms as models for personal spiritual development can be found in the "Christian History and Christian Psycho-Biography" chapter of *NS,* 46–56.

29. Aubrey De Vere, *Essays, Chiefly on Poetry,* 2 vols. (London: Macmillan, 1887), 1.263.

30. Herbert Lindenberger, "For the 1805 *Prelude,*" 17 (1986): 3.

31. J. Robert Barth, "Visions and Revisions: the 1850 *Prelude.*" *Wordsworth Circle* 17 (1986): 19. Let me remind readers that Barth himself denies the express Christianity of both the 1805 and 1850 text, remarking that Wordsworth himself "at no point in his life is what I would call a traditional Christian, because he had no belief that is discernible to me—even in *The Excursion*—of central Christian doctrine" (Barth, 21).

32. As Wu contends, following up a suggestion by Owen, in *FBP,* 111n.24.

33. See James Chandler's *Wordsworth's Second Nature: A Study of the Poetry and Politics* (Chicago: University of Chicago Press, 1984), passim; and Johnston's recent *The Hidden Wordsworth: Poet, Lover, Rebel, Spy* (New York: Norton, 1998), especially 669. Johnston's case for Wordsworth's conservatism does not depend upon his speculation that the poet worked in 1798–99 as a government agent.

Writing the Self/Self Writing

William Wordsworth's Prelude

ANNE K. MELLOR

◆　◆　◆

Writing the Self

ASCULINE ROMANTICISM has traditionally been identified with
the assertion of a self that is unified, unique, enduring, capable of
initiating activity, and above all aware of itself as a self. The construction
of such self-consciousness was the project of one of the most influential literary autobiographies ever written, William Wordsworth's *The Prelude*. Responding to Locke's sceptical insistence that since human consciousness is
mutable, constantly receiving new sensations and ideas, so also must human identity be discontinuous, Wordsworth attempted to represent a unitary self that is maintained over time by the activity of memory, and to
show that this self or "soul" is defined, not by the body and its sensory experience, but by the human mind, by the growth of consciousness. In the
last decade, however, deconstructive critics, most notably Paul de Man and
those influenced by his work, have rightly argued that Wordsworth's project was undercut by his own recognition that language can never be more
than an alienating "garment," can never be "the air we breathe." They have
tracked the way images of an achieved unitary self give way in *The Prelude* to
figures of effacement and defacement, to images of a lost boy, a self "bewildered and engulfed," and the "broken windings" of the poet's path.[1]

However fragile and tenuous the self linguistically constructed in *The Prelude,* the poem's overt rhetorical argument and structure locate it, as Meyer Abrams argued, within the genre of "crisis autobiography," a secularization of seventeenth- and eighteenth-century religious autobiographies grounded in a narrative of confession and conversion, of retrospection and introspection, based on the literary model of St. Augustine's *Confessions.*[2] It tells the story of Wordsworth's fall and possible (but never certain) redemption. Or more precisely, as Herbert Lindenberger argued, Wordsworth constructs his past as a series of moments in which he experienced a separation from all that he felt to be most sacred and from which he was restored, however momentarily, to a sense of wholeness and well-being.[3] The most traumatic episodes for Wordsworth are stealing the boat on Lake Ullswater, which left him, he claimed, with a sense of a power in Nature outside of his own mind, of "huge and mighty forms that do not live / Like living men" (I, 424–5);[4] his residence at Cambridge University, during which his "imagination slept" and he was reduced to an aimless wanderer, a "floating island, an amphibious thing, / Unsound, of spungy texture" (III, 340–1); and his political commitment to the French Revolution, to an abstract theory of social justice that was denied by historical events. This last produced in Wordsworth what he portrayed as the crisis of the true believer, a radical disillusionment that resulted in an allegiance to pure reason, mathematics, and an aesthetic theory which deadened both his feelings and his ability to perceive imaginatively. But Wordsworth's falls, couched in tropes borrowed from Milton's *Paradise Lost,* are represented as potentially fortunate. As he asserts in moments of high rhetorical confidence, they have led him to an ever subtler understanding and more profound conviction of his poetic vocation, of the "one life" that flows between his mind and nature, and of the enduring coherence of his self, the tenuous bridge strung by memory over the abyss between his past existence and his present writing self, over that

> vacancy between me and those days
> Which yet have such self-presence in my mind
> That sometimes when I think of them I seem
> Two consciousnesses—conscious of myself,
> And of some other being.
>
> (II, 29–33)

Wordsworth bases the construction of his self or poetic identity upon a genetic, teleological model, one that establishes three developmental stages of consciousness, beginning with the unself-consciousness of the child who experiences the external world and his own being as one ("I communed with all that I saw as something not apart from, but inherent in, my own immaterial nature"), progressing through the growing self-consciousness of the schoolboy ("more like a man / Flying from something that he dreads, than one / Who sought the thing he loved"), and arriving finally at the realization of the power of consciousness as such, at the achievement of that "philosophic mind" which is the "counterpart" of Nature's own creative power (XIII, 88). The self thus empowered is imaged positively in many ways during the poem: as a river or stream, now visible, now hidden, that gathers force as it flows (XIII, 166–80); as a circuitous path or journey that leaves home only to return, spiralling upward, at a higher level of knowledge; as a wanderer or tourist exploring the "cabinet or wide museum" of nature and society (III, 653); and as an organic growth ("Fair seed-time had my soul," I, 305). Each of these tropes, of course, has negative implications that are also figured in the poem: the stream can be turned aside or dry up, the circuitous path can return only pointlessly to its own beginning, the tourist-wanderer can remain an alien, organic growth can produce mutations and monstrous abnormalities. These attempts to stage the growth of the self, and the role played by language in the construction of this subjectivity, have been fully described by numerous Wordsworth scholars, most notably Geoffrey Hartman,[5] and I need not dwell upon them longer here.

What I wish to emphasize is the way in which the self or consciousness linguistically constructed by William Wordsworth, as both the subject and the author of *The Prelude,* is not the "higher"—and potentially universal—self he dreamed of, but rather a specifically *masculine* self. This self is represented as the struggling hero of an epic autobiography in which Wordsworth asserts without irony that the growth of the poet's mind can represent the growth of the common *man.* Marlon Ross has identified the tropes of heroic quest and conquest that structure the poet's efforts in *The Prelude,* and Alan Liu has tracked the subtle discourses in which Wordsworth rhetorically envelops Napoleon's achievements within his own.[6] The goal of Wordsworth's epic quest, his "heroic argument and genuine prowess" (III, 183–4), is nothing less than the triumph of the maker of the social contract, the construction of the individual who owns his own body, his own mind, his own labor, and who is free to use that body and labor as he chooses, the achievement of "Man free, man working for himself, with choice / Of time and place, and object" (VIII, 152–3). As Wordsworth enthuses, "Now I am free, enfranchis'd and at large, / May fix my habitation where I will" (I, 9–10).

Moving from the level of the rhetorical to the psychological, we can recognize with Richard Onorato the Oedipal pattern of exclusively masculine childhood development and regression that is embedded in *The Prelude*.[7] Wordsworth conceives the development of the poet's self as dependent first upon a definitive separation from the mother, imaged both as a pre-Oedipal source of primal sympathy or "first-born affinities" for the "blessed babe" and, after his own mother's death by which "I was left alone" (II, 292) and "destitute" (V, 259), as the "ministry of beauty and of fear" provided by a female Nature to whose "care" he was "entrusted" (V, 451). This childhood separation produces in Wordsworth a never-satisfiable desire for reunion with that originating mother. His desire, Marlon Ross has argued,is contoured by its rivalry with other males, be they powerful father figures (troped in Wordsworth's poem as either the divine creative power and authority of "God" or as numerous isolated male figures of resolution and independence—the old soldier, the blind beggar, the good shepherd) or as challenging peers (especially Coleridge, to whom *The Prelude* is anxiously addressed). This Oedipal model operates at both a psychological and a discursive level, as what Harold Bloom has called an "anxiety of influence" that produces strong misreadings of earlier prophet-poets, of Spenser, Milton, and the Bible.[8] The result, announced by Wordsworth in *The Prelude* in a moment of surpassing confidence, is the construction of an autonomous poetic self that can stand alone, "remote from human life" (III, 543), face to face with Nature and the poet-prophets of the past, "as I stand now, / A sensitive, and a *creative* soul" (XI, 255–6).

This egotistical sublime, as Keats named Wordsworth's portrait of his heroic masculine self, depends upon the conventions of classical Western literary narrative: it has a beginning, a middle, and an end; it is the "story of my life" (I, 667). To achieve coherence and endurance, this self or subjectivity must transcend the body and become pure mind, become a consciousness that exists only in language. It is the imagination that climactically reveals to Wordsworth not only the "glory" of his own soul, but the conviction that the "destiny" of *every* soul, its "nature" and its "home," is "with infinitude" (VI, 538–9). Whether or not we as readers can accept Wordsworth's appropriation of the general or royal we in *The Prelude,* it is crucial to see that the soul or self he constructs is bodiless. Despite Wordsworth's myriad sensory interactions with nature as child and man, his minute and detailed recollections of what he saw and heard and felt, his self remains curiously disembodied—we never hear whether he is hot or cold, whether he washes himself or defecates, whether he has sexual desires or intercourse.[9] Only rarely does he mention that he eats or sleeps—and when he does, these quotidian details are either heightened into Shakespearean allusion, as when the "noise of waters" outside his hotel near Lugarno makes "innocent sleep / Lie melancholy among weary bones" (VI, 579–80), or they function to demonstrate Nature's "sterner character," that admonitory power which serves to rouse the poet's heroic efforts, as when, on the banks of Lake Como, "the stings of insects" remind the poet that

> Not prostrate, overborne—as if the mind
> Itself were nothing, a mean pensioner
> On outward forms—did we in presence stand
> Of that magnificent region.
>
> (VI, 642–3, 666–9)

The Wordsworthian self thus becomes a Kantian transcendental ego, pure mind or reason, standing as the *spectator ab extra,* the detached observer both of Nature—that scene spread before his feet at the top of Mount Snowdon that becomes "the perfect image of a mighty Mind"—and of his own life.

> . . . Anon I rose
> As if on wings, and saw beneath me stretched
> Vast prospect of the world which I had been,
> And was; and hence this song, which like a lark
> I have protracted, in the unwearied heavens
> Singing. . . .
>
> (XIII, 377–82)

Deliberately denying his material physicality, even his mortality, Wordsworth represents his poetic self as pure ego, as "the mind of man," which thereby

> . . . becomes
> A thousand times more beautiful than the earth
> On which he dwells, above this frame of things
> (Which, 'mid all revolutions in the hopes
> And fears of men, doth still remain unchanged)
> In beauty exalted, as it is itself
> Of substance and of fabric more divine.
>
> (XIII, 446–52)

Precarious indeed is this unique, unitary, transcendental subjectivity, for Wordsworth's sublime self-assurance is rendered possible, as many critics have observed,[10] only by the arduous repression of the Other in all its forms: of the mother, of Dorothy, of other people, of history, of nature, of "unknown modes of being," of that very gap or "vacancy" which divides his present from his past identity. To sustain such a divine intellect, un-speaking female earth must be first silenced, then spiritually raped (as in *Nutting*), colonized, and finally completely possessed. By the end of *The Prelude,* female Nature is not only a thousand times less beautiful than the mind of man but has even lost her gendered Otherness.

But Wordsworth's masculine control of the female remains as problem-atic as his possession of an enduring self. Wordsworth consistently genders Nature and "the earth" as female; he also assigns the feminine gender to the moon and to flowers. He specifically identifies the small or hidden aspects of Nature with Dorothy:

> thou didst plant its [my soul's] crevices with flowers,
> Hang it with shrubs that twinkle in the breeze,
> And teach the little birds to build their nests
> And warble in its chambers.
>
> (XIII, 233–6).[11]

On the other hand, he assigns the masculine gender to the river Derwent, to the sea (I, 596), and to the sun (II, 175); and he appropriates the sterner dimensions of nature to his masculine self:

> My soul, too reckless of mild grace, had been
> Far longer what by Nature it was framed—
> Longer retained its countenance severe—
> A rock with torrents roaring, with the clouds
> Familiar, and a favorite of the stars. . . .
>
> (XIII, 228–32)

The immaterial soul or mind of man thus exists in tension with material Nature. Wordsworth initially genders the mind as feminine, taught by a female Sovereign Intellect that manifests herself through the "bodily im-age" of earth and heaven (V, 10–17). But as the poem progresses, the mind or soul is increasingly identified with an imagination gendered as neuter, a *sui generis* or "unfathered" power (VI, 525–42). As the mind moves ever further away from, or above, nature, it finally becomes simultaneously masculine and feminine: "the mind / Is *lord* and *master,* and that outward sense / Is but the obedient servant of *her* will" (XI, 270–2, italics mine).

Gender is thus rhetorically implicated in Wordsworth's philosophical and psychological struggle to establish a stable linguistic relationship between the mind and nature, to construct a masculine identity distinct from that of the mother. In the climactic ascent of Mount Snowdon, Wordsworth finally wrestles gender to the ground—only to have the repressed rise up again. Having defined poetic genius as definitively male in book 12, existing in productive interchange with female Nature (XII, 6–14), he confidently climbs Mount Snowdon, representing the scene before his feet and the mighty mind of which it is an image as a neutral "it." But what gender is creative power? When Nature exerts a domination upon the outward face of things, that domination is gendered as feminine. But when the higher mind of the poet exercises that same power, it is first neutered—"in the fullness of *its* strength / Made visible" (my italics)—and then, remarkably, regenerated as specifically masculine. Even Nature's power becomes masculine, the "Brother" of the poet's imagination (XIII, 89). At this moment, Nature is effectively both repressed and cannibalized by the male poet, who now defines himself as a "sovereign" power "from the Deity" (XIII, 114, 105). "Oh, who is *he* that hath *his* whole life long / Preserved, enlarged, this freedom in *himself?*" (XIII, 120–1, my italics). When Nature reemerges in the poem as a sexual other, she is but "A handmaid to a nobler than herself" (XIII, 240), subservient to the masculine poetic genius.

But Wordsworth recognizes that his hold on male supremacy is as insecure as his hold on his autonomous self. At the very end of this poem dedicated to a revelation of the male poet's possession of a godlike imagination "in all the might of its endowments" (VI, 528), Wordsworth acknowledges that this very imagination, "the main essential power" which throughout *The Prelude* he has tracked "up her way sublime" (XIII, 290), is resistantly female. Wordsworth thus reveals the stubborn Otherness of all that he has labored so long and hard to absorb into his own identity: the originary power of the female, of the mother, of Nature.

Wordsworth's attempt to represent an autonomous self with clearly defined, firm ego boundaries, a self that stands alone, "unpropped" (III, 230), entirely self-sufficient and self-generating, both unmothered and unfathered, is undercut by Wordsworth's own slippery pronouns as a heuristic fiction, a "story." Hence the hortatory mode of the following:

Here must thou be, O man,
Strength to thyself—no helper hast thou here—
Here keepest thou thy individual state:
No other can divide with thee this work,
No secondary hand can intervene
To fashion this ability

(XIII, 188–93)

Although Wordsworth himself acknowledged its fictive nature, the existence of the autonomous individual self Wordsworth once so boldly claimed—"Behold me then / Once more in Nature's presence, thus restored" (XI, 392–3)—has become one of the enduring myths of modern Western culture.[12]

Wordsworth's *Prelude* rhetorically depended upon, and has been read by Meyer Abrams and many others as giving additional authority to, the historical emergence of the individual (male) self of social contract theory and economic capitalism, that "every Man" who, in Locke's famous formulation, "has a *Property* in his own *Person.*"[13] More important, Abrams' influential way of reading *The Prelude* through the 1960s and 1970s helped to shape the genre of literary autobiography, to determine the linguistic conventions by which the viable self has been represented in contemporary critical discourse. Although studies of autobiography as a genre have tended to focus on works in prose, taking as seminal texts Augustine's *Confessions,* Rousseau's *Confessions,* and Goethe's *Dichtung und Wahrheit, The Prelude* has been hailed as the first work to present the writing of a single man's life within the conventions of the classical epic, thus elevating the genre of autobiography to the highest aesthetic status.

Contemporary theorists of autobiography have wrestled with the very problems that Wordsworth foregrounded in his poem, the uncertain relation between the self-as-lived and the self-as-imagined, between the referential and the written self, the gap or vacancy between "two consciousnesses." If the writing self can remember how it felt but what it felt remember not, to what degree can it claim referential authority for its memories? To what degree is the written self always already a metaphor, in James Olney's phrase?[14]

Even as they debate whether an autobiography can claim a special truth status, or whether it is only a literary fiction,[15] too many of the leading theorists of autobiography have assumed that the self constructed either by memory or by figurative language is finally unified, coherent, and capable of agency. Georges Gusdorf argued that autobiography arose in the eighteenth century out of a combined Christian and Romantic belief in the value and uniqueness of the individual life. Structurally, he asserted, autobiography "requires a man to take a distance with regard to himself in order to reconstitute himself in the focus of his special unity and identity across time" and is thus "a second reading of experience," one that "is truer than the first because it adds to experience itself consciousness of it."[16] Explicit in Gusdorf's influential formulation of the genre is the assumption that the self so reconstituted will express "a complete and coherent" image of "inmost being," what Gusdorf calls "my destiny"; implicit in his formulation is a capitalist ideology that defines value in terms of material possession—"in narrating my life," Gusdorf claims, "I give witness of myself even from beyond my death and so can preserve this *precious capital* that ought not disappear" (my italics).[17]

Philippe Lejeune and Elizabeth Bruss, in their highly regarded efforts to codify the conventions or literary rules of autobiography, also assumed that the subject revealed in autobiography is unified. Lejeune famously defined autobiography as a "retrospective prose narrative written by a real person concerning his own existence, where the focus is his individual life, in particular the story of his personality,"[18] a definition that implies that the self has a structure and chronological development that can be narrated, that coherence exists between the present and the past (a "retrospective" of "his own existence"), and that the ontological presence of this self (this "real" person) is not in doubt. Elizabeth Bruss also assumed that a written autobiography requires a "unity of subjectivity and subject matter—the implied identity of author, narrator, and protagonist,"[19] the identity marked by what Lejeune has called the "autobiographical pact," the identity of the signature on the title page with that of the subject of the narrative.[20] Despite poststructuralist and deconstructive critiques of the existence of a referential self or an author outside of the linguistic text, Bruss continued to regard the autobiographical self as "an arbitrary cultural fact but *not* a delusion."[21] Drawing on speech-act theory, she defined the "fundamental identification (or conflation) of two subjects—the speaking subject and the subject of the sentence" as "crucial to the autobiographical project, to the unity of observer and observed, the purported continuity of past and present, life and writing."[22]

Wordsworth's *Prelude,* for the most part read too simplistically by theorists of autobiography, nonetheless helped to establish the generic conventions of autobiography, conventions that predicate the existence of a subjectivity that is coherent over time, that can be represented linguistically as a bounded image, a completed "soul," and that can exist beyond the confines of the physical body, beyond death. This is the self which in several canonical masculine Romantic texts was glorified as the creator of reality, as the "human form divine":

> So was it with me in my solitude;
> So often among multitudes of men.
> Unknown, unthought of, yet I was most rich,
> I had a world about me; 'twas my own,
> I made it; for it only liv'd to me,
> And to the God who look'd into my mind.
>
> > (*The Prelude*, 1805, III, 139–44)

Notes

1. For readings of Wordsworth which emphasize his hermeneutic and rhetorical doubts, see Paul de Man, "The Rhetoric of Temporality," in *Interpretation: Theory and Practice,* ed. Charles S. Singleton, pp. 173–209, *Blindness and Insight,* and *The Rhetoric of Romanticism;* Cynthia Chase, *Decomposing Figures;* Jonathan Arac, "Bounding Lines: *The Prelude* and Critical Revision," *Boundary* 7 (1979), pp. 31–48; Susan Wolfson, *The Questioning Presence—Wordsworth, Keats, and the Interrogative Mode in Romantic Poetry;* William Galperin, *Revision and Authority in Wordsworth—The Interpretation of a Career;* David Simpson, *Irony and Authority in Romantic Poetry;* Tilottama Rajan, *Dark Interpreter—The Discourse of Romanticism;* and Frances C. Ferguson, *Wordsworth: Language as Counter-Spirit.*

2. M. H. Abrams, *Natural Supernaturalism,* see esp. pp. 71–140.

3. Herbert Lindenberger, *On Wordsworth's Prelude.*

4. All references to Wordsworth's *Prelude* are to the 1805 edition, *The Prelude— 1799, 1805, 1850,* ed. Jonathan Wordsworth, M. H. Abrams, and Stephen Gill (New York: Norton, 1979). Cited hereafter in text.

5. Geoffrey Hartman, *Wordsworth's Poetry, 1787–1814.*

6. Marlon B. Ross, *The Contours of Masculine Desire—Romanticism and the Rise of Women's Poetry,* see esp. pp. 15–55; Alan Liu, *Wordsworth—The Sense of History.*

7. Richard J. Onorato, *The Character of the Poet—Wordsworth in The Prelude,* see esp. pp. 174–82. Here I accept the arguments of Nancy Chodorow (in *The Reproduction of Mothering*), Juliet Mitchell (in *Psychoanalysis and Feminism*), and other feminist psychologists that the Oedipal complex applies *only* to male children, and that females follow a very different model of psychic maturation than the one posited by Freud as the "Electra-complex," a model that discourages the development of strong ego boundaries.

8. Harold Bloom, *The Anxiety of Influence—A Theory of Poetry.*

9. Wordsworth's sexual liaison with Annette Vallon is of course never mentioned in *The Prelude,* and is rhetorically displaced into the love story of Vaudracour and Julia; even the "slight shocks of young love-liking" that he attributes to the festal company of maids and youths whom he joins during his summer vacation is rhetorically depersonalized: they "mounted up like joy into *the* head, / And tingled through *the* veins" (not *my* head, *my* veins; IV, 325–8, italics mine).

10. For discussion of the way Wordsworth precariously represses the Other, see Susan J. Wolfson, *The Questioning Presence: Wordsworth, Keats, and the Interrogative Mode in Romantic Poetry;* Cynthia Chase, *Decomposing Figures: Rhetorical Readings in the Romantic Tradition,* chaps. 2–3; Mary Jacobus, *Romanticism, Writing and Sexual Difference: Essays on the Prelude;* and E. Douka Kabitogou, "Problematics of Gender in the Nuptials of *The Prelude,*" *Wordsworth Circle* 19 (1988) pp. 128–35.

11. Kurt Heinzelman discusses this passage as a *locus amoenus* in which Wordsworth's male body becomes the landscape which Dorothy's feminine art of gardening refines and improves, in "The Cult of Domesticity—Dorothy and William Wordsworth at Grasmere," in *Romanticism and Feminism,* ed. Anne K. Mellor, p. 66.

12. Although they approach the issue from very different methodological perspectives, both the traditional historian of ideas Karl Joachim Weintraub, in *The Value of the Individual—Self and Circumstance in Autobiography,* and Michel Foucault, in his enquiry into "the archaeology of knowledge" initiated in *The Order of Things* (1966), concur in defining the late eighteenth century as a pivotal moment in the evolution of the idea of the self, the beginning of an episteme in which the individual has a new sense "of something taking place in himself, often at an unconscious level, in his subjectivity, in his values, that traverses the whole of his action in the world" (*Michel Foucault: The Will to Truth,* pp. 82–3). It is probably not accidental that this is also the historical moment when the very word "autobiography" is coined, by the poet Robert Southey in 1809.

This modern self is assumed as a given in the canonical Victorian autobiographies by John Stuart Mill, Cardinal John Henry Newman, John Ruskin, and Edmund Gosse; for studies of the Victorian/modern self, see Linda H. Peterson, *Victorian Autobiography—The Tradition of Self Interpretation;* Avrom Fleischman, *Figures of Autobiography—The Language of Self-Writing in Victorian and Modern England;* Susanna Egan *Patterns of Experience in Autobiography;* Jerome Hamilton Buckley, *The Turning Key—Autobiography and the Subjective Impulse since 1800;* and Heather Henderson, *The Victorian Self—Autobiography and Biblical Narrative.* For other modes of Victorian subjectivity, see Regenia Gagnier's study of Victorian working-class autobiographies in her *Subjectivities: A History of Self-Representation in Britain, 1832–1920.*

13. Carole Pateman has demonstrated the way in which the individual assumed capable of entering into the social contract in both classical and modern social contract theory is exclusively male, in *The Sexual Contract;* John Locke's equation of

the individual with the ownership of his own capacities, attributes, and physical body occurs in his *Two Treatises of Government,* ed. P. Laslett, 2nd ed., II, p. 27.

14. "Metaphors . . . are that by which the lonely subjective consciousness gives order not only to itself but to as much of objective reality as it is capable of formalizing and controlling," writes James Olney in *Metaphors of Self—the Meaning of Autobiography,* p. 30. Despite its rhetorical status. Olney argues that the self so constituted in metaphor is "a coherent and integral self, potential at first and destined, though no one can foredraw the exact shape of destiny, to be realized through many experiences until it shall become this one, and no other, self" (p. 326).

15. The most subtle studies of the relationship between the fictive and the referential self in autobiography are by Paul John Eakin, *Fictions in Autobiography— Studies in the Art of Self-Invention and Autobiography as a Referential Art*; Huntington Williams, *Rousseau and Romantic Autobiography*; William C. Spengemann, *The Forms of Autobiography—Episodes in the History of a Literary Genre*; and the essays collected in two volumes edited by James Olney, *Autobiography: Essays Theoretical and Critical* and *Studies in Autobiography.*

16. Georges Gusdorf, "Conditions and Limits of Autobiography," trans. James Olney, in James Olney, ed., *Autobiography: Essays Theoretical and Critical,* p. 38.

17. Gusdorf, pp. 35, 39, 29.

18. Philippe Lejeune, *On Autobiography,* foreword by Paul John Eakin, trans. Katherine Leary, p. 4. This definition first appeared in Lejeune's *Autobiographie en France* (Paris: A. Colin, 1971).

19. Elizabeth W. Bruss, "Eye for I: Making and Unmaking Autobiography in Film," in Olney, *Autobiography: Essays Theoretical and Critical,* p. 297. Bruss first proposed her generic rules for autobiography in her *Autobiographical Acts—The Changing Situation of a Literary Genre,* pp. 10–8.

20. Lejeune, "The Autobiographical Pact" and "The Autobiographical Pact (*bis*)," in *On Autobiography,* pp. 3–30, 119–37.

21. Bruss, "Eye for I," p. 298n.

22. Bruss, "Eye for I," p. 301.

Wordsworth and the Conception
of *The Prelude*

HOWARD ERSKINE-HILL

◆   ◆   ◆

T HE 1798–99 *The Prelude* opens abruptly with a rhetorical question
the antecedent of which is never formally identified: 'Was it for this
| That one, the fairest of all rivers loved | To blend her murmurs with
my nurse's song...' (I, 1–3).[1] This question, well known in eighteenth-
century poetry and carrying with it a series of heroic and mock-heroic
associations, goes back in its English form to Harington's version of Ariosto's *Orlando Furioso*.[2] (Wordsworth carried an Ariosto with him to read
during his tour of France and Switzerland in 1790.[3] The context from
Orlando Furioso, and from the suggestive analogue in the opening of Mil-
ton's *Samson Agonistes* ('For this did the angel twice descend? For this |
Ordained thy nurture holy...?' (ll. 361–2), invokes a destined hero or
heroic enterprise, apparently in utter defeat. In lines closely following
this opening description of *The Prelude,* but dropped after 1799, Wordsworth, thinking of himself, alludes to those similarly marked out by
higher powers:

> I believe
> That there are spirits which, when they would form
> A favoured being, from his very dawn

> Of infancy do open out the clouds
> As at the touch of lightning . . .
>
> (I, 69–72)[4]

After the addition of the preamble to *The Prelude* as completed in 1805, it seemed obvious that the disappointment in 'Was it for this . . . ?' stemmed only from Wordsworth's awareness of poetic talent so far unfulfilled,

> Like a false steward who hath much received
> And renders nothing back.
>
> (1805, I, 270–1)[5]

In view, however, of the poet's writing in the earlier 1790s, it seems possible that the rhetorical question out of Ariosto had become attached to the revolutionary hopes of 1790, and probable that 'Was it for this . . . ?' in the 1799 *Prelude* referred rather to political dismay than poetic unfulfilment, and thus accorded with the famous affirmation (answering the appeal of Coleridge)[6] with which part 2 ended:

> —if, in this time
> Of dereliction and dismay, I yet
> Despair not of our nature, but retain
> A more than Roman confidence . . .
>
> (II, 486–9)[7]

This was a passage similar in its rhetorical patterning to the opening repetitions, 'for this' being now supplanted by 'If this . . . ', 'If', 'If', 'If', 'if in this time . . . ' (II, 465–92)[8] This concluding exordium makes it clear that the 1799 *Prelude* (whether Wordsworth originally envisaged its subsequent extension or not) had as its goal the consolation available for those who have undergone political disappointment, and the reorientation of faith in—something radical perhaps for the times—Human Nature.[9]

If the antecedent of 'this' is left undefined in 1799, what follows the question is notable for its suggestive direction: the recollection of an early childhood in rural Cumberland by Derwentside.

> Was it for this
> That one, the fairest of all rivers, loved
> To blend his murmurs with my nurse's song,
> And from his alder shades and rocky falls,

And from his fords and shallows, sent a voice
That flowed along my dreams?

(I, 1–6)[10]

This recalls the image of 'a naked boy' among the river pools, and concludes with the related but different image of 'A naked savage in a thunder
shower' (i. 26).[11] There was nothing subtle or recondite in the choice of
this image. From Montaigne to Dryden and Rousseau, it conveyed a controversial sense of primal freedom, with implications for the origin and
nature of human government.[12] If primitive man had not been born into
patriarchy then he enjoyed pure, perilous freedom until contract established magistracy.[13] The concept is so pervasive that it is probably instructive to cite an example from a late eighteenth-century work of political
controversy:

> But hear, ye sons and daughters of liberty, the sounds which the winds
> are wafting from the Western continent. The Americans are telling one
> another, what, if we may judge from their noisy triumph, they have
> but lately discovered, and what yet is a very important truth. "That
> they are entitled to life, liberty and that they have never ceded to any
> sovereign power whatever a right to dispose of either without their
> consent."
>
> While this resolution stands alone, the Americans are free from sin-
> gularity of opinion; their wit has not yet betrayed them to heresy. While
> they speak as naked sons of Nature, they claim but what is claimed by
> other men, and have withheld nothing but what all with-hold. They
> are here upon firm ground, behind entrenchments which never can be
> forced.[14]

Thus far Johnson will concede the claims of the American colonists. But
if the colonists have ever enjoyed the protections of government, whether
before leaving England or after arriving in the Western Continent, then
the authority of the London government cannot be gainsaid. Johnson's
argument sets history and common law above Nature; in his recollection
of early childhood Wordsworth finds something of Nature's precontractual
freedom in his own early life. The growth of this poet's mind will evoke
some of the stages of the general progress of the human mind, as recently
sketched, in unmistakably Lockeian manner, by Condorcet.[15] Condorcet
opens his *Sketch* with the statement that 'Man is born with the faculty of
receiving sensations' and later defines man as *'a being endowed with sensation'*

(pp. 1, 231); combinations of pain and pleasure, recognized by reason, later lead him to morality. Wordsworth's whole passage is, of course, infused with the joy of sheer physical sensation. The episode appeals to the tactile imagination above all, in its sensations of warmth and cold, rest and action, 'Basked in the sun, or plunged into thy streams, | Alternate' (I, 20–1).[16] The description works toward the expression of a separate but not individualized life: in touch through perception with 'crag and hill, | The woods, and distant Skiddaw's lofty height' the boy 'stood alone, | A naked savage in a thunder-shower'.

That plunge back to the primal once past, the story of boyhood resumes, 'when upon the mountain slope | The frost and breath of frosty wind had snapped | The last autumnal crocus' (I, 28–30),[17] but the implications of the word 'savage' still reverberate, if with some indulgent retrospective irony:

> That time, my shoulder all with springes hung,
> I was a fell destroyer.
>
> (I, 34–5)[18]

> Sometimes strong desire
> Resistless overpowered me, and the bird
> Which was the captive of another's toils
> Became my prey . . .
>
> (I, 42–5)[19]

Almost unnoticed, packed safely back into childhood memory, these images of killing, predatory pursuit, and theft emanate from the 'naked savage'. This picture is not one of innocent childhood. Boyhood adventure is soon a matter of theft and death, albeit only of birds, yet with analogies to a cruel adult world ('What! all my pretty chickens and their dam | At one fell swoop?' *Macbeth,* 4.3. 218–9). But, as before, the idyllic natural setting and form of childhood memory control the theme of menace borne by the lines. This was, after all, no more than the part sporting, part gainful activity of a young country boy.

In subsequent famous episodes the themes of killing and theft are picked up in the boy's bird-nesting and nocturnal rowing. 'In the high places, on the lonesome peaks, | Among the mountains and the winds' (I, 54–5) he was 'a rover' with 'inglorious' views (I, 53, 56)—the episode is to be made more explicit in 1805. In its turn the rowing boat episode takes up the theme of wrong to tell how the mysterious forces of nature ('low breathings coming after me' in the trapping, the 'strange utterance' of the wind in the bird-nesting) are more powerful and more moral than before. Here the adventure is cut short; the 'huge cliff Rose up between me and the stars' and 'like a living thing | Strode after me', so that the boy turns back in fear. As in all these episodes in part 1 of the 1799 *Prelude,* however, the moral aspect of the account, though developing, is relatively subordinated, partly in the diminishing of retrospect, but more through the repeatedly dramatic emphasis upon the alien, mysterious, but not purposeless presences of Nature: its sublimity or otherness.

The next episode, that of the skating, prompting or prompted by a letter from Coleridge, around 14 January 1799, is remarkable in being the first communal episode of *The Prelude,* in 1799 as in the later versions.[20] Opening with sunset and lighted cottage windows, the tolling of the village clock establishes human time and setting. The image of the horse, the first in *The Prelude,* beautifully strikes the mean between untrained and subordinate:

> I wheeled about
> Proud and exulting, like an untired horse
> That cares not for its home.
> (I, 155–7)[21]

The pride and freedom of the mettlesome horse, likely to have carried for Wordsworth the associations given it in the unpublished 'Llandaff', do not form the experience of a solitary creature, such as the bathing, trapping, or bird-nesting boy. This skating is a collective sport, and the horse leads on to images of the hunt and headlong gregarious exertion:

> All shod with steel
> We hissed along the polished ice in games
> Confederate, imitative of the chace
> And woodland pleasures, the resounding horn,
> The pack loud bellowing, and the hunted hare.
> (I, 156–60)[22]

This, for the moment, is the foreground, but in the distance other presences wait to make themselves felt:

> With the din,
> Meanwhile, the precipices rang aloud;

> The leafless trees and every icy crag
> Tinkled like iron; while the distant hills
> Into the tumult sent an alien sound
> Of melancholy, not unnoticed . . .
>   (I, 163–7)[23]

The episode now wonderfully conveys the sensation of individual independence:

> I retired . . .
>   . . .
> . . . . leaving the tumultuous throng,
> To cut across the shadow of a star
> That gleamed upon the ice.
>   (I, 170, 172–4)[24]

And again, 'When we had given our bodies to the wind . . . then at once |
Have I, reclining back upon my heels | Stopped short' (I, 175, 178–80):[25]
the skater is not checked in full career, like the rower, but arrests his own
course within the throng, and at that moment seems to see the movement
of the earth itself in its slow revolution, as his senses slowly readjust to
his individual stillness. The notable diminuendo 'Till all was tranquil as a
summer sea' (contrasting strangely with the winter scene and perhaps
reinforcing the sense of heavenly motion) is a complete catharsis in the
sense that all the energy of social and solitary movement is spent as this
serene clemency supervenes. This is noticeably different from earlier conclusions, the 'naked savage' with its potential energy, the haunting 'almost
as silent as the turf they trod', and the more clearly psychological 'and
were a trouble to my dreams'. Here the vigour of the boy has been spent
without injury to others, constraint from society, or alienation from it.
The vision of physical life in relation to society and nature which this
yields, a moving spectacle of freedom, is the fullest human experience yet
conveyed in this, Wordsworth's earliest *Prelude*.

At this point it may be asked what has become of affairs of state, those
clear and conspicuous political events, the avowed focus of the present
book? The early episodes of the 1799 *Prelude* are indeed not political (nor
apolitical), but prepolitical. They are physical experiences, sporting activi-
ties, but with spiritual and moral awareness growing out of sensation and
energy. Yet they also have political implications. They concern the primal
awareness of the untaught human being ('the naked savage'), the earliest

predatory impulses, conscious guilt, enterprise, and rebuff, free enjoyment both social and solitary. They contain the germs of political ideas capable of being experienced later in practice, in specific historical situations, later still of being meditated upon and generalized. As a point of biography, the evidence available to us does not confirm whether these episodes are (as presented) close factual and emotional records, or exemplary episodes, loosely based on childhood memory and fortified by more recent experience, designed to explore and respond to current political anxiety and error by offering the early ground for adult political attitudes and belief.

The notable advent in *The Prelude* of affairs of state proper, in the children's card-games of part 1, tends to confirm the latter interpretation, especially since the episode was added to part 1 late, and it therefore seems deliberately, in the period of composition of the two-part *Prelude*.[26] The metaphor of politics as a game of cards remained fully current: as Burke had put it in his *Letters on a Regicide Peace* (1795): 'What signifies the cutting and shuffling of cards, while the Pack still remains the same?'[27] This is another social episode, and another sport, this time an indoor one:

> I would record with no reluctant voice
> Our home amusements by the warm peat fire
> At evening . . .
> We schemed and puzzled, head opposed to head,
>
>   . . . sate in close array,
> And to the combat—lu or whist—led on
> A thick-ribbed army, not as in the world
> Discarded and ungratefully thrown by
> Even for the very service they had wrought,
> But husbanded through many a long campaign.
>   (I, 206–19)[28]

Consistently with the view that *The Prelude* of 1799 is a poem seeking the fount of political engagement in early experience, the card-game embeds in childhood recollection a series of images for high affairs of state. Consistently, too, with the democratic nature of much of Wordsworth's earlier verse, the first reference here is popular, and invokes what we know to have been the subject of the recent, unpublished, poem on the Discharged Soldier (Jan.–Feb. 1798). 'Discharged' or 'dismissed' now become 'Discarded', and Wordsworth's narrative reflects upon an ungrateful world that presses its manpower into military campaigns only to discharge it, later, into hospitals or penury. ('The Old Man Travelling' is as relevant here as 'The Discharged Soldier'.) This political allusion is now systematically extended:

> Oh, with what echoes on the board they fell—
> Ironic diamonds, hearts of sable hue,
> Queens gleaming through their splendour's last decay,
> Knaves wrapt in one assimilating gloom,
> And kings indignant at the shame incurred
> By royal visages.

$$(I, 220–25)^{29}$$

If the plebeian cards in Wordsworth's account carry the allusion suggested, so surely do the court cards. 'Queens gleaming through their splendour's last decay' is an ironic rejoinder to Burke's presentation of Queen Marie Antoinette in the celebrated passage of his *Reflections on the Revolution in France* (1790). Burke lamented the situation of the Queen, 'once glittering like the morning star, full of life, and splendour, and joy', now with 'disasters fallen upon her'.[30] Wordsworth's first response had been to describe the passage with some sarcasm as a 'philosophic' lamentation over the extinction of chivalry' in the unpublished 'Letter to the Bishop of Llandaff' (1793). Now he gives the humble card-game of the lakeland children a pastoral rôle in prefiguring the downfall of regal splendour. The poet, one might suggest, had seen and felt the 'assimilating gloom' of Robespierre's ascendency, and witnessed the reaction among other crowned heads at the imprisonment and execution of Louis XVI. Quietly and with some humour, without revolutionary zeal, the card-game marks the two-part *Prelude's* awareness of itself as the poem of a revolutionary era. The episode has enough in common with other communal sports to belong in the narrative, but is sufficiently different to constitute some kind of pointer to the poet's concern. More, it is a wholly 'artificial' passage: its domestic intimacy contrasts not only with the tragedies of high politics, but with ferocious natural forces outside, where the 'splitting ice', no longer sustaining the delights of skating, sent forth 'its long | And frequent yellings, imitative some | Of wolves that howl along the Bothnic main' (I, 229–34).[31]

The concluding stretch of part 1 of the 1799 *Prelude* is dominated by the two powerful and mysterious 'spots of time' episodes, the girl with the pitcher on the Beacon, and the news of the poet's father's death. These, and these two only, are designated 'spots of time' in the poem. Part of their power lies in paradox. Introduced always as possessing some fertile or restorative virtue, their immediate imaginative impact is rather daunting than cheering, and in the 1799 *Prelude* it is especially obvious that they belong with episodes of check and chastisement, such as that of the stealing of the rowing boat. They are located here, significantly, immediately after the recovery of the drowned man's body from Esthwaite Water (I, 263–88).[32] Here is another variation on beauty and fear, security and exposure, fulfilment and denial. And here too is a link between the drowned man, 'such tragic facts | Of rural history' (I, 282–3)[33] and the 'spots of time' in the resilience and resource of the assimilating mind: 'images to which in following years | Far other feelings were attached . . . ' (i. 284–5)[34]

Part 2 of the 1799 *Prelude* turns from the Sublime to the Beautiful, and from Nature to, in greater measure, the works of man. In this way one is tempted to simplify the relationship, and there is some truth in saying so. Thus, in part 2, the 'smart assembly-room' supplants the 'stone | Of native rock' in the centre of Hawkeshead; thus ruins of an earlier age blend into the scenes of modern boys' activities. In each case a sense of specific historical change is introduced, complementary to the more primitive moments generally comprising part 1. This development is, in one way, taking the cue offered by the card-game; the words and goals of men, some of them heavenly, are now, in relics and icons, part of the theatre of youthful life. Competitive impulse, whether in theft, race, or game, is, in this part, transcended in scenes redolent of a more holy time. 'To beat along the plain of Windermere | With rival oars . . . ' was 'such a race, | So ended', on a hermit's island, that 'We rested in the shade, all pleased alike, | Conquered or conqueror' (II, 55–67).[35] The salient episode of part 2, the expedition to 'the antique walls | Of a large abbey' (Furness Abbey), picks up both the energy and the reconciliation of these lines. The early part of this narrative is fresh with energetic arrangement: food, time, horses. And what emerges from all this is, first, the sheer physical pleasure and movement—'To feel the motion of the galloping steed (II, 102)—and then the presence all around of the remains of a historic antiquity,

> . . . the antique walls
> Of a large abbey, with its fractured arch,
> Belfry, and images, and the living trees—
> A holy scene:
>
> (II, 108–11)[36]

The fracture of historical wrong, the revolution that dissolved the monasteries, is, without concealment, made good by the marks of peace:

> Along the smooth green turf
> Our horses grazed. In more than inland peace,
> Left by the winds that overpass the vale,
> In that sequestered ruin trees and towers—
> Both silent and both motionless alike—
> Hear all day long the murmuring sea that beats
> Incessantly upon a craggy shore.
>
> (II, 109–17)[37]

The feeling of the abbey in the late eighteenth century as a place of respite, 'sequestered', is given in the treatment of the winds 'that overpass the vale' and the 'murmuring sea' whose energy is heard but at a distance, beating 'Incessantly upon a craggy shore': gales and sea are here the agents of violent change, and the word 'murmur', while on the face of it having a gentle and lulling effect, is not quite without its earlier sense of a restless and resentful power.[38] Neither wind nor sea violate this holy scene, but the boys on horseback do:

> Our steeds remounted, and the summons given,
> With whip and spur we by the chantry flew
> In uncouth race, and left the cross-legged knight
> And the stone abbot, and that single wren
> Which one day sang so sweetly in the nave
> Of the old church that, though from recent showers
> The earth was comfortless, and, touched by faint
> Internal breezes, from the roofless walls
> The shuddering ivy dripped large drops, yet still
> So sweetly 'mid the gloom the invisible bird
> Sang to itself that there I could have made
> My dwelling-place, and lived for ever there,
> To hear such music. Through the walls we flew
> And down the valley, and, a circuit made
> In wantonness of heart . . .
>
> (II, 118–32)[39]

This is much more than a picturesque backdrop for a further episode of rural sports. The 'smooth green turf' is, in a way, a field of energies in which old things and young life assume a dynamic relation one with another. The rough vigour of the boys on horseback is in dramatic counterpoint to the cold, still, and silent effigies of 'the stone abbot' and 'the

cross-legged knight', icons of a feudal order, fallen supremacies. As Wordsworth was to put it in his 'Reply to Mathetes': 'Youth has its own wealth
and independence; it is rich in health of Body and animal spirits . . . above
all . . . in the possession of Time, and the accompanying consciousness of
Freedom and Power.'[40] Knight and abbot, the life of action and the life of
God, once had their power too, but, sketched in here with the most
delicate sensibility, is a Protestant awareness, in which to disturb, if not
desecrate, images and 'holy scene', by 'whip and spur' and the impetuous
pleasure of youth, is the purest freedom. Shakespeare, alluding to the more
recently despoiled monasteries, wrote of 'Bare ruined choirs, where late
the sweet birds sang';[41] here the voice sounding from amidst what we think
of for the first time in the passage as the horrors of antiquity—'The
shuddering ivy dripped large drops'—is not that of the monks of ancient
devotion, but of 'the single wren', 'the invisible bird'. In a brilliant intervention of nature poetry, 'the invisible bird' is witness to the invisible world
for which the church was originally built. A voice of Nature, in the song
of the wren, seems to fulfil the vocation desecrated by history. It transcends
the impetuous but harmless violation of the horseriders and leads to the
'still spirit of the evening air' which inspires them on the steeps of the
hills or when, in a final assertion of physical power, '[they] beat with
thundering hoofs the level sand' (II, 39).[42]

The political implications of this episode are rather more than latent,
though they will in any case be recalled at two more explicitly political
moments, the visit to the Grande Chartreuse and the news of the death
of Robespierre, in the later *Prelude* (1805, VI, 414–25; 1850, VI, 407–89; 1805,
X, 559–67).[43] Taken as a whole it is an image of historical revolution, in
which the young express their freedom from the past though they do it
no wrong. Indeed they may keep some larger faith, within a natural spirit
of overthrow and survival, licensing iconoclasm within a larger reverence.

Part 2 of the 1799 *Prelude* moves through further scenes of youthful life
in a partly man-made and social environment to a summarizing personification skilfully stripped of the poetic dress which would have rendered
it 'poetical' in much of the verse of the late eighteenth century: 'Blessed
the infant babe . . . | Nursed in his mother's arms . . . '. The expressive
unvatic idiom of this crescendo is partly achieved by the enhanced presence
here of Coleridge as the addressee ('Thou my friend, art one | More deeply
read in thy own thoughts . . . (II, 249–67; cf. I, 447–9), partly by the well-
judged prosaic parentheses and explanations: 'For with my best conjectures
I would trace | The progress of our being—' (II, 267–9).[44] There is a
convincing feeling of having arrived at a source of wisdom even as such

explanation is sceptically disclaimed ('who shall parcel out | His intellect
... Who that shall point as with a wand, and say | "This portion of the
river of my mind | Came from yon fountain" ' (II, 242–9).[45] What 'hath
no beginning', Wordsworth writes to Coleridge, is here given a peculiarly
Coleridgeian form, picking up the theme of infancy and parenthood from
many of Coleridge's poems, notably 'Frost at Midnight', to which Wordsworth will shortly allude. This turning to Coleridge as in the mode of a
conversation poem takes on further meaning as Wordsworth reaches the
overtly political peroration of his work:

> If in my youth I have been pure in heart,
> If, mingling with the world, I am content
> With my own modest pleasures, and have lived
> With God and Nature communing, removed
> From little enmities and low desires,
> The gift is yours; if in these times of fear,
> This melancholy waste of hopes o'erthrown,
> If, 'mid indifference and apathy
> And wicked exultation, when good men
> On every side fall off we know not how
> To selfishness, disguised in gentle names
> Of peace and quiet and domestic love—
> Yet mingled, not unwillingly, with sneers
> On visionary minds—if, in this time
> Of dereliction and dismay, I yet
> Despair not of our nature, but retain
> A more than Roman confidence, a faith
> That fails not, in all sorrow my support,
> The blessing of my life, the gift is yours
> Ye mountains, thine O Nature.
>
> (II, 473–92)[46]

The argument of this passage, and even some of the keywords ('domestic',
'visionary') coincides with, if it does not necessarily derive from, Coleridge's
letter to Wordsworth of *c,* 10 September 1799, of which, unfortunately, the
well-known fragment is all that has been preserved:

> I wish you would write a poem, in blank verse, addressed to those, who,
> in consequence of the complete failure of the French Revolution, have

thrown up all hopes of the amelioration of mankind, and are sinking into an almost epicurean selfishness, disguising the same under the soft titles of domestic attachment and contempt for visionary *philosophes*. It would do great good, and might form a part of 'The Recluse,' for in my present mood I am wholly against the publication of any small poems.[47]

If this request arrived soon after the date stated, and without anticipation in earlier correspondence or conversation, it came perfectly to cap Wordsworth's emerging design. His peroration seems to arise naturally from the body of the poem, the chief episodes of which powerfully militate against apathy and despondency. The rhetoric of the poem flows between 'Was it for this?' and 'Ah, not in vain . . . ' (I, 1, 130).[48] To speak of 'the sudden entrance into the poem of a concern with "hopes o'erthrown" ', as the Norton editors do,[49] is to ignore the emotion of 'Was it for this . . . ?' at the outset, a lament not identified in the 1799 text with poetic unfulfilment.

We should beware of assuming that Coleridge had hitherto no idea of what Wordsworth was doing in the 1799 *Prelude,* or that the suggestion of the younger poet was totally novel to the recipient. Torn from its original context it may seem to have a rather contrived aptness, but however that may be, the two poets had at this time minds well attuned to one another's concerns. Further, several passages of what came to be the 1799 *Prelude,* including the rowing boat and skating episodes, were sent to Coleridge by Dorothy Wordsworth when all three were in Germany. Thus when Coleridge requested a poem 'in blank verse' he will not only have had in mind the quasi-philosophic vein and mental preoccupation of 'Tintern Abbey' but the most recent—and finest—examples of blank verse from Wordsworth's hand. Is it too much to suppose that Coleridge saw, in the check to adventure in the rowing boat episode, and the alternation of communal and solitary in the skating, something that bore upon political engagement and disappointment? I think not, for in Coleridge's own *France: An Ode* (1798) the liberty betrayed when revolutionary France invades that fountain-source of freedom, republican Switzerland, withdraws into the spaces and energies of Nature:

> Thou speedest on thy subtle pinions,
> The guide of homeless winds, and playmate of the waves!
> And there I felt thee!—on that sea-Cliff's verge,
>   Whose pines, scarce travelled by the breeze above,

Had made one murmur with the distant surge!
Yes, while I stood and gazed, my temples bare,
And shot my being through earth, sea, and air,
   Possession all things with intensest love,
   O Liberty! my spirit felt thee there.

(ll. 97–105)[50]

By comparison with Coleridge's total turn in this ode, from the arena of history to the world of Nature, Wordsworth, in the early *Prelude* episodes, presents human and natural far more closely intertwined. In so doing he explores the blending of public, personal, and instinctive within experience more fully, and in a way more able to meet the challenge of Coleridge's request.

To return to the psychological and political image of the horse, considered at the opening of this chapter, how may we characterize the horses in the boys' expedition to Furness Abbey? The answer, it may be thought, discloses something of the relation of historical, personal, and natural in Wordsworth. Living creatures that gallop, graze, and pause for breath, they are more than merely mounts, borrowed from an innkeeper. They are extensions of the energies and exploring enterprise of their riders; their speed can be produced by whip and spur, they can be directed, but their momentum and power become, temporarily, those of youth, those of the poet, when

We beat with thundering hoofs the level sand.

They will not always convey such harmonious energy.

Notes

1. *The Prelude, 1799, 1805, 1850,* ed. Jonathan Wordsworth, M. H. Abrams, and Stephen Gill (New York: Norton, 1979), 1.

2. Howard Erskine-Hill, 'The *Prelude* and its Echoes', *Times Literary Supplement* 3837 (Sept. 1975), 1094; Norton 1. Wordsworth's reading of *Orlando Furioso* is recorded in Duncan Wu, *Wordsworth's Reading,* 1770–1799 (Cambridge 1993), 7 (item 13).

3. Gill, *Wordsworth,* 45, 431; Wordsworth to Sir George Beaumont 17 Oct. 1805, *The Letters of William and Dorothy Wordsworth. The Early Years 1787–1805,* ed. Chester L. Shaver (Oxford: Clarendon Press, 1967), 529.

4. Norton, 3; cf. *Samson Agonistes,* ll. 23–36.

5. Norton, 42.

6. Coleridge to Wordsworth, *c* Sept. 1799, in S. T. Coleridge *Collected Letters*, ed. E. L. Griggs (Oxford, 1956), i. 527. It is much to be regretted that only so much of so important a letter of Coleridge should survive as Wordsworth chose to excerpt. On the political implications of this moment, see Nicholas Roe, 'Wordsworth, Milton, and the Politics of Poetic Influence', in J. R. Watson (ed.), *The French Revolution in English Literature and Art* (1989), 112–26.

7. Norton, 26.

8. Norton, 25–6.

9 Alan Bewell, *Wordsworth and the Enlightenment* (1989).

10. Norton, I.

11. Ibid.

12. Michel Eyquem de Montaigne, *Essaies* (1588), 24, 'Of Canibals'; John Dryden, *The Conquest of Granada* (1670), I, i.i. 209; *Works*, xi. 30; Jean-Jeacques Rousseau, 'Discours sur les sciences et des arts (1750), 'Discours sur l'origine et les fondements de l'linégalité parmi les hommes' (1755).

13. For this classic debate in European political theory see Quentin Skinner, *The Foundations of Modern Political Thought* (Cambridge, 1978), ii chs. 7 and 9. For the intervention into this debate of a great English poet, Alexander Pope, see Howard Erskine-Hill, 'Pope on the Origin of Society', in Pat Rogers and George Rousseau (eds.), *The Enduring Legacy: Tercentennial Essays on Alexander Pope* (Cambridge, 1988), 79–93.

14. Samuel Johnson, *Taxation No Tyranny*, in *Works*, x. *Political Writings*, ed. Donald Greene (New Haven, 1977), 428.

15. Marquis de Condorcet, *Esquisse d'un tableau historique de progrès de l'esprit humain* (Paris, 1794–5); *Outlines of an Historical View of the Progress of the Human Mind*, translated from the French (1795).

16. Norton, 1.

17. Norton, 2.

18. Ibid.

19. Ibid.

20. Griggs (ed.), *Collected Letters*, i. 462.

21. Norton, 5.

22. Ibid.

23. Ibid.

24. Ibid.

25. Ibid.

26. Norton, 514.

27. Burke, *Works*, iv. 65.

28. Norton, 6.

29. Norton, 6–7.

30. Burke, *Works,* v. 149. For recent essays on Wordsworth's card-game in the tradition of poems of political allusion, see Howard Erskine-Hill, 'The Satirical Game at Cards in Pope and Wordsworth', in Claude Rawson and Jenny Mezciems (eds.), *English Satire and the Satiric Tradition* (1984), 183–95, and Nicholas Roe, 'Pope, Politics and Wordsworth's *Prelude*', in David Fairer (ed.), *Pope: New Contexts* (1990), 189–204. Roe presents further evidence for the currency of the card-game metaphor in the 1790s. Jerome McGann, *Don Juan in Context* (Chicago, 1976), 91–3, misses the point, perhaps, of so salient a late addition to the 1798–9 text.

31. Norton, 7.

32. Norton, 8.

33. Ibid.

34. Ibid.

35. Norton, 15.

36. Norton, 16.

37. Ibid.

38. Cf. Milton, *Paradise Lost,* IV, 1015; and Dryden, *Absalom and Achitophel,* l. 45.

39. Norton, 16–17.

40. *Prose Works,* ii. 13.

41. The probable recollection of Shakespeare's Sonnet 73, l. 4, is noted by Jonathan Wordsworth, *William Wordsworth,* 118–19. On this scene in *The Prelude,* see Geoffrey Hartman, *The Unremarkable Wordsworth* (1987), 10–11.

42. Norton, 17.

43. Norton, 208–11, 388.

44. Norton, 20, corrected by the Cornell Edition.

45. Norton, 19–20.

46. Norton, 26.

47. Coleridge, *Collected Letters,* i. 527.

48. Norton, 1, 4.

49. Norton, 26.

50. S. T. Coleridge, *Complete Poetical Works,* ed. E. H. Coleridge (Oxford, 1912), i. 247.

'Some Other Being'

Wordsworth in The Prelude

RICHARD GRAVIL

❖   ❖   ❖

> I have said that poetry is the spontaneous overflow of powerful
> feelings; it takes its origin from emotion recollected in tran-
> quillity; the emotion is contemplated till by a species of re-
> action the tranquility gradually disappears, and an emotion,
> kindred to that which was before the subject of contemplation,
> is gradually produced and does itself actually exist in the mind.
>
> Preface to Lyrical Ballad

> A tranquillising spirit presses now
> On my corporeal frame, so wide appears
> The vacancy between me and those days
> Which yet have such self-presence in my mind,
> That, musing on them, often do I seem
> Two consciousnesses, conscious of myself
> And of some other Being.
>
> The Prelude, II, 27

THERE IS—ON the face of it—no doubt that three revolutionary
books of the 1850 text of *The Prelude* are intended to present a spectacle
of woe, an illustration of human ignorance and guilt. They constitute a
confession that Wordsworth (like Coleridge, the poem's addressee, who is
now recuperating in the Mediterranean) has been capable of being parted
from his better self. He too has experienced nightmares of incrimination,
and periods 'Of sickliness, disjoining, joining things | Without the light of
knowledge' (VIII, 436–7).[1] He has been taught to 'tame the pride of intellect'. Wordsworth presents himself as 'lured' into France (IX, 34), over-
confident in his capacity to understand the course of history, and 'en-

chanted' by revolutionary illusions.[2] Man, he comes to feel, is mocked by possession of the 'lordly attributes of will and choice', having in himself no guide to good and evil (XI, 306–20).

Yet no one who reads *The Prelude* attentively can fail to notice that Wordsworth's presentment of his earlier self has a candour which contrasts strikingly with Coleridge's lack of it in *Biographia Literaria.* Wordsworth is so bold to look on painful things that it becomes harder, the more familiar one becomes with the procedure of his account, to avoid the impression that while one of Wordsworth's consciousness is concerned to present himself as prey to delusions, another is anxious to present Coleridge with an image of one whose loyalty to the revolution—well after the Great Terror of 1794, and by implication right up to the Coronation of Napoleon in 1804—is, as a form of natural piety, a matter of self-congratulation.

The manner of Wordsworth's self-presentation was well debated in *The Critical Quarterly* in 1976/77 by George Watson, John Beer, and David Ellis.[3] Since then it has been more minutely examined by Michael Friedman and James Chandler.[4] This essay agrees substantially with each of these contributions. I accept, with George Watson, that Wordsworth intends his account as a warning against allowing oneself to be seduced into political malignancy by the ardour of undisciplined benevolence. I accept with David Ellis that the rhetoric of *The Prelude* none the less sometimes works harder to enforce than to criticize the classical argument for political terror. I accept with Chandler that Wordsworth is quite clearly arguing in Burkean terms, even in the 1805 text, that 'upstart Theory'—whether French or Godwinian—is counter-humanist.

I am not here concerned with the arguments of Chandler and Friedman, that Wordsworth's politics is—even in *Lyrical Ballads*—that of a convert to Burke, or that he is by this date (ensconced in Grasmere) well on the way to becoming a 'tory humanist'.[5] My concern is rather with what is created in the rhetorical structure of books 9, 10, and 11: and initially, at least, with the way in which *The Prelude* embodies within its critique of the ardour of undisciplined benevolence, a more powerful argument against those who were not, at the time, capable of such 'indiscipline'.

As one reads *The Prelude* it becomes very hard to escape the impression that as Wordsworth recollects, in tranquillity, the year of the terror, 'an emotion, kindred to that which was before the subject of contemplation, is gradually produced and does itself actually exist in the mind' so that the persona who addresses us from the midst of these events is a revolutionary persona, and if not a 'Terrorist', then certainly, in the phrase implausibly used of Coleridge by John Thelwall, a 'man of blood'.[6] In book

4, Wordsworth's subject is the rediscovery of a true self beneath the Cambridge patina so recently interposed between the world and himself. In book 2, more famously, Wordsworth finds such 'self-presence' of the past that 'often do I seem | Two consciousnesses, conscious of myself | And of some other Being'. What creates the difficulty for the reader of the revolutionary triad is the 'self-presence', alongside the autobiographer, of a Robespierrean *alter ego* who is capable of thrusting aside whatever attempts Wordsworth may make to sustain a tone of apologetics. This *alter ego* is related of course to those other manifestations of Wordsworth's revolutionary persona, the Solitary of *The Excursion* and Oswald in *The Borderers*, in whose mouths Wordsworth places many of his own best lines.

The recollected revolutionary self is younger, and more self-confident, than the writer. He may of course be more Satanic, but he may also be, as Wordsworth twice recognizes, 'a child of nature' (XI, 168), for youth maintains 'Communion more direct and intimate | With Nature,—hence, ofttimes with reason too— | Than age or manhood even' (XI, 29).[7] One of Wordsworth's major themes is that of loyalty to the self or recovery of a self that has become 'bedimmed and changed | Both as a clouded and a waning moon' (XI, 344). It would be perverse to argue that *The Prelude* consciously entertains any doubt as to which is the 'true self', for that self is explicitly associated with 'the feelings of my earlier [i.e. prerevolution] life' (*1805*, X, 924—not in *1805*), yet the possibility constantly presents itself that the self of 1792/93, the imaginative self, which usurps, by a special reaction, upon the recollecting poet, may be in some sense 'truer' than the one it has left behind.

'Human Nature Seeming Born Again'

The problems begin as early as book 6. Wordsworth's excursion through France and the Alps with Robert Jones is 'chartered' (an interesting term, given its status in the revolution debate) by Nature. Nature being sovereign in his mind, her 'mighty forms . . . had given a charter to irregular hopes'. Logically one would suppose the forms alluded to to be the Alps, but tropically, and in context (VI, 333–41) they turn out to be a trinity of personifications—namely those of

> Europe . . . thrilled with joy,
> France standing on the top of golden hours,
> And human nature seeming born again.

There is little doubt that in *The Prelude* the devil has all the best images, even if these images must be read with the caution called for when reading Satan's rhetoric in *Paradise Lost*. Wordsworth presents himself as beset, and ensures that the reader is beset, with countless cases of seeming. Implicit in the fairground figure of France standing on the top of golden hours is a prefiguring of subsequent decline. The 'seeming' of 'seeming born again' is read to begin with as meaning merely 'as if': only later does one understand it to signify deception. The Wordsworth who tells us later that 'I had approached, like other youths, the shield | Of human nature from the golden side' expects us to recall the mediaeval fable of knights in combat over the true colour of a shield which was in reality silver on one side and gold on the other. But even if we do, chivalry is chivalry and silver is silver. We may think him mistaken, but we will hardly think him culpable. Each of these images is designed to tell the truth twice: the truth of enthusiasm and the truth of disenchantment.

The millennial 'born again' image is followed, in any case, by an extended picture of rejoiced humanity. This passage, with its wondering record of 'How bright a face is worn when joy of one | Is joy for tens of millions', its register of 'benevolence and blessedness | Spread like a fragrance everywhere', of 'amity and glee' and continuous dance, is vivid enough to remain as a reminder of a contrary state of the human soul depicted in London in book 7. The long dance-like traverse of regenerated France (VI, 342–408) is Wordsworth's most Blakean vision of human possibility. It much surpasses the glimpse of 'Helvellyn fair' which, as the opening of book 8 (II. 1–69) is more often noted as the contrary to unregenerate St Bartholomew's (VII, 675–730).

Wordsworth's architectonics are much underrated, perhaps because they are so understated. In what might be called the second quatrain of the fourteen-book structure (the first quatrain having to do with the building of Wordsworth's own selfhood), book 5 concerns itself with the culture man creates, and with the culture of man, including his ways of imagining other ways of being. Books 6, 7, and 8 appear to be designed to follow this theoretical introduction by counterpointing three successive visions of actual human life. 'Human nature seeming born again' (VI, 341) is contrasted in book 7 with Londoners 'melted and reduced | To one identity' (VII, 726). In book 8 the central figure is a Cumbrian shepherd 'wedded to his life | Of hope and hazard', whose feet 'Crush out a livelier fragrance from the flowers | Of lowly thyme'. The third vision of human possibility refers back, not surprisingly, to the patriarchal Swiss ('to hardship born and compassed round with | Danger' (VI, 509–10). More surprisingly perhaps it also refers forward, though only in the more carefully articulated *1850* text, to book 9's introduction of Michel Beaupuy as a man whose nature 'Did breathe its sweetness out most sensibly, | As aromatic flowers on Alpine turf, | When foot hath crushed them'.

The introduction of Beaupuy is, however, contextualized by two strains echoed from book 8, and this conjunction creates a remarkable ambivalence. Shepherdlike he may be, in ll. 294–8, but in 298–302 he appears as a character wandering in perfect faith through a realm of Romance. Might Beaupuy, like Wordsworth in book 8, be guilty of excessive exercise of 'that first poetic faculty | Of plain Imagination and severe' and consequently of 'wilfulness of fancy and conceit'? 'From touch of this new power', Wordsworth had said of his own imagination, 'Nothing was safe' (VII, 365–77). The phraseology is ominous, and weighty enough to be applied to that later and greater 'work | Of false imagination' (*1805*, X, 848) his Godwinian new man. Beaupuy, however, is not presented, as Coleridge is in book one 'in endless dreams | Of sickliness, disjoining, joining, things | Without the light of knowledge' (l. 435). Wordsworth and Beaupuy *beheld* a 'living confirmation' of their theories and their aspirations, and

> saw in rudest men,
> Self-sacrifice the firmest; generous love,
> And continence of mind, and sense of right,
> Uppermost in the midst of fiercest strife.
>
> (IX, 386)

They were steadied in their speculations by having real and solid forms about them.

The most striking 'form' of this book, the hunger-bitten girl of Blois, licenses Wordsworth's most positive enunciation of a political manifesto. The girl is employed, as every reader of *The Prelude* knows, as a mobile object to which a heifer can be conveniently tethered, an emblem of the utmost human degradation. What Wordsworth tethers to her, within the same long sentence, is first the unsurprising hope that 'poverty | Abject as this would in a little time | Be found no more' and then a striking series of constitutional demands. The 'heartless' girl releases in him a hope to see

> All institutes for ever blotted out
> That legalized exclusion, empty pomp
> Abolished, sensual state and cruel power

> Whether by edict of the one or few;
> And finally, as sum and crown of all,
> Should see the people having a strong hand
> In framing their own laws; ...

What we have here is, in effect, a recollected Rousseauistic preview of the politics of the *Letter to the Bishop of Llandaff*.[8]

Wordsworth's tale up to this point in book 9 projects a young man only slowly deciding upon his stance and sympathies. Lured (IX, 34) into a 'theatre, whose stage was filled | And busy with an action far advanced' (IX, 94) he was 'unprepared with needful knowledge'. The National Synod, and the Bastille, are tourist attractions, like but less powerful than 'the painted Magdalen of le Brun' (IX, 42–80). Only by a species of reaction to Royalist feeling and opinion does he discover that 'The soil of common life, was, at that time, | Too hot to tread on'. His political science, before Beaupuy, amounts to a feeling that 'the best ruled not, and feeling that they ought to rule', a position rooted in his schooltime experience of 'ancient homeliness' in Lakeland's admittedly untypical 'nook'. The events of France seem to have happened 'rather late than soon'. Identifying with the French in their desire to share in such ancient homeliness as Cumbrians enjoy, and with the 'bravest youth of France' enlisting in defence of their revolution, he thunderously concludes that no one could resist their cause

> Who was not lost, abandoned, selfish, proud,
> Mean, miserable, wilfully depraved,
> Hater perverse of equity and truth.

There is, then, little in book 9 except its frame to suggest that this is a cautionary tale. The framing should be noted, however. Book 9 began with an ominous image: that of the poet fearing to press on for fear of the 'ravenous', or in *1805* 'devouring', sea that lies in wait (IX, 4). It ends, in *1805,* with the narrative of Vaudracour and Julia as an oblique instance of impatience, illegitimacy, and untethered mind.

'Domestic Carnage'

In October 1792 the fierce metropolis finds Wordsworth—now bound for England—by no means as indifferent to late events as he had been the previous year. The account given in the first paragraph of book 10, of the historical state of play, leaves one in no doubt which side Wordsworth is on. The revolutionary state has a high and fearless soul, and is a republic in body as well as in name. The late and lamentable crimes are past, and 'the plains of liberty' seems a suitable periphrasis for French soil. In daylight, however, the Carousel is no more affecting than was the Bastille a year before: he seems still unable to unlock the meaning of Parisian stones. Only at night, in his lonely garret room, does the carnage of the previous month, in the September Massacres, seem close enough to touch. Or rather, for this is Wordsworth's most manufactured 'spot', the events can be made to yield a 'substantial dread' by one willing to work and to be wrought upon by apocalyptic incantations and tragic fictions and appropriate echoes of Shakespeare. The brilliant, if over-literary, vision ends by grafting Burke's 'swinish multitude' onto Blake's revolutionary tigers to produce a sense of Paris as a place 'Defenceless as a wood where tigers roam' (IX, 93).

One's suspicion that this dread is somewhat factitious, a product of Burke's intoxicating bowl, is reinforced by its slight effect on Wordsworth's daytime consciousness. True, he attributes to himself foresight of widening terror, but the immediate consequence is that he toys with the idea of summoning an international brigade to descend on France 'from the four quarters of the winds' to compel her to be free. In such a cause he would have been prepared to offer 'Service however dangerous'. When he reflects that

> A spirit thoroughly faithful to itself,
> Is for Society's unreasoning herd
> A domineering instinct
>
> (X, 167)

it is not entirely clear whether he sees himself as the needful bellwether merely expressing willingness, as an insignificant stranger, to serve other 'paramount mind'.

At home in England, Wordsworth presents himself as no woolly-minded liberal but a strident revolutionary—more Stalinist than Hegelian—indifferent to the outcome of Clarkson's campaign against the slave-trade not because slavery isn't a rotten business, but because it is fatuous to concern oneself with pruning a tree which is on the point of being felled.

> for I brought with me the faith
> That if France prospered, good men would not long

Pay fruitless worship to humanity,
And this most rotten branch of human shame.
Object, so seemed it, of superfluous pains,
Would fall together with its parent tree.

(X, 257)

This systemic metaphor should caution one against any reading of Wordsworth's convictions at this date based upon a compendium of good causes:
the 1805 text expresses derision for disappointed campaigners awaiting the
next fashionable 'caravan', just as the 1850 introduces a barbed reference
to English liberals experiencing 'a novel heat of virtuous feeling'. Unless
the metaphor is loosely chosen, slavery is here envisioned as part of a
shameful system of exploitation, based upon division, ownership, and the
failure to recognize the good of humanity as an end in itself. Wordsworth's
relative indifference to it as a single issue indicates a confidence in the
imminent fall of all social organizations based upon any but *'equity* and
justice'.[9] 'Such was my then belief' (*1805* continues), 'that there was one,
| And only one, solicitude for all.'

There follows 'the conflict of sensations without name' brought about
by the declaration of war between Britain and France. Britain's rulers could
not see that to test old-fashioned 'patriotic love' at the very moment when
the volcano of revolution was bringing to birth a new and higher loyalty,
to human freedom itself, was akin to deifying John the Baptist and spurn-
ing the Christ. The implication of this outrageous analogy is that responsibility for the crucifixion of humanity that follows must be laid at the
door of English idolaters. Should we miss that implication it does not
matter, because Wordsworth's account of the Great Terror begins, at line
331, by arraigning Pitt for provoking it.

Nothing in *The Prelude,* in either text, exculpates Pitt. There were of
course men in France who 'for their desperate ends had plucked up mercy
by the roots', but only Pitt's goad could have created the coalition of
temperaments necessary to the instigation and the continuance of revolutionary terror. In describing the terror, which began in June 1794, Wordsworth uses the oddest of his exculpatory tropes: the guillotine whirls like
a windmill, with a kind of macabre innocence. The infant revolution, we
are invited to conclude, exemplifies like any other infant the recurring
Wordsworthian theme of 'the might of souls . . . while yet the yoke of earth
is new to them' (III, 180), and the desirable 'eagerness of infantine desire'.
One of Wordsworth's selves parenthetically questions the image, but does
not censor it:

Domestic carnage now filled the whole year
With feast-days; old men from the chimney nook,
The maiden from the bosom of her love,
The mother from the cradle of her babe,
The warrior from the field—all perished, all—
Friends, enemies, of all parties, ages, ranks,
Head after head, and never heads enough
For those that bade them fall. They found their joy,
They made it proudly, eager as a child,
(If light desires of innocent little ones
May with such heinous appetites be compared),
Pleased in some open field to exercise
A toy that mimics with revolving wings
The motion of a windmill; though the air
Do of itself blow fresh, and make the vanes
Spin in his eyesight, *that* contents him not,
But, with the plaything at arm's length, he sets
His front against the blast, and runs amain,
That it may whirl the faster.

(X, 356)

The edict which released the worst phase of the Terror was passed on 10 June 1794. Two days before that, on 8 June 1794, Wordsworth told Mathews (with whom he was planning a somewhat Fabian organ of reform to be called *The Philanthropist*) that he 'recoiled from the bare idea of a revolution'. He described himself as 'a determined enemy to every species of violence'.[10] Ten years later *The Prelude* certainly expresses in these lines a horror of violence, but Wordsworth seems equally capable of finding images expressive of something which is not merely horror, but a kind of dreadful fascination. Either Wordsworth the philanthropist was not, in fact, as 'determined' an enemy to 'every species of violence' as he pretended, or Wordsworth the poet has become aware, whether in writing *The Prelude* or at some point in between, that the rage for destruction is something he had shared.

A second 'childhood' image is introduced at line 391, dignified association with both classical and English myth: 'The Herculean Commonwealth had put forth her arms and throttled with an infant godhead's might | The snakes about her cradle'. Part of its function is to prepare for the curious usage of the terms 'treachery' and 'desertion' in the nightmare passage which follows: Wordsworth presents himself as tortured 'through

months, through years, long after the last beat | Of those atrocities' (well
into the Racedown period, that is) by nightmares of imprisonment, nightmares in which he appears to plead before unjust tribunals 'with a
voice | Labouring, a brain confounded, and a sense, | Death-like, of treach-
erous desertion, felt | In the last place of refuge—my own soul'. The
ambiguity is of the sharpest order: would it be more treacherous to plead
against the victims of the terror, or on their behalf? The function of the
'Herculean Commonwealth' image, and the repeated child motif, is to give
weight to the less expected sense, that the treachery is to the infant commonwealth, the rough beast that born-again human nature turns out to be.

Can human nature in its 'dog-day' aspect be worshipped as physical
nature had been worshipped in its tumultuous states? The answer to that
strange question (if that is what the paragraph X, 416–36 means) appears
to be yes. Wordsworth identifies with those (briefly alluded to at X, 340)
who see the terror as part of the wrath of providence, a sublime retribution: he experiences 'daring sympathies with power', sympathies whose
'dread vibration is to this hour prolonged' (X, 457–60—the final phrase in
1850 only). The devouring sea, threatened at the beginning of book 9, is
now (X, 470–80) understood as a 'deluge' of ancient guilt, spreading its
loatsome charge, to fertilize (if one may extrapolate the image as Wordsworth does elsewhere) the plains of liberty.

That being so, it is hard to see why Robespierre, prime strangler of the
snakes about the cradle of the commonwealth, and lancer of the boils of
ancient guilt, should come in for such rhetorical vengeance as he receives
at Wordsworth's hands in X, 481–603. If those of the Poole circle in 1794
could view Robespierre as 'a ministering angel of mercy, sent to slay thos-
ands that he might save millions' why should Wordsworth react so differently?[11] That he did rejoice so immoderately one may doubt. But even as
an instance of editorial self-exculpation, a distancing, it is quite out of
character with the rest of the account. The extent of Wordsworth's alleged
glee is puzzling. The reference to Robespierre as 'chief regent' of 'this foul
Tribe of Moloch' might be understood as an ironic adoption of fiercely
anti-Jacobin sentiments except that no irony seems to be present. Or we
might see Robespierre as having given too many hostages to Tory propa-
gandists and having fuelled counter-revolutionary zeal. But there is a further consideration. Robespierre appears as having incarnated Wordsworth's
own revolutionary self, a self which was far closer to the reality of the
'angel of death' so lightly spoken of in Nether Stowey, and which the poet
of 1805 is relieved to lay to rest.

The letter to Mathews already quoted contains—presumably by coincidence—the very image Coleridge would use in 1795 to describe Robes-pierre. Wordsworth in June 1794 can see himself as one who 'in [his] ardour to attain the goal, [does] not forget the nature of the ground where the race is to be run': Coleridge sees Robespierre as one whose eagerness to reach the 'grand and beautiful' prospect ahead of him caused him to 'neglect the foulness of the road'.[12] Whether or not Wordsworth has Robes-pierre in mind, in choosing his image, it is clear that he does not choose to present himself to Mathews as one who has already been seduced into excessive hatred, or undisciplined benevolence, or discovered to what ex-treme consequences his conversion, by the innocent Godwin, to schemes of social engineering, could lead him.

'Come now, ye Golden Times'

The death of Robespierre is prepared for and concluded by the most com-plex assortment of motifs. It begins with a paragraph of recollection of the joys of Arras (Robespierre's birthplace) in 1790, and ends with a reprise of the Furness 'spot' from Wordsworth's own boyhood. It tells of a visit to the burial-place of William Taylor the wise instructor (Taylor stands in perhaps for that later tutor Michel Beaupuy, but also contrasting with him, as the one who set Wordsworth on the safer path of poetry). It includes a description of ethereal mountains observed from the Leven sands, mountains reminiscent of the 'dawn dedication' passage, and pauses to make ironic reference to the 'great sea . . . at a safe distance far retired', having momentarily suspended its ravages.

The announcement, by a passing traveller, of Robespierre's death oc-casions from Wordsworth a 'hymn of triumph', and (in *1805*) 'glee of spirit' and 'joy in vengeance'. It is presented as reawakening and reactivating Wordsworth's sense of himself as a power: his boyhood mastery of the horses of Furness usurps upon the fading echoes of the horsemen of apoc-alypse. The Wordsworth who with his boyhood associates 'beat with thun-dering hoofs the level sand' now sees himself, with his political associates, cleansing the Augean stables by more patient means than those of Her-cules, tranquillizing the 'madding factions', and furthering 'the glorious renovation'. The shadow has passed, and its passing is recorded in a dawn image, which Wordsworth orchestrates as deliberately for humanity as Coleridge once orchestrated a sublime sunset for Lamb in 'This Lime-Tree Bower': 'Come now, ye golden times . . . as the morning comes | From out the bosom of the night come ye'.

The reprise of 'We beat with thundering hoofs the level sand' makes so resonant a conclusion to book 10 in the 1850 text that it can obscure the fact that the 'dawn' image is not yet finished with. The death of Robespierre marks in fact a rite of passage for Wordsworth's revolutionary self— all things have second birth—and he looks now (August 1794) for the republic to enjoy triumphs which will be 'Great, universal, irresistible'. Lines 19–27 of book 11 recognize that he was mistaken, but the revolutionary self is permitted an uncensored claim that what is at work, once again, is Nature's self. Wordsworth seems confident that the acquittal of Thelwall, Hardy, and Tooke in the treason trials of December 1794 is a victory for Nature, Justice, and Liberty over those who, in England, appeared intent on importing terror in the cause of repression.

Less clear is what happens when Wordsworth returns 'from those bitter truths' about Pitt's persecutions to continue his own history. On the face of it, book 11, lines 75–104, which review his development as a political thinker, could be dealing solely with the summer of 1792, when under Beaupuy's tutelage he was led to take 'an eager part | In arguments of civil polity'. Arguably, however, the same passage could be surveying his political development through to the end of 1794 when, with Mathews, he is striving to learn to what extent the happiness of nations depends 'Upon their laws, and fashion of the state'.

Most readers have, quite reasonably, taken the passage beginning

> Bliss was it in that dawn to be alive,
> But to be young was very Heaven!

to refer unambiguously to France's 'standing on the top of golden hours' in the period between 1790 (the walk to Como) and 1792 (the friendship with Beaupuy). The fact that the lines were separately published under the title 'Feelings of an Enthusiast upon the Commencement of the French Revolution' appears to confirm that view, as indeed does the reflection that Wordsworth in 1794 is not thought to have known much 'bliss'.

In context, however, in *The Prelude*, the antecedent dawn is that which breaks in August 1794 upon the sands of Leven. One of the most impressive features of *The Prelude*, especially in *1850*, is Wordsworth's articulation of image to image: Snowdon and Simplon are linked by usurpation of vapours, the Shepherd and Beaupuy by herbal fragrances, and so on. Could a poet who links widely separated episodes by such means *miss* the fact that the logical antecedent of 'that dawn' is the dawn of hope in 1794, a mere 134 lines before? Simply *by placing the passage where he places it,* Wordsworth invites the question whether he found in the early period of maximum political involvement following the terror the climax of his bliss.

Moreover, the reference in this famous passage to 'Reason' seeming to assert her rights 'When most intent on making of herself a prime enchantress', seems to fit the Godwinian period of 1794 rather better than any moment before that, as indeed does the imagery of plasticity (IX, 138) and of moulding and remoulding (XI, 150) the world one inherits. If this 'dawn' is that of 1789 or 1790, Wordsworth's description of himself as politically committed in *that* dawn is thoroughly misleading. If it is the summer of 1792, it is hard to see what the 'licence' of II, 163 refers to, or why he refers to himself as

> Not caring if the wind did now and then
> Blow keen upon an eminence that gave
> Prospect so large into futurity.

As an image for one who has come to terms with the need for political violence, this has the merit of somewhat chilling understatement: as an image for one who knows of nothing worse than the fall of the Bastille, or the need to repel invaders massing upon the borders, it simply misses the mark.

What prevents one from concluding that the 'blissful dawn' is biographically as well as textually subsequent to rather than prior to the death of Robespierre is, of course, the resumption of relative chronological clarity at XI, 173. 'In the main outline, such it might be said | Was my condition, till with open war | Britain opposed the liberties of France'. This statement would certainly appear to restrict the 'blissful dawn' to a period before February 1793. Even this, however, is five months after the September Massacres. In any case the event which is blamed for clouding the blissful dawn, and bringing to an end this 'condition' of rapture is not, in the first place, Robespierre's terror but Pitt's military action against France.

No doubt Coleridge, as auditor-elect, was better equipped than we to know precisely what the landmarks were in Wordsworth's political development. For whatever reason, the frequency of Wordsworth's references to time in book II does nothing to make them more distinct. 'But now', Wordsworth continues, in XI, 206, 'become oppressors in their turn, | Frenchmen had changed a war of self-defence | For one of conquest'. It is not possible to date this 'now' any earlier than May 1794, when the French began a summer of offensive military campaigns, or to know what it signifies. Dire though the news is, it makes France no worse than the autocratic powers opposing her. Wordsworth is unlikely to have sided with those fighting against France any earlier than Tom Poole (who was welcoming Napoleon's victories in May 1797);[13] and he seems to have taken most of France's martial adventures prior to the second invasion of Switzerland in his stride. War merely prompts him to adhere 'more firmly to old tenets'.

And 'this was the time' (XI, 223) when Godwin's philosophy arrived to complete the work Pitt had begun: the stopping of the passages through which the ear converses with the heart. The poet's goaded mind takes on the mantle of Robespierre, dragging 'all precepts, judgements, maxims, creeds, | Like culprits to the bar' (XI, 295) and probing (in *1805*) 'the living body of society | Even to the heart (*1805,* X, 875).

'Studied vagueness' understates what Wordsworth is doing with chronology throughout the first 305 lines of book 11. They lead up to an undateable moral and intellectual crisis, some time between the joint depredations of France and Godwin in 1794 and the beginnings of recovery in late 1795 under Dorothy's influence at Racedown: a crisis most probably associated with political activity during the period of residence in the great city in 1795. In any case, if one examines the images employed, even as hastily as here, one cannot but notice that something more than a haziness about dates is involved. The poetry seems designed to induce a real confusion about the sequence of events and responses, rather than merely about their intervals. Confusion has its attraction, of course, for if 'Bliss' cannot be dated, neither culpability nor apostasy can be established. But the confusion in this case seems to stem from something else: a recognition that the famous cantata to revolutionary enthusiasm seems to Wordsworth to apply with equal force to two quite separate phases in his political development, and to express two quite different states of being.

One of those states is the one which generates in the course of the narrative that striking sequence of tropes designed to rob terror of its sting: the child with his windmill, Hercules in his cradle, and the wind upon an eminence. Each figure exhibits, arguably, that use of language Wordsworth deplored in the Essays upon Epitaphs, as 'a counter-spirit, unremittingly and noiselessly at work to derange, to subvert, to lay waste, to vitiate, and to dissolve' (*Prose Works,* 2:85). More pertinently, perhaps, Wordsworth's prefatory essay to *The Borderers* directly addresses the tendency of revolutionaries to employ style to diminish atrocities. He remarks of the revolutionary mind that it will tend to 'chequer & degrade enterprises great in their atrocity by grotesque littleness of manner and fantastic obliquities' (*Prose Works,* 1:78). This is not through lack of imagination. Minds such as Oswald's possess powerful imagination, as the preface observes. The presence of powerful imagination is perhaps appropriately signified in the 'windmill' simile and the mountaintop metaphor by their common element, the correspondent breeze.

'A Veil Had Been Uplifted'

In book 9, lines 224–320, Wordsworth develops his account of the intellectual crisis which ends his revolutionary career. Godwinian philosophy, the philosophy 'That promised to abstract the hopes of man | Out of his feelings', but which in fact allowed the passions to work disguised as pure reason seduces Wordsworth into the experience he dramatizes in his 'Oswald'. (Wordsworth's distrust of the reason may be Burkean, as Chandler argues, but it can also be heard as strikingly Nietzschean). What both experience is masterful personal liberty,

> Which, to the blind restraints of general laws
> Superior, magisterially adopts
> One guide, the light of circumstances, flashed
> Upon an independent intellect.

The career of 'Oswald' shows this guide to be a will-o'-the-wisp—an abstraction operating upon a delusion—and line 248 speaks of Wordsworth's understanding as 'inflamed'. None the less, the desire that man should 'start out of his earthy, worm-like state' still appears to Wordsworth 'A noble aspiration!' To the 1805 declaration that 'yet I feel the aspiration', the 1850 text adds 'nor shall ever cease | To feel it'. What he criticizes himself for is the desire to accomplish that transformation 'by such means as did not lie in nature'.

If the enlightenment dream of the man to come, parted as by a gulph from him who has been (XII, 59–60) is a work of 'false imagination' it is none the less justified by the upholders of 'ancient Institutions'.

> Enough, no doubt, the advocates themselves
> Of ancient Institutions had performed
> To bring disgrace upon their very names;
> Disgrace, of which, custom and written law,
> And sundry moral sentiments as props
> And emanations of those institutes,

Too justly bore a part. *A veil had been*
Uplifted; why deceive ourselves? 'twas so,
'Twas even so; and sorrow for the man
Who either had not eyes wherewith to see,
Or, seeing, hath forgotten!

(*1805*, X, 849; my italics)

Moreover it is at this point that Wordsworth describes himself as having been mentally let loose, 'let loose and goaded', a trope which combines an image earlier used of the French leaders in 1794 (goaded into terror by Pitt's ministrations, X, 336), with one used in the *Letter to the Bishop of Llandaff* of the French people themselves: 'The animal just released from its stall will exhaust the overflow of its spirits in a round of wanton vagaries'.[14] He thereby gratuitously associates himself with the Mountain and the People, and absolves all three.

Wordsworth's hymn of triumph at the passing of the shadow, Robespierre, one may conclude, is only partly occasioned by what he felt about the death of Robespierre himself. A major element is relief, felt at the time of writing, at the dethroning of his Godwinian self whose depredations upon the living body of society and nature's holiest places are quite clearly presented as an internalization of Robespierre's practices. Yet that self, even amid these confusing obsequies (confused by images of dawn and consecration and mingled origins at Arras and Hawkshead) asserts itself sufficiently to see the 'dawn' of Robespierre's death as the blissful dawn of its own experience.

Its continued co-presence as co-author in 1804 is responsible, one has to feel, for the fact that Wordsworth, although largely restored to his milder self, by nature and 'all varieties of human love', twice employs language of the utmost vituperation in books 10 and 11. First in the reference to Pitt's verminous Tory cabinet, and its imitative bloodlust, and second in his account of the coronation of Napoleon in 1804.

This last opprobrium *when we see the dog*
Returning to his vomit; when the sun
That rose in splendour, was alive, and moved
In exultation among living clouds
Hath put his function and his glory off,
And turned into a gewgaw, a machine,
Sets like an Opera phantom.

The sun is dead and France has killed it.

Wordsworth had been of the devil's party. In so far as to be a man of blood is to be of the devil's party, he remains one in book 12 and 13. It has been part of my intention to suggest that Wordsworth in *The Prelude* justifies the little terror, and partially excuses the great terror, just as he presents the character of Oswald, in *The Borderers,* as a blend of himself and Robespierre. Imagination resuscitates past selves and their loyalties.

But this explanation is too simple. It is not necessary, after all, that it should be a strictly revolutionary self that in the *1805* and *1850* texts continues to legitimate a certain connoisseurship of blood. It might also be an apocalyptic one. We see that self emerging, in fact, in the curious rhetoric of book 10 where Wordsworth notes among the observers of the terror who 'doubted not that providence had times of vengeful retribution' (X, 340), and suggests that some spirit fell on him that linked him with the ancient prophets who

> Wanted not consolations . . .
> > when they denounced
> On towns and cities, wallowing in the abyss
> Of their offences, punishment to come
> > > (X, 440)

Wordsworth's youthful and revolutionary selves were certainly more imaginative than his editorial self. The youthful imagination is unafraid of contemplating 'a world how different from this', or 'something evermore about to be'. It is pleased that a midnight storm can grow darker 'in the presence of my eye', and delights in witnessing—in the Snowdon vision—how the real sea gives up its majesty in the face of an imaginative usurpation, the sea of mist on whose shore Wordsworth finds himself. Similarly, the revolutionary self is able to share the excitement of a Robespierre, or a Godwin, as they contemplate 'the man to come, parted as by a gulph from him who had been', or try to bring to birth 'a world how different from this', or drive man more rapidly along what Coleridge called the imaginative 'ascent of being'.

Most accounts of Wordsworth's imagination, however, leave out the quality of dread, which while present elsewhere emerges most clearly in the negative sublime of the Salisbury Plain spot, whose topography is associated with another of Wordsworth's literary self-projections in the 1790s, the benevolently murderous sailor of *Guilt and Sorrow.* In book 13, lines 279–349, in a major argument too little attended to in this context, Wordsworth presents himself as wandering across Salisbury Plain in a state of confidence that he has the power to perceive things unseen before, and to create works that because they arise 'from a source of untaught things' might 'become a power like one of Nature's'. There, like his sailor in *Guilt and Sorrow,* he 'paced the bare white roads | Lengthening in solitude their dreary line'. For him, however, time fled backward until he saw 'multitudes of men, and here and there, | A single Briton clothed in wolfskin vest' and heard 'The voice of spears':

> I called on darkness—but before the word
> Was uttered, midnight darkness seemed to take
> All objects from my sight; and lo! again
> The desert visible by dismal flames;
> It is the sacrificial altar, fed
> With living men—how deep the groans! The voice
> Of those that crowd the giant wicker thrills
> The monumental hillocks, and the pomp
> Is for both worlds, the living and the dead.

Such wickers, according to Frazer, formed part of traditional midsummer processions in some regions of Europe, and particularly France and Belgium, until well into the early years of the nineteenth century. In Brie a wicker giant was burnt annually on Midsummer's Eve. In Paris and elsewhere the preferred date was the nearest Sunday to 7 July. In many areas animals—usually cats—were substituted for the human sacrifices that according to Caesar and Strabo were offered by the ancient Gauls. For contemporary cartoonists the wicker was negatively associated with the iconography of terror: Wordsworth, however, seems able to sympathize with the sublimity of sacrifice.

While Chandler boldly deals with the early spots of time as Burkean, in that they have to do with the discipline of place, he has less to say about this spot, except to call it—none too helpfully, it seems to me—'a sublime dream of Burke's immemorial British past'.[15] The meaning of this reverie concerning benign druidic sacrifice may not be welcome, but it is clear: the imaginative mind 'stands by Nature's side among the men of old' and may indeed 'boldly take his way among mankind | Wherever nature leads' (XIII, 296), whether it leads to contemplation of the stars or to 'the sacrificial altar, fed | With living men' (ll. 331–2).

Imagination is geared to the sublime in so extraordinary a degree that in 1816 Wordsworth will celebrate the bloodshed of Waterloo as both a votive offering and a martial feat on a scale sufficient to satiate Imagination. The 'Ode: 1815' made many tremble, not least for the lines on the deity which Wordsworth advisedly cut:

> But Thy most dreaded instrument,
> In working out a pure intent,
> Is man arrayed for mutual slaughter,
> Yea, Carnage is thy daughter

But these lines of 1816 are not, it seems to me, an aberration. They continue in a direct line from the Salisbury Plain spot, in which Wordsworth offered his definitive statement of what it means to be a child of nature and to stand by Nature's side. A veil had indeed been uplifted in the 1790s, but there was more behind it than revolutionary sympathy. There was also the curious perception, attributed to Ovid in Geoffrey Hill's poem ('Ovid in the Third Reich', *King Log*, 1968), that those who stand near 'the ancient troughs of blood', though they may be damned, 'harmonise strangely with the divine love'.

Notes

1. All quotations from *The Prelude* are from the Penguin edition and from the *1850* text except where noted.

2. The reference to enchantment is surely an allusion to Coleridge's reference to France in *France; an Ode* as 'disenchanted'.

3. See George Watson, 'The Revolutionary Youth of Wordsworth and Coleridge', *Critical Quarterly*, 18, no. 3, 49–66, John Beer, 'The "Revolutionary Youth" of Wordsworth and Coleridge: Another View', *Critical Quarterly*, 19 (1976), 79–86, and David Ellis, 'Wordsworth's Revolutionary Youth: How We Read *The Prelude*,' *Critical Quarterly*, (1976), 59–67.

4. See Michael Friedman's illuminating account, in *The Making of a Tory Humanist* (New York, 1979), of Wordsworth's friendship with Beaupuy and the nature of Wordsworth's confusion in imagining that he shared Girondin's objectives, and James K. Chandler's often persuasive account of the Burkean basis of Wordsworth's political views, in *Wordsworth's Second Nature: A Study of the Poetry and the Politics* (Chicago and London, 1984).

5. Both of these Burkean theses seem to me to rely on a very partial reading of the later Wordsworth—in the *The Convention of Cintra* and the *Postscript* for instance.

6. In the 1976 debate in the *Critical Quarterly* neither George Watson nor John

Beer referred to the evidence of the Poole family regarding Coleridge's sentiments in 1794. Either Coldridge [*sic*] or Southey is alleged to have greeted the news of the death of Robespierre with the remark that 'Robespierre was a ministering angel of mercy, sent to slay thousands that he might save millions'. Mrs Sandford, *Thomas Poole and his Friends,* 2 vols. (London, 1888), 1, p. 105.

7. In 'Tintern Abbey' Wordsworth's 'though changed no doubt from what I was' alludes, Tony Brinkley has suggested, to the fallen Satan while invoking the unchanged Milton. See 'Vagrant and Hermit: Milton and the Politics of *Tintern Abbey', Wordsworth Circle,* 16 (1985), pp. 126–33.

8. It is hard to know whether 'edict of the few' could in this instance include the idea of representative government (to which Rousseau was opposed, but which his reading of Paine persuaded Wordsworth to accept as sensible), or whether 'the people' meant some of the people (as it did to the Girondins) or all of the people (as it did to Robespierre and to Wordsworth in *A Letter to the Bishop of Llandaff*). But the 'studied vagueness' here is not merely poetic: it is appropriate after all to Wordsworth in 1793, a Wordsworth taking his first steps in political science, and 'untaught' in 'nice distinctions'.

9. *1805* says the issue never 'fastened on' his affections; *1850* is surely more credible when it says the issue did not 'rivet itself' upon those affections.

10. *The Letters of William and Dorothy Wordsworth. The Early Years 1787–1805,* ed. E. de Selincourt. Second ed. rev. Chester L. Shaver (Oxford, 1967), p. 124.

11. See note 6 above.

12. S. T. Coleridge, *Lectures 1795 on Politics and Religion,* ed. L. Patton and P. Mann (1971), p. 35.

13. Mrs. Henry Sandford. *Thomas Poole and His Friends.* 2 vols. London: Macmillan, 1888, i, 219.

14. *Prose Works,* I, p. 38.

15. James K. Chandler, *Wordsworth's Second Nature.* Chicago: University of Chicago Press, 1984, 139.

A Transformed Revolution

The Prelude, *Books 9–13*

ALAN LIU

◆ ◆ ◆

Shapeless Eagerness

BECAUSE THE REVOLUTION BOOKS are among the most difficult sections of the poem to grasp as a whole, it may be useful to
begin with an overview of their design. A look at the strangely shapeless
river that opens book 9 will point the way:

> As oftentimes a River, it might seem,
> Yielding in part to old remembrances,
> Part sway'd by fear to tread an onward road
> That leads direct to the devouring sea
> Turns, and will measure back his course, far back,
> Towards the very regions which he cross'd
> In his first outset; so have we long time
> Made motions retrograde, in like pursuit
> Detain'd. But now we start afresh; I feel
> An impulse to precipitate my Verse.
> Fair greetings to this shapeless eagerness,
> Whene'er it comes, needful in work so long,
> Thrice needful to the argument which now
> Awaits us.
>
> (IX, 1–14)

From the hypothetical river in book 1 whose floating twig points the poet's way (I, 31–2) to the figurative Nile in book 6, rivers have throughout imaged Wordsworth's act of touring. What makes the river in book 9 more than ordinarily interesting, however, is that in a historical context the image is not just another insignia of inspiration. Wordsworth's character-istic river of history, as Barbara T. Gates has identified the image ("Words-worth and the Course of History"), is here an inspiration especially oblique to actual history.

Imagine, for example, what the poet would have seen in the river had his drift been toward realism. He would have had good reason to be "Part sway'd by fear." Like the Street, the River was one of the most celebrated killing grounds of the Revolution. As Cobb and others have noted, it was the bloodbath not only of popular violence but of the organized violences that allowed the Mountain to suppress the Vendéan counterrevolution. Popular riots thus began so frequently on river banks (and seaports) that the French police became "obsessed" with keeping rivers under surveillance (Cobb, *Police,* p. 16). And in the Vendée, late 1793 saw some of the most infamous of all French violences: the *Noyades* on the Loire as well as other deaths-by-water.[1]

In this direction Wordsworth's shapeless eagerness must not turn. Rather, with a touch of the pen that is his Moses' rod, he stains the water clear. The shapeless eagerness of his Revolution books will indeed carry a full freight of violence—a stream of disassociated names, events, topics that even at the time of writing (and certainly in our time) are finally only as interesting as drowned corpses: distended with irrecoverable mean-ing. But shapeless eagerness washes away such debris of realism by at last converting history into myth. The myth is a story of deluge followed by lyric peace. As we will see, Wordsworth's shapeless eagerness is the very genius of transform [*sic*] allowing him at last to deny the deluge of revo-lution—to recover the antediluvian Loire he knew firsthand in 1792 and to prophesy the postdiluvian zone at Leven Sands.

We can chart the precise route of shapeless eagerness in books 9–10 against the course of waters in two other histories of the poet's revolu-tionary involvement. On the one hand, there is the devouring sea in *The Borderers.* Rivers is a Robespierre-figure who, in the action antecedent to the play's main action, arrives at a sea figuring mental, moral, and social over-throw, suffers a sea change, and returns to show Mortimer the land's end of all order (4.2). The barely stageable plot and style of *The Borderers* are themselves a turbulent river, a type, indeed, of disordered Rivers. When we as readers puzzle over plot, motive, and sometimes even the sense of sentences, we enter into the character of Mortimer asking Rivers repeatedly, "What hast thou seen?" "What do you mean?" (1.1.234, 249). Except in those passages that verge toward lyric (when irony-become-affection, as we have seen, anticipates full subjectivity), the play exhibits a narrative turbulence that refuses to let us stand at a reflective or emotionally "recollective" distance: it is *enactive.*

On the other hand, there are the still waters of book 3 of the later *Excursion* (*The Poetical Works of William Wordsworth,* ed. Ernest de Selincourt and Helen Darbishire, (1940–49, 5: 75–108).[2] Following Shakespearean precedent, *The Borderers* had achieved closure by calling for a future stately recapitulation: Mortimer, we remember, instructs his band to "Raise on this lonely Heath a monument / That may record my story" for warning (5.3.262–3). In a sense, it is an even more mortified Mortimer that then reappears as the Solitary in book 3 of *The Excursion,* where he becomes his own historian erecting the final memorial to the revolutionary spirit. In a natural amphitheater with stones like "monumental pillars" (l. 57), the Solitary renders his tale of personal and political disillusion in the aftermath of the French Revolution with nearly marmoreal composure. For just a moment, the enclosure converts into a theater proper, and he becomes a Mortimer projecting his agony: he spoke "As skill and graceful nature might suggest / To a proficient of the tragic scene" (ll. 465–6). But the moment of narrative enactment passes, and the Solitary becomes a historian condensing his life's story into schematic chapters pointed with studied or mock exclamations. Past joy surfaces only as "faint echoes from the historian's page" (l. 603), and past grief survives archaeologically: "Only by records in myself not found" (l. 705).

At the last, the narrative urgency of the Solitary's tale fades entirely into the lyric brilliance of the stream at the end of book 3. His present life, he says in an outpouring of imagery as lyrical as any in Wordsworth's work, is like "a mountain brook / In some still passage of its course." The brook is wholly reflective, recalling only in murmurs the echoes of past precipitations:

> The tenour
> Which my life holds, he readily may conceive
> Whoe'er hath stood to watch a mountain brook
> In some still passage of its course, and seen,
> Within the depths of its capacious breast,
> Inverted trees, rocks, clouds, and azure sky;
> And, on its glassy surface, specks of foam,

And conglobated bubbles undissolved,
Numerous as stars; that, by their onward lapse,
Betray to sight the motion of the stream,
Else imperceptible. Meanwhile, is heard
A softened roar, or murmur; and the sound
Though soothing, and the little floating isles
Though beautiful, are both by Nature charged
With the same pensive office; and make known
Through what perplexing labyrinths, abrupt
Precipitations, and untoward straits,
The earth-born wanderer hath passed; and quickly,
That respite o'er, like traverses and toils
Must he again encounter.—Such a stream
Is human Life; and so the Spirit fares
In the best quiet to her course allowed.

(ll. 967–88)

Fulfilling the call of *The Borderers* for monumental finish, the star-struck, hushed lyricism of the Solitary's narration becomes itself a kind of still passage. The river of stars that is its figure-within-a-figure functions like some actual constellation to awe him into composed acceptance of mortal process—into an idealization by which stories of mortal struggle and pain are transmuted into tracings of eternal peace above.[3] On the strength of a recent paradigm for Wordsworth's poetry, we may call such reflective lyricism "epitaphic."[4] To raise a monument, Wordsworth writes in his first "Essay upon Epitaphs" (composed in 1809–10), "is a sober and a reflective act," and the passions in the inscription "should be subdued, the emotions controlled; strong, indeed, but nothing ungovernable or wholly involuntary" (*The Prose Works of William Wordsworth,* ed. W. J. B. Owen and Jane Worthington Smyser, 1974, 2: 59–60). Such could be the very definition of lyrical "emotion recollected in tranquillity." When Revolutionary history vanishes, what remains is a lyric inscription whose zero-degree story—like the bare name, span of dates, or short verses of an epitaph—points away from the buried narrative to an imagined, eternal history.[5] "My particular current," the Solitary thus anticipates at the close of book 3 of *The Excursion,* will soon "reach / The unfathomable gulf, where all is still!" (ll. 990–1).

The Revolution books of *The Prelude,* I suggest, flow in form from the troubled waters of *The Borderers* to the milky way of *The Excursion* at its best—from enactive narrative to epitaphic lyric. The bulk of books 9–10 is enactive because Wordsworth engages the reader in his younger self's perpetual confusion about the kind of agon the Revolution is and the kind of narrative appropriate to tell it. He portrays himself wandering at first into an inaugural tour poem of history. But descriptive form is suddenly appalled by irrepressible stories of Revolution. Like a curtain on the proscenium stage, description splits in two to reveal a bewildering succession of story forms—most importantly, romance, drama, and epic. Each generic frame in turn rifts apart in its effort to grasp the two aspects of the Revolution, the bright and the dark; and the overall accumulation of genres merely accentuates a sense of shapeless eagerness. Such shapelessness—really an excess of shapes—reduces the distance between the reader and the "I" on the page. We enact the character of the young Wordsworth whose bewilderment the poem figures as the reading, or misreading, of history. He came to look upon the Revolution, the poet says,

> as doth a man
> Upon a volume whose contents he knows
> Are memorable, but from him lock'd up,
> Being written in a tongue he cannot read,
> So that he questions the mute leaves with pain
> And half upbraids their silence.
>
> (X, 49–54)[6]

Yet shapeless as much of books 9–10 may be, a peculiar grace of lyric at last subsumes their enactive agony. As we will see, shapeless narrative first stops at Leven Sands to lyricize the death of Robespierre and that of a beloved teacher, William Taylor. "I" mourn and "I" prophesy, the orphic self sings. The narrative then resumes, but only to lead once more to an orphic moment, an elegy-become-prophecy, devoted to the sick Coleridge. Again the "I" is paramount: "I feel for Thee, must utter what I feel," the poet laments (X, 986). Like Edward King in Milton's *Lycidas,* Robespierre, Taylor, and Coleridge are stand-ins. Each moment of lyric recollection really records the poet in the act of celebrating the death of his own revolutionary spirit and the triumph of his true self. Such are Wordsworth's fetes to end all fetes, his postrevolutionary holidays celebrated in moments of sandy peace when the tide of history has gone out.

Having surveyed the overall terrain, we can now focus on the precise march of genres leading to poetic Thermidor and the regime of terminal fetes that Wordsworth will next institute: the spots of time.

The Beauty of the Revolution

The river inspiring book 9 is just the first signal that history in the Revolution books begins as a tour poem: cities, people, and events are a landscape to be described. Wordsworth depicts his younger self as a "sauntering traveller," for example, leaving the "field" of London with its bookstalls like "Wild produce, hedge-row fruit" (IX, 31–4) to enter France in an exclusively tourist frame of mind. "Through Paris lay my readiest path," he says, "and there / I sojourn'd a few days, and visited / In haste each spot of old and recent fame" (IX, 40–2). Such spots include those that disappoint the naive enthusiast. At the site of the demolished Bastille, for example, the young poet retrieves a souvenir more to follow the etiquette of enthusiasm than because, like Childe Harold in the Colosseum, he feels any grand response to history's ruins:

> Where silent zephyrs sported with the dust
> Of the Bastille, I sate in the open sun,
> And from the rubbish gather'd up a stone
> And pocketed the relick in the guise
> Of an Enthusiast, yet, in honest truth
> Though not without some strong incumbences;
> And glad, (could living man be otherwise)
> I look'd for something that I could not find,
> Affecting more emotion than I felt.
>
> (IX, 63–71)[7]

Already the tourist of political France senses a disjunction between his expectations and the actual lay of the land. The rubble of the Bastille "Seem'd less to recompense the Traveller's pains" (IX, 75) than did a single painting: "the Magdalene of le Brun, / A Beauty exquisitely wrought, fair face / And rueful, with its ever-flowing tears" (IX, 78–80).

The Magdalene is the genius of the landscape Wordsworth tours. He saw Charles Le Brun's *Repentant Magdalene* in its original setting at the Carmelite convent in Paris soon after his arrival in 1791 and before the convent's art works were seized the next year.[8] The painting shows three sets of subjects related emblematically: the overthrown riches and trappings of the Magdalene's life (epitomized by the spilled jewel box at her feet), the Magdalene herself partly reclining upon a seat and facing away from a mirror at the extreme right, and a landscape with tower visible through the window at the left. The congruence of the three subjects brings out their significance. Just as brilliant gems and pearls pour out of the rectilinear confines of the jewel box, so the brilliantly lit Magdalene—herself a kind of jewel or "Beauty exquisitely wrought"—pours across the Cartesian grid of the room's groundplane with a Baroque fluidity repeated in her clothes and hair. The Magdalene, indeed, escapes the figurative jewel box of her past life entirely by turning away from the darkened mirror of *vanitas* that might have boxed her beauty within its frame. And just as both the gems and the Magdalene represent brilliant beauty escaping worldly confines, so the landscape in the background of the recession through the window illustrates the liberation of light. The real reflection of the Magdalene is not in the mirror but in the miraculously released atmosphere of the landscape. Radiance near the horizon refuses to stay boxed in the window, but spills according to the conventions of fresco into the room itself as a suggestion of glory borne upon clouds.

Furthermore, there is a striking way in which Le Brun's painting reached out of its frame to involve the viewer in its subject. *The Repentant Magdalene,* along with six less famous paintings also illustrating the saint's life (designed but not executed by Le Brun), hung in a chapel devoted to the Magdalene. Facing the ensemble and set upon a large, boxlike pedestal was Jacques Sarrazin's kneeling statue of the Cardinal de Bérulle (Eriau, p. 88 and his pl.). Not only did the statue's expression emulate the Magdalene's, but its total form—white marble leaning slightly along diagonals across the pedestal's rectilinear coordinates—imitated the painting's subjects: gems, woman, and radiance escaping worldly confines. The statue provided a model for viewer response to the painting. We can imagine that the viewer—and Wordsworth—would place himself in mind in the emulative posture of the Cardinal and so in alignment with the painting's upward series of subjects culminating in landscape.

Together, then, painting and statue form a tableau allowing us to sketch the traveler's world the young Wordsworth expects and the response he wants this world to unlock in himself. He wants to see a revolutionary country in which liberation arrives, not with the pike thrusts of violence, but with the soft, fluid undulations of a necklace spilling from a box, of clouds rolling through a window, or of the clothes, hair, tears, and body of a woman flowing out of old constraints.[9] In the pictorial terms available to Wordsworth—for whom "Baroque" was not a possibility—Revolutionary France should embody the *beautiful* (the "intricate" side, that is, of the picturesque).[10] Set beside a radiant landscape, the Magdalene's "fair face . . . with its ever-flowing tears" is a paradigm of beauty standing in for such native belles as the Lake District widow "Wetting the turf with never-ending tears" in *Prelude* VIII, 533–41. The young Wordsworth, in sum, has not truly left home upon arriving in France in 1791: he seeks to glimpse an idealized land of childhood watched over by a weeping feminine genius. Only there, in a land like Blake's Beulah, could he achieve self-liberation; only there could he assume the posture of the kneeling Cardinal de Bérulle releasing himself from worldly cares. We should remember, after all, the poet's anxieties at this time about worldly maintenance and his thoughts of entering the clergy. The search for a "relick" at the Bastille leads him directly to the Carmelite convent; the tour through France becomes a pilgrimage toward a Madonna's beauty bypassing historical reality.

But the point of *The Prelude,* surely, is that the traveler of 1791 misread *The Repentant Magdalene* and the beauty of the revolution. Of crucial importance in the painting is not beauty without context, but the condition or aspect in which beauty appears. The 1805 *Prelude* records the young traveler's impression of a sentimental beauty in the condition of ruefulness. The 1850 poem, which details "hair / Dishevelled" and "gleaming eyes," comes closer to the truth by introducing a touch of wildness. In fact, Le Brun's painting depicts beauty, not in the aspect of sentimental sorrow, but in the act of being emotionally ravished or violently transported. The Magdalene's face duplicates most closely the expression of Ravishment or Rapture (similar in many respects to Acute Pain) in Le Brun's widely known illustrations of the passions, and differs markedly from the physiognomies of Sadness or Dejection. Approximating Le Brun's paradigmatic Sadness more closely (coupled, perhaps, with Veneration) is his *Le Repas chez Simon,* also known as *La Madeleine aux pieds de Jésus Christ.* This latter painting, apparently unnoticed by Wordsworth, hung in the church nave of the same convent and shows the Magdalene kneeling before Christ with head lowered and eyes closed.[11] It could have displayed to Wordsworth a truly gentle revolution of spirit before the consoling Son. The contrasting figure in *The Repentant Magdalene,* we might say, expresses in her upward look only a violent revolution of spirit before the fearsome Father. Even the landscape in *The Repentant Magdalene* is at best only darkly beautiful, showing a Claudian radiance near the horizon that must be acted upon by storm clouds before it can be sublimed into the nebular glory overhead.

In Burke's terms, what the young Wordsworth has difficulty seeing is that *The Repentant Magdalene* really illustrates not so much beauty as the rape of beauty by the *sublime,* the other pole of picturesque experience.[12] Jewels, Magdalene, and light are being liberated not by gentleness but by a cataclysmic, "masculine" revolution forcing the Magdalene with her ever-flowing tears into the mold of a punished Niobe. Indeed, it is helpful to notice that *The Repentant Magdalene* bears interesting resemblances to a famous "sublime" painting that Wordsworth probably did not see until 1806 but read about in Reynolds's *Discourses* between July and December 1804, possibly during his autumn work on books 9 and 10: the Wilton-Beaumont version of Richard Wilson's *Destruction of Niobe's Children*.[13] The latter is a kind of *Repentant Magdalene* in which landscape is writ large. Where the Le Brun work shows spilled jewels, the upward-looking Magdalene, clouds projecting past a tower into the foreground, and a hint of supernatural glory above, the Wilson shows Niobe's offspring spilled in death, the figure in the center foreground looking upward in an attitude like the Magdalene's, storm clouds jutting over a fearful landscape into the foreground (there is a tower in the distance), and Apollo upon the clouds shooting arrows. In terms Wordsworth would have known after mid-1804, after he read Reynolds and placed himself under the informal guidance of Sir George Beaumont, *The Repentant Magdalene* is like Wilson's painting in exposing beauty not to a Claudian but to a Salvatorean or Burkean setting—a landscape that suggests violation by rough forces.[14]

The older Wordsworth, we should note, knew that his younger self would soon be implicated in the violation of France's feminine genius. Part of the fame of Le Brun's painting rested upon popular belief that it was a masked portrait of Louise de la Vallière, a maid of honor who became Louis XIV's mistress, suffered from court intrigue, and retired at the age of thirty into the Paris Carmelite convent.[15] Like Julia forced into a convent at the end of book 9, the Magdalene is a type of Annette Vallon (the fact that both Vallon and La Vallière came from Blois further links the two). Looking at the Le Brun painting in 1791, the young Wordsworth half falls in love with a Madonna, but really spies a violable Mary who will come to represent a violated land.

Now we can better understand his strange mental state at the site of the Bastille, a condition not so much of disaffection as of suppressed, unfamiliar emotion on a taboo spot of violation. Just as the young traveler misreads Le Brun's painting, so *The Prelude* shows him misjudging the overall type of pictorial experience political France offers. The razed Bastille is a signature, not of beauty ("something that I could not find"), but of sublime violence, and it affects him with "strong incumbences"—powers incumbent or pressing down from overhead like Apollo on Niobe. The young Wordsworth would suppress such incumbencies under a shield of "gladness." "Could living man be otherwise," he half states, half asks in a strange parenthesis. Yet such gladness rings hollow. Everywhere the traveler looks, he sees a landscape contoured like the rubble of the Bastille and mandating that he be indeed otherwise than glad; everywhere the beautiful Revolution is violated by the characteristic earthquakes and storms of the sublime. "I saw the revolutionary Power / Toss like a Ship at anchor, rock'd by storms" (IX, 48–9), he says. In a seeming lull in the political climate, he observes that "the first storm was overblown, / And the strong hand of outward violence / Lock'd up in quiet" (IX, 109–11). The lull passes, and the eruptions of history continue: "The soil of common life was at that time / Too hot to tread upon" (IX, 169–70); "The land all swarm'd with passion, like a Plain / Devour'd by locusts" (IX, 178–9); and the names of politicians were "Powers, / Like earthquakes, shocks repeated day by day, / And felt through every nook of town and field" (IX, 181–3). No longer a picture of beauty exquisitely wrought, France comes to resemble a John Martin canvas in which whole populations succumb to devastations of sea, sky, and land.

As a tour poem, in sum, the first portion of book 9 surveys a land that has undergone a revolution of terrain before the traveler's eyes. The challenge for the tour mode of perception—as for any framework—is to explain a Revolution beginning in golden promise and ending in dark upheaval. But such radical transition between the greatest "two points" yet faced by his tour framework distresses Wordsworth because he now possesses only an outmoded generic frame no longer able to hold rough sublimity and intricate beauty together in the same world of the picturesque.[16] We might think in terms of the complementary model of loco-description. Just as landscape in a poem such as Denham's "Cooper's Hill" touches off miscellaneous historical or political reflections, so historical events in the tour sections of the Revolution books generate scattered images of landscape. The reversal of ground and figure does not so much indicate difference of kind as nostalgia for an established principle of organization. Wordsworth as he portrays himself in 1791 wants to fix history to a linear route able to index otherwise unrelated sights. But in book 9, the merely associative coordination of the sublime and beautiful no longer suffices. It is now precisely because he cannot find "a regular Chronicle" explaining the origin and development of "the main Organs of the public Power" that events in France appear "loose and disjointed," leaving his affections "without a vital interest" (IX, 101–8). Challenged by changes in historical topography, Wordsworth's younger persona suddenly comes to the point where it yearns to see history, not as a loose variety of beauty and sublimity, but as an organic whole.

The Prelude, of course, argues that in the realm of actual landscape the poet of 1791 had already formulated a philosophy of nature able to integrate the beautiful and sublime at a deep level. (The critique of the tyranny of the eye in book II, indeed, accounts the picturesque to the period *after* France.) The beautiful and sublime in nature became organically linked because they participated in forming, and in being formed by, his self. In the Lakes, "beauteous forms or grand" (I, 573) thus cooperated to influence his growth. Reciprocally, his fancy, as in VIII, 542–86, made landscape even more beautiful while his imagination, as in the Simplon passage, enhanced sublimity. Landscape came to compose a single, coherent picture washed by consciousness in which nurturing and chastising, beautiful and sublime elements complemented each other. Only in such a view of nature where all chastisement is borne with awareness of consolation can the sublime transcend mere horror.

But for the bulk of the Revolution books, the traveler through France not only cannot apply his philosophy of nature to history but seems unaware of any such philosophy separate from what I have called the verificatory nature of the Revolution itself—the time's own idiom of storms, earthquakes, and so forth. One example will demonstrate this point clearly. As remembered in the early books of the poem, beauty and sublimity in the Lakes complemented each other such that a child hanging over a raven's nest could surrender to sublime winds trustingly, mindful of balancing forces (I, 341–50). But *history's* sublime winds cause vertigo, a total loss of balance and trust. After England declares war on France,

> I, who with the breeze
> Had play'd, a green leaf on the blessed tree
> Of my beloved Country; nor had wish'd
> For happier fortune than to wither there,
> Now from my pleasant station was cut off,
> And toss'd about in whirlwinds.
>
>   (X, 253–8)

Wordsworth's conceit merely witnesses the random destruction of beauty by the sublime. Contrary to the hindsight of book II, a fully organic philosophy of nature does not arise until after the Revolution makes it necessary.[17]

Bad Stories

With the failure of description, the curtain rises on the underlying narrative scene. The genre of the tour poem extends into the succeeding portions of the Revolution books: "All else was progress on the self-same path / On which . . . I had been travelling," the poet says, "this a stride at once / Into another region" (X, 238–41). But increasingly, Wordsworth disrupts the facade of description with narrative genres enacting his younger self's shapeless perception of events. Altogether, the kinds of books 9–10 form a layered structure conducting us toward lyric, as shown in Fig. 1. Concentrating for the present on the three narrative genres of romance, drama, and epic, we can see that each produces a version of the tour poem's inadequate split-image of the Revolution: each first projects a golden-world France, then limns a terrible iron age. Or rather, each genre follows the pattern of the travel poem in representing the sudden appearance, not of an iron age conceptually related to the golden past, but of a whirlwind energy—call it gothic, tragic, or hellish—canceling the line of history and confronting the perceiver with a merely monstrous experience.

We might think by contrast of the Revolutionary "ideology of combat," which had organized the forces of liberty and tyranny in a structured agony constitutive of the state. The rift in each of Wordsworth's narrative genres marks something like agon—a combat, for example, between the chivalric and gothic revolutions. But such agon potentially mimetic of historical combat is never comprehended as such. Rather, the moment an agony occurs sharp enough to focus a coherent narrative of revolution, the frame of generic expectation shifts and the lines of combat must be

Genre	*Paradigm Shift in Genre*		
Tour poem	Beautiful——(Picturesque)→Sublime		
Narrative genres			
Romance	Chivalric ————————→Gothic		
Drama	Comic ————————→Tragic		
Miltonic epic	Millennial ————————→Hellish		
Lyric	Elegiac ————————→Prophetic		

FIGURE I The contest of genres in books 9 and 10 of *The Prelude*.

redrawn. The contest of genres in books 9–10 is thus a denied mimesis of revolutionary combat. It flinches back from one genre after another in search of some perfectly purgative narrative form—a tragedy beyond tragedy—able to make acceptable the underlying facts of combat. But a purgation so complete that agony hurts not at all is unimaginable in narrative. Abandoned in mid-performance in all its available narrative forms, history in the Revolution books thus becomes only what we know it intuitively to be: a bad story.

Chivalric romance dominates the middle portion of book 9 before yielding to its dark gothic brother.[18] In what we can call the "Beaupuy Tale" (IX, 294–555), Michel Beaupuy appears as a knight wandering "through a Book, an old Romance or Tale / Of Fairy" (IX, 307–8) and inspires the young Wordsworth to recall "each bright spot" of "truth preserv'd and error pass'd away" (IX, 373–5). Wordsworth thoroughly romanticizes the history seen under this bright spotlight. First, his younger self "slipp'd in thought" to the marvelous realm of Ariosto's Angelica, Tasso's Erminia, and Spenser's Satyrs where enchanted woods replace the tourist's landscape of history (IX, 445–64). After imagining Spenser's Satyrs dancing about "A mortal Beauty, their unhappy Thrall" (probably Una),[19] he slips to the cognate actual sight of a "Convent in a meadow green" violated by "violence abrupt" (IX, 468–81). Finally he is fired with "chivalrous delight" (IX, 503) after visiting a castle near Chambord where Francis I once wooed a mistress "bound to him / In chains of mutual passion" (IX, 481–93). Altogether, this rapid montage creates a composite bright spot focused upon helpless ladies or symbols of innocence awaiting champions. Book 9 acquires such an aura of romance, indeed, that it is easy to see the succeeding scene as the epitome of the romantic bright spot: " 'Tis against *that* / Which we are fighting," the outraged Beaupuy declares at the sight of a "hunger-bitten Girl," a damsel-in-distress or secular version of the weeping Magdalene (IX, 511–20).

Yet the romantic story cannot continue. One of the spots of romance, we notice, is anomalous because it does not contain a simple example of innocence awaiting her champion. At the castle near Chambord, Francis I, a traditional courtly lover, is both villain and champion, both the seducer and defender of his mistress—probably a maid of honor like Louise de la Vallière. Just surfacing in Wordsworth's younger mind on this spot is recognition that the chivalric world is the very emblem of the *ancien régime* that necessitated revolution in the first place. The castle, the poet says, commemorates not only the "better deeds" but the "vices" of kings (IX, 496). If we may vary Marie Antoinette's dictum, to love romance in this case is to have one's cake and eat it too: to temporize on politics. On spots of royal vice, Wordsworth says, his "Imagination" would thus often need to "mitigate" the "virtuous wrath," "noble scorn," and "civic prejudice" of his "youthful Patriot's mind" (IX, 494–501). But the compromise between romance and revolution is stillborn, its narrative climax unimaginable. When Wordsworth's hero declares " 'Tis against *that* / Which we are fighting," he throws down his glove in challenge to invisible antagonists as if *this* were the moment the combat of the Revolution should come to a point. But Wordsworth's romance necessarily misses the point because it cannot grasp the underlying nature of Revolutionary combat. Urging the good fight between a Childe and a clearly identifiable enemy, it cannot comprehend that the purpose of Revolutionary fighting is to *establish* (test, fix, confirm) identity in the first place. Which is the enemy, after all, the aristocrat or his foe? And in insisting upon a fight to the finish, Wordsworth's romance then compounds its error. As we have seen, a revolution in which protagonists in one phase of action turn antagonists in the next necessarily perpetuates the state of war as the very condition of its being. Thus, for example, an event that will completely mystify the young poet: "become oppressors in their turn, / Frenchmen . . . changed a war of self-defence / For one of conquest" (X, 791–3).

In the event, then, no enemy appears to pick up Wordsworth's gauntlet; and the Beaupuy tale simply stops. Beaupuy indeed dies fighting; but he dies in an *anti*climatic battle (as Wordsworth believed) against the "deluded Men" of the Vendéan civil war.[20] This meaningless death is buried early in Wordsworth's tale (IX, 431) so that, like the Redcrosse Knight fighting the great dragon, Beaupuy can seem to come vividly to life again. But he lives to no purpose; there is no final canto of triumph.

Wordsworth then appends to the Beaupuy Tale the episode of Vaudracour and Julia, and romance turns gothic. Vaudracour, a romantic hero like Beaupuy, attempts a doomed revolution against social and political institutions represented by his father.[21] "Arabian Fiction," Wordsworth says, "never fill'd the world / With half the wonders that were wrought for him" (IX, 584–5). But failure plunges Vaudracour into a much darker kind of romance—an increasingly gothic tale much like *Caleb Williams,* where, to use Godwin's words, the plot consists of "a series of adventures of flight and pursuit; the fugitive in perpetual apprehension of being overwhelmed with the worst calamities, and the pursuer, by his ingenuity and resources, keeping his victim in a state of the most fearful alarm." Like the hero of Godwin's quasi-gothic novel, Vaudracour both flees from and is drawn to the father figure, experiences the gothic horrors of prison, and (as in the original conclusion of the novel) ends in madness. We come to recognize in his "dark and shapeless fear of things to come" (IX, 749) and his "savage" appearance to visitors ("he shrunk, / And like a shadow glided out of view"; IX, 925–6) the characteristic demeanor of what Peter Thorslev calls the gothic villain-hero. Godwin's novel makes an especially apt analogue because in its original state it leaves its hero in unmitigated horror, refusing to liberate him from dungeons of the soul. The shift from the Beaupuy to the Vaudracour romance, in sum, duplicates exactly that from the beautiful to the sublime Revolution. Like the sublime, the gothic of history ultimately appears to the young Wordsworth as an isolated, monstrous detour from history breaking with, rather than developing from, the *ancien régime* of the romantic past. Such a freak horror must be kept at a distance, and so becomes for Wordsworth merely a tale "I heard" perhaps "worth memorial" (IX, 553).[22] The romance framework, whether chivalric or gothic, cannot comprehend the Revolution as historical phenomenon.

Complementing and, indeed, overlapping with the genres I have traced so far is a dramatic frame staging a shift from comic to tragic Revolution. The Vaudracour and Julia romance serves to announce the theater at hand because it is itself simultaneously a special kind of "tragic Tale" (IX, 551). Wordsworth opens this tale in line 559 with an allusion to *Romeo and Juliet,* 2.2.15, goes on to give Julia/Juliet her own balcony scene (IX, 626–34), and even refers, explicitly to Shakespeare's play (IX, 635–42). Like *Romeo and Juliet,* the Vaudracour and Julia episode is a play profoundly transitional between comedy and tragedy. "Oh! happy time of youthful Lovers!" (IX, 556), Wordsworth says, establishing expectations of a comic universe in which love triumphs over insubstantial woes. But as in Shakespeare's play, such expectations perish as the full tragic implications of the plot unfold. The structure of society victimizes Vaudracour/Romeo and poisons his life. So pronounced is the wrench in expectations from comic to tragic that Vaudracour changes scripts entirely to become villain rather than victim, a malcontent rather than Romeo. "From that time forth he never utter'd word / To any living" (IX, 912–3), Wordsworth says, echoing Iago's last words in *Othello:* "From this time forth I never will speak word."

An allusion-filled passage near the beginning of book 10 then restages the shift from comedy to tragedy and initiates the strong emphasis on tragedy in the rest of the Revolution books. This is the passage centered in the Paris hotel room (X, 38–77). The scene is "a spot" in Paris evoking the same blend of strong incumbencies and too-eager gladness evident at the site of the Bastille (or of patriotic wrath and chivalrous delight near Chambord). Keeping watch like Hamlet on his castle or Brutus in his tent, the young Wordsworth allows "true history" to dematerialize (at the touch of "pressing" incumbencies) into a phantasmal, dramatic chorus (see Peterfreund, "Metamorphic Epic," p. 462). The chorus begins by quoting the first scene of *As You Like It,* in which Orlando complains that his tyrannical brother treats his horses better than his sibling. Then, turning specifically tragic, it rehearses a topos of such plays as *Julius Caesar* and *Hamlet:* a catalog of unnatural perturbations in earth, sky, and ocean heralding apocalyptic doom. A climactic allusion finishes the scene. Wordsworth hears the regicide Macbeth crying, "Sleep no more." Altogether, this passage shows Revolution changing from a comedy such as *As You Like It,* in which an Arden world can reform political tyranny, to a tragedy such as *Macbeth,* in which the very woods must be uprooted in a cataclysmic battle against oppression.

After the Paris-hotel passage, tragedy then seizes center stage in book 10. Wordsworth, who read *Hamlet* again in March 1804 shortly before beginning the Revolution books, crowds the pages with allusions not only to *Hamlet* (X, 313–4), but to *Julius Caesar* (X, 167), *King Lear* (X, 462), and *Samson Agonistes* (X, 377). All revolutionary incidents come to seem staged. Appearing so soon after the "Sleep no more" cry, for example, Louvet seems an avenging Macduff confronting Robespierre/Macbeth (X, 91–100). "I, Robespierre, accuse thee!" Louvet says in much the same tone as Beaupuy declaring, " 'Tis against *that* / Which we are fighting."[23] Yet, of course, Louvet is a failed Macduff. The young Wordsworth continues seeking a Macduff figure—"one paramount mind" that "Would have abash'd those impious crests, have quell'd / Outrage and bloody power" (X, 179–81). But Macduff cannot appear in book 10 because the tragedy so carefully staged refuses to yield cathartic release. Just as the sublime and the gothic of revolution seem merely terrifying when perceived in isolation from their counterparts, so the tragic climax of book 10 remains perpetually unfinished, thoroughly Jacobean, when viewed as canceling rather than complementing the possibility of comedy. The revolutionary tragedy refuses to purge dark elements from society in order to allow restoration of a bright, comic universe. Book 10 is the bloody fifth act of a Shakespearean play in which the duel or battle never ceases; or again, it is a *Samson Agonistes* in which freedom cannot be achieved through any number of temple destructions. Drama is no more able than romance to comprehend the Revolution.

Superimposed upon the dramatic frame of book 10 is then the last of the narrative genres of revolution I will consider: a Miltonic epic that shifts disturbingly from what may be called the millennial to the hellish (see

Peterfreund on the Miltonic allusions of the Revolution books, "Metamorphic Epic," pp. 461–6). Book 10 opens with a millennial story that stresses the insignificance of evil and the importance of a special heroism in achieving immediate human regeneration. In the first lines, Wordsworth perceives the Revolution's foreign enemies through a Miltonic lens:

> say more, the swarm
> That came elate and jocund, like a Band
> Of Eastern Hunters, to enfold in ring
> Narrowing itself by moments and reduce
> To the last punctual spot of their despair
> A race of victims, so they seem'd, *themselves*
> Had shrunk from sight of their own task, and fled
> In terror.
>
> (X, 13–20)

The phrase "punctual spot" derives from *Paradise Lost,* VIII, 23, but the simile as a whole echoes the similes concluding Milton's first book, in which the devils suddenly swarm like bees and play jocund music like fairy elves. As in Milton's similes, in other words, the opening of book 10 diminishes evil and predicts "confidence / And perfect triumph to the better cause" (X, 22–3). Wordsworth's opening simile, however, only introduces the millennial form of revolution. The theory of evil it contains makes no link between evil's fall and good's rise: evil declines by itself because it is a terrorism that can only redound upon the terrorist's head. Wordsworth follows the opening simile by predicting a similar fate for the Revolution's domestic terror: "lamentable crimes" of violence are "Ephemeral monsters ... / Things that could only shew themselves and die" (X, 31–7). But as book 10 continues, Wordsworth shows himself developing a full theory of good as well. Repeating the essence of Milton's argument, he pictures the triumph of good over evil as the shift from a violent martial ethos—in which the "senseless sword/Was pray'd to as a judge" (X, 33–4)—to one of Christian heroism. Wordsworth prepares for someone like Milton's Messiah, a savior confident in himself and God. In Wordsworth's terms, the Revolution requires a "Spirit thoroughly faithful to itself," endowed with "desires heroic" and with invincible "self-restraint, ... circumspection and simplicity" (X, 146–57). The young poet's trust that "the Godhead which is ours" will triumph over "tyrannic Power" is so strong, indeed, that it has "a revelation's liveliness" (X, 158–75). Such millennial expectation amounts to a creed that France will be "Redeem'd according to example given / By ancient Lawgivers" (X, 187–8).

Yet here the millennial epic ends as Wordsworth encounters betrayal, apostasy, and the declaration of war between England and France. Suddenly, the Revolution is no longer a *Paradise Lost* heralding redemption but instead a *Paradise Lost* in which no hint of salvation mitigates the calamitous history of Michael's vision. Alluding to book 4, lines 393–4, of Milton's work, Wordsworth recalls that "Tyrants, strong before / In devilish pleas were ten times stronger now" (X, 309–10). The implications of the opening simile of Book 10 are reversed: the devils grow rather than shrink. Now the Christian heroism of the just and faithful becomes indistinguishable from "the blind rage / Of insolent tempers, the light vanity / Of intermeddlers," and the "steady purposes / Of the suspicious" (X, 315–26). Now Wordsworth sees everywhere a return to the old violent code of justice: "The Herculean Commonwealth," he says in a recapitulation of the Fete of Unity and Indivisibility of 1793, had "throttled with an infant Godhead's might / The snakes about her cradle" (X, 362–4). Instead of heralding a Messiah, the Revolution gives birth to a pagan destroyer, a Hercules or Satanic Robespierre who, as Wordsworth says with an echo of *Paradise Lost,* (VI, 370, "Wielded the sceptre of the atheist crew" (X, 457). (We might remember here with some irony the the "herculean mace" the poet picks up at the close of *Salisbury Plain.*) This is a vision of the hellish Revolution.[24] Like the sublime, gothic, and tragic Revolutions, it cancels rather than complements its happier counterpart and provides not so much a form of history as a frightening terminus to history. It is a vision of the origin of Death. "Domestic carnage now fill'd all the year" (X, 329), Wordsworth says, beginning his tribute to the guillotine. Epic can no more comprehend the Revolution than Adam and Eve can understand the personified shapeless eagerness that is Milton's Death.

A Dead History

Yet, of course, this is not the end of Wordsworth's account of revolution. Book 10 goes on to envision a new shape of history about to begin—a history signaled by allusion to Milton but not achieved in the framework of Miltonic epic or, indeed, of any of the narrative frameworks I have sketched. A tragedy beyond tragedy or perfect purgation, as I earlier called it, is imaginable only in lyric form. It will be instructive to focus on a preliminary passage in which narrative history reaches its height of generic clash, then watch the formation of an island moment on Leven Sands witnessing the death of history and the birth of lyric.

At X, 439, there is a figurative "deluge" of guilt and ignorance over the land. In the next verse paragraph Wordsworth shows us the remains of old history. There are remnants of a tour-poem landscape:

> And as the desert hath green spots, the sea
> Small islands in the midst of stormy waves,
> So that disastrous period did not want
> Such sprinklings of all human excellence.
>
> (X, 440–3)

There is an echo of the language of romance we heard in book 9: Wordsworth recalls "those bright spots, those fair examples ... / Of fortitude, and energy, and love" (X, 445–6). There is a stage scene: Arras, the town that fathered Robespierre, seems a Lear reproaching the winds (X, 462). And there is Miltonic epic: Robespierre appears the leader of the "atheist crew" (X, 457) and, a little later, "chief Regent" of the "foul Tribe of Moloch" (X, 468–9). Genre piles upon genre in a storm of narrative contradiction: "human excellence" and "fair examples" clash with types of Lear's madness and Satan's foulness. The whole form of this passage of history is a contradiction and "mocks" the poet under a "strange reverse" (X, 465). Narrative history can no more contain the deluge (the "devouring sea" predicted at the opening of book 9) than the false "rainbow made of garish ornaments" at Arras (X, 452) can shape the Covenant.

But the false passage of history acts as prelude to the new. In the three verse paragraphs following his strange reverse, Wordsworth launches a "separate chronicle" (X, 471), a fresh kind of history. The deluge-sea recedes, and he shows us his younger self walking home in 1794 over Leven Sands estuary beneath a prospect of Miltonic splendor: "Creatures of one ethereal substance, met / In Consistory, like a diadem / Or crown of burning Seraphs" (10, 480–2).[25] But the prospect of Miltonic glory is not the core of the experience. Prospect originates in a retrospective moment that makes "fancy more alive" (X, 488): the poet's morning visit to Cartmel Priory and the grave of his Hawkshead teacher, William Taylor. At the center of this retrospection is his reading of a special kind of history on Taylor's tombstone:

> A plain Stone, inscribed
> With name, date, office, pointed out the spot,

To which a slip of verses was subjoin'd,
(By his desire, as afterwards I learn'd)
A fragment from the Elegy of Gray.
A week, or little less, before his death
He had said to me, "my head will soon lie low;"
And when I saw the turf that cover'd him,
After the lapse of full eight years, those words,
With sound of voice, and countenance of the Man,
Came back upon me; so that some few tears
Fell from me in my own despite.

(X, 495–506)

This is epitaphic, or self-epitaphic, history. The passage, we notice, begins by alluding to a pastoral elegy sealing off, rather than releasing, the history of the dead. Taylor's tombstone adds to a plain chronology of events a close variant of the last four lines in the self-epitaph closing Gray's "Elegy Written in a Country Churchyard":

His Merits, Stranger, seek not to disclose,
Or draw his Frailties, from their dread Abode.
There they alike, in trembling Hope, repose,
The Bosom of his Father, and his God.[26]

Such an epitaph is not far removed from the purely prophylactic variety (e.g., the verses guarding Shakespeare's grave: "Bleste be the man that spares thes stones, / And curst be he that moves my bones"). But precisely because the epitaph is a *self*-epitaph, it allows the reader to pick up the bones of the dead in a different way. The nature of the self-epitaph is to trigger further stages of self-epitaphic consciousness in the reader himself. Viewing the stone in Cartmel Priory with its allusion to Gray, Wordsworth in 1794 thus first recalls Taylor's self-epitaphic words, "my head will soon lie low," and then goes on to write what is really the epitaph for his own passed-away self. Taylor "loved the Poets," he says,

and if now alive,
Would have loved me, as one not destitute
Of promise, nor belying the kind hope
Which he had form'd, when I at his command,
Began to spin, at first, my toilsome Songs.

(X, 510–4)

Thrice-compounded as if in some magic spell, self-epitaphic consciousness at last wholly seals off the enactive quality of narrative history, causing
a shift of perspective by which the self, caught up in the deluge of contemporary events, suddenly elegizes itself in past tense. When the 1794
Wordsworth reads the stone in Cartmel Priory, it is not so much that he
brings to mind his 1786 self in the year of Taylor's death (and, indeed, an
even younger self spinning its first songs) as that he abruptly gains eight
years' distance on himself in 1794. Epitaphic history creates such a sense
of elegiac finish, that is, that even the present becomes *as if* past. Only in
such a moment of temporal *ekstasis,* a standing outside the present self, can
strong incumbencies force the 1794 poet into an attitude of mourning like
that of the repentant Magdalene ("some few tears / Fell from me in my
own despite"). And only such *ekstasis* can then transform elegiac mourning
into the profound, rather than superficial, gladness of Miltonic ecstasy on
Leven Sands. Only epitaphic historical consciousness, in sum, can lay the
past to rest with acceptance of loss because it lays to rest the present—
with all its hopes and fears—as well.

But Wordsworth's wake for history is not simply elegiac. Rather, in both
the self-epitaph (by its very nature) and the tradition of pastoral elegy
generally, elegy wakes to prophecy. Just as Gray looks forward to a supernatural realm in his last line, so the 1794 Wordsworth, after meditating
Taylor's epitaph, reenters immediate reality on the estuary to celebrate
Robespierre's death in a hymn of supernatural prophecy. He spies a "rocky
Island" grounding a ruined "Romish Chapel, where in ancient times /
Masses were said" (X, 517–22). This is the new island of history: the point
of Ararat in the Revolution books. Here, while the "great Sea" of the
deluge "Was at safe distance" (X, 528–9), the poet learns of Robespierre's
death and launches a "Hymn of triumph" (X, 543) celebrating the passing
of the revolutionary daemon. "Come now ye golden times," he begins as
if the present were part of times so ancient as to be biblical (X, 541). Thus
does he fulfill the spirit he had assumed just before the Leven Sands episode: that of one of the "ancient Prophets" (X, 401–10).

We now come to the burden of our argument. Modulating in this
fashion from pastoral elegy to prophetic hymn, Wordsworth's epitaph contains in seed the whole span of his characteristic lyricism. The oscillation
from pastoral elegy to prophetic hymn, after all, mirrors his general oscillation in this period between classical and Hebraic or near-Hebraic forms
(including the psalm-like form of the ballad, whose common measure was
identical with that of the hymn).[27] Writ large in early 1804 in the "Immortality" ode, for example, the alternation between pastoral and pro-

phetic, elegiac and hymnal, and classical and Hebraic assumes the dignity of the very epitome of passionate oscillation: the Pindaric ode (as it was conceived at the time). Indeed, the first three kinds of lyric listed in Wordsworth's later classification of genres in the preface of 1815 encapsulate the span of lyricism I sketch here: "The Lyrical," he says, contains "the Hymn, the Ode, the Elegy" (together with "the Song, and the Ballad") (*Prose*, 3: 27).[28] Of course, much closer study of the interplay of lyric genres must accompany any description of the matrix of Wordsworth's lyricism in this period. What we should witness at present is that the epitaphic mood, which will at last be reified in such clear-cut genres as the sonnet (my crowning example of the poet's lyricism) is really the potential for a whole symphony of lyric.[29]

We might compare the epitaph buried in the Leven Sands episode, indeed, to the shell's "loud prophetic blast of harmony" or "Ode" in the Arab-Quixote dream (V, 96–7).[30] As in the case of this latter Ur-lyric as well, the function of lyric poetry is to sound the death of history. In particular, the lyricism introduced in epitaph lays history to rest through precise strategies designed to transform the scene of collective authority into that of the poet's original self. Its basic strategy is a strangely selfish manner of allusion. From the perspective of the Revolution itself, we have seen, the story of combat was supervised by the collective People. It was the People who governed the process of splitting constitutive of the state agonistes. In the Revolution books, however, the People are a mob of allusion. Here I venture upon a purely literary-historical aspect of authority and originality that I have so far underemphasized. It is indisputable that in the Revolution books and elsewhere Wordsworth wrestles with such "strong" poetic ancestors as Milton. But in the case of Wordsworth, I believe, anxiety of influence is secondary to fear of a more direct influence. In Harold Bloom's terms, a great, invisible trope underlies the system of swerves by which Wordsworth rereads his predecessors. This is the trope by which the entire system of misreading swerves away from something not even on its map: the influence of the People—of that frightful, pervasive, yet all but anonymous author of events that Furet and Cobb title Rumor or Opinion. Where the rumored People once governed the splitting of the state, now only a madding crowd of allusions seems to govern the splitting apart of narrative genres that is the misprision of the Revolution books.[31]

How to reauthorize and individuate the collective authority that compels allusion? It is suggestive that the last, redemptive swerve in Bloom's system is *apophrades*, or "the return of the dead" (*Anxiety*, pp. 139–55). Epitaphic lyric, of course, is Wordsworth's version of the return of the dead—of a mode of return that is more than simple recurrence. We can take our paradigm here from the common type of epitaph in which, as Wordsworth knew, the actual voices of the dead seem to utter again from a transformed world. Wordsworth comments in his first "Essay upon Epitaphs":

> The departed Mortal is introduced telling you himself that his pains are gone; that a state of rest is come; and he conjures you to weep for him no longer. He admonishes with the voice of one experienced in the vanity of those affections which are confined to earthly objects, and gives a verdict like a superior Being, performing the office of a judge, who has no temptations to mislead him, and whose decision cannot but be dispassionate. Thus is death disarmed of its sting, and affliction unsubstantialised. (*Prose,* 2:60)

In the context of the Revolution books, we may add: thus is *history* "unsubstantialised." The function of Wordsworth's lyric return of the dead is to allow the voice of past history to utter again only in the service of leading us into a purer, eternal history ruled by a transcendent authority. In actual epitaphs, of course, the realm of eternity is heaven and its authority God. But in Wordsworth's epitaph for Revolutionary history, there is a new heaven and God: nature and self. By modulating from pastoral elegy to prophetic hymn, epitaph in the Revolution books introduces a nature compounded from idyllic nature and supernature—the inheritors of picturesque beauty and the sublime, respectively. Such heavenly nature is what I have called Wordsworth's other, or historically alienating, nature, and its genesis in the Revolution books leads directly to a new, transcendental authority of history: Wordsworth's "I."

Here we may look once more to the detail of the Leven Sands episode. "Other nature" in the episode, of course, is assimilated to the Lakes (the true other nature in the Gallic world of books 9–10). Such a historically alienated nature makes possible the new, individual authority of the self by "quoting" collective allusion according to a process exactly like Bloom's *apophrades:* as if collective allusion were really *an allusion to the poet himself.*[32] The power of the whole episode thus originates in the fact that Wordsworth never alludes *directly* to Gray or any other precedent of pastoral elegy. Rather, he seizes upon a natural scene in the Lakes that allows Gray to be quoted by Taylor, the spirit-medium who can bring the wayward ghost back to native haunts. When the poet then wakes from his seance, the collective authority that mobs the rest of the Revolution books is thus suddenly recentered within a field of purely personal meaning. Just as Gray becomes Taylor, so Taylor at last becomes no more than an excuse for the poet to cite himself.

The prophetic hymn that closes the Leven Sands episode then completes the process of individuation precisely by allowing Wordsworth to allude to himself. Indeed, we need only listen to the hymn in full to confirm that the entire process of Revolutionary emergency—its Herculean narratives, its bloody scenes of natural verification, and its culminating ideology of justice—is now reincarnated in the poet's "I":

> Great was my glee of spirit, great my joy
> In vengeance, and eternal justice, thus
> Made manifest. "Come now ye golden times,"
> Said I, forth-breathing on those open Sands
> A Hymn of triumph, "as the morning comes
> Out of the bosom of the night, come Ye:
> Thus far our trust is verified; behold!
> They who with clumsy desperation brought
> Rivers of Blood, and preached that nothing else
> Could cleanse the Augean Stable, by the might
> Of their own helper have been swept away;
> Their madness is declared and visible,
> Elsewhere will safety now be sought, and Earth
> March firmly towards righteousness and peace."
> Then schemes I framed more calmly, when and how
> The madding Factions might be tranquillised,
> And, though through hardships manifold and long,
> The mighty renovation would proceed;
> Thus, interrupted by uneasy bursts
> Of exultation, I pursued my way
> Along that very Shore which I had skimm'd
> In former times, when, spurring from the Vale
> Of Nightshade, and St. Mary's mouldering Fane,
> And the Stone Abbot, after circuit made
> In wantonness of heart, a joyous Crew
> Of School-boys, hastening to their distant home,
> Along the margin of the moonlight Sea,
> We beat with thundering hoofs the level Sand.
>   (X, 539–66)

Whose voice, we may ask, sings out, "Come now ye golden times"? Surely not Wordsworth's so much as that of a whole assembly of other speakers, past and present, poetic and prosaic, scriptural and secular. By naturalizing the voice within his childhood landscape, however ("Along that very Shore which I had skimm'd / In former times"), the poet succeeds in capturing it within his own orbit—so fully, indeed, that his refrain is a line from earlier in *The Prelude* itself. "We beat with thundering hoofs the level Sand," he says, reciting from book 2, line 144.

Thereafter, the next portion of book 10 (which becomes a separate book in the 1850 poem) recapitulates the descriptive and narrative genres of revolution, fashioning an enactive history specifically of the poet's intellectual development up to the time of the writing of the poem. The young political thinker, for example, approaches "the Shield / Of human nature from the golden side" (X, 662–3) as if he were a knight and enters upon social philosophy as if on a quest through "a Country in Romance" (X, 696). Again he becomes a tourist of historical landscape, describing contemporary society in terms of beautiful prospects (X, 701–7) and historical winds (X, 749–51). He anticipates a time "When some dramatic Story may afford / Shapes livelier" to convey his thoughts (X, 879–81). And again he alludes often to Milton and an intellectual, millennial story turning hellish.

But book 10 then culminates in a coastal region much like Leven Sands—a zone of epitaphic rather than enactive history where lyric resumes its song of pastoral elegy and prophetic hymn. In X, 940–1038, Wordsworth displaces his "grief" for Napoleonic France (X, 954) into an elegiac lament for the sick Coleridge at Syracuse—a "pastoral interlude," as Lore Metzger has shown, woven from strands of Theocritean idyll and Miltonic elegy. The overall movement of this pastoral elegy reproduces that of the Leven Sands episode. First there is a vision analogous to the earlier deluge: Wordsworth imagines in Sicily "a Land / Strew'd with the wreck of loftiest years" (X, 959–60). "How are the Mighty prostrated!" he exclaims (X, 951). Then there is a glorious prospect like that on Leven Sands, where angels met in consistory. "There is / One great Society alone on earth," the poet says, opening to view a new earth of "The noble Living and the noble Dead" (X, 967–9).[33] But like the Miltonic prospect earlier, this view also looks back to retrospect. In the next verse paragraph, Wordsworth reads what is essentially an epitaph for Coleridge parallel to that for Taylor:

> Thou art gone
> From this last spot of earth where Freedom now

Stands single in her only sanctuary,
A lonely wanderer, art gone, by pain
Compell'd and sickness, at this latter day,
This heavy time of change for all mankind.

(X, 980–5)

As in the Leven Sands episode, the home chord of pastoral elegy sounded in this epitaph (with its allusion to line 37 of *Lycidas:* "But O the heavy change, now thou art gone") causes Wordsworth suddenly to memorialize a lost version of self. "Child of the mountains, among Shepherds rear'd," he remembers, "Even from my earliest school-day time, I loved / To dream of Sicily" (X, 1006–8). Like Taylor's epitaph, in sum, the elegy for Coleridge finally guides the poet back to Hawkshead school days. But having reached the depths of elegy, self-epitaphic consciousness then at last ascends once more to a mountain vision of prophecy at the conclusion of book 10. "Thou will stand / Not as an Exile but a Visitant / On Etna's top," Wordsworth predicts to Coleridge, and "Shalt linger as a gladsome Votary, / And not a Captive, pining for his home" (X, 1031–8).

We might perform a simple addition to evaluate the cumulative effect of books 9–10. There are spots of enactive history—the tourist's "spot" of the Bastille, the romantic "bright spot," the dramatic "spot" in the Paris hotel, and the epic "punctual spot"—over which flows a riverlike shapeless eagerness, a historical version of the breeze's "redundant energy" inaugurating *The Prelude* as a whole (I, 46). Such spots are instinct with the energies that will characterize the gibbet mast and blasted hawthorn episodes to come in book II.[34] Yet they remain unrealized, merely redundant. Only when they are removed from the enactive flow of narrative history-made-present can they be seen to sum up on the essentially single spot of time, of denied history, repeating itself in Wordsworth's poetry without fear of redundancy. On this "last spot of earth," as the poet names freedom's sanctuary at the close of book 10, the shapeless eagerness of the sense of history gathers into the strength of Wordsworth's poetry at its most powerful. There is muscular poise in this poetry, a sense that the whole story of history has been folded into passages of utterly lyric peace. Repose is come again.

Indeed, it would be possible at this point to refer back to "repose" in the penultimate line of Gray's self-epitaph. But it will be more useful to point ahead in our argument by reciting a stanza from the "Ode to Duty" of early 1804. In DC MS. 44 of the time:

From no disturbance of my soul
Or strong compunction in me wrought,
I supplicate for thy controul;
But in the quietness of thought:
Me this perpetual freedom tires;
I feel the weight of chance desires:
My hopes no more must change their name,
I wish for a repose that ever is the same.

(P2V, p. 106 and appar. crit.)

Picturesque repose, we saw, had projected a carefully controlled freedom. Now repose must be reconstituted under a new control of freedom: duty.

Notes

1. Mathiez describes the *Noyades* organized by Jean-Baptiste Carrier at Nantes as follows: "Lighters or rafts were got ready, in which scuttle-holes had previously been pierced; Carrier's guard crowded them first with priests and afterwards with Vendéans, floated their human cargoes into the middle of the Loire, opened the scuttle-holes, and sank them.... At the lowest computation the Noyades accounted for two thousand victims" (pp. 402–3). On violence in Lyons, "with its two rivers, and a dozen or so bridges," see Cobb, *Police,* p. 41.

2. In comparing the Revolution books of *The Prelude* with book 3 of *The Excursion,* Lindenberger finds that the former are "dramatic" and "immediate" in their presentation of mental struggle, while the latter displays emotions and attitudes that seem "to reecho only as reconsidered passion, recollected in perhaps too rigidly imposed a tranquillity" (*On Wordsworth's "Prelude,"* p. 260). I have benefited from Lindenberger's chapter "The Non-Visionary Books" as a whole, and from its discussion of the unique features of Wordsworth's historical consciousness in France within the context of the poet's overall social vision. What Lindenberger calls "dramatic" I have called "enactive."

3. We might be reminded here of the Druids in *Salisbury Plain* pointing from the ground to the stars, or perhaps of the "image of tranquillity" upon which the Pedlar reflects in *The Ruined Cottage.*

4. My development of the historical consciousness implied by the epitaph is influenced by several works on Wordsworth and epitaphic poetry beginning with Bernhardt-Kabisch's essays and Hartman's "Wordsworth, Inscriptions, and Romantic Nature Poetry." Hartman traces the link between the poet's work and the inscription that "points to" rather than "evokes" the landscape (p. 221). Ferguson,

p. 33, further suggests that the poet makes the epitaph the "epitome of poetic language" and creates "a kind of power vacuum within words themselves, so that they can only 'speak of something that is gone.' " And Fry, p. 433, argues that for Wordsworth (and Byron) the epitaphic mode accomplishes the "burial of voice"; it is the "gravesite" of "sublime" communication. Conceived as epitaph, these readers thus suggest, poetic language remains inevitably removed from its buried subject; it can only point stiffly and briefly to a once "living" portion of experience that has vanished. As a historical tool, it constitutes an elaborately ritualized way of *not* presenting the immediacy of the past, of resigning the speaker and hearer (communing over the carved inscription) to the fact that the subject of their thoughts and feelings must remain sealed in silent memory. Whereas enactive history strives to make the historian proximate to and contemporary with his subject, epitaphic history—as I will go on to argue—resigns him to being distant from and posterior to historical "life." Or, rather, if enactive history brings the past into the present, epitaphic history effects precisely the reverse: it displaces even the living present into the undisturbed past.

5. We may instance here a moment near the close of the third "Essay upon Epitaphs" where Wordsworth interrupts his mode of critical discourse for a meditation upon the barest epitaph possible: "In an obscure corner of a Country Church-yard I once espied, half-overgrown with Hemlock and Nettles, a very small Stone laid upon the ground, bearing nothing more than the name of the Deceased with the date of birth and death, importing that it was an Infant which had been born one day and died the following. I know not how far the Reader may be in sympathy with me, but more awful thoughts of rights conferred, of hopes awakened, of remembrances stealing away or vanishing were imparted to my mind by that Inscription there before my eyes than by any other that it has ever been my lot to meet with upon a Tomb-stone" (*Prose*, 2:93).

6. Spivak discusses Wordsworth's transformation of the Revolution into a literary-historical and "iconic" text in her intriguing essay on "Sex and History" in the closing books of *The Prelude*.

7. Compare Wordsworth's experience and vocabulary with Gibbon's upon entering Rome: "My temper is not very susceptible of enthusiasm, and the enthusiasm which I do not feel I have ever scorned to affect. But at the distance of twenty five years I can neither forget nor express the strong emotions which agitated my mind as I first approached and entered the *eternal City*. After a sleepless night I trod with a lofty step the ruins of the Forum; each memorable spot where Romulus *stood*, or Tully spoke, or Caesar fell was at once present to my eye; and several days of intoxication were lost or enjoyed before I could descend to a cool and minute investigation" (p. 134).

8. For information about the painting, the convent, and the "liberation" of Le Brun's work from the Carmelites during the Revolution, see Jouin, pp. 493–4; *Charles Le Brun,* pp. 43, 67; Eriau, pp. 97–99 and *passim;* and *Inventaire Général,* I: 22–23, 2: 18, 38. The painting was taken from the convent in late 1792 first to the Petits Augustins and then to the *Musée central des arts* in early 1793.

9. Recusant priests imprisoned at the Carmelite convent, we may note, were among the most prominent victims of the pike during the September Massacres. The *Times* for 10 Sept. 1792, reports: "The number of Clergy found in the Carmelite Convent was about 220. They were handed out of the prison door two by two into the *Rue Vaugerard,* where their throats were cut. Their bodies were fixed on pikes and exhibited to the wretched victims who were next to suffer. The mangled bodies of others are piled against the houses in the streets." See also Mathiez, p. 181, and Lenotre.

10. Burke's analysis of beauty, indeed, stressed fairness of hue and curvature of line, and was equally applicable to landscapes and women (Sublime and Beautiful, esp. pp. 114–17). Boulton in his introduction to that work, p. lxxv, cites those who have noticed the "femininity" of Burke's concept of beauty. See Burke's passage on p. 115 on the "beautiful woman." Regarding "Baroque": the OED traces the usage of the term from the mid–nineteenth century. The specifically Baroque air of Le Brun's painting must be seen by Wordsworth as a complexity of "beauty" and—as we will see below—"sublimity."

11. For British reproductions of Le Brun's illustrations of the passions contemporary with Wordsworth, see *Heads Representing the Various Passions* and *Elements of Drawing.* Among other signal differences between Rapture and Sadness is the fact that in the latter, the head is literally "dejected," or faced downwards. On *Le Repas chez Simon,* see *Charles Le Brun,* p. 47; Jouin, pp. 470–71; and Eriau, p. 95.

12. My thinking on the aesthetics of revolution was spurred on by Paulson's wide-ranging talk, "Burke's Sublime and the Representation of Revolution," at Stanford University, January 19, 1978. The paper has since appeared in Perez Zagorin, ed., *Culture and Politics from Puritanism to the Enlightenment* (Berkeley, Calif., 1980) and in revised form in Paulson, *Representations.* Focusing on Burke amid other figures, Paulson follows the use of vegetable, sexual, and other imagery to depict the Revolution's violent release of energy and then relates such imagery to Burke's own concept of the sublime. As Paulson suggests, "Burke's solution to the confrontation with this unthinkable phenomenon, the French Revolution . . . was to fit it into the framework of aesthetic categories he had worked out himself thirty years before" (*Representations,* p. 68). He then sketches a psychological model of response to the Revolution based on the sexual dynamics of the sublime. For another suggestive study of the aesthetics of history, see Kroeber, "Romantic Historicism."

For Kroeber, a signal feature of Romanticism is "a dialectical engagement with confusingly open-ended experiences," an effort to represent "sublime" historical subjects that the writer or artist already knows "cannot be represented" (p. 164).

13. The painting hung in Beaumont's collection, and Wordsworth probably saw it in 1806 when he also first saw Claude's *Hagar and the Angel.*

14. Telling evidence of Wordsworth's increasing mastery of aesthetic categories—especially of the sublime—may be found in the letter to Coleridge of 6 Mar. 1804, in which Dorothy recounts her brother's discovery of the "slip" farther up the rill at Rydal Lower Falls: "William found it out by himself—it is a little slip of the River above Rydale that makes the *famous* waterfalls—about two hundred yards in length, it is high up towards the mountains where one would not have expected any trees to be, and down it tumbles among Rocks and trees, trees of all shapes, elegant Birches, and ancient oaks, that have grown as tall as the storms would let them, and are now decaying away, their naked Branches like shattered lances, or the whole tree like a thing hacked away and dismantled, as William says to impale malefactors upon. . . . With these are green hollies, and junipers, a little waterfall, endless, endless waterbreaks—now a rock starting forward, now an old tree enough to look at for hours, and then the whole seen in a long prospect. It is a miniature of all that can be conceived of savage and grand about a river, with a great deal of the beautiful. William says that whatever Salvator might desire could there be found. He longed for Sir George Beaumont, but if it is not seen in winter it would be nothing" (*Letters*, I:449). What is clear here is that the picturesque "miniature" of the Falls and its environs is being reanalyzed by brother and sister (under the tutelary spirit of Beaumont) to fit the schema of the beautiful and of the Salvatorean "savage and grand."

15. See *Charles Le Brun*, p. 67; and Eriau, pp. 98–9. It is improbable that Le Brun actually depicted La Vallière, whom he did not meet until later and who, in any case, was a child at the time of the painting's composition. For more information on La Vallière, her infamous seduction by the king, and the sensational ceremony in which she took the veil, see Lair, esp. pp. 60–86, 306–28; and Wolf, pp. 290–304.

16. It would be interesting to take the purely pictorial aspect of the problem to its logical end. We can speculate that in order truly to paint the agon of revolution, in which sublimity and beauty combat, an artist would need to utilize some compositional framework expressive of struggle. Rectilinear stasis on the model of Hubert Robert's picture of the storming of the Bastille would not be adequate (a point I owe to William Pressly, formerly of the History of Art department, Yale University, with whom I cotaught a course on the Age of Revolution). Neither would straight-line recession serve, whether of the direct or diagonal variety. Rather, we would need at least a double-diagonal model able to create a binary composition (as in Rubens's *Chateau Steen* or, with the diagonals

transposed onto the vertical plane as a gigantic "X," in Martin's *The Deluge*). Or we would need to follow Turner's lead in choosing an orbicular scheme (evident in Martin's *Deluge* as well) framing color antagonism.

17. See Woodring's thesis, *Politics in English Romantic Poetry*, p. 49 and *passim*, that Wordsworth and other Romantics faced a dilemma posed "by discrepancies between the intellectual principles underlying [their] first political assents and [their] romantic intuitions of organic wholeness made apparent by the creative, unifying imagination."

18. Since the appearance of this portion of my argument in earlier form, J. Chandler, pp. 203–6, has published excellent commentary on the Beaupuy segment of book 9. Also relevant to my following discussion is Paulson's fuller consideration of the relation between gothic fiction and the French Revolution (*Representations*, pp. 215–47), which appeared too late for me to make use of it here. Since the topic of the gothic is only a small part of my argument in this chapter, I have not attempted to go back and reinforce my discussion with Paulson's insights. Particularly relevant would be his discussion of *Caleb Williams* and—by way of *Frankenstein*—of the monstrous.

19. In identifying Wordsworth's allusions and literary references, I am guided throughout by Selincourt's notes in *Prel.* (supplemented by WAG and Maxwell's notes in his edition of *The Prelude*). Here, for purposes of comparison, Selincourt cites passages from *The Faerie Queene* depicting Una and Hellenore (*Prel.*, p. 294). But Hellenore (*Faerie Queene*, 3.10) seems an unlikely candidate because she is certainly not an "unhappy Thrall."

20. As Selincourt notes, Wordsworth was mistaken that Beaupuy died in the Vendée. In fact, he was only wounded and did not die until the battle of the Elz in 1796 (*Prel.*, p. 293).

21. I deal here with the Vaudracour and Julia segment by linking literary form to historical allegory. An alternative would be to link the historical allegory to the biographical relationship between Wordsworth and Annette Vallon, for which see Erdman, "Wordsworth as Heartsworth."

22. In the 1850 poem, Wordsworth relates the Vaudracour and Julia episode more closely to the Revolution, but then does not tell the full tale.

23. See Jacobus, " 'That Great Stage,' " p. 363, on the link between Robespierre and Macbeth in *The Prelude*.

24. On Burke's similar use of Milton in condemning the Jacobin Hell, see Paulson, *Representations*, pp. 66–71.

25. Selincourt identifies the Miltonic echoes here in his note to lines 479–86 (*Prel.*, p. 303).

26. This epitaph, which still exists in the graveyard at Cartmel Priory, varies Gray's lines only slightly. The "Elegy" closes: "No farther seek his merits to disclose,

/ Or draw his frailties from their dread abode, / (There they alike in trembling hope repose) / The Bosom of his Father and his God." In quoting the tombstone, I have not normalized capitalization or punctuation (cf. *Prel.*, p. 303).

27. On common measure ($a^4 b^3 a^4 b^3$), see Deutsch, pp. 34–35. Needless to say, I am arguing very broadly here in situating Wordsworth's lyricism at the intersection of classical and Hebraic forms. The simplification, however, has the advantage of allowing his early lyricism to be seen as cognate with that of other lyrical hermeneutics—as it might be called—designed to reinterpret the classical in the light of the Hebraic. Christopher Smart's negotiation between the Psalms and Horace's Odes in his translations is a case in point (see my "Christopher Smart's 'Uncommunicated Letters' ").

28. In this list, it is useful to read Ode as mediational between Hymn and Elegy. Song and Ballad may then be read as the popular or lay forms of the structure: Hymn ← Ode → Elegy. This is why the ode-like turns and counterturns of a poem like "Tintern Abbey" seem to the poet perfectly assimilable to the rest of the *Lyrical Ballads*. The strophe, antistrophe, and epode of ode in the high style— so well suited to modulating the transition between what I have called the elegiac and the hymnal—become separate voices in the low-style ballads (in the manner Bialostosky calls Wordsworth's "dialogism"; see esp. pp. 105–59): first there is the turn of the narrator's voice, then the counterturn of encounter with another, often vulgar voice, and finally the epode-like "stand" of a narrator left at rest. It is in this manner, for example, that the narrator's elegiac mood at the opening of "Resolution and Independence" (1802) modulates through the intervention of the Leech-gatherer's voice into the hymnal strain in the final stanza (see Bialostosky's treatment of the poem at the close of his chapter "Dialogic Personal Anecdotes," pp. 148–59).

29. We can notice that in the Preface of 1815 Wordsworth assigns epitaph and sonnet, along with locodescription and the epistle, to his fourth category, the "Idyllium." Appended after the first three categories of narrative, drama, and lyric, epitaph and sonnet must thus be presumed to denote lyricism of a special kind. Recalling my discussion elsewhere of locodescription and georgic as mediational forms, we can speculate that epitaph and sonnet for Wordsworth are also mediational in function. They are not just lyrics but transformational lyrics designed to organize, reverse, or otherwise adjust the relations between the narrative, dramatic, and lyric. Wordsworth's sonnet form thus serves to subordinate narrative history to lyric or personal history.

30. My reading of the shell's song as pan-lyric—or perhaps a panic of lyric—is indebted to Miller's reading of the shell as containing "the original and originating Word, source of all language, which is yet no word because it holds all words undistinguished within it" (*Linguistic Moment*, p. 67).

31. There is much more to my historicization of Bloom's theory of poetry than can be explored here. It would be useful, for example, to read Bloom's system of swerves in relation to the process of faction formation in the Revolution.

32. For a fuller study of *apophrades* or metalepsis in rhetorical tradition, see Hollander, pp. 133–49. Hollander stresses the fact that the term has had an exceptionally tangled history.

33. With J. Chandler's book in mind, we may think here of the contract between the living and dead in Burke's *Reflections*.

34. Cf. J. Chandler's reading of the romantic "bright spot" in the context of Wordsworth's spots of time (pp. 205–6).

35. On repetition in *The Prelude*, see Lindenberger, *On Wordsworth's "Prelude,"* pp. 188–97. Throughout this section of my chapter dealing with books 9–10 in *The Prelude*, I am indebted to Lindenberger for much early encouragement and advice. See "The Poetry of Revolution" in *On Wordsworth's "Prelude"* (pp. 252–70) for a sustained discussion of the Revolution books consonant with mine.

References

Bernhardt-Kabisch, Ernest. "The Epitaph and the Romantic Poets: A Survey." *Huntington Library Quarterly* 30 (1967): 113–46.

————. "Wordsworth: The Monumental Poet." *Philological Quarterly* 44 (1965): 503–18.

Bialostosky, Don H. *Making Tales: The Poetics of Wordsworth's Narrative Experiments.* Chicago, 1984.

Bloom, Harold. *The Anxiety of Influence: A Theory of Poetry.* London, 1973.

Boswell, James. *A Philosophical Enquiry into the Origin of Our Ideas of the Sublime and Beautiful.* Ed. James T. Boulton. Notre Dame, Ind., 1958; rpt., 1968.

Chandler, James K. *Wordsworth's Second Nature: A Study of the Poetry and Politics.* Chicago, 1984.

Cobb, Richard. *The Police and the People: French Popular Protest, 1789–1820.* Oxford, 1970.

Deutsch, Babette. *Poetry Handbook: A Dictionary of Terms.* Rev. and enl. ed. NewYork, 1962.

Erdman, David V. "Wordsworth as Heartsworth: or, Was Regicide the Prophetic Grounds of Those 'Moral Questions'?" In Donald H. Reiman, Michael C. Jaye, and Betty T. Bennett, eds., with Doucet Deven Fischer and Ricki B. Herzfeld, *The Evidence of the Imagination: Studies of Interactions between Life and Art in English Romantic Literature.* New York, 1978.

Eriau, J.-B. *L'Ancien Carmel du Faubourg Saint-Jaques (1604–1792).* Paris, 1929.

Ferguson, Francis. *Wordsworth: Language as Counter-Spirit.* New Haven, Conn.: 1977.

Fry, Paul H. "The Absent Dead: Wordsworth, Byron, and the Epitaph." *Studies in Romanticism* 17 (1978): 413–33.

Furet, François. *Interpreting the French Revolution.* Trans. Elborg Forster. Cambridge, 1981. (First published in French as *Penser la Révolution Française.* Paris, 1978.)

Gates, Barbara T. "Wordsworth and the Course of History." *Research Studies* 44 (1976): 199–207.

Gibbon, Edward. *Memoirs of My Life.* Ed. Georges A. Bonnard. New York, 1969.

Hartman, Geoffrey H. "Wordsworth, Inscriptions, and Romantic Nature Poetry." In *Beyond Formalism: Literary Essays 1958–70.* New Haven, Conn., 1970.

Harvey, G. M. *Inventaire Général des Richesses d'Art de la France, Archives de Musée des Monuments Français.* Vol. 1. Paris, 1883. Vol. 2. Paris, 1886.

Hollander, John. *The Figure of Echo: A Mode of Allusion in Milton and After.* Berkeley, Calif., 1981.

Jacobus, Mary. " 'That Great Stage Where Senators Perform': Macbeth and the Politics of Romantic Theatre." *Studies in Romanticism* 22 (1983): 353–87.

Jouin, Henry. *Charles Le Brun et les arts sous Louis XIV: Le premier peintre, sa vie, son oeuvre, ses écrits, ses contemporains, son influence d'après le manuscrit de Nivelon et de nombreuses pièces inédites.* Paris, 1889.

Kroeber, Karl. *British Romantic Art.* Berkeley, Calif., 1986.

Lair, Jules. *Louise de La Vallière and the Early Life of Louis XIV.* 3d. ed. Trans. Ethel Colburn Mayne. London, 1881.

Lenotre, G. *The September Massacres: Accounts of Personal Experiences Written by Some of the Few Survivors of the Terrible Days of September 2nd and 3rd, 1792, Together With a Series of Hitherto Unpublished Police Reports.* London, n. d.

Lindenberger, Herbert. *On Wordsworth's "Prelude."* Princeton, N.J., 1963.

Mathiez, Albert. *The French Revolution.* Trans. Catherine Alison Phillips. New York, 1964.

Miller, J. Hillis. *The Linguistic Moment: From Wordsworth to Stevens.* Princeton, N. J., 1985.

Moorman, Mary. *William Wordsworth: A Biography.* 2 Vols. Oxford, 1957, 1965.

———. "Wordsworth and His Children." In Jonathan Wordsworth, ed., with Beth Darlington, *Bicentenary Wordsworth Studies in Memory of John Alban Finch.* Ithaca, N.Y., 1970.

Paulson, Ronald. *Representations of Revolution (1789–1820).* New Haven, Conn., 1983.

Peterfreund, Stuart. "*The Prelude*: Wordsworth's Metamorphic Epic." *Genre* 14 (1981): 441–72.

Reed, Mark L. *Wordsworth: The Chronology of the Middle Years 1800–1815.* Cambridge, Mass., 1975.

Spivak, Gayatri Chakravorty. "Sex and History in 'The Prelude' (1805): Books Nine to Thirteen." *Texas Studies in Literature and Languages* 23 (1981): 324–60.

Thorslev, Peter L., Jr. "Wordsworth's *Borderers* and the Romantic Villain-Hero." *Studies in Romanticism* 5 (1966): 84–103.

WAG. Wordsworth, Jonathan, M. H. Abrams, and Stephen Gill, eds. *"The Prelude": 1799, 1805, 1850.* Norton Critical Edition. New York, 1979.

Wolf, John B. *Louis XIV.* New York, 1968.

Woodring, Carl. *Politics in English Romantic Poetry.* Cambridge, Mass., 1970.

A Language That Is Ever Green

JONATHAN BATE

◆ ◆ ◆

D URING HIS HIGHLY PRODUCTIVE residence at Racedown in Dorset and then at Alfoxden in Somerset, Wordsworth worked on 'The Ruined Cottage', a poem Coleridge took to be one of the most beautiful in the language. Over the last twenty years this poem has come to look absolutely central to Wordsworth's achievement, and its narrative is now highly familiar to students: owing to failed harvests and high prices, Margaret's husband enlists as a paid recruit; he does not return, Margaret and her family decline and die, nature reencroaches upon her cottage plot until all that is left is an overgrown ruin. For the poet and the character— originally called the Pedlar, later the Wanderer—who narrates Margaret's tragedy, the ruined cottage provides an image of consolation. Wordsworth tells of how he

> traced with milder interest
> That secret spirit of humanity
> Which, 'mid the calm oblivious tendencies
> Of nature, 'mid her plants, her weeds, and flowers,
> And silent overgrowings, still survived.[1]

The Pedlar responds by saying that he too has gained consolation and a sense of tranquillity, an inner peace that leads to an acceptance of suffering, from the weeds:

> The purposes of wisdom ask no more;
> Be wise and chearful, and no longer read
> The forms of things with an unworthy eye.
> She sleeps in the calm earth, and peace is here.
> I well remember that those very plumes,
> Those weeds, and the high spear-grass on that wall,
> By mist and silent rain-drops silvered o'er,
> As once I passed did to my heart convey
> So still an image of tranquillity,
> So calm and still, and looked so beautiful
> Amid the uneasy thoughts which filled my mind,
> That what we feel of sorrow and despair
> From ruin and from change, and all the grief
> The passing shews of being leave behind,
> Appeared an idle dream that could not live
> Where meditation was. I turned away
> And walked along my road in happiness.
>
> ('The Ruined Cottage', 509–25)

Wordsworth has always provoked widely differing responses. With this passage in mind, I want to consider two contrasting reactions in the Victorian era. First, here is Thomas De Quincey, in his essay on Wordsworth's poetry, originally published in *Tait's Edinburgh Magazine* in 1845:

It might be allowable to ask the philosophic wanderer who washes the case of Margaret with so many coats of metaphysical varnish, but ends with finding all unavailing, 'Pray, amongst your other experiments, did you ever try the effect of a guinea?' Supposing this, however, to be a remedy beyond his fortitude, at least he might have offered a little rational advice, which costs no more than civility. Let us look steadily at the case. The particular calamity under which Margaret groaned was the loss of her husband, who had enlisted—not into the horse marines, too unsettled in their head-quarters, but into our British army. . . . Here it is that we must tax the wandering philosopher with treason to his obvious duty. He found so luxurious a pleasure in contemplating a pathetic *phthisis* of heart in the abandoned wife, that the one obvious word of counsel in her particular distress, which dotage could not have overlooked, he suppresses. And yet this one word, in the revolution of a week would have brought her effectual relief. Surely the regiment into which her husband had enlisted bore some number: it was the king's 'dirty half-hundred', or the rifle brigade, or some corps known to men and the Horse Guards. Instead, therefore, of suffering poor Margaret to loiter at a gate, looking for answers to her questions from vagrant horsemen . . . the Wanderer should at once have inquired for the station of that particular detachment which had enlisted him. This *must* have been in the neighbourhood. Here, he would have obtained all the particulars. That same night he might have written to the War-Office; and in a very few days, an official answer, bearing the indorsement, *On H. M.'s Service*, would have placed Margaret in communication with her truant. To have overlooked a point of policy so broadly apparent as this, vitiates and nullifies the very basis of the story. Even for a romance it will not do, far less for a philosophic poem, dealing with intense realities.[2]

And, by way of contrast, here is John Stuart Mill, in his *Autobiography* of 1873, recollecting how in 1828, twenty-two years old and in the depths of depression, he read Wordsworth for the first time. Granted, he has been reading the short poems, not *The Excursion* into which 'The Ruined Cottage' was incorporated, but the poet's and the Wanderer's reflections are among the best examples of that aspect of Wordsworth which Mill emphasizes:

In the first place, these poems addressed themselves powerfully to one of the strongest of my pleasurable susceptibilities, the love of rural objects and natural scenery; to which I had been indebted not only for much of the pleasure of my life, but quite recently for relief from one of my longest relapses into depression. . . . But Wordsworth would never have had any great effect on me, if he had merely placed before me beautiful pictures of natural scenery. Scott does this still better than Wordsworth, and a very second-rate landscape does it more effectually than any poet. What made Wordsworth's poems a medicine for my state of mind, was that they expressed, not mere outward beauty, but states of feeling and of thought coloured by feeling, under the excitement of beauty. They seemed to be the very culture of the feelings, which I was in quest of. In them I seemed to draw from a source of inward joy, of sympathetic and imaginative pleasure, which could be shared in by all human beings . . . I needed to be made to feel that there was real, permanent happiness in tranquil contemplation. Wordsworth taught me this, not only without turning away from, but with a greatly increased interest in the common feelings and common destiny of human beings. . . . The result was that I gradually, but completely, emerged from my habitual depression, and was never again subject to it.[3]

These passages are the products of two different kinds of reading. De Quincey's is materialistic and realistic, sceptical and interrogative, ultimately political. Mill's is spiritual and emotive, sympathetic and engaged, ultimately medicinal. In one, the reader tells the poet what he should have done; in the other, the reader allows the poet to do something to him. Neatly reversing our expectations, De Quincey has produced a Utilitarian reading, Mill a Romantic one.

The most influential recent readings of Wordsworth are in the tradition of De Quincey's, though they are, alas, nowhere near so comic as his. They seem to demand of poetry that it should attempt to solve political and social problems; they forget Chekhov's advice that it is the business of art to pose questions in interesting ways, not to provide answers.[4] Jerome McGann is annoyed with Wordsworth for finding consolation in nature when he ought to be attending to economic conditions. He is also annoyed with Keats for attending to swallows instead of Corn Laws in 'To Autumn', just as Marjorie Levinson is annoyed that Wordsworth doesn't talk about coal-barges on the river Wye and vagrants in the ruins of Tintern Abbey.[5] In an essay in which George Crabbe is praised for looking rural poverty squarely in the face, McGann argues that the relationship with nature in poems such as 'The Ruined Cottage' is a matter of 'compensatory justice', 'Romantic displacement', and 'the "fond illusion" of Wordsworth's heart that some uncertain hope presides over all disastered things'.[6] 'Displacement' is the key term here: comfort in nature is read as an escape from, or even an active suppression of, socio-political reality.

> Wordsworth's Nature 'upholds and cherishes' suffering humanity 'first and last and midst and without end'. Ecological nature is Wordsworth's fundamental sign and symbol of his transcendent Nature because the objective natural world—the field of chemistry, physics, biology—contains for human beings, whose immediate lives are lived in social and historical fields, the images of permanence which they need. Like Coleridge, however, Wordsworth translates those ecological forms into theological realities: nature as Nature, the Active Universe and manifest form of the One Life.[7]

So it is that Alan Liu feels a need to do away with this transcendent Nature: 'there is no nature except as it is constituted by acts of political definition made possible by particular forms of government'.[8] Since the work of John Barrell, critics of Romantic representations of rural nature have become increasingly interested in questions of landownership.[9] David Simpson looks at parish records and agricultural histories in order to establish the real state of sublunary nature in the Vale of Grasmere during the early nineteenth century and to consider how true or false Wordsworth's representation of it is in his poetry.[10] In a book aimed at the student market, Roger Sales advances an angry reading of 'Michael' which accuses the poem of ignoring where economic change comes from. Towards the end of the poem we learn of Michael's cottage that 'the ploughshare has been through the ground / On which it stood'; according to Sales, Wordsworth's phrasing effects a cunning evasion of the identity of the driver of the plough— rural change is made to seem like an inevitable process of nature, not a depredation brought about by the aristocracy. Wordsworth suppresses the role of the large landowners in the decline of the smallholders, the 'statesmen' whom he so admired; already in 'Michael' he is implicitly toeing the line of the local grandees, the powerful Lowther family to whom he will later openly toady in his 1818 by-election addresses.[11] Critics in this mould like to point out that a majority of statesmen did not really own their land, but held it under a system of 'customary tenure' which allowed it to revert to the lord of the manor if certain payments ('feudal obligations', Sales calls them[12]) were not made. One looks in vain in such books as Sales's for reference to the process of enfranchisement which enabled many statesmen to become genuine freeholders.

There is a constant implication in all this work that Wordsworth *ought* to have written about real economic conditions; hence the analogy with De Quincey's comments on what the Wanderer *ought* to have done about Margaret's unfortunate position. But where De Quincey was playful, others are in deadly earnest. In a recent study of *Pastoral and Ideology*, Annabel Patterson says of a chapter on 'Michael' by a critic of an older generation that it is 'an attractive but overly generous reading'.[13] The critic's superiority to the poet is proclaimed by that 'overly generous'. We know about ideology and economic reality, therefore to read 'Michael' with Wordsworth's own emphasis on the shepherd's bond with nature, rather than his bondage to the aristocracy, is to read over-generously. What, one wonders, does Annabel Patterson make of John Stuart Mill's reading of Wordsworth? Is it 'overly generous' to read a poet in such a way that he pulls you through a nervous breakdown?

De Quincey's witty dismantling of 'The Ruined Cottage' was in fact an aberration in his criticism. In his more characteristic mode he juxtaposed Wordsworth and Crabbe in the way that McGann does, but came down firmly on the side of Wordsworth. Responding to a comparison in a letter by John Clare,

> The Opium-Eater wondered that [Clare] should think of comparing Wordsworth and Crabbe together, who had not one thing in common in their writings. Wordsworth sought to hallow and ennoble every subject on which he touched, while Crabbe was anything but a poet. His pretensions to poetry were not nothing, merely, but if they were represented algebraically, the negative sign must be prefixed. All his labours and endeavours were unpoetical. Instead of raising and elevating his subjects, he did all he could to make them flat and commonplace, to disrobe them of the garb in which imagination would clothe them, and to bring them down as low as, or even to debase them lower than, the standard of common life. Poetry could no longer exist if cultivated only by such writers as Crabbe. Wordsworth's aim is entirely the reverse of this.[14]

It is this disrobing and debasement that attracts McGann to Crabbe; in their algebraic representations of poetry, modern neo-Benthamites prefix the negative sign to Wordsworth precisely because of his elevation and imagination. Contemporary criticism forces us to choose between a materialist response to poetry from which it can only follow, as Bentham had it in *The Rationale of Reward* (1825), that poetry is of no more value than push-pin, and a response more akin to that of De Quincey and Hazlitt, for whom it was an article of faith that 'Poetry is that fine particle within us, that expands, rarefies, refines, raises our whole being'.[15]

The latter quotation is from the first of Hazlitt's *Lectures on the English Poets*. In the same lecture, Hazlitt suggests that the word 'poetry' should not be confined to something found only in books, contained in lines of ten syllables; rather, poetry is 'the universal language which the heart holds with nature and itself'; further, 'wherever there is a sense of beauty, or power, or harmony, as in the motion of a wave of the sea, in the growth of a flower that "spreads its sweet leaves to the air, and dedicates its beauty to the sun,"—*there* is poetry, in its birth.'[16] In Romantic poetics, poetry is to be found not only in language but in nature; it is not only a means of verbal expression, it is also a means of emotional communication between man and the natural world. John Clare's poem 'Pastoral Poesy' begins with a manifesto remarkably similar to Hazlitt's:

True poesy is not in words
But images that thoughts express
By which the simplest hearts are stirred
To elevated happiness

Mere books would be but useless things
Where none had taste or mind to read
Like unknown lands where beauty springs
And none are there to heed

But poesy is a language meet
And fields are everyone's employ
The wild flower neath the shepherd's feet
Looks up and gives him joy

A language that is ever green
That feelings unto all impart
As awthorn blossoms soon as seen
Give May to every heart.[17]

For Clare, himself a farm-labourer, not a 'gentleman' like Wordsworth, 'pastoral poesy' is the life and the beauty in nature. It is available to give joy 'unto all', to elevate even the 'simplest hearts'; when the shepherd's heart lifts with joy at the sight of a wild flower, that is poetry. Pastoral poetry has a permanent, enduring power—it is an *ever*green language.

For modern criticism, however, pastoral poetry is historically and socially specific. *Pace* Clare, it is not really written by shepherds, it is a comforting aristocratic fantasy that covers up the real conditions of oppression and exploitation in feudal and neo-feudal agrarian economies. Raymond Williams writes with honest indignation: 'It is not easy to forget that Sidney's *Arcadia*, which gives a continuing title to English neo-pastoral, was written in a park which had been made by enclosing a whole village and evicting the tenants.'[18] Roger Sales lashes out with less measure: 'Pastoralism covers a multitude of economic sins. Literary criticism ought, therefore, to take the form of a brutal strip-tease. Pastoralism should be divested of its silver-tongued language and myths of the golden age.'[19] A major count in the critical indictment of Wordsworth is that he was among the many conspirators in the Great Pastoral Con Trick.

Of course it is to be welcomed that literary critics should have begun to question easy generalities about nature, should now be attending to walls and fences and No Trespassing signs. Alan Liu's claim that 'there is no nature except as it is constituted by acts of political definition made possible by particular forms of government' is arresting. Almost everywhere on this earth, the land is owned—or claimed—by someone. In a small country like Britain the pressure of landownership has always been exceptionally acute. In international law, even much of the sea is owned. As I write, the issue of the *privatization of water* is politically highly charged. But here one sees the limitation of Liu's argument: not even the most ardent advocate of entrepreneurship and the free market can privatize the air we breathe. Governments may legislate about what we emit into the air, and in that sense the constitution of nature is determined by government and industry, but we cannot parcel out the air as we parcel out the land. And water can only be privatized in a limited sense. The particles of water which form clouds—and we need no reminding of how important clouds were to Wordsworth, as they were to Ruskin—cannot be possessed or sold.

What, then, are the politics of our relationship to nature? For a poet, pastoral is the traditional mode in which that relationship is explored. Pastoral has not done well in recent neo-Marxist criticism, but if there is to be an ecological criticism the 'language that is ever green' must be reclaimed. 'Why did Wordsworth build into the *The Prelude* a minihistory of pastoral that contrasts the past with the present, central Europe with northern England, and concludes with an accolade to the hard but noble life of the *working* shepherd?' The question is asked by Annabel Patterson in *Pastoral and Ideology* (p. 272). She goes on to pose a choice as to whether Wordsworth's version of pastoral was the product 'of a man whose social and political instincts were outraged by the hardships attributable to the industrial and agrarian revolutions' or whether it was, rather, a subtle contribution 'to the counter-revolutionary programs of the British government, promoting a conservative ideology based on the "georgic" values of hard work (by others), landownership (Wordsworth became a freeholder in 1803), and, above all, the premise that hardship is to be countered by personal "Resolution and Independence" rather than social meliorism' (pp. 272–3). I would say that it was neither; I would suggest instead that Wordsworth built an account of the pastoral into the pivotal retrospective eighth book of *The Prelude* in order to forge a link between the holistic values of his native vales and the 'social meliorism' that underlay the French Revolution. If this is so, then we must abandon the model of Wordsworth the young radical with his 'outraged' social and political instincts sooner or later (sooner in most current readings[20]) becoming Wordsworth the 'counter-revolutionary' promoting a conservative ideology. An 'ideology' based on a harmonious relationship with nature goes beyond, in many ways goes deeper than, the political model we have become used to thinking with. By recuperating the Wordsworthian pastoral, we may begin to reconfigure the model.

Book 8 of *The Prelude*, 'Retrospect: Love of Nature leading to Love of Mankind', was written before book 7, but in the structure of the completed poem it is crucial that it comes after it. Book 7, 'Residence in London', contains Wordsworth's fundamental apprehension concerning the city:

> Above all, one thought
> Baffled my understanding, how men lived
> Even next-door neighbours, as we say, yet still
> Strangers, and knowing not each other's names.
> (VII, 117–20)

This key perception about alienation in the modern urban world is picked up toward the end of the book:

> How often in the overflowing streets
> Have I gone forwards with the crowd, and said
> Unto myself, 'The face of every one
> That passes by me is a mystery.'
> (VII, 595–8)

From here, Wordsworth proceeds to his description of the blind beggar wearing a written paper explaining his life story:

> it seemed
> To me that in this label was a type
> Or emblem of the utmost that we know
> Both of ourselves and of the universe.
> (VII, 617–20)

Recent theorists have tended to treat the beggar as the poet's double and to relate this encounter to the sublime bafflement of the moment when the light of sense goes out in the Simplon Pass section of book 6.[21] But such a reading gives insufficient due to the fact that Wordsworth's vision of human life reduced to the status of data that can be written on a label is located in the city. A little later in book 7 the poet enters Bartholomew Fair, with its shows and freaks: 'O, blank confusion, and a type not false /

Of what the mighty city is itself' (VII, 696–7). The 'type' of the city is very different from the 'types and symbols of eternity' which Wordsworth sees in the landscape of the Alps (VI, 571): here, 'blank confusion' springs not from the inward mental blockage associated with the Kantian sublime but from the distortion of social relations effected by the economy of the city.

For Wordsworth, the distinction between being in the city and being in nature is cardinal; so it is that the move from book 7 to book 8 is from negative types to positive ones. As 'Residence in London' ends with Bartholomew Fair, so 'Retrospect' begins with Grasmere Fair. In contrast to the unknown faces in the city, the community gathered in Grasmere for the annual fair is a 'little family'. The only patriarch is the mountain itself. The Vale of Grasmere is imagined as a visionary republic; as Wordsworth put it in his *Guide to the Lakes*, it is a 'pure Commonwealth; the members of which existed in the midst of a powerful empire like an ideal society or an organized community, whose constitution had been imposed and regulated by the mountains which protected it'.[22] The language here—'Commonwealth', 'ideal society', 'organized community'—is from a tradition of radical republicanism that goes back to the English civil war.[23] To summon up English republicanism was to declare allegiance to the French Revolution; it therefore follows that, by associating Grasmere Vale with republicanism, Wordsworth was retrospectively finding a seedbed for his own revolutionary enthusiasm in the rural communities that he had known since his earliest years. In contrast to the competitive chaos of Bartholomew Fair, the sheep pens of Grasmere Fair are ordered and equally distributed. 'Booths are there none' (VIII, 25): there are no freak shows and callous entertainments, the fair is not based on economic exploitation. Wordsworth notes the absence of booths in order to make a specific contrast with the London fair, where

> Tents and booths
> Meanwhile—as if the whole were one vast mill—
> Are vomiting, receiving, on all sides,
> Men, women, three-years' children, babes in arms.
> (VII, 692–5)

The parenthetic simile sustains the critique of industrialization and urbanization. Whereas in the city the family is subordinated to the system of getting and spending, in Grasmere the people are 'embraced' maternally by the hills around. Nature serves as *both* parents; the imagery thus sidesteps the patriarchalism of Tory models of both family and state.

Wordsworth argues that it was only when he went to the city that he fully and consciously apprehended his debt to nature, and in particular how his sense of human brotherhood came from his early encounters with Lakeland shepherds. In a spirit of visionary republicanism, he represents his native vales as paradise. As Milton in *Paradise Lost* says where the true paradise is *not* before he says where it is ('Not that fair field of Enna . . . '[24]), so Wordsworth begins with false paradises, rejecting 'Gehol's famous gardens', an emperor's pleasure-garden like Kubla Khan's (VIII, 123ff.). He then turns to his origins:

> But lovelier far than this the paradise
> Where I was reared, in Nature's primitive gifts
> Favored no less, and more to every sense
> Delicious, seeing that the sun and sky,
> The elements, and seasons in their change,
> Do find their dearest fellow-labourer there,
> The heart of man; a district on all sides
> The fragrance breathing of humanity,
> Man free, man working for himself, with choice
> Of time, and place, and object.
>
> (VIII, 144–53)

Here man is a 'fellow-labourer' with nature, working in harmony with the elements and the seasons. Furthermore, he is free, 'working for himself, with choice / Of time, and place, and object'. Marx argued that when we work for someone else we become alienated: 'the worker relates to the product of his labour as to an alien object'.[25] But Wordsworth's shepherds are free, they work for themselves, they represent the spirit of unalienated labour. In his unpublished 'Letter to the Bishop of Llandaff', Wordsworth wrote of 'that most important part of property, not less real because it has no material existence, that which ought to enable the labourer to provide food for himself and his family'.[26] In Marx's account of 'Alienated Labour' in the Economic Manuscripts of 1844, 'for the worker who appropriates nature through his work, this appropriation appears as alienation, his own activity as activity for and of someone else, his vitality as sacrifice of his life, production of objects as their loss to an alien power' (p. 86), but in Wordsworth's Grasmere the shepherds retain their vitality, and nature is *not* appropriated. In the original manuscript draft of this section of book 8, Wordsworth proposed that there can be such a thing as 'a tract / Boundless of unappropriated earth'.[27]

Despite the absence of alienation and appropriation, Wordsworth's image is not that of a pre-lapsarian Eden. This is a *working* paradise. In an important passage, the pastoral is hardened and differentiated from that of literary tradition:

> And shepherds were the men who pleased me first:
> Not such as, in Arcadian fastnesses
> Sequestered, handed down among themselves,
> So ancient poets sing, the golden age;
> Nor such—a second race, allied to these—
> As Shakespeare in the wood of Arden placed,
> Where Phoebe sighed for the false Ganymede,
> Or there where Florizel and Perdita
> Together danced, Queen of the feast and King;
> Nor such as Spenser fabled.
>
> (VIII, 182–91)

Wordsworth transposes the pastoral from the fictional Arcadian golden age to the severe life and landscape that he knew:

> the rural ways
> And manners which it was my chance to see
> In childhood were severe and unadorned,
> The unluxuriant produce of a life
> Intent on little but substantial needs,
> Yet beautiful—and beauty that was felt.
> But images of danger and distress
> And suffering, these took deepest hold of me,
> Man suffering among awful powers and forms.
>
> (VIII, 205–13)

The poem itself performs the act Roger Sales demands of literary criticism: it divests pastoral of its silver-tongued language and myths of the golden age. It is the fortitude of the Lakeland shepherd that Wordsworth singles out for praise. At this point he inserts in the 1805 version of *The Prelude* the 'Matron's Tale' that he had originally written for 'Michael', a humble but heroic story of a boy trying to rescue a sheep and himself being rescued by his father. After this narrative, Wordsworth continues in his vein of differentiation. His shepherds are not only unlike those of Renaissance pastoral, they differ also from those of classical poetry:

Smooth life had flock and shepherd in old time,
Long springs and tepid winters on the banks
Of delicate Galesus—and no less
Those scattered along Adria's myrtle shores—
Smooth life the herdsman and his snow-white herd,
To triumphs and to sacrificial rites
Devoted, on the inviolable stream
Of rich Clitumnus; and the goathered lived
As sweetly underneath the pleasant brows
Of cool Lucretilis, where the pipe was heard
Of Pan, the invisible God, thrilling the rocks
With tutelary music, from all harm
The fold protecting.

                                    (VIII, 312–24)

Wordsworth suggests that such a soft pastoral world still exists on the German plains he had seen from Goslar, but he prefers his craggy, harsh northern landscape:

                                    Yet hail to you,
Your rocks and precipices, ye that seize
The heart with firmer grasp, your snows and streams
Ungovernable, and your terrifying winds,
That howled so dismally when I have been
Companionless among your solitudes!
There, 'tis the shepherd's task the winter long
To wait upon the storms: of their approach
Sagacious, from the height he drives his flock
Down into sheltering coves, and feeds them there
Through the hard time, long as the storm is 'locked'
(So do they phrase it), bearing from the stalls
A toilsome burthen up the craggy ways
To strew it on the snow.

                                    (VIII, 353–66)

Weather, work, and plain language—note the use of the shepherd's own term for the 'locking' of the storm—ensure that this pastoral is no aristocratic fantasy. Indeed, the aristocracy have no place in this 'Ungovernable' world. Amidst the grand forms of the mountains, the shepherd is free and self-sufficient: 'He feels himself, / In those vast regions where his service is / A freeman' (VIII, 385–7). As at the fair below Helvellyn, the only master the shepherd serves is nature; there is no feudal landlord. Furthermore, the image of the working paradise evokes a tradition of anti-feudal protest that goes back to Wat Tyler and the Peasants' Revolt of 1381, in which John Ball produced the slogan 'When Adam delved and Eve span / Who was then a gentleman?'

Wordsworth's ideal pastoral mountain republic is not exclusively 'northern'. The image of the Grasmere shepherd is comparable to the reality of the Swiss shepherd. In the (unsent) 'Letter to the Bishop of Llandaff', Wordsworth nudged his anti-republican ecclesiastical antagonist: 'If your lordship has travelled in the democratic cantons of Switzerland you must have seen the herdsman with the staff in one hand and the book in the other.'[28] The poet himself had first-hand experience of what he was talking about; indeed, he devoted a substantial section of his *Descriptive Sketches*, published in 1793, the year of the 'Letter', to an account of the Swiss shepherd, 'The slave of none', living in the mountains where he is taught 'to feel his rights'.[29] The system of democratic representation in the *Landesgemeinde* of the higher cantons of Switzerland, with their elective assemblies, showed that Wordsworth's ideal of political emancipation ultimately derived from unity with nature could actually be brought into practice. The Lake District is seen as the nearest approach to it in Britain: there, as in Switzerland, Wordsworth envisions what Coleridge called 'a particular mode of pastoral life, under forms of property, that permit and beget manners truly republican'.[30] As late as 1901, G. W. Kitchin, well known for his liberal and anti-imperial pronouncements, could write in 'The Statesmen of West Cumberland', 'They answer nearly to the free farmers of Switzerland and Norway; they too keep alive, as the Norse and Swiss also do, the love of liberty and simple independence, bred in the blood of men of mountain regions.'[31] According to this model, pastoral life begets republicanism, and, by the same account, pastoral poetry as redefined by Wordsworth begets both reverence for nature and political emancipation.

The Wordsworthian shepherd represents man 'in his primaeval dower' (*Sketches*, 526). He is a figure of terrific magnitude who looms a giant size in the fog, his sheep like Greenland bears; at the time of the setting sun he is a vast Blakean spiritual form, comparable to an enormous aerial cross stationed high on the Grand Chartreuse, not some 'Corin of the groves' (VIII, 420). He is 'man Ennobled' (VIII, 410–11): true nobility is to be found amongst not the nobles but the working shepherds. In all this, Wordsworth is fulfilling the demand he made of himself in *Home at Grasmere* to write a poetry of rural life as it is lived, not as it is sung in literary tradition (note the acknowledgement here of 'real evil', the refusal to indulge in a moral idealization):

> Is there not
> An art, a music, and a stream of words
> That shall be life, the acknowledged voice of life,
> Shall speak of what is done among the fields,
> Done truly there, or felt, of solid good
> And real evil, yet be sweet withal,
> More grateful, more harmonious than the breath,
> The idle breath of sweetest pipe attuned
> To pastoral fancies?
>
> (*Home at Grasmere*, 620–8)

Two questions may be asked about this new project for pastoral: does it offer a valid account of the previous pastoral tradition and does it offer a valid account of real Grasmere shepherding? The answer to the first question is no. It is only valid for a simplified reading of pastoral. In particular, Wordsworth was reacting against the neo-classical version of pastoral, so popular in the eighteenth century, which insisted that the genre should concern itself only with shepherds in a state of innocence in the Arcadian golden age; for Pope, the art of pastoral lay 'in exposing the best side only of a shepherd's life, and in concealing its miseries'.[32] When Wordsworth alludes to 'Shakespeare in the wood of Arden' he emphasizes the courtiers who play at pastoral, the 'false Ganymede' who is really the noble Rosalind in disguise. But Arden also contains a Corin, and he most emphatically does not live 'For his own fancies' or 'dance by the hour / In coronal, with Phyllis in the midst' (VIII, 420–2). He is no neo-classical Arcadian; his hands are greasy, and he has to perform such unsavoury tasks as the application of tar to the wounds of his sheep. As for his attitude to his work, in this Corin foreshadows Wordsworth's unalienated shepherd: 'Sir, I am a true labourer. I earn that I eat, get that I wear; owe no man hate, envy no man's happiness; glad of other men's good, content with my harm; and the greatest of my pride is to see my ewes graze and my lambs suck' (*As You Like It*, 3.2. 71–5). Shakespeare, as always, is supremely multidimensional. He is not just wilier than the idealizing soft pastoralists, he is also more complex than the idealizing image-makers of unalienated labour, for Corin, despite his content in his work, is shepherd to another man and does not shear the fleeces that he grazes—he is sold along with a piece of property, transferred from churlish master to master-mistress Rosalind.

In Spenser, too, the situation is more complex than Wordsworth's allusion implies. In his lines about the world that Spenser fabled—'maids at sunrise bringing in from far / Their May-bush', 'Tales of the maypole dance', and so on (VIII, 193–203)—Wordsworth is alluding to the May eclogue of the *Shepheardes Calender* where Palinode 'saw a shole of shepeheardes outgoe, / With singing, and shouting, and jolly chere . . . to the greene Wood they speeden hem all, / To fetchen home May with their musicall'. 'O that I were there,' wishes Palinode, 'To helpen the Ladyes their Maybush beare.'[33] But the May eclogue is a dialogue in which the sceptical voice of Piers answers back at Palinode,

> Perdie so farre am I from envie,
> That their fondnesse inly I pitie.
> These faytours little regarden their charge,
> While they letting their sheepe runne at large . . .
> ('Maye', 37–40)

Piers goes on to discuss questions of hire and payment in shepherding. Besides, a political and ecclesiastical allegory runs through the whole dialogue—Piers's is a Protestant voice. Pastoral has always been a form in which 'under the vaile of homely persons and in rude speeches' poets 'insinuate and glaunce at greater matters'.[34] Thus Wordsworth's allusion to the smooth life of classical shepherds smooths over the political complexity of Virgil's pastoral.

The rivers Galesus and Clitumnus, cited in *The Prelude*, occur not in Virgil's *Eclogues*, with their easeful *otium*, but in his *Georgics*, in which there is every bit as much hard work as in Wordsworth. Galesus is in the fourth *Georgic*:

> where dark Galaesus waters his yellow fields, I saw an old Corycian, who had a few acres of unclaimed land, and this a soil not rich enough for bullock's ploughing, unfitted for the flock, and unkindly to the vine. Yet, as he planted herbs here and there among the bushes . . . he matched in contentment the wealth of kings, and, returning home in the late evening, would load his board with unbought dainties.[35]

This unalienated old Corycian bears a remarkable resemblance to Wordsworth's statesmen: scraping a living from poor-quality land, but self-sufficient and happy. Again, 'Lucretilis' alludes to the hill above Horace's Sabine farm, but its context in the *Odes* (1.17) suggests not so much pastoral *otium* as surrounding dangers such as wolves.

But, although Wordsworth glosses over some of the complexities of previous pastoral, his distinction in terms of landscape stands. Arden is an enchanted forest, Clitumnus a pleasant river; the hill above the Sabine farm is a far cry from Helvellyn in winter. In dramatic contrast to those of the Arcadian places, Wordsworth's harsh northern names are characterized by rugged 'r' sounds more than sylvan sibilance:

> Helvellyn, a superior mount
> With prospect underneath of Striding Edge
> And Grisedale's houseless vale, along the brink
> Of Russet Cove . . .
>
> (VIII, 238–41)

The pastoral is removed from its traditional *locus amoenus* to a landscape such as men do live in. In terms of the distinction that was popularized by Edmund Burke, the aesthetic category of traditional pastoral is the beautiful, while that of the Wordsworthian is the sublime.

The tendency of recent criticism has been to suggest that Wordsworth's sublime representation of his shepherds contrived to distort historical reality for literary effect every bit as much as the *otium* of traditional pastoral had done. It is easy to undermine the vision of book 8 of *The Prelude*. Quite apart from the question of how many statesmen really were freeholders, it could be argued that the market economy is in full swing at Grasmere fair. A 'sweet lass of the valley' is to be seen selling apples and pears (VIII, 36–43)—'and who that sees her would not buy?' asks Wordsworth in a line into which could be read a dark hint of prostitution or even of the woman-selling that took place at country fairs like that in Hardy's *Mayor of Casterbridge*. Those who see Wordsworth as Burkean not only in an aesthetic of the sublime but also in a politics of patriotism and patriarchy will find in a line like 'The home and ancient birthright of their flock' (VIII, 263) notions of tradition and rootedness which seem to spring from a belief in values of family and home that are the core of Burkean conservatism then and now. After all, it was when he was revising books 7 and 8 of *The Prelude* in 1832 that Wordsworth inserted his apostrophe to the Burke who

> the majesty proclaims
> Of Institutes and Laws, hallowed by time;

> Declares the vital power of social ties
> Endeared by Custom.
>
> (1850, VII, 525–8)

I shall return to what might be described as 'the politics of home', but here it must be pointed out that Wordsworth built into book 8 an apostrophe to those readers who refuse to believe his vision of Grasmere Vale:

> Call ye these appearances
> Which I beheld of shepherds in my youth,
> This sanctity of Nature given to man,
> A shadow, a delusion?
>
> (VIII, 428–31)

The problem with such readers, he suggests, is that they are nurtured by the dead letter of theory, not the spirit of life. They are Malthusians and Benthamites,

> ye who are fed
> By the dead letter, not the spirit of things,
> Whose truth is not a motion or a shape
> Instinct with vital functions, but a block
> Or waxen image which yourselves have made,
> And ye adore.
>
> (VIII, 431–6)

Hazlitt saw that for Benthamites the *'idea of a perfect commonwealth'* was not the kind of human community Wordsworth envisioned, but a society 'where each member performs his part in the machine, taking care of himself, and no more concerned about his neighbours, than the iron and wood-work, the pegs and nails in a spinning-jenny. Good screw! good wedge! good ten-penny nail!' Benthamites and modern neo-Benthamites wish 'to strip the cause of Reform (out of seeming affection to it) of every thing like a *misalliance* with elegance, taste, decency, common sense, or polite literature'; they 'leave nothing intermediate between the Ultra-Toryism of the courtly scribes and their own Ultra-Radicalism'.[36] With their deadening, materialist emphasis on the wedges and nails of economic reality, such readers leave no room for the *effect* the image of the shepherd has on poet and, by extension, reader. They read in the way De Quincey read 'The Ruined Cottage', not the way Mill read Wordsworth.

For Wordsworth, to demand 'realism' or 'reportage' from poetry is to mis-apprehend its function; the purpose of book 8 of *The Prelude* is not so much to show shepherds as they are but rather to bring forward an image of human greatness, to express faith in the perfectibility of mankind once institutions and hierarchies are removed and we are free, enfranchised, and in an unmediated, unalienated relationship with nature. The radical humanism of book 8 proposes the 'human form' as 'an index of delight, / Of grace and honour, power and worthiness' (414–6). In book 7 the institution of the established church is attacked by means of satire in the portrait of a mincing clergyman, 'a comely bachelor', 'pretty shepherd, pride of all the plains', preaching to his 'captivated flock' (VII, 547–66). He is a false pastor whereas the working Lakeland farmer, free from institu-tional constraint, is a true shepherd of the people. By virtue of his rela-tionship with his environment he represents human potential wrought to its uttermost.

Nevertheless, even if we turn away from economic reality and toward the shepherd's role as an inspirational figure, there is still the possibility of a critique. Wordsworth's most powerful images of the shepherd are those of the man alone on the mountainside. One cannot help thinking that he sees in the solitary shepherd an image of his solitary self. He seems to project on to the shepherd feelings that really belong to himself, which is to say the feelings of someone like Rousseau's solitary walker:

> Night was coming on. I saw the sky, some stars, and a few leaves. This first sensation was a moment of delight. I was conscious of nothing else. In this instant I was being born again, and it seemed as if all I perceived was filled with my frail existence. . . . I felt throughout my whole being such a wonderful calm, that whenever I recall this feeling I can find nothing to compare with it in all the pleasures that stir our lives.[37]

Renato Poggioli writes of the Romantic development of pastoral:

> As the pastoral poet replaces the labors and troubles of love with an exclusive concern for the self, he changes into a new Narcissus, contem-plating with passionate interest not his body but his soul. At this point, he deals only, in Whitman's words, with 'the single, solitary soul', and the pastoral becomes the poetic vehicle of solipsism. . . . What Rousseau terms 'rêverie' is a state of passive introspection, by which the pastoral psyche reflects its shadow in nature's mirror, fondly and blissfully losing its being within the image of itself.[38]

Wordsworth, it might accordingly be argued, is overabsorbed in his *own* relationship with nature; he makes the shepherd into a symbol of his personal sublime, what Keats called the 'wordsworthian or egotistical sublime'. He is not interested in the shepherd but in what the shepherd provides him by way of both inspiration and admonition; 'He sees nothing but himself and the universe. . . . His egotism is in some respects a madness', as Hazlitt said so devastatingly in his lecture on the living poets.[39]

Raymond Williams drew attention to the phrase 'the very culture of the feelings' in Mill's account of his reading of Wordsworth. He argued that here Mill removed 'culture' from 'society' by appropriating the term in the name of the private experience of art: 'These paragraphs [in his *Autobiography*] are now the classical point of reference for those who decide that the desire for social reform is ultimately inadequate, and that art, the "source of inward joy", is fortunately always there as an alternative.'[40] But Mill did not propose the reading of Wordsworth as an 'alternative' to the desire for social reform. He claimed that Wordsworth taught him to commune with nature 'not only without turning away from, but with a greatly increased interest in the common feelings and common destiny of human beings'. Here one must consider the full implication of the structure of *The Prelude*'s eighth book: love of nature *leads* to love of mankind. In a defensive moment, Wordsworth recognizes that, while a traditional, poeticizing pastoral will speak of a woodman languishing from the pangs of disappointed love, real woodmen die of disease 'From sleeping night by night among the woods / Within his sod-built cabin' (612–13). Such a critique of 'love' is built into all the best hard pastoral—Rosalind in *As You Like It* claims that Leander in the Hellespont died of cramp not love, that 'Men have died from time to time, and worms have eaten them, but not for love' (4.1. 99–101). Wordsworth replaces illusions of romantic love with the philanthropy explicit in the phrase 'love of mankind'. Such a move necessitates a critique of the traditional kind of history that is written from above: he will not accept those 'high-wrought modern narratives' that are 'Stript of their humanizing soul, the life / Of manners and familiar incidents" (VIII, 774–6). He will write instead a history of working people and local communities. To aggrandize the common man, to write the shepherd into history in this way, is a radical move.

The love of nature leads Wordsworth to be able to love and to see love even in the city. At the end of book 8 he returns to his memory of London. He sees a man sitting

> with a sickly babe
> Upon his knee, whom he had thither brought

For sunshine, and to breathe the fresher air.
Of those who passed, and me who looked at him,
He took no note; but in his brawny arms
(The artificer was to the elbow bare,
And from his work this moment had been stolen)
He held the child, and, bending over it
As if he were afraid both of the sun
And of the air which he had come to seek,
He eyed it with unutterable love.

(VIII, 849–59)

(In the final text of *The Prelude* Wordsworth transferred these lines to book 7, one of his major structural misjudgements.) This old man is the obverse, the redeemed image, of the blind beggar. That redemption has been achieved by means of the retrospective account of Grasmere shepherds; Wordsworth is now prepared to move on. Books 7 to 9 form a carefully structured triptych: book 7 concerns 'Residence in London', 8 is the pivot, and 9 concerns 'Residence in France'. The pivot is such that the three-book sequence should be read as a progression from alienation in the city through love of nature to the recognition of individual human love and tenderness in the city to the general love of humanity in the revolutionary spirit of book 9, seen at its most powerful in such moments as the one when Wordsworth's friend Beaupuy points to a hunger-bitten girl and says ' " 'Tis against that / Which we are fighting" ' (IX, 519–20). The principle of the 'love of mankind' to which the 'love of nature' leads is of a piece with the rhetoric of the revolutionary declaration of the universal rights of man. It is no coincidence that for the Romantics Rousseau was a prophet both of nature and of the French Revolution.

To return to Annabel Patterson's choice: she ultimately comes down on the side of the view that Wordsworth's pastoral promotes a conservative ideology based on the premise that hardship should be countered by personal 'Resolution and Independence' rather than social meliorism. This conclusion ignores the cardinal fact that book 8 is the prelude to book 9. It also ignores an important point about the function of the pastoral: the purpose of the Arden perspective in *As You Like It* is to bring about the melioration of the court, the overthrow of a corrupt regime. When Thomas Babington Macaulay read *The Prelude* on its publication in 1850, he recorded in his journal: 'The poem is to the last degree Jacobinical, indeed Socialist. I understand perfectly why Wordsworth did not choose to publish it in his life-time.'[41] That 'last degree' is worth pondering, not least because Macaulay had total recall of everything he read and would therefore have held the whole poem in his mind. In summarizing *The Prelude*, he spoke not only of 'the story of the French Revolution, and of its influence on the character of a young enthusiast', but also of 'the old raptures about mountains and cataracts; the old flimsy philosophy about the effect of scenery on the mind'. If the poem is to the last degree Jacobinical, then these latter features, characteristics of such books as the eighth, are part of its Jacobinism. The 'politics of home', of the small organic community based on frugality, hard work, and 'domestic affections'—the phrase is from the letter to Charles James Fox of 14 January 1801 in which Wordsworth commended 'The Brothers' and 'Michael' to the attention of the leading opposition politician of the day—would then be Jacobinical, indeed socialist, and by no means Burkean.

In one of the most famous passages of the *Reflections*, Burke argued that 'To be attached to the subdivision, to love the little platoon we belong to in society, is the first principle (the germ as it were) of public affections. It is the first link in the series by which we proceed towards a love to our country, and to mankind.'[42] But the three links in Wordsworth's chain are not the same as those in Burke's: where the latter has local community, country, and mankind, Wordsworth has nature, local community, and mankind. Wordsworth goes straight from nature and Grasmere to mankind, and in particular to the aspirations for mankind that were given voice in the ideals of the French Revolution. The inclusion of nature and the exclusion of a Burkean sense of nation, of an established order under threat in England, are equally significant. The progression suggests that the 'socialism' of Wordsworth's republican pastoral is of a highly distinctive kind. Its vision of 'fullness and completeness of life', to use William Morris's fine phrase, is dependent on integration with, not subjugation of, nature. The politics of Grasmere Vale are ultimately based on a relationship to the environment, a marriage of humankind to the natural world—'the very world which is the world / Of all of us, the place in which, in the end, / We find our happiness, or not at all' (X, 725–7)—and such a relationship transcends the politics of both Paine and Burke, both the French Revolution and the counter-revolution in England. To go back to nature is not to retreat from politics but to take politics into a new domain, the relationship between Love of Nature and Love of Mankind and, conversely, between the Rights of Man and the Rights of Nature. The language of *The Prelude* is fleetingly red but ever green.

In the spirit of John Stuart Mill's way of reading, let us ask what Wordsworth's pastoral may do for us. Poems do not send people out on to barricades, but they do have the capacity to alter mentalities. Wordsworth can help us to rethink the nature of politics. The thrust of Mill's reading is that the beauty, stability, and endurance of nature are necessary prerequisites for human social and psychological well-being. In Jerome McGann's terms, 'Ecological nature . . . contains for human beings, whose immediate lives are lived in the social and historical fields, the images of permanence which they need.' The criticism of the 1980s was vigorous and effective in its critique of Wordsworth's handling of the social and historical fields. But McGann's position, even though it was articulated a mere decade ago, now seems curiously outdated. Ecological nature no longer looks like an image of permanence. In the 1990s we will have to learn to live not just in the social and historical fields but also, perhaps pre-eminently, in the ecological field. I want to conclude this chapter where I began it, with the ending of 'The Ruined Cottage'; let me sketch a reading of that ending for the 1990s.

In the final section of the poem, nature's processes are seen as inexorable. The weeds go on growing, oblivious of human suffering, but for Wordsworth an indefinable 'spirit of humanity' insinuates its way into that growth. Paradoxically, nature's very indifference seems to guarantee humanity's survival. 'Survived' is the climactic word in Wordsworth's lines, and knowing what weight he attached to words we need to remember its Latin root—sur-vive, *super vivere*, to live beyond. Wordsworth's intensely immanent religion—we may perhaps allow ourselves to say his 'pantheism'—is at work here. There is no sense of Margaret 'living beyond' in heaven; not until very late in life did Wordsworth rewrite part of this ending in the language of orthodox Christianity. What we do sense is that since the vegetation lives beyond, lives on, her spirit somehow survives too. As in 'A slumber did my spirit seal', the dead female achieves new life in earth's diurnal course. Humanity only survives *in nature*. Human survival and the survival of nature are therefore co-ordinate with one another.

In the Pedlar-Wanderer's meditation on this theme, the crucial point to note is, I think, that it is the weeds and the spear-grass which are found beautiful and which accordingly bring comfort. At funerals we console ourselves with flowers. There is something more robust about the Pedlar's emphasis; he is a realist in that he knows that weeds will always win in the garden. Indeed, his lines seem to be a plea for the claims of wildness, of wilderness. Behind the whole passage there is the startling idea that where wilderness reasserts itself there the spirit of humanity survives. Orthodox thought defines man through his mastery over nature; 'The Ruined Cottage' proposes that the survival of humanity comes with nature's mastery over the edifices of civilization. Wordsworth reminds us that a claim can be made for the weeds. It is a claim that John Clare also made:

for him, Eden was to be found not in a garden but amidst 'flat swampy vallies unholsome'. Clare recognized the importance of the 'refuse of nature'; one of his early poems sings of his love for the 'commons left free in the rude rags of nature', for 'Swamps of wild rush beds and sloughs squashy traces / Grounds of rough fallows wi thistle and weed'.[43] And it is a claim reiterated in Gerard Manley Hopkins's stanza, written in the 1880s as if with foreknowledge of the 1990s:

> What would the world be, once bereft
> Of wet and of wilderness? Let them be left,
> O let them be left, wildness and wet;
> Long live the weeds and the wilderness yet.[44]

Notes

1. 'The Ruined Cottage', 502–6, in *The Oxford Authors: William Wordsworth*, ed. Stephen Gill (Oxford, 1984). Unless otherwise stated, Wordsworth's shorter poems are quoted from this edition.

2. Repr. in *De Quincey as Critic*, ed. John E. Jordan (London, 1973), pp. 407–9.

3. Mill, *Autobiography* (repr. London, 1924), pp. 125–6.

4. To A. S. Suvorin, 27 October 1888, in *Letters of Anton Chekhov*, ed. Avrahm Yarmolinsky (London, 1974), p. 88.

5. See McGann, 'Keats and the Historical Method in Literary Criticism', repr. in *The Beauty of Inflections* (Oxford, 1988); Levinson, *Wordsworth's Great Period Poems* (Cambridge, 1986).

6. 'The Anachronism of George Crabbe', in *The Beauty of Inflections*, p. 310.

7. McGann, *The Beauty of Inflections*, p. 300.

8. *Wordsworth: The Sense of History* (Stanford, 1989), p. 104.

9. See in particular Barrell's influential discussion of enclosure in *The Idea of Landscape and the Sense of Place 1730–1840: An Approach to the Poetry of John Clare* (Cambridge, 1972).

10. *Wordsworth's Historical Imagination: The Poetry of Displacement* (London, 1987).

11. Sales, *English Literature in History 1780–1830: Pastoral and Politics* (London, 1983), chap. 3.

12. *English Literature in History*, p. 58.

13. *Pastoral and Ideology: Virgil to Valéry* (Oxford, 1988), p. 275n.

14. 'Notes of Conversations with Thomas De Quincey', in James Hogg, *De Quincey and his Friends* (London, 1895), p. 92. I owe this reference to Rob Morrison.

15. 'On Poetry in General', in *The Complete Works of William Hazlitt*, ed. P. P. Howe, 21 vols (London, 1930–4), v. 2.

16. *Complete Works*, v. 1.

17. Clare, *Selected Poetry*, ed. Geoffrey Summerfield (London, 1990), p. 163.

18. *The Country and the City* (London, 1973, repr. 1975), p. 33.

19. *English Literature in History*, p. 77.

20. James K. Chandler, for instance, argues in *Wordsworth's Second Nature: A Study of the Poetry and Politics* (Chicago, 1984) that Burkean political values are already implicit in the supposedly 'radical' poetics of *Lyrical Ballads*.

21. See, for example, Neil Hertz, 'The Notion of Blockage in the Literature of the Sublime', in his *The End of the Line: Essays on Psychoanalysis and the Sublime* (New York, 1985), pp. 40–60, especially the closing pages.

22. *Wordsworth's Guide to the Lakes. The Fifth Edition (1835)*, ed. Ernest de Sélincourt (Oxford, 1906, repr. 1977), p. 68.

23. For Wordsworth and this tradition, see further Z. S. Fink, 'Wordsworth and the English Republican Tradition', *Journal of English and Germanic Philology*, 47 (1948), 107–26.

24. *Paradise Lost*, IV, 268ff.

25. 'Economic and Philosophical Manuscripts', in *Karl Marx: Selected Writings*, ed. David McLellan (Oxford, 1977), p. 78.

26. *The Prose Works of William Wordsworth*, ed. W. J. B. Owen and J. W. Smyser, 3 vols. (Oxford, 1974), i. 43.

27. MS Y, *The Prelude 1799, 1805, 1850*, ed. Jonathan Wordsworth, M. H. Abrams, and Stephen Gill (New York, 1979), p. 505.

28. *Prose Works*, i. 39.

29. *Descriptive Sketches*, 519–61, in *Wordsworth's Poetical Works*, ed. Ernest de Sélincourt and Helen Darbishire, 5 vols (Oxford, 1940–9, corrected ed., 1952–8), i. 72–4.

30. *Biographia Literaria*, ed. James Engell and W. Jackson Bate, in *The Collected Works of Samuel Taylor Coleridge*, VII, 2 vols. (Princeton, 1983), ii. 45.

31. Kitchin, *Ruskin in Oxford and Other Studies* (London, 1904), p. 56.

32. 'A Discourse on Pastoral Poetry', in *The Poems of Alexander Pope*, ed. John Butt (London, 1963), p. 120. Pope is following Fontenelle's theory of pastoral (1688). See further, J. E. Congleton, *Theories of Pastoral Poetry in England, 1684–1798* (Gainesville, 1952), and the discussion of Wordsworth and the pastoral tradition in chap. 5 of S. M. Parrish, *The Art of the Lyrical Ballads* (Cambridge, Mass., 1973).

33. *The Shepheardes Calender*, 'Maye', 19–36, in *Spenser's Minor Poems*, ed. Ernest de Sélincourt (Oxford, 1910), pp. 47–8.

34. George Puttenham, *The Arte of English Poesie* (1589), bk. 1, chap. 18.

35. *Georgics*, iv. 126–33, trans. H. Rushton Fairclough in Loeb ed. (London and Cambridge, Mass., 1916).

36. Hazlitt, 'The New School of Reform', in *The Plain Speaker—Complete Works*, xii. 182–3.

37. *Reveries of the Solitary Walker*, Second Walk, trans. Peter France (Harmondsworth, 1979), p. 39.

38. Poggioli, *The Oaten Flute: Essays on Pastoral Poetry and the Pastoral Ideal* (Cambridge, Mass., 1975), p. 22.

39. *Complete Works*, v. 163. Keats coined the phrase 'egotistical sublime' in a letter to his friend Woodhouse written on 27 October 1818, a few months after he heard Hazlitt's lecture.

40. Williams, *Culture and Society 1780–1950* (London, 1958; repr. Harmondsworth, 1963), p. 80.

41. Macaulay's *Journal*, 28 July 1850, quoted in *The Prelude 1799, 1805, 1850*, p. 560.

42. *Reflections on the Revolution in France* (London, 1790; repr. 1910 [Everyman ed.]), p. 44.

43. 'Song', *The Oxford Authors: John Clare*, ed. Eric Robinson and David Powell (Oxford, 1984), pp. 46–7.

44. Hopkins, 'Inversnaid' (1881).

Suggested Reading

Study of *The Prelude* cannot be undertaken in isolation; this guide to additional materials therefore includes a few titles that will be found helpful for fuller Wordsworth study. For the most part, books and articles already referenced in the notes to the introduction are not included; nor are the books from which the extracts in this collection are taken.

Scholarly Resources

Two bibliographical surveys of great value are: Nicholas Roe's entry on Wordsworth in *Literature of the Romantic Period: A Bibliographical Guide*, ed. Michael O'Neill (Oxford: Clarendon Press, 1998) and Keith Hanley's similar entry in *The Cambridge Companion to Wordsworth*, ed. Stephen Gill (Cambridge: Cambridge University Press, 2003).

Wordsworth's poetry is being edited in full in the Cornell Wordsworth series, general editor Stephen Parrish (Ithaca, N.Y.: Cornell University Press, 1975–). The previously standard edition remains in use: *Poetical Works*, ed. Ernest de Selincourt and Helen Darbishire, 5 vols. (Oxford: Clarendon Press, 1940–49). The standard edition of the prose is *The Prose Works of William*

Wordsworth, ed. W. J. B. Owen and Jane Worthington Smyser, 3 vols. (Oxford: Clarendon Press, 1974), and that of the letters is *The Letters of William and Dorothy Wordsworth,* 8 vols. (Oxford: Clarendon Press, 1967–93). Individual volumes are: *The Early Years 1787–1805,* ed. Chester L. Shaver (1967); *The Middle Years, Part 1: 1806–1811,* ed. Mary Moorman (1969); *The Middle Years, Part 2: 1812–1820,* ed. Mary Moorman and Alan G. Hill (1970); *The Later Years, Part 1: 1821–1828,* ed. Alan G. Hill (1978); *The Later Years, Part 2: 1829–1834,* ed. Alan G. Hill (1979); *The Later Years, Part 3: 1835–1839,* ed. Alan G. Hill (1982); *The Later Years, Part 4: 1840–1853,* ed. Alan G. Hill (1988); *A Supplement of New Letters,* ed. Alan G. Hill (1993).

Biography

Mark L. Reed's two volumes of chronology are indispensable: *Wordsworth: The Chronology of the Early Years 1770–1799; Wordsworth: The Chronology of the Middle Years 1800–1815* (Cambridge, Mass.: Harvard University Press, 1967 and 1975). The standard single-volume biography is Stephen Gill, *Wordsworth: A Life* (Oxford: Clarendon Press, 1989). For a fuller account of the poet domestically, see Mary Moorman, *William Wordsworth: A Biography. The Early Years: 1770–1803; The Later Years: 1803–1850* (Oxford: Clarendon Press, 1957; 1965); and Juliet Barker, *Wordsworth: A Life* (London: Viking, 2000). Two important biographical-critical studies that concentrate on the poet's earlier years are Kenneth R. Johnston, *The Hidden Wordsworth* (New York: Norton, 1998), and Duncan Wu, *Wordsworth: An Inner Life* (Oxford: Blackwell, 2002).

General Scholarship and Criticism

Chandler, James K. *Wordsworth's Second Nature: A Study of the Poetry and Politics.* Chicago: University of Chicago Press, 1984.

Devlin, D. D. *Wordsworth and the Poetry of Epitaphs.* London: Macmillan, 1980.

Gravil, Richard. *Wordsworth's Bardic Vocation, 1787–1842* Basingstoke, England: Palgrave Macmillan, 2003.

Hodgson, John A. *Wordsworth's Philosophical Poetry 1797–1814.* Lincoln: University of Nebraska Press, 1980.

McFarland, Thomas. *Romanticism and the Forms of Ruin: Wordsworth, Coleridge, and Modalities of Fragmentation.* Princeton, N.J.: Princeton University Press, 1981.

Roe, Nicholas. *Wordsworth and Coleridge: The Radical Years.* Oxford: Clarendon Press, 1988.

Simpson, David. *Wordsworth's Historical Imagination: The Poetry of Displacement.* London: Methuen, 1987.

Thomas, Keith G. *Wordsworth and Philosophy: Empiricism and Transcendentalism in the Poetry.* Ann Arbor: UMI Research Press, 1989.

Books Devoted to or with Useful Chapters on *The Prelude*

Chase, Cynthia. *Decomposing Figures: Rhetorical Readings in the Romantic Tradition.* Baltimore: Johns Hopkins University Press, 1986.

Clancey, Richard W. *Wordsworth's Classical Undersong: Education, Rhetoric and Poetic Truth.* Basingstoke, England: Macmillan, 2000.

Ellis, David. *Wordsworth, Freud and the Spots of Time.* Cambridge: Cambridge University Press, 1985.

Gill, Stephen. *William Wordsworth: The Prelude.* Landmarks of World Literature series. Cambridge: Cambridge University Press, 1991.

Harvey, W. J., and Richard Gravil. *Wordsworth: The Prelude.* Casebook series. London: Macmillan, 1972.

Janowitz, Anne. *England's Ruins: Poetic Purpose and the National Landscape.* Oxford: Blackwell, 1990.

Jarvis, Robin. *Romantic Writing and Pedestrian Travel.* Basingstoke, England: Macmillan, 1997.

Johnston, Kenneth R. *Wordsworth and "The Recluse."* New Haven, Conn.: Yale University Press, 1984.

Kneale, J. Douglas. *Monumental Writing: Aspects of Rhetoric in Wordsworth's Poetry.* Lincoln: University of Nebraska Press, 1988.

Lindenberger, Herbert. *On Wordsworth's "Prelude."* Princeton, N.J.: Princeton University Press, 1963).

McConnell, Frank D. *The Confessional Imagination: A Reading of Wordsworth's Prelude.* Baltimore: Johns Hopkins University Press, 1974.

Nichols, Ashton. *The Revolutionary "I": Wordsworth and the Politics of Self-Presentation.* Basingstoke, England: Macmillan, 1998.

Onorato, Richard J. *The Character of the Poet: Wordsworth in "The Prelude."* Princeton, N.J.: Princeton University Press, 1971.

Roe, Nicholas. "Revising the Revolution: History and Imagination in *The Prelude,* 1799, 1805, 1850." In *Romantic Revisions,* ed. Robert Brinkley and Keith Hanley. Cambridge: Cambridge University Press, 1992, 87–102.

Williams, John. *William Wordsworth.* Critical Issues series. (Basingstoke, England: Palgrave, 2002.

————. *Wordsworth.* New Casebooks series. (Basingstoke, England: Palgrave, 1993.

Wolfson, Susan J. *The Questioning Presence: Wordsworth, Keats, and the Interrogative Mode in Romantic Poetry.* Ithaca, N.Y.: Cornell University Press, 1986.

Wood, Nigel, ed. *The Prelude: Theory in Practice.* Philadelphia: Open University Press, 1993.